Taking Faith Seriously

Taking Faith Seriously

Edited by
Mary Jo Bane
Brent Coffin
Richard Higgins

Harvard University Press
Cambridge, Massachusetts, and London, England   2005

Library of Congress Cataloging-in-Publication Data

Taking faith seriously / edited by Mary Jo Bane,
Brent Coffin, and Richard Higgins.
    p.   cm.
Includes bibliographical references and index.
ISBN 0-674-01710-2 (alk. paper)
1. Christian sociology—United States.
2. Christianity and politics—United States.
3. Church and social problems—United States.
I. Bane, Mary Jo.   II. Coffin, Brent.
III. Higgins, Richard, 1952–

BR517.T35 2005
261.8′0973—dc22   2004042350

Contents

Preface

This book grew out of an intense conversation over three years that reshaped our sense of the boundaries of our disciplines, which range from religion to public policy to social science. Eleven of us came together in 2000 under the auspices of Harvard's Hauser Center on Nonprofit Organizations to examine the relationships between religion and American life in overlapping contexts that included congregations, voluntary groups, service organizations, and political movements. Our seminar was part of a larger Hauser program to develop a deeper understanding of the social roles of the nation's "voluntary" sector. We included theologians Brent Coffin and Ronald Thiemann, public policy analysts Mary Jo Bane, who chaired the group, and Mark Moore, and sociologists of religion Nancy Ammerman, Omar McRoberts, and Ziad Munson. The others were Martha Minow, a legal scholar, Peter Dobkin Hall, a historian, and two other sociologists, Julie Wilson and Christopher Winship. Writer and editor Richard Higgins joined us in 2002 to help frame and put together this book.

Each of us undertook to study religion in public life, using his or her discipline as the basis for engaging others in dialogue—trying as we did so to keep our theoretical observations grounded in studies of lived religion. Most members of the seminar are represented in this volume by individual chapters or, in the case of Winship, by one coauthored with Amy Reynolds. The roles of Moore and Minow were broader. As a political scientist and a legal scholar, Moore and Minow continually challenged us to assess the multiple roles of religion both in theory and in practice from the standpoint of the polity and to do so without viewing religion merely as an instrumental resource for the policy. Their contributions enriched all the chapters of this book.

There were two stages in our intellectual orientation. The first was to recognize religion as not only an important but also an integral part of American life. Moore and others studying nonprofit organizations at the Hauser Center insisted that they could not talk about that sector without including religious organizations. A substantial amount of the money in the nonprofit sector comes from or goes to religious entities of various kinds. Nor can one evaluate social capital in America without considering religious groups: more Americans belong to religious congregations than to any other kind of voluntary association. Religious participation in American politics is a fact that cannot be ignored, as has been amply demonstrated in books and articles at least since the rise of the Religious Right in the 1980s. The simple fact of the pervasiveness of religious beliefs, practices, and organizations in American civic and political life compelled attention from a center with a focus on the nonprofit sector. This fact brought us together and provided the broad context for our work.

As part of this first stage, we sought to develop frameworks to evaluate the various roles, the obvious and the many more subtle ones, that religious practice and religious organizations play. We, like policymakers and other scholars, were intrigued by the role that "faith-based organizations" might play in the delivery of social services. Welfare and social services policy are a research and teaching interest for many of the contributors; we found ourselves trying to make sense of the potential benefits, costs, and impacts of the increasing efforts in public policy to direct more public dollars to faith-based social services providers. We were distressed by the lack of evidence on the effectiveness of such efforts and disturbed by the possibility that religious organizations might be called on to do the impossible: to pick up the pieces of the safety net that had been dropped by government.

But we also realized that the provision of help to those who need it was but one of the contributions that religious organizations made to public life. Urged on by Moore, we sought to address the equally important contributions religion makes to the development of civic virtue and character, to social capital, to moral discourse, and to the development of both skills and opportunities for participation in the political process. Robert Putnam estimates, for example, that half of all the social capital in the United States is developed in congregations and other religiously affiliated groups. As another example, we considered the work of Sidney Verba and his colleagues documenting the importance of religious groups as places where people, especially lower-income and less-educated men and women, have learned to organize, to plan, and to participate in collective action. These insights about the different important roles that religion plays broadened the scope of our inquiry and reinforced our sense of the importance of the religious sector.

The second stage came as a corrective: being reminded by members of our group that religious faith, in its many forms, is not about performing useful functions for society but is instead concerned with its own reality and mission. Viewing religion in purely instrumental terms has long been a flaw in social science research about religion. We began to share the stories of our own religious identities, practices, and commitments, which for many of us are central features of our lives as praying and practicing believers. Members of our group include a Baptist, a Catholic, an Episcopalian, two Jews, two Lutherans, and one Presbyterian. Rather than viewing our personal commitments as "biases" to ignore or deny, we sought to articulate them more fully to one another and to expose them to the scrutiny of our respective academic disciplines.

There were also two levels in our cumulative research and dialogue. One was the writing of nine case studies by individual authors that combined, to various degrees, narrative and functional analysis. Emboldened by sharing both our own religious stories and the tools from our various disciplines, we each explored an example of religious interaction with American civic life, the understanding of which required us both to take religious practice seriously in its own right and to look at the effects it had on civic and political society in more functional terms. Our selection of cases was inevitably idiosyncratic and driven by both interest and convenience. All come from the Christian tradition, which in no way deemphasizes the importance of Judaism, Islam, Hinduism, and Buddhism in America's increasingly diverse religious landscape. And we have chosen to do our research in the Northeast, given our location and our desire to do the work ourselves. To keep our focus manageable, we also could not examine such important organizations or activities as the new faith-based community organizing movements in the United States, twelve-step groups, religiously mobilized political lobbying, or religious programs in prisons. Nonetheless, the diversity of the cases we present in this book yields insights about the myriad roles and activities of congregations, the complexities of faith-based social services, and the interaction of religion and politics. And we believe that the analytical framework we present contributes to the broader project of finding better ways to recognize and evaluate the social roles of religion.

On a second level, we examined our cases to see if there were broader empirical and normative implications. In this process we asked how policymakers and religious leaders should assess and react to our analyses. For example, Bane's finding that Catholic involvement in social service and social justice is less than one might expect raises questions about how the organizational and activity patterns of parishes might be interfering with the church's own mission. As another example, Munson's study showing that most pro-life activists remain committed to the democratic process raises the possibility of allowing or even welcoming the expansion of religious voices in political discourse.

Our normative discussions took place in the context of a changing legal climate, as interpreted by our constitutional scholar, Minow. Rigid devotion to the principle of the separation of church and state has given way to a doctrine requiring more accommodation and flexibility on the part of the state toward religion. This approach sees a positive role for religion—as long as one religious view is not privileged over others, and no religious view is privileged over a nonreligious one. This evolved doctrine is based on the recognition of the importance of faith in American life and a conviction on the part of some, including ourselves, that religion contributes to the flourishing of our democracy.

This conviction frames our normative stance. We are encouraged by the rise in some religious traditions of a theological argument that democracy is necessary for the exercise and expression of faith. We are also heartened that democracy's fostering of religious tolerance and volunteerism has strengthened American religious institutions and made possible the vitality of American religious life generally. Thus it is not only the case that religiously mobilized social action (as in the case of civil rights, war, or economic injustice) has made contributions to public debate, but that the freedoms heralded by the Constitution have been good for religion: those freedoms have sustained religious practices by slaves and freed slaves, by immigrants, by Americans founding new religions, and by Americans reinvigorating old ones.

It is in the hope of better understanding the possibility for mutual enrichment of religion and American democracy, in the context of appropriate safeguards that recognize their differences, that we have undertaken this book.

Acknowledgments

Mark H. Moore inspired the conversation that led to this book by convening "The Intellectual Foundations Seminar on the Social Role of Faith-Based Organizations." This project was funded by the Atlantic Philanthropies and was part of a larger effort at the Hauser Center for Nonprofit Organizations to identify the intellectual foundations of the public roles of the American voluntary sector. The center enlivened our work with a collegial atmosphere that sparked exchanges and constructive arguments across established lines.

Our initial discussions were broadened and enriched by contributions from Mark Chaves, Karen Fields, Anna Greenberg, James Gustafson, J. Bryan Hehir, Evelyn Brooks Higginbotham, David Hollenbach, Reuven Kimelman, Karen King, David Little, Linda Loury, Martha Minow, Richard Parker, Theda Skocpol, Bernard Steinberg, Jim Wallis, Preston Williams, and James Wind.

Our research has been part of the Hauser Center's Program on Religion and Public Life, which has been generously supported by Parker Montgomery. We thank Margot Murphy for providing staff support that enabled our effort. Our gratitude goes especially to Anne Mathew, assistant director of the Program on Religion and Public Life, without whose personal dedication and outstanding project management our work as a group would have been far more difficult and far less enjoyable.

Taking Faith Seriously

Taking Faith Seriously

DESPITE a longtime reluctance in the academic and public policy world to engage the very subject, it is increasingly apparent that religion, and all the questions it poses for a democratic society, cannot be ignored. From 2000 to 2003, the contributors to this book engaged in a dialogue to articulate a coherent, empirically grounded perspective on the relationship of religion and liberal democracy in the United States. Our aim has been to find an analytical approach that would provide better ways both to recognize and to evaluate the public face of religion, which includes its extensive social contributions as well as the inescapable challenges it poses for a diverse civil society and evolving democracy. We believe the strategy we have developed contributes to the emerging debate and has significant implications for future research and practice. It is on the basis of it that we challenge ourselves and others, including scholars, public officials, and citizens, to take faith seriously. By this we do not mean superficially asserting the importance of religion, as has become de rigueur in electoral politics, but developing tools of thought that permit us to see the public aspect of religion in all its subtlety and complexity and to begin to analyze it.[1]

This book has two goals. The first is to enhance understanding of the complex ways in which religious beliefs, practices, and organizations influence public life. In the chapters that follow, we look at how different kinds of Americans connect—or disconnect—religion, democracy, and the public world. Our second goal is normative. We aspire to help shape the debate over the appropriate role of religious language and practice, and religious institutions, in contributing to the well-being of our society.

Why Rethink Religion in American Liberal Democracy?

How do we understand, or fail to understand, the complex social effects of religion on liberal democracy in the United States? Given that the majority of Americans profess a form of Christianity, is the United States a "Christian nation," where one faith undergirds national values and institutions? Or, to draw from an opposite perspective, does American liberal democracy require a secular society in which markets, media, and the state consign religious practices to the private sphere, as the secular left assumes? Or could it be that both of those positions are wrong, and that the United States, among the most religiously diverse societies in the world, offers models of how religious communities can contribute to vibrant civil society and democratic participation? It is this third possibility, we suggest, that requires greater attention. Before proceeding to it, however, we examine the first two viewpoints. Neither, we believe, offers adequate perspectives for evaluating the roles of religion in public life.

Faith-based boosterism. In the first camp are those who would valorize or boost the public role of religion, in particular the traditional public roles it has played, such as serving the poor. This position, which President George W. Bush champions through his faith-based initiatives, has become dominant in public policy. Certainly it merits the careful attention it is receiving from scholars, policymakers, and community leaders. School vouchers allowing parents to use public dollars for children to attend sectarian schools and public-private partnerships involving faith-based service providers are focal points of the changing relationship between public religion and liberal democracy—constitutionally, politically, and programmatically. Yet this viewpoint, and the debate over it, is too narrowly focused. The material betterment of individual lives and the mending of our society's frayed safety net is noble work, but these goals only skim the surface of the civic and cultural influence of religious traditions that engage the deepest beliefs and values of tens of millions of Americans.

The current political focus on faith-based social services is both dangerous and inadequate. It is dangerous because it misrepresents the capacities of religious organizations to carry the burden of social welfare for the nation's disadvantaged citizens, families, and communities. It is inadequate because this narrow focus distorts the identity and priorities of religious organizations themselves. It fails to recognize fully that the essential independence and intrinsic faith commitments of religion limit its usefulness to the polity. Such distortions prevent secular leaders from recognizing other important contributions that religious organizations can offer. These roles include increasing moral and spiritual capacities, inspiring citizens to serve neighbors, building relationships across barriers of race and income, and providing a vision of what kind of society we are called to be. This book sheds light on such contributions by suggesting ways in which scholars and practitioners can recognize and evaluate the multiple facets of religion more adequately.

Dogmatic secularism. If the first paradigmatic approach includes religion or a sectarian version of it too uncritically, the second excludes it equally uncritically. Not only does the dogmatic secularist approach devalue the effects of religious practices on democratic life, it does not even evaluate them, for it construes them as private, subjective phenomena that need not be taken seriously. By dogmatic secularism, we hasten to add that we do not mean the functional secular ethos that characterizes many public settings of liberal democracy. All Americans—those who are deeply religious, those with scant or no religious beliefs, and those with antipathy toward religion—find it necessary in everyday social interactions to withhold the full range and depth of their convictions in order to maintain mutual respect, cooperation, and civility in public settings. In doing so, they are not necessarily denying their convictions. Indeed, as the case studies in this volume illustrate, citizens transport their convictions from religious to secular settings in a variety of ways. Yet the second paradigmatic approach, dogmatic secularism, wrongly equates a public ethos of tolerance and civility with the absence of religious commitments. In so doing, it fails to recognize the multiple roles that religion does play in public life.

In recent years significant scholarly work has challenged this prevailing academic indifference toward religion.[2] This book broadens these efforts, which seek to move the American academy out of an ironic predicament. The rooting of religious practices in the soil of democratic freedom has been a great achievement in the United States, both for religion and for democracy. Yet many parts of the academy have neglected the historical sources and continuing practices that sustain this very achievement. Many scholars have adopted the "separation of church and state" and "secularization" as uncritical dogma. Further, some have assumed that a secularist approach is the only valid intellectual foundation acceptable in a liberal democracy. (We would argue that forms of Enlightenment secularism are comprehensive belief systems which, like their religious counterparts, should not be privileged as the unifying basis of liberal democracy.)[3] Consigning religion to the private sphere of individual subjectivity or private association, many consider religion to be "the single subject about which many intellectuals can feel free to be ignorant."[4] Such dogmatism is empirically obtuse in a society where approximately half of all social capital is religiously related, and in which eight out of ten Americans report that religion is important in their lives.[5]

Nevertheless, we recognize that there are solid reasons for caution about the role of religion in democracy, and we believe that these potential flashpoints are not to be lightly dismissed in the interest, for example, of forging public-private partnerships with faith-based service providers. The reasons for caution include doubts about the capacity of religiously based service organizations to take on a significant share of the task of social provision, the low or uneven level of accountability in such organizations, and the absence of sound empirical research on the effectiveness of such efforts. It is furthermore appropriate to be concerned about direct or indirect proselytizing, especially of clients who are vulnerable, by faith-based providers and the potential social implications of exempting such organizations from laws banning discrimination in hiring employees on the basis of religion.

Despite these legitimate concerns, we find the dogmatic secularist posture inadequate for four reasons. First is the issue of respect for beliefs and values that a majority of Americans reports are of deep importance to them. Empirical data showing the United States to be a religious nation need to be taken seriously, if for no other reason than to respect the identities and values of the American citizens who are the source of these data. Second, moving beyond the black-and-white certainties of dogmatic secularism creates opportunities to reenvision and realign the boundaries between public and private, secular and sacred, for-profit and nonprofit. Third, screening out the influence of religion disables the United States from responding adequately to the challenge of growing religious pluralism, both at home and abroad. Legal strategies adopted over time to deal with mainline Protestantism, Catholicism, or Judaism may not be useful in dealing with the many other religions, new and old, taking root in American soil.[6]

A final reason to rethink religion in the context of liberal democracy is a more pragmatic one. Taking faith seriously is the work of public sector practitioners as well as scholars. As political and policy changes raise expectations for the nonprofit sector to meet social needs, a growing number of organizations in communities across America find themselves competing with one another in a chaotic ground game. Like their for-profit counterparts, nonprofit organizations, both religious and secular, compete for "brand recognition," shares of the customer market, financial resources, and legitimacy. And the ground game is becoming more complex as the boundaries between public and private or for-profit and nonprofit actors erode.[7] In this environment, public and nonprofit leaders seek ways to form partnerships in order to achieve greater results or to reach broader communities. But for cross-sector partnerships to prove effective, they will require fresh insight into what religious organizations can and cannot bring to the table. For all these reasons, it is time to rethink the social contributions of religion in liberal democracy.

The Constitutional Structure of Liberal Democracy

Before presenting a framework to elucidate religion's public roles, we wish to put them in context with a brief look at the fundamental structure of liberal democracy. It is the constitutional right to free exercise of religion and the constitutional ban on establishment, along with other rights and principles, that give life to the practice of religion in the United States. The First Amendment of the Constitution states: "Congress shall make no law respecting an establishment of religion, or prohibiting the free exercise thereof; or abridging the freedom of speech, or of the press, or the right of the people peaceably to assemble, and to petition the government for redress of grievances." The constitutional structure of American liberal democracy thereby guarantees to all citizens the freedoms of religion, speech, and association.

From the perspective of democratic polity, constitutional rights are guaranteed claims that impose upon government both obligations to act in certain ways and restraints on acting in certain other ways. The various branches and levels of government have the obligation to safeguard the freedoms of religion, speech, and association—particularly on behalf of minority groups that lack political power and are thereby more vulnerable to the tyranny of the majority. Constitutional rights at the same time impose essential limits on the powers and scope of government, such as any action that would appear to grant rights to one religion over another—limits not to be transgressed even for the sake of popular purposes. The constitutional structure of liberal democracy is thus a system of perpetual tensions engendered by conflicting interpretations of constitutional rights, by rights in conflict with other rights, and by the noninstrumental sanctity of rights conflicting with the pursuit of instrumental private and public interests.

Over the last decade, the constitutional and legal climate in the United States has entered a period of change, particularly with regard to the religion clauses of the First Amendment. Since the mid-1990s the courts have construed legal doctrine forbidding governmental establishment of religion to require not a complete separation of church and state but rather evenhandedness and impartiality on the part of the state toward religion and religious organizations. Jurisprudence involving the First Amendment's Establishment Clause has, in effect, emphasized neutrality and equal treatment of religion and secularism. The state may not privilege secularism over religion but must ensure that adherents of any religious tradition or of no religion receive the same opportunities— whether to participate in a school choice program, to use public facilities, or to obtain public aid. Coupled with the ongoing constitutional protection for individual free exercise of religion, this evolving doctrine recognizes a positive role for religion and even permits aid to religious activities as long as: (a) religious ideology and practice are not privileged over secular, and (b) no religion is privileged over others.[8]

The watershed Supreme Court decision for the evolving legal doctrine is the Cleveland School voucher case in 2000, which authorized the use of public funds in the form of vouchers for education in pervasively religious as well as public and private nonsectarian schools. Yet the changing climate does not mean that the old safeguards have less salience. In 2002 a federal panel ordered the chief justice of the Alabama Supreme Court to remove a monument of the Ten Commandments from the courthouse rotunda, and when he refused to do so, the court ordered the removal of the justice from his post.[9]

Viewed from the standpoint of religious communities, the constitutional structure of liberal democracy is equally definitive and just as complex. Many religious citizens regard freedom of worship, speech, and association as rights endowed by their Creator that are safeguarded but not conferred by the Constitution. For many, the freedom to worship is the supreme right safeguarding human freedom and limiting the proper authority of government. If human beings owe their being and ultimate allegiance to God, in this perspective, they must be free to exercise their sacred obligations of faith;

and political institutions have no legitimate authority to define, impose, or interfere with the sacred obligations of free citizens. But religious citizens understand their religious commitments in different ways. Therefore the liberal democratic structures that protect basic human liberties also protect the space of a wider civic culture in which a plurality of cultural and religious identities may flourish. Liberal democracy is both the child and the parent of the deep pluralism generated by religion and other sources of identity.

An Analytical Framework

The constitutional structure of liberal democracy sets the context in which religion performs multiple functions in public life. A number of schemes have been developed to analyze religion in democracy, often focusing on a single role. Using a broader framework, we have chosen six interrelated roles or functions of religion within the constitutional structure of liberal democracy.

1. Fostering expression: religion fosters expression of personal beliefs and identity.

2. Forming identities: such expression shapes the identities, virtues, and commitments of communities, organizations, and individuals.

3. Creating social bonds: religious groups and practices create and sustain social bonds and networks.

4. Shaping moral discourse: religious groups and practices shape the character and quality of moral discourse.

5. Enabling participation: religious affiliation and practice enable civic engagement and political participation.

6. Providing social services: religious groups and organizations serve as providers of social services.

Each of these roles or functions can be analyzed from different vantages in society and through different lenses. They can be recognized or described from the standpoint of the polity, secular organizations, or religious organizations. They can also be evaluated from each of these stances in different but equally valid ways: the interpretive analysis of narrative, identity, and mission; and the functional analysis of resources, actions, and outcomes. This broader analytical framework advances the book's two purposes. It provides relatively clear categories that focus attention on significant features of religious practice; it contributes to the ongoing evaluation and dialogue of researchers and practitioners.

1. *Fostering expression.* In part because religious practice is well protected by our form of government, it has been a primary vehicle for self-differentiation and expression in American society. Religious adults may choose from among a variety of forms of worship, modes of moral discourse, and religious associations to give voice to the deep sources of their individual identities. While the freedom to worship as one pleases is particularly important in the United States, it is widely recognized as a fundamental human right in international law.

This function can be described from different perspectives. To members of faith communities, such expression may have little to do with personal choice or the exercise of rights. Religious persons may regard worship as a duty to which they are called by God. Worship emerges from a relationship with the holy that utterly transcends the constitutional structure of any polity. Policymakers, leaders of secular organizations, and other persons who may stand outside a faith perspective may recognize this function differently. They may see religious expression as a social good, because it satisfies individuals' desires for religious experience. They may describe it as a means to achieve a higher level of social welfare in a liberal society, that higher level being the result of giving individuals freedom to define what they value and want to do and also to structure opportunities to satisfy those desires.

This expressive function can also be evaluated either instrumentally or theologically by the polity, secular organizations, or faith communities. Antiabortion activists, to take one example, may view their right to lobby legislators and to protest in public to be instrumentally useful in achieving their political goals. On a narrative level, they may also interpret such rights and opportunities as a divinely ordained means of developing and acting on deep theological convictions.

2. *Forming identities.* Growing out of the expressive function is the role religion plays in shaping our identities, allegiances, preferences, and obligations. Religion not only allows individuals to express preexisting desires and values but also provides enduring social and cultural resources through which individuals inherit their particular identities, make choices that shape their lives, and influence whom the next generation will become. Formation operates not only at the individual level of analysis; it also applies to communities and to political and social movements. Indeed, as Peter Dobkin Hall shows in Chapter 1, nineteenth-century Protestant social efforts created templates of voluntary associations that persist in civil society today. The success of myriad religious organizations in formation is empirically documented by the highly diverse religiosity of the American people and by the deep pluralism of liberal democracy.

Religious formation can be evaluated through different lenses. From the normative standpoint of faith, it provides opportunities for faithfulness and discipleship. At the same time, religious communities cannot avoid functional analysis to assess if they are being faithful, whether by transmitting faith to their children or helping the poor.

Religion's formative role may be evaluated normatively from a secular standpoint as well—but for a different reason, namely the assumption that the state must not control the voluntary associations through which free citizens express their identities, whether the desires of citizens are for consumer products or salvation. But it is also important to note that the formative function can shape preferences or commitments that benefit society and those that do not, including fear and hatred of those who are different or the justification of inequity and violence. A secular analyst may find it necessary to evaluate the formative role of religion instrumentally, as when the state has an overriding interest in protecting children from abuse or educating them for civic tolerance, or when public officials must determine how best to use limited social service funds.

3. *Creating and sustaining social bonds and networks.* Social scientific research has increasingly recognized the role that religious congregations and organizations (like other voluntary associations) play in fostering bonds of reciprocity and trust among similar citizens and creating networks of social relationships, a phenomenon that some have called social capital.[10] In some cases, those bonds may encourage members of religious communities to reach across barriers of race, ethnicity, and economic and social opportunity in pursuit of a common theological perspective or social effort, a phenomenon that Robert Putnam has described as bridging social capital. But it is also true that social bonds based on religion may, in many cases, reinforce those same divisions.[11]

Religion promotes social capital through rituals, narratives of meaning, shared experiences, the building and sustaining of physical locations for worship, and holy days and life-cycle events that afford repetition, regularity, and scaffolds for mutual aid and concern. These efforts provide both utility and pleasure, and they underwrite much of the connectedness of American society. Different religious traditions teach different narratives about how they interact with the broader world, so there is no one style of social capital associated with religion. The social bonds and networks fostered by liberal Protestant churches differ markedly from those of conservative evangelical traditions. Across the spectrum, however, church life generates a social force. It is well documented that people most involved in religious congregations are the citizens most engaged in serving the community. Yet religious congregations cannot be adequately understood solely in terms of bonding and bridging social capital, as Nancy Ammerman shows in Chapter 5. A more careful analysis is also required to explain the different patterns of participation that Hall finds in different religious traditions in previous centuries.

Evaluated from the perspective of the polity, religion's role in creating social capital may be assessed as being good or bad for democracy. Yet the same role may be evaluated quite differently from the perspective of faith communities. To them, social capital may be seen as simply a by-product, albeit a good one, that grows out of commitments and allegiances formed in their desire to be faithful in their relationship with God.

4. *Shaping moral discourse.* The exploration of serious moral issues is central both to the ideal of deliberative democracy and to the practice of many religious communities. This is a potential synergy between democracy and religion that has received insufficient attention. As Brent Coffin writes in Chapter 4, religion helps to shape what he calls thick moral discourse, deliberation in community that shapes identity and judgment, being and doing, through stories, rituals, and symbols of transcendence.

The polity may evaluate this role in terms of its usefulness to liberal democracy, finding, for example, that citizens who are empowered to articulate their moral viewpoint are more likely to participate in public life. The same angle of vision may produce a different evaluation of this role: the fear that discourse driven by religious fervor unleashed in the public square will undermine reason and respect and make things worse rather than better.

From a religious perspective, this role may be evaluated as a way to go beyond abstract or fixed beliefs and engage with others in dialogue that can lead to concrete actions or decisions that are in accordance with, for example, the Christian moral ideal of the "Kingdom of God." Analyzing this function from a religious standpoint leads Mary Jo Bane to conclude, in Chapter 2, that Catholicism's rich tradition of social and moral discourse is an underused resource in Catholic parishes and has not produced a level of social engagement commensurate with its potential. As Bane demonstrates, this assessment further requires a functional analysis from the perspective of Catholic faithfulness: what resources are needed for parishes to transmit social teachings into civic life?

5. *Enabling participation.* Religious groups play a significant role in developing the skills needed for participation in the political process and in providing outlets for that participation, as has been shown by Sidney Verba and colleagues.[12] Verba finds that religious

congregations and organizations provide three kinds of help that enable involvement in political, electoral, and legislative affairs: information, resources, and opportunity. For Americans with lower levels of income or education, religious communities are sometimes the primary place where they learn how to organize a social initiative, as was demonstrated in the American South during the civil rights movement of the 1960s. But the link between religious activity and civic engagement is old; in New England, it reaches back to the establishment of the first communities of English settlers, in which the "church" was, quite literally, the meetinghouse and seat of town government.

As with the other roles with which it overlaps, the role of enabling civic engagement may be recognized by religious groups in the narrative or theological sense as an opportunity for discipleship and what progressive Catholics call *praxis:* putting faith into action. Or this role may be recognized instrumentally. An example would be urging members of a religion to vote for a candidate who has pledged to fulfill the social agenda articulated by the leaders of that tradition.

From a secular viewpoint, this role may be seen as helping to create a stable feature of any liberal democracy: the political participation of its citizens. Those who are active in churches, synagogues, temples, and mosques turn out to be quite active in politics more generally. Yet this role has long raised concerns about the manipulation of the political process by religion, sufficient to make John F. Kennedy promise Protestant pastors in the 1960 presidential campaign not to take orders from the pope. Such a pledge may seem quaint against the contemporary standard of on-your-sleeve religion that has arisen in national politics, but today the concerns about the influence of religiously mobilized political movements on national issues such as defining the nature of marriage are no less real.

6. *Providing social services.* While we have placed this most familiar role of religion in public settings last, it has long been a major one in the social welfare of our society. It spans Thomas Jefferson's decision as president to pay Jesuit missionaries to teach

English to the new Americans living in the areas of the Louisiana Purchase to the most recent efforts to allocate federal tax dollars to small faith-infused organizations that provide social services to the needy. Such providers are the dominant focus of current discourse on religion's role in American public life, although, as we have said, that focus is too narrow and potentially distorting of the nature of communities of faith.

Religious and secular organizations recognize both dangers and opportunities in this role. Dangers include the lack of solid empirical data on the success of religious groups as social providers and also the temptation to strain the limited resources of those organizations. Opportunities include adding another dimension to current treatment modalities, reaching out more effectively to at-risk children and families, and reducing the economic burden of social provision on the public treasury.

Religious organizations evaluate this role theologically when they ask if a particular social service truly expresses faithfulness to their traditions. A Catholic organization may, for substantive, narrative reasons, rule out working with government organizations that offer social services that conflict with Catholic teaching on abortion or birth control, while receiving public funds to serve the needy in other ways. The same Catholic group may evaluate its social service role in a different light: is this program or activity serving the interest of making the Church's voice heard in the halls of public policy? Alternatively, conservative Protestant churches that judge faithfulness in terms of serving and converting the destitute may be unwilling to enter into any public-private partnerships for fear of relinquishing their religious autonomy. Evaluation not only depends on the vantage of institutional sectors; it must be seen in the context of particular organizations and social settings.

The Cases

The nine empirical studies in *Taking Faith Seriously* form three groups. Peter Dobkin Hall's opening chapter, which takes a historical perspective, stands by itself in Part One. He traces the rise and influence of the Protestant civic engagement tradition by show-ing how the beliefs and practices of early Congregationalists shaped their secular activities and the public face of their church. Hall re-minds us that religion, far from having suddenly emerged in the public square, has always been there. Chapter 1 presents in differ-ent historical contexts all six roles in our framework and thus lays the foundation for the contemporary cases to follow. Voluntary or-ganizations are seen as rooted in liberal Protestant theology, and participation in them is seen to have both a formative and an ex-pressive function. Faith-based social services are present, as are the risks inherent in them: here, lack of accountability and bigotry (anti-Catholicism). The formative function of religion is highly visi-ble as Hall shows how Protestantism shaped the architecture of nonprofit organizations as the vehicles through which religious but nonsectarian citizens pursued common public goals.

The next four chapters form Part Two. In these we present case studies taking different perspectives on the public roles and func-tions of religion as it appears in congregations and communities. These cases take us beyond the myth of privatized religion in Amer-ica's communities in order to examine religious practices and social interactions in different locations.

Mary Jo Bane begins Part Two with her study of the empirical re-alities of social capital and moral discourse in Roman Catholic par-ishes. Bane asks why it is that Catholics, as measured according to several indices, are less involved than are Protestants in both reli-gious and civic activities. She examines this puzzle against the back-drop of what should presumably boost Catholic civic engagement: the church's teachings on social justice. Bane proposes several rea-sons why that tradition has remained an underused resource in Catholic parish life.

In Chapter 3, Omar McRoberts looks at a cluster of black con-gregations that make up what he calls a religious district in a rela-tively poor Boston neighborhood. His case study focuses on the for-mative function of religion and how it enables civic engagement and reaching out to those at risk. McRoberts explores different reli-gious attitudes and orientations to the street and the world outside, and he shows how these attitudes affect the ways in which church members relate to one another and their neighbors.

In Chapter 4, Brent Coffin studies moral discourse in the congregations and community life of an affluent Boston suburb. He tracks the different ways three Protestant congregations use social capital to generate thick moral deliberation that shapes conflicting identities and moral orientations toward public issues. The question to be evaluated is whether deep religious differences, in this case over the inclusion of gays and lesbians, can be addressed in public without injuring the civic values of tolerance, mutual respect, and democratic deliberation.

In the last chapter of Part Two, Nancy Ammerman uses survey data to examine and evaluate styles of civic engagement within several mainline Protestant traditions. She begins by highlighting the importance of religious narratives and practice in shaping personal identity and, in turn, the importance of religious beliefs and activity as predictors of civic involvement. She then shows how specific traditions provide members with stories, activities, and practices that link them to the world in different forms of participation.

Part Three presents three cases that examine religion in larger and more diffuse settings, such as institutions and faith-based programs and movements. Together these chapters demonstrate the diversity of faith-based organizations and the complexities involved in trying to understand the faith factor in organizations.

Ronald Thiemann looks in Chapter 6 at the history of two Lutheran child-serving agencies in Pennsylvania, and shows how the interaction of Lutheran theology and externally driven constraints has shaped the mission and practice of a merged agency. Thiemann shows how the formative function and social provision role of religion in public settings overlap. A theologian, he focuses on the distinctiveness of church-based social efforts and their allegiance to their mission as communities called into being by God.

In Chapter 7, Julie Wilson examines the roles of religion in the care of the elderly, also in Pennsylvania. Her study focuses on for-profit, secular nonprofit, and religious nursing homes that hold relatively stable market shares in a competitive industry. She finds interesting hints of differences in the operations and quality of care among religious and nonreligious homes, differences that could be elaborated further, she argues, if other researchers employed the framework we propose to take religion and faith seriously.

In Chapter 8, Chris Winship and coauthor Amy Reynolds present an evaluation of four programs in Boston directed at teenage girls. One program is secular, and three have varying degrees of religious ties. The authors document the complicated ways in which faith interacts with program design and outcomes, and they also find overlap among the formative and social provision roles.

In Chapter 9, Ziad Munson studies a controversial political phenomenon, the pro-life movement. He examines the attitudes and beliefs of the participants about both abortion and democracy, providing an analysis of the role of religion in enabling political participation. The individuals interviewed by Munson make strong claims for the absolute truth of their positions—and yet they remain committed to democratic processes. Munson analyzes this seeming paradox.

In the concluding chapter, we elaborate the usefulness of our analytical framework, as demonstrated by the cases, and propose three theses that are consistent with our research. Our main argument is to "take faith seriously" by rethinking the relation of religious practices and democracy, and to encourage the use of a broader and deeper toolbox for doing so. This approach models a flexible but constructivist process for recognizing faith in the different contexts of liberal democracy and for evaluating religious interactions with public life from multiple perspectives—the polity, religious communities, and secular organizations. It is a framework that offers a promising way for researchers, practitioners, and citizens to take seriously the contributions of faith—and faiths—to American democracy.

part one

Religious Roots

PETER DOBKIN HALL'S chapter traces how nineteenth-century Protestant theology, practices, and polity shaped the structure and mission of the voluntary associations and service organizations that play a large role in America's civic life today. This section thus lays the historical groundwork for the eight contemporary empirical chapters to follow in several ways. It shows that religion, far from having burst on the public scene with the rise of the Moral Majority in the 1980s, has been a social force in America since colonial times and that its values have shaped civic, cultural, and economic organizations. All six roles or functions in our analytical framework—the formative and expressive functions of religion and its roles in building social capital, shaping moral discourse, influencing civic participation, and providing direct service—are present in the story Hall traces.

Focusing on New England Congregationalism, in particular the leadership of Lyman Beecher and others who inherited the eighteenth-century evangelical movement begun by Jonathan Edwards, Hall shows how religious citizens adapted to the challenge posed by America's new liberal democracy: they created new civic structures to exercise Christian moral responsibility while remaining nonsectarian. The result was a gradual shift among these Protestants to secular organizations as the primary venues for the exercise and development of faith.

chapter 1

The Rise of the Civic Engagement Tradition

Peter Dobkin Hall

HOW RELIGIOUS BELIEF and practice shape the ways that people view the world and behave in public life, and how belief and practice also influence the structure of religious or civic organizations that faithful people create, are not only questions for contemporary America. They have enormous historical resonance, as this account of the rise of the Protestant tradition of civic engagement demonstrates. Indeed most of the public roles and functions of religion that are examined in the eight contemporary studies that follow are present in this analysis of the voluntary principle in nineteenth-century Protestantism. I explore, among other elements, examples of faith-based social services as a preferred means to meet social needs, porous boundaries between the secular and religious worlds, participation in religious voluntary associations as both expressive and formative influences, problems of accountability, the socially divisive aspect of religion, and, most centrally, the theological grounding of voluntary social efforts.

Earlier studies have found provocative answers to such questions. Lloyd Warner and Paul Lunt's 1941 investigation of the associational life of Newburyport, Massachusetts, focused on notable differences in types and degrees of civic engagement among religious groups. They identified significant connections between the patterns of voluntary engagement by congregations and the overall associational architecture of the community.[1] Of special note were the differences between congregations that now would be labeled theologically liberal (Congregationalist, Episcopalian, Presbyterian, and Unitarian Universalist) and those that would be called theologically conservative (Baptist, Methodist, and Roman Catholic).

The liberal Protestants were exceptional not only for the extensiveness and intensity of their associational ties, but also for their willingness to sponsor civic groups like the YMCA, Boy Scouts, and Campfire Girls, which served the whole community rather than only their own members. In contrast, the more conservative Protestant congregations in Warner and Lunt's "Yankee City" (Methodists and Baptists) displayed in proportion to their size the fewest formal (interorganizational) and informal (membership) ties to other associations in the community. On the formal level, they were not sponsors of youth and athletic groups or civic associations. Their members were the least likely of Yankee City's residents to be members of broadly inclusive civic associations. Parishioners in Yankee City's second-largest faith community, Roman Catholics, were associationally active but almost exclusively in organizations in which only Catholics were permitted to participate. They were far less likely than liberal Protestants to participate in broadly civic organizations.

Aware that these findings might be artifacts of the liberal Protestants' historical domination of community life or of the extent to which their greater wealth gave them the leisure to be active in civic life, Warner and Lunt examined the patterns of involvement by members of different socioeconomic groups in these congregations. The fact that lower-middle-class members displayed nearly identical patterns of associational participation as upper-class members did suggested that religion topped socioeconomic factors in influencing civic engagement.

More recent studies have affirmed and expanded on Warner and Lunt's findings. E. Digby Baltzell's 1979 study of the impact of variants of Protestant belief on the contributions of two American cities, *Puritan Boston and Quaker Philadelphia*, offered compelling historical evidence for the role of religious values in shaping civic, cultural, and economic leadership. Baltzell argued that Bostonians made vastly greater contributions to national life, despite Philadelphia's unquestionably greater wealth and natural advantages, because of the ways in which religious beliefs and practices shaped the uses of wealth and preferences for forms of collective action.[2] These differences were evident as early as 1800, when Massachusetts accounted for 18 percent of the nation's corporate charters, whereas Pennsylvania accounted for a mere 7 percent.[3]

Sidney Verba, Kay Lehman Schlozman, and Henry Brady's important 1994 study of the origins of civic engagement, *Voice and Equality,* highlighted the role of religious congregations as venues for acquiring civic values and competencies. In particular, they called attention to the varying capacities of religious groups in this regard: religious bodies that encouraged involvement in congregational governance and worship produced higher levels of civic engagement than those in which such involvement was less important. Overall, they found that religion was more important than education, wealth, or status in eliciting civic engagement.

Robert Putnam's work generally confirms these insights in different contexts. In an early book, *Making Democracy Work,* he and his colleagues looked at the role Italian civil society plays in the effectiveness of government institutions and economic enterprise in that country.[4] Putnam and his coauthors found that, in Italy, religion, rather than promoting civic engagement and political participation, served as an alternative to it. This inverse relationship between religion and civic engagement is entirely consistent with the hierarchical and authoritarian character of Old World Roman Catholicism.

Yet Putnam's work on American civil society in 2000 produced quite different conclusions. Even though he found that church membership was in decline, he called attention to the powerful connections between religion and civic engagement: "faith communities in which people worship together are arguably the single most important repository of social capital in America," Putnam writes in *Bowling Alone.* Such communities, he notes, serve as incubators for "civic skills, civic norms, community interests, and civic recruitment."[5] Not only did he find that religion itself was important as a locus for giving, volunteering, and participating, church members were more likely than nonmembers to participate in secular organizations and activities. *Bowling Alone* echoes *Voice and Equality*'s insight on the potential significance of newer religious differences: members of evangelical and "New Age" churches are more likely than members of mainline bodies to devote their giving and volunteering to their own congregations or religion-related causes rather than to the community as a whole or to secular social and political initiatives.[6]

The findings of all these scholars are correlative. They call attention to the significant associations between religion and civic engagement but shed little light on *how* religious beliefs and practices shape either the public role of religious bodies or the secular activities of their members. Valuable insights into these mechanisms have been offered by theologian and organizational scholar Thomas Jeavons, who has explored the ways that religious beliefs shape structure and process in a variety of domains within Christian service organizations.[7] These domains include organizational self-identification, sources of financial support, goals, products and services, information and decision-making processes, allocation and exercise of power, employment practices, and interorganizational relations and organizational fields. Jeavons finds that organizations representing themselves as being religious varied significantly in the extent to which religious beliefs shaped them. Some nominally religious organizations were indistinguishable from secular entities. In others, religiosity shaped every aspect of organizational behavior, including sources of funding and personnel, products and services, how decisions were made, who had authority within the organization, and relations with other organizations.

Complementing Jeavons's research into the ways in which religion shapes organizational structure and process are studies of the influence of belief and practice on giving and volunteering by the faithful. Laurence Iannacone's study "Why Strict Churches Are Strong" finds that "strictness increases commitment, raises levels of participation, and enables a group to offer more benefits to current and potential members."[8] "Compared to members of other Protestant denominations," he writes, members of strict congregations "contribute more money and attend more services, hold stronger beliefs, belong to more church-related groups, and are less involved in secular organizations."[9] In other words, members of theologically liberal bodies (Episcopalian, Unitarian-Universalist, United Church of Christ, Presbyterian, and Quaker) are more likely to donate to and participate in secular organizations than their conservative counterparts.

Iannacone's findings are confirmed by investigations of the religious affiliations of directors and trustees of secular nonprofit organizations. David Swartz's study of the religious affiliations of nonprofit hospital trustees in six major American cities from 1931 to 1991 found that members of theologically liberal denominations were consistently overrepresented: "Only the older more established Protestant denominations have significant board representation . . . Thus, Baptists, who make up a broad and diverse base of Protestant representation in the United States are hardly more represented than the small Unitarian faith tradition. Further, only one trustee is identified from the less socially elite and less institutionalized but rapidly growing religious movements such as the Assemblies of God."[10]

An ongoing historical study of the religious affiliations of trustees of all types of nonprofit organizations drawing on the same data shows that while liberal Protestants made up 7 percent (1931), 10 percent (1961), and 4 percent (1991) of the religious populations of the six cities, they made up 33 percent (1931), 26 percent (1961), and 14 percent (1991) of all directors and trustees.[11] Conservative Protestants, though vastly more numerous than liberals, were surprisingly underrepresented: though accounting for 21 percent (1931), 32 percent (1961), and 24 percent (1991) of all members in the seven cities, they formed only 26 percent (1931), 16 percent (1961), and 10 percent (1991) of directors and trustees. Roman Catholics were even more dramatically underrepresented: though constituting 21 percent (1931), 25 percent (1961), and 28 percent (1991) of adherents in the six cities, they made up only 2 percent

(1931), 3 percent (1961), and 7 percent (1991) of nonprofit board members.

The persistence of these differences over time suggests, as earlier studies have found, that religious belief and practice are more powerful than socioeconomic factors in shaping engagement. Jews were as likely to be victims of social exclusion in 1931 as Catholics, but Jews were more than three times as likely to serve on boards as Catholics in all three periods. Although Catholics were likely to be as affluent and educated as other Americans by 1991, they were far less likely to serve on boards than even conservative Protestants.

The fact that connections between religious affiliation and civic engagement are persistent over time suggests the value of historical inquiry into their origins. To this end, I will examine a branch of American Calvinism particularly notable for its associational activity—the body of beliefs and practices developed by the self-identified followers of theologian Jonathan Edwards (1703–1758) under the rubric of the "New Divinity" in the eighteenth century and the "New Haven Theology" in the nineteenth.

The evolution of this strand of evangelical religiosity spanned an epoch of fundamental economic, social, and political change: the American Revolution, the creation of constitutional governments that guaranteed religious freedoms, and the rise of capitalist economies. These dramatic events challenged adherents' beliefs, requiring their accommodation to new circumstances. But these accommodations were not merely passive adjustments: change was viewed through the lens of faith and, on the basis of what was seen, the faithful and their leaders identified and chose among opportunities.

Certainly agitation for the separation of church and state, which gathered momentum after the Revolution, constituted the greatest challenge faced by New England Congregationalism. If it could not depend on laws requiring church attendance and levying taxes for its support, Congregationalism would have to compete on equal terms with other sects and persuade people to voluntarily attend services and support their faith. Congregationalists were divided over how to adapt to these circumstances. Would they follow the "gathered church" model of the Baptists, in which membership was restricted to those who could profess a living faith and demonstrate an upright character? Or should they follow the "territorial church" or parish model, in which everyone living within the community was considered eligible for membership?

Certain tenets of New England Congregationalism made the gathered church model attractive: Edwards and his followers were notorious for refusing communion to persons regarded as spiritually unsound or morally reprehensible. The Great Awakening of the mid-eighteenth century was not intended to convert the unchurched, but to more deeply evangelize and purify the existing church. But the territorial church tradition was an equally strong aspect of Congregationalism: nearly two centuries as a state church had produced a theology that viewed private belief as having important public consequences and that projected public roles both for the church and for the faithful.

The American Revolution and the establishment of political democracy served to rekindle awareness of the linkage between public and private. Democratic self-government would require a virtuous and informed electorate, and the Congregationalists, with their long tradition of involvement in education as founders of colleges and schools, saw themselves as having a particularly central role to play in public life. Even after disestablishment (in Connecticut in 1818; in Massachusetts in 1833) had dashed Congregationalism's hopes of being an organ of government, its conviction that religion in general—and itself in particular—had public responsibilities remained a cornerstone of Congregational belief and practice. This conviction led its adherents to seek ways of exercising public influence independent of state authority, namely, through voluntary associations that could act on public opinion and shape public values, preferences, and priorities.

At the outset, Congregationalist leaders did not know that associations could serve these purposes. They shared most Americans' inexperience with—and hostility toward—such "self-created corporations."[12] But when early experiments with associations proved startlingly successful, as in the case of the temperance movement, both clergy and laity were quick to use them for all sorts of purposes, religious and secular. The Congregationalists were hardly alone in their willingness to embrace voluntary associations. But they did so far more often and to far greater effect than any other religious group. One thing that differentiated them was the extent to which their use of associations was not limited by a "gathered church" perspective: Congregationalist associations were intended to serve as broad and inclusive a constituency as possible rather than merely co-religionists. This difference was rooted in theology, not in the opportunity structure—though their theology unquestionably led them to see and act on opportunities to which others were blind.

Ultimately the Congregationalists' inclination to use voluntary associations came from deeper beliefs about the nature of moral agency. These involved not only notions about the public dimensions of belief, but also more fundamental convictions about the capacity of humanity to choose between good and evil. In denying man's ability to choose the good, Calvinism, in its original form, promoted political fatalism; yet as reformulated by Edwards and further developed by his followers, it enabled the faithful to sacralize their work in the world and to mobilize their energies to change and improve it.

Although Congregationalism can hardly be given sole credit for the role voluntary associations came to play in American public life, exploring its part in this process helps us to understand what Tocqueville meant when he wrote, "Religion in America takes no direct part in the government of society, but it must be regarded as the first of their political institutions; for if it does not impart a taste for freedom, it facilitates the use of it. Indeed, it is in this same point of view that the inhabitants of the United States themselves look upon religious belief. I do not know whether all Americans have a sincere faith in their religion—for who can know the human heart?—but I am certain that they hold it to be indispensable to the maintenance of republican institutions."[13]

Order and Authority in the New Republic

In describing the evolution of American polity during his lifetime as an "experiment in republican institutions," the great nineteenth-century evangelist Lyman Beecher was referring to the struggle of citizens since the achievement of independence to resolve central dilemmas of self-government.

The most pressing of these involved the legal status of religion. Liberty of conscience had been a central theme in Anglo-American democratic discourse since the seventeenth century. It had been embodied in the ban against establishment of religion by the federal government and the protection of free exercise of religion in the First Amendment and in the declarations of rights in many state constitutions. Though affirmed in principle even by church leaders in states that maintained religious establishments, abandoning matters of faith to the marketplace—to the voluntary willingness of individuals to support it—was unsettling. What might have seemed an enlightened sentiment in the flush of revolutionary optimism looked quite different after the years of domestic turbulence and gory reportage of the excesses of the French Revolution. The question of whether democratic institutions could survive an ignorant and irreligious citizenry was foremost in the minds of the "men of property and standing" who wrote the federal Constitution.

The Constitution was a conservative document. It proposed representative institutions intended to curtail popular passions and to empower the wealthy, learned, and respectable. It even permitted individual states to decide for themselves whether to keep established churches. But the founders did not foresee popular opposition to this decision or to their efforts to impose education on citizenry. By 1800 religious disestablishment, a rallying point for Jeffersonians, had become so popular that only two states—Connecticut and Massachusetts—still had established churches. No state would have a universal common school system until the 1830s. Even in the newer states being carved out of the Northwest Territory, where federal law set aside land in every town for public education, there was no means of enforcing this provision or determining who would benefit from it. The South lagged behind the rest of the new nation. When Virginia governor Thomas Jefferson proposed the establishment of a common school system, lawmakers considered it too costly and refused to pass the legislation. As late as 1850 fewer than half of American children between the ages of five and twenty were attending school. The federal census of 1840 found that while the overall national literacy rate was very high, there were significant regional variations: nearly 100 percent of white males in the Northeast were literate, but the rate was considerably lower in the South.[14]

The legal situation of religion was no more reassuring. In states like Massachusetts and Connecticut, where churches were tax supported and church attendance mandatory, every town supported several congregations. But in the poor neighborhoods of cities like Boston, New York, and Philadelphia, and in states outside New England, religion languished. Timothy Dwight, the Congregational theologian, evangelist, and scholar, calculated that the ratio of clergy to population in Connecticut in 1798 was 1:1 and that "South of New-England," as he termed it, the ratio was 1:13.[15] Conservatives worried that, unless steps were taken, the republic would not last long. And their worries intensified as religious dissenters began to organize politically to disestablish religion in their own states and to assert public authority over church-controlled institutions like Harvard and Yale.

The Challenge of Disestablishment

It is profoundly ironic that New England Protestantism, which had contributed so much to the idea of religious voluntarism, should have ultimately fought so fiercely to defend state churches. The struggle was especially intense in Connecticut, where church and state had been bound together with particular vigor to defend political and religious orthodoxy. In 1706 the colony's churches had adopted what was, in effect, a Presbyterian ecclesiastical polity, which subjected ministers and congregations to oversight by "associations" and "consociations" made up of clergymen and church elders. The colony also delegated major tasks to ecclesiastical societies, including responsibility for public education.[16] As a result religious controversies inevitably became political ones and vice versa.[17]

Massachusetts, by contrast, though maintaining a Congregational establishment and suffering the same religious turbulence as

Connecticut, lacked the institutional mechanisms for defining or enforcing orthodoxy. As a result, religious tensions such as congregational conflicts and pamphlet wars between leading clergymen generally played themselves out without becoming major sources of political division.

Conflicts over religion broke out more frequently and raged with greater intensity after the Revolution, as citizens began to translate the abstractions for which they had fought into lessons for guiding their own lives. Reflecting the importance of religious toleration and liberty of conscience on the revolutionary agenda, virtually all the new states enacted statutes protecting religious rights and permitting sectarian diversity.[18] States differed, however, in their understanding of what this meant. Some, like Virginia, completely dismantled the Anglican establishment, not only depriving it of all of its historical privileges but also confiscating properties, such as poor and education funds, which had been entrusted to it.[19] Jefferson's and Madison's arguments to the Virginia legislature in the course of the debate on disestablishment became—and remain today—the definitive rationale for the separation of church and state.[20]

Both Massachusetts and Connecticut enacted tolerance statutes, but they were far less liberal than Virginia's. While granting individuals freedom of conscience and the freedom to form dissenting congregations, both retained their religious establishments and continued to tax citizens for support of the "public worship of God."[21] Article III of Massachusetts's Constitution of 1780, affirming that "the happiness of a people, and the good order and preservation of civil government, essentially depend upon piety, religion, and morality," empowered the legislature to "establish and support public worship and religious training."[22]

Connecticut's toleration act granted the least freedom of all, requiring every citizen to belong to some "regular" congregation and empowering citizens of municipalities to decide by majority vote which church would receive tax support. Dissenters were permitted to form their own churches and could be exempted from paying the taxes that supported the establishment by presenting to authorities a "certificate of their dissent."[23] In practice, this proved to be oppressive. Forcing dissenters to apply for such exemption from the taxes that supported the established churches exposed them to "hard and rigorous usage" by courts and juries that were almost always packed with the orthodox.[24]

Connecticut's 1784 quasi-disestablishment defined the state's political battle lines for the next three decades. The Congregational establishment, insisting that tax-supported religion was essential to free institutions, would fight fiercely to maintain its prerogatives by using the certificate system to effectively disenfranchise religious dissenters. In doing so, it not only alienated powerful groups like the Episcopalians, who shared many of the establishment's political and economic views, but ever larger numbers of independent-minded citizens who, with active assistance from Jefferson's Democratic Republican organization, were increasingly willing to mobilize against it.

Rationalizing Establishment

By the late 1780s orthodox ministers and magistrates, in sermons, pamphlets, and speeches, were already calling attention to the "rise of Infidelity" in Connecticut. They decried declining church attendance, the increasing activity of dissenting sects, and the open expression of both anticlerical and outright agnostic and "deistic" opinions. The actual extent of "infidelity" and dissent remains an open question, since those who seemed most troubled by it—especially the "New Divinity" faction of the Congregationalists—also happened to be the group offering itself and its doctrines as the solution to it.

No one articulated these ideas more forcefully than the multi-talented Dwight (1752–1817), who, in addition to his religious accomplishments, was also a poet, naturalist, politician, and president of Yale from 1795 to 1817. He was also Edwards's grandson. In his 1788 poem "The Triumph of Infidelity," he recounted a dark vision of a society divided between "decent Christians" and individuals unrestrained by religious belief.[25] For Dwight, the corrective to unrestrained individualism was orthodoxy. "On uniformity depends, / all government that gains its ends," he wrote in 1793, reiterating the role of the church in nurturing the individual morality essential to the survival of democracy.[26] But he was too sophisticated to believe in enforced uniformity: however intensely he and his contemporaries believed in the importance of maintaining religious establishment, as "New Light" descendants of the Great Awakening, they also understood the futility of external compulsion. Just as good works were empty gestures unless undergirded by faith, so moral agency, to be genuine, had to proceed from internal conviction. Though fearing the consequences of religious diversity, they thus permitted the passage of the state's 1784 General Toleration Act, which, at least formally, permitted citizens to worship according to the dictates of their consciences.

Dwight and his allies viewed the rise of religious diversity as a challenge to their powers of persuasion. They unleashed a torrent of sermons, pamphlets, and letters to newspapers and, by the 1790s, began creating entirely new kinds of organizations whose purpose was to stem the rising tide of infidelity both in Connecticut and in the nation at large.[27] At the same time, they turned their own churches into battlefields, purging members suspected of being doctrinally or morally weak in order to turn those who remained into disciplined groups of committed believers.

While transforming the churches into sectarian instruments, Dwight and his followers with increasing force advanced a rationale for the public role of religion. They vigorously denied that Connecticut supported an ecclesiastical establishment, arguing that the Act of 1784 had placed "all classes of Christians on the same level"—with equal rights to worship as they pleased and, if they could muster an electoral majority, to obtain tax support for their churches.[28]

Dwight's chief argument in favor of Connecticut's system was pragmatic: religion, he believed, was demonstrably "indispensable to the welfare of a free country." "It is wiser, more humane, and more effectual, to prevent crimes than to punish them," Dwight declared. "Religion is the only great preventive of crimes; and contributes more, in a far more desirable manner, to the peace, and good order, of Society than the Judge and the sheriff, the goal and the gibbet, united . . . He who would willingly lessen this influence is a fool; he who would destroy it, a madman."

Continuing in this pragmatic vein, Dwight addressed himself to those who objected to religious establishment on equity grounds: "There are men, who may, and in all probability will, say, that, however good and useful the public worship of God may be, they do not wish to avail themselves of its benefits; and owe, therefore, no contributions to its support." He responded to them by holding up the example of those who claimed exemption from supporting schools or roads and bridges because they either did not send children to the former or did not travel over the latter: "The list of individual enjoyments is as much or more valuable in a community, where Religion prevails, than where it does not, as the safety, peace, and pleasure of civilized society are more desirable than the exposure, discord, and misery, produced by the furious and malignant passions of uncultivated man."

Dwight grounded his political and historical defense of establishment with scriptural arguments about the nature of moral agency and salvation. Dismissing as specious the gospel passage in which Jesus claims "his kingdom not to be of this world," Dwight replied: "When Christ declared his kingdom not to be of this world, he had not even the remotest reference to the subject in hand. He merely replied to the accusation, which the Jews brought against him to Pilate, viz. that he claimed to be a king, and was therefore a rebel against the government of Caesar."

Though Dwight conceded that "in the fullest sense, that the kingdom of Christ is not of this world," he argued that human actors and, more significantly, human institutions like the state played a vital role in advancing the kingdom of Christ. "Miracles have ceased," Dwight asserted. "The extraordinary, and immediately perceptible, agency of Christ in this business cannot, therefore, be expected; and will not be employed. Whatever is to be done, except the work of sanctification, which man cannot do, is to be done by man as the instrument of his Maker. Man is to plant, and water; and then, and then only, is warranted either to hope, or to pray, that God will give the increase." "Men are to build churches," Dwight continued,

> to qualify themselves to become Ministers of the Gospel; to preach the Gospel; to settle Ministers; to support them, when they are settled; to secure to them that support, that they may be enabled to fulfil the duty of providing for their own households, and thus be safe from the charge of having denied the faith, and being worse than infidels . . . In this manner only, will they secure themselves and their children from being left to the guidance of ignorant men, who, instead of being qualified to teach, are neither able, nor willing, to learn.

As a practical matter, Dwight had little faith in supporting churches through the voluntary support of their members. Because only large towns had sufficient population and wealth to support churches, small towns and villages would be left unchurched. Even in large towns, he feared, the burden of support would fall upon a few individuals. Besides, he continued, citing Paul, taxes not only spread the burden of support more equally among citizens, but ensured that every citizen would have access to the benefits of religion.

The clincher for Dwight's argument was the evidence he offered to show that without government support, religion would languish. Citing statistics of church membership, he pointed out that Connecticut had 209 churches and 189 ministers for its population of 251,002 inhabitants, while "States South of New-England," with a population of 4,033,775, had only 430 congregations and 242 ministers. Thus, if the "States South of New-England . . . contained congregations, and were supplied with ministers in the same proportion as Connecticut; the whole number of congregations would be 3,344; and the whole number of ministers, settled and supported would be 3,024." "In Connecticut," he concluded, "every inhabitant . . . may hear the gospel, and celebrate the public worship of God, every Sabbath." In the states where religion was not tax supported, "it is not improbable, that a number of people, several times as great as the census of Connecticut, have scarcely heard a sermon, or a prayer in their lives."

The "establishment of the public worship of God" in Connecticut and Massachusetts, Dwight argued, produced measurable civic benefits: "the peace; the good order; the regular distribution of justice; the universal existence of schools; the universal enjoyment of the education which they communicate; and the extension of superior education."

Dwight contrasted civil society in Connecticut and Massachusetts with the situation in Rhode Island, where religion had long been disestablished. Because the churches were financially weak, they could not attract first-rate candidates to the ministry, which left communities without the moral leadership to establish strong civic institutions. Schools, Dwight noted, "usually go parallel with ministers, and churches." Noting that "schools in this State can hardly be said to exist," Dwight declared, "without churches men will be vicious . . . ; without schools they will be ignorant; and ignorance and vice are sufficiently melancholy characteristics of the people, in whom they are united."

Although Dwight's rationale for government support of religion was an entirely pragmatic notion of religion as a public good that prevented poverty and crime, fueled economic prosperity, promoted education, and maintained the values "indispensable to free institutions," its roots were theological. Public order and prosperity were subsidiary components of a broader process of spiritual redemption. As a Calvinist, Dwight could not assert either that public order and prosperity were good in themselves or that they could bring about spiritual redemption (which, as he reminded his readers, was something only God could do). Rather, he had to argue that the obedience that God demanded of his people—regardless of ultimate rewards or punishments—depended on mankind's creation of social institutions such as churches and schools that ensured them equal access to God's word.

Beyond Establishment: Lyman Beecher and the "Voluntary System"

Having been reared in a political age (he graduated from Yale in 1776), it is not surprising that Timothy Dwight viewed the church as a political actor and worried about the impact of crusades that "might transcend the sanction of public sentiment" and in doing so further alienate political support for the establishment. If anything, such caution became more evident as the battle over church establishment in New England intensified after 1810.

Lyman Beecher (1775–1863), one of Dwight's most energetic protégés, had no such compunctions. Although publicly committed to defending the Congregational establishment, he privately conceded that the church would (and perhaps should) be disestablished and had set about preparing for the challenges that would lie ahead under those circumstances.

Like other avatars of the Second Great Awakening, Beecher participated enthusiastically in purging his congregation of doubtful individuals, in order to transform it into a voluntary body of committed "saints." At the same time, he became active in promoting a variety of voluntary organizational efforts to promote nondenominational Christianity. Writing to his best friend, the Reverend Asahel Hooker, in January of 1811, he described the assortment of associational efforts in which he and his congregation were involved, including purging his church ("we have received three confessions for intemperance . . . and there is to be an excommunication next Sabbath") and getting subscriptions for the Connecticut Bible Society, which he noted was "the most popular of any public charity ever attempted in Connecticut."[29]

As Beecher began to broaden his focus from the role of religion in regulating private morality to the role of the church and the faithful in public life, he became interested in the problem of temperance. It seems clear from his own account that his actions were intuitive rather than deliberate. Moved by indignation, he merely acted. And the significance of what he had done only occurred to him later when, on reflection, he characterized his "report" to the General Association of the Connecticut Congregational Church as "the most important paper that I ever wrote."

Describing the proceedings of the ordination of a colleague at Plymouth, Connecticut, Beecher mentioned the "broad sideboard covered with decanters and bottles, and sugar, and pitchers of water." As the ministers and the Consociation arrived to drink before the public services and returned afterward to continue their carouse, "the sideboard, with the spillings of water, and sugar, and liquor, looked and smelled like the bar at a very active grog shop. None of the Consociation were drunk; but that there was not, at times, a considerable amount of exhilaration, I can not affirm."

A few days later Beecher attended another ordination, this time in Goshen, Connecticut. "There was the same preparation," he noted, "and the same scenes acted over, and then afterwards still louder murmurs from the society at the quantity and expense of liquor consumed." "These two meetings were near together," he continued, "and in both my alarm and shame, and indignation were intense. 'Twas that that woke me up for the war. And silently I took an oath before God that I would never attend another ordination of that kind. I was full. My heart kindles up at the thoughts of it now."

When church leaders proved unresponsive to his concerns, he demanded that a committee be created "to report at this meeting the ways and means of arresting the tide of intemperance." The committee was appointed, with Beecher as chairman. The following day he presented his report. Pointing to the "deadly effect" of "undue consumption of ardent spirits" on health and intellect as well as "family, society, civil and religious institutions," in "nullifying the means of grace and destroying souls," and in loss of property, he urged the clergy to take a stand by preaching against intemperance, setting an example by abstaining themselves, circulating of literature on the evils of alcohol, and forming "voluntary associations to aid the civil magistrate in the execution of the law."

Beecher took particular offense at the passivity and fatalism of the original report to the General Association. Very much in the spirit of Dwight's defense of public support for religion, Beecher argued that believers could not wait passively for God's intervention and pointed to the crucially important role of human agency in the process of spiritual redemption. "Had a foreign army invaded our land to plunder our property and take away our liberty, should we tamely bow to the yoke and give up without a struggle?" Beecher asked. He compared intemperance to a "band of assassins scattering poison," "venomous reptiles and beasts of prey, destroying in our streets the lambs of the flock before our eyes." "If we make a united exertion and fail of the good intended," Beecher concluded, "nothing will be lost by the exertion . . . But if, as we confidently expect, it shall please the God of our fathers to give us the victory, we may secure to millions the blessings of the life that now is, and the ceaseless blessings of the life to come."

Dwight responded coolly to the younger Beecher's enthusiasm. Though Dwight "approved of our zeal," Beecher wrote, "he was not without some apprehension that in their great and laudable earnestness his young friends might transcend the sanction of public sentiment; but, with a smile peculiarly his own, and heavenly, he added, 'If my young friends think it best to proceed, God forbid that I should oppose or hinder them, or withhold by suffrage.' "

Despite Dwight's doubts, the temperance movement took off. The following year, Beecher was able to report to the General Association that spirits had been

> banished from ecclesiastical meetings; ministers had preached on the subject; the churches generally had approved the design; the use of spirits in families and private circles had diminished; the attention of the community had been awakened; the tide of public opinion had turned; farmers and mechanics had begun to disuse spirits; the legislature had taken action in favor of the enterprise; a society for Reformation of Morals had been established, and ecclesiastical bodies in other states had commenced efforts against the common enemy. The experience of one year had furnished lucid evidence that nothing was impossible to faith.

Twenty years later, Tocqueville would point to the temperance movement as a powerful example of the unique ways in which Americans used voluntary associations.

> As soon as several of the inhabitants of the United States have taken up an opinion or a feeling which they wish to promote in the world, they look out for mutual assistance; and as soon as they have found one another out, they combine. From that moment, they are no longer isolated men, but a power seen from afar, whose actions serve for an

example and whose language is listened to. The first time I heard in the United States that a hundred thousand men had bound themselves publicly to abstain from spirituous liquors, it appeared to me more like a joke than a serious engagement, and I did not at once perceive why these temperate citizens did not content themselves with drinking water by their own firesides. I at last understood that these hundred thousand Americans, alarmed by the progress of drunkenness around them, had made up their minds to patronize temperance. They acted in just the same way as a man of high rank who should dress very plainly in order to inspire the humbler orders with a contempt of luxury. It is probable that if these hundred thousand men had lived in France, each of them would singly have memorialized the government to watch the public houses all over the kingdom.[30]

The rapid success of the early temperance movement pointed to a revolutionary transformation of the public role of religion. Since a disestablished church could no longer compel people to obey its teachings, it would have to learn how to persuade them to do so. Beecher's willingness to focus on moral reforms that cut across sectarian differences was not merely pragmatic, it was also theologically consistent with New England Calvinism's belief that sinners had to be prepared—through education and appropriate social and political institutions—to hear and accept the word of God. Joining the work of saving souls to a mission to transform the world in this way shifted moral agency from the church as an institution to individual believers in their capacities as parents, voters, and economic actors. In moving the church out of a compulsory role in politics, Beecher expanded Dwight's ideas about secular reform as a ministry of the church. For Dwight, it was enough to build churches and schools to save Americans from infidelity and ignorance; for Beecher, the work of preparation required the faithful to energetically overcome ignorance, poverty, drunkenness, ill health, or anything else that stood in the way of citizens' access to God's word.

By mobilizing people of faith to join with the unchurched to promote secular reforms that transcended sectarian and political interests, Beecher created what his contemporary (and critic) William Ellery Channing would call a "mighty engine."[31] It was a brilliant move. Disestablishment deprived Congregationalism of any governmental authority, making it one of many sects competing for public favor. Broadening its ministry to include education, moral reform, and social welfare enabled the faithful to dominate areas of public discourse and collective action in which the state was unwilling to involve itself and which rival sects eschewed. Beecher intuited that there was a vast domain lying between government and its citizens—a domain in which the values, beliefs, and opinions that underlay economic and political action were up for grabs. The rest of his career would be spent moving clergy and the faithful to create secular institutions that sought to shape the public's moral agenda—and, in doing so, to bring it closer to Christ's kingdom.

"Applying Christianity Directly without the Intervention of the State"

Beecher understood that intemperance and infidelity were only symptoms of the more fundamental threat that unrestrained individualism posed to republican institutions. In a passionate sermon delivered in 1812, he warned:

> Our institutions, civil and religious, have outlived that domestic discipline and official vigilance in magistrates which rendered obedience easy and habitual. The laws are now beginning to operate extensively upon necks unaccustomed to the yoke, and when they shall become irksome to the majority, their execution will become impracticable . . . The mass is changing. We are becoming another people. Our habits have held us long after those moral causes that formed them have ceased to operate. These habits, at length, are giving way. So many hands have so long been employed to pull away the foundations, and so few to repair the breaches, that the building totters. So much enterprise has been displayed in removing obstructions from the current of human depravity, and so little to restore them, that the stream at length is beginning to run. It may be stopped now, but it will soon become deep, and broad, and rapid, and irresistible.[32]

Beecher grasped the consequences of a people "emancipated from moral restraint" by political democracy, the marketplace, the unraveling of traditional communities, and the decline of religion.

Government could legislate morality, but it could not enforce it against "necks unaccustomed to the yoke." Without individual moral reform, "all the daring enterprise of our countrymen, emancipated from moral restraint," would "be attended with miseries such as the sun has never looked upon" and would let "loose upon our land the crimes and miseries of hell." But, he argued, men and women of faith, acting associationally in the public sphere, could avert "the great earthquake that is to sink Babylon [that] is shaking the nations."

Inspired by the success of his efforts, Beecher sought to broaden the temperance initiative into a general movement for the "reformation of morals and the suppression of vice." Once again he moved beyond the church, seeking to build a coalition of like-minded clergy and influential laymen as leaders and basing his plans organizationally on "local auxiliary societies."

In his effort to "apply Christianity directly to man and to society," Beecher broadened the evangelical fervor of the Second Great Awakening to a variety of secular reforms. In doing so, he transformed the public influence of religion beyond its traditional purposes (missionary, Bible, tract, and Sunday school societies) to include nonpolitical secular ends as well (promoting temperance, public morality, public health, and education). "They say ministers have lost their influence," Beecher wrote later in life.

> The fact is, that they have gained. By voluntary efforts, societies, missions, and revivals, they exert a deeper influence than ever they could by queues, and shoe-buckles, and cocked hats, and gold-headed canes . . . The great aim of the Christian Church in relation to the present life is not only to renew the individual man, but also to reform human society. That it may do this needs full and free scope. The Protestantism of the Old World is still fettered by the union of the Church with the State. Only in the United States of America has the experiment been tried of apply Christianity directly to man and to society without the intervention of the state.

The power of Beecher's ideas about moral agency and the efficacy of voluntary action, as well as his effectiveness as a speaker and publicist, were such that his reputation grew rapidly beyond Connecticut. In 1826 he was called to take charge of the Hanover Street Church in Boston. In this new and more cosmopolitan setting, he continued his experiments with the "voluntary system."

"When I came to Boston," he later recalled, "evangelical people had no political influence there, and in civil affairs those who joined them had but little chance. All offices were in the hands of Unitarians—perhaps a Baptist occasionally; hence, as young men came in from the town, there was a constant stream of proselytes to them. But as the revival went on, I had a large number of young men that joined the church . . . the finest set you ever laid eyes on." He invited a young parishioner to his parsonage, where he explained "to him the operation of political patronage." "The whole influence of Unitarianism IS a poisonous bribery," he declared, "it must be stopped, or we shall be stopped."

Beecher gathered a group of twelve young men. He explained to them that the Unitarians' political power stemmed from the fact that the Trinitarians stayed aloof from politics. "Now organize a society," he told them. "Go to primary meetings; go to this and that man, and persuade them to go and *do up* the business." The youngsters did not stop at mobilizing co-religionists. They built alliances with like-minded people from other denominations, and their efforts were dramatically successful.

The young men met monthly as the Hanover Association of Young Men, organized in January 1827. They organized a committee to which they delegated responsibility for "various important matters relating to [the] state of [the] city and things needing to be done." They wrote a report on lotteries that they sent to the legislature and which became the basis for the prohibition of that form of gambling. "Nobody ever knew where that movement came from," Beecher cackled; "they never knew what hit 'em." Other projects included banning the sale of liquor on Boston Common, pressuring authorities to enforce Sunday closings of businesses, and special missions for the "colored population," the Irish, and sailors. By the end of the year there were four similar associations in the city.

Beecher's efforts to teach young people the power of voluntary action were, as his account suggests, very successful. But Beecher did not confine himself to denominational, political, or public morality issues alone. As Benjamin Franklin had discovered three quarters of a century earlier, the empowering character of voluntary action made it difficult to restrict it to any one sphere of action. Amasa Walker, one of the twelve founders of the Hanover Street Association, went on to become an abolitionist and founder of the Free Soil Party; lectured at Amherst, Oberlin, and Harvard; served as Massachusetts secretary of state; and was a Republican congressman during the Civil War.

In 1850 Walker proudly recalled the association's early support for the American lyceum movement, programs of educational public lectures on science, history, and edifying topics that began in central Massachusetts in 1826 and served as a moral alternative to the saloon or theater. The lyceums were open to women as well as to men, were an immediate success, and were soon imitated nationwide. They spread to fifteen states by 1835, and by 1860 there were 3,000 local lyceums across the country. Walker wrote that the Hanover Association had endorsed the movement during its infancy, in late 1828.

> It is quite difficult to realize the great importance of this Lyceum effort in changing the public state, and in giving a higher and better tone to the public mind. Individual voluntary associations pass away, but ideas become impressed upon society never to be obliterated. Lyceums, however transient as organizations, have produced a social revolution in a most essential particular, and the several lecturers who now traverse the broad territory of the United States, entertaining thousands with their eloquence, have been created by the new tastes generated by the Lyceum movement.

Walker went on to summarize what he regarded as Beecher's "vast influence" in Boston "through the various agencies he set in motion." The young men's associations he created gave "such an impetus to the public mind that societies of young men were formed for a great variety of kindred objects." Walker described a "grand display" of these on July 4, 1833, when some three dozen societies gathered to pay tribute to Beecher. They included the Boston Lyceum, the Franklin Debating Society, the Boston Young Men's Society, the Boston Young Men's Marine Bible Society, the Boston Laboring Young Men's Temperance Society, the Lyceum Elocution and Debating Society, the Mercantile Library Association, the Mechanics Library Association, the Young Men's Temperance Society, and the Mechanics Lyceum.

Beecher's strategic location within the evangelical movement encouraged the rapid spread of his ideas. The domestic missionary societies, created at the beginning of the century, were intended to ensure that the evangelical message was carried not only to the new settlements on the frontier but into the cities. Vitality for these efforts came in part from privately funded "education societies," which made scholarship funds available to pious and indigent young men who, after completing their degrees, went on to become ministers or laymen active in the evangelical movement.[33]

Wherever they went, the New England evangelicals used their organizational abilities both to promote their own fortunes and to work for what they defined as the public good. And though physically isolated from one another, they remained closely linked, not only through the comings and goings of itinerant evangelical preachers, but also through the newspapers, periodicals, and, eventually, lyceum lecture circuits. As historian Mary P. Ryan observed in her study of civic life in antebellum New York, towns and villages were "overrun" with voluntary associations. The village directory for Utica in 1828 listed "twenty-one religious or charitable societies, three reform societies, five benefit associations, six fraternal orders, and six self-improvement associations."[34]

The real power of these associations lay in the fact that, despite their sectarian origins, most quickly accommodated themselves to the reality of pluralism and recruited members without respect to their religious affiliations and formed alliances with groups founded by other denominations. In an important way, Beecher had reversed Dwight's formulation of the relation between religion and voluntary associations. For Dwight, religious faith empowered people to act effectively in civil society. For Beecher, voluntary activity became a means of leading people toward faith.

"Experimental Knowledge of Free Institutions"

Beecher himself eventually decided to go west and arrived in Cincinnati in the fall of 1832. Appointed as president and professor of theology at Lane Seminary, he quickly found the greater part of his time taken up by practical rather than theological matters—especially fund-raising for Lane and other western institutions. He soon was back in the East, touring in search of donors.

In the sermon prepared for this purpose, *A Plea for the West* (1835), Beecher broke new ground. His mentor Dwight had despaired of the efficacy of voluntary action and doubted that civic virtue could be maintained across vast expanses of territory, among "casual collections of mankind" who had settled according to "no fixed or regular scheme of colonization," who were united by no common object, and whose religious beliefs were varied or nonexistent.[35] Beecher, in contrast, saw the West as a challenge—and as the ultimate proving ground for the realization of nationhood through the "voluntary system." "What nation is blessed with such experimental knowledge of free institutions," Beecher asked,

> with such facilities and resources of communication, obstructed by so few obstacles, as our own? There is not a nation upon earth which, in fifty years, can by all possible reformation place itself in circumstances so favorable as our own for the free unembarrassed application of physical effort and pecuniary and moral power to evangelize the world.

"It is plain," Beecher went on, "that the religious and political destiny of our nation is to be decided in the West," which would soon be the center of the growing nation's population, wealth, and political power.[36]

But if the West was God's chosen ground for perfecting "experimental knowledge of free institutions," it also posed particular challenges. The population there was "assembled from all the states of the Union, and from all the nations of Europe . . . rushing in like the waters of the flood." Required for the West's "moral preservation" was "the immediate and universal action of those institutions which discipline the mind, and arm the conscience and the heart."

> So various are the opinions and habits, and so recent and imperfect is the acquaintance, and so sparse are the settlements of the West, no homogeneous public sentiment can be formed to legislate immediately into being the requisite institutions . . . A nation is being 'born in a day,' and all the nurture of schools and literary institutions is needed, constantly and universally, to rear it up to a glorious and unperverted manhood.

Beecher laid out the mechanics of constructing these institutions. An educated ministry, he said, was the "central luminary in each sphere." It "sends out schools and seminaries as its satellites by the hands of sons and daughters of its own training." A land served by able clergy would "of course be filled with schools, academies, libraries, colleges, and all the apparatus for the perpetuity of republican institutions." Education was the key. "We must educate!" Beecher declared, "or we must perish by our own prosperity. If we do not, short from the cradle to the grave will be our race. If in our haste to be rich and mighty, we outrun our literary and religious institutions, they will never overtake us; or come up after the battle of liberty is fought and lost, as spoils to grace the victory, and as resources of inexorable despotism for the perpetuity of our bondage."

In describing the urgency and the difficulty of the task, Beecher stressed the inadequacy of political institutions. The power of legislation, he argued, was minimal compared with that of an "undivided, earnest, decided public sentiment" and "well systematized voluntary associations." He warned in melodramatic language of the crisis posed by an ignorant and unchurched electorate:

If we do fail in our great experiment of self-government, our destruction will be as signal as the birthright abandoned, the mercies abused, and the provocation offered to beneficent Heaven. The descent of desolation will correspond with the past elevation. No punishments of Heaven are so severe as those for mercies abused; and no instrumentality employed in their infliction is so dreadful as the wrath of man. No spasms are like the spasms of expiring liberty, and no wailings such as her convulsions extort. It took Rome three hundred years to die; and our death, if we perish, will be as much more terrific as our intelligence and free institutions have given to us more bone, and sinew, and vitality. May God hide me from the day when the dying agonies of my country shall begin! O, thou beloved land! bound together by the ties of brotherhood and common interest and perils, live forever—one and undivided!

Having embraced the West, Beecher now extended his thinking in surprising ways. A conventional theme of American missionary rhetoric in the early nineteenth century had been the role of the East in redeeming the uneducated West. He played on these themes in *Plea for the West* (which was, after all, written as an appeal for donations). He then moved on to focus on the influx of foreign immigrants and the role that the West might play in redeeming the East.

Citing 1830 census figures, Beecher estimated that nearly three million Americans, adults and children, were illiterate. Many states, East and West, made no effort to provide public education. "Such masses of ignorance," he argued, "are most dangerous to liberty; for, as a general fact, *the uneducated mind is educated vice.*" The safety of the republic, he declared, was imperiled by "a million of voters without intelligence, or conscience, or patriotism, or property" who, "driven on by demagogues," may, "in our balanced elections, overrule all the property, and wisdom, and moral principles of the nation." The danger posed by native-born illiterates, Beecher continued, was compounded by "the rapid influx of foreign immigrants, unacquainted with our institutions, unaccustomed to self-government, inaccessible to education" and easily drawn to unscrupulous demagogues. "What is to be done," he asked, "to educate the millions which in twenty years Europe will pour out upon us?"

The remaining two-thirds of Beecher's *Plea for the West* were devoted to a highly inflammatory exploration of this issue—in particular the dangers posed to republican institutions by Roman Catholics. Interestingly, his fears centered around their ability to use voluntary associations to their own questionable ends. This was in no sense a diminishing of Beecher's faith in the possibilities of his "voluntary system." Rather, it emphasized his view that moral agency was not a property of institutions, but of the individuals who created and used them.

Like Madison's denunciation of faction in *The Federalist,* Beecher's depiction of the Catholic influence contained strange echoes of self-accusation. No one knew better than Beecher—the "ambitious ecclesiastic" who had forged the twelve young men of the Hanover Association into a force that revolutionized Boston politics—the power of "a corps of men acting systematically and perseveringly." Yet he worried that, in the case of Catholic associations, priests could manipulate "a community unapprised of their doings."

Beecher was not being disingenuous in his criticism of Catholic associations. Over the years, he had come to understand that the survival of the republic required *churches* and their ministers to step back from acting in the political arena as such, while at the same time requiring clergy to inspire and empower church *members* to act as moral agents. Thus, for all of his alarm about the potential power of Catholicism, he did not urge that the tide of immigration be stopped or that the immigrants be deprived of their rights as citizens. The problem, in his view, was not Catholic citizens, but the Catholic Church as an institution, which rejected democracy and, in claiming to be the one true church, rejected religious pluralism. Catholics posed no threat so long as they accepted such fundamental rules of civil society as toleration of other sects and separation of church and state.

Beecher's almost prescient attention to the problem of immigration (prescient because the influx of the 1830s was but a trickle compared with the deluge that would occur with the Irish in the 1840s) was only one of the remarkable aspects of *Plea for the West*. Of perhaps greater significance was Beecher's whole-hearted acceptance and evocation of evangelicalism's responsibility for the welfare of the nation as a whole. Accompanying this intense nationalism was an acceptance of the essentially secular nature of the evangelicals' task: despite his invocation of Edwards and his emphasis on the role of the clergy in the establishment of civil and literary institutions, Beecher's goal seemed to be essentially secular. He seemed to be saying that to establish institutions that enabled people to make free and informed political and religious choices was to create the preconditions for the Millennium to follow the Second Coming.

Finally, Beecher explicitly engaged the issue of public versus private support for the institutions he deemed vital to the republic's survival. Not only did he accurately point out the overall failure of states to make adequate provision for education (Ohio, for example, had established a number of colleges and then let them languish; Virginia had successfully started its university, but failed to appropriate funds for common schools), but he also pointed out the vulnerability of publicly supported institutions to the instability of the popular will. Stable institutions required the determined and committed support of a "republican phalanx" of private individuals, a "willing multitude to give and toil till intelligence and holiness . . . cover the land as the water cover[s] the sea."

His *Plea for the West* summarized the reasoning that had led evangelicalism first to advocate philanthropy and voluntarism and then to articulate the role of religion in civil society. At the same time, it pointed to a new set of challenges, which would be primarily secular in nature. The most important of these, Beecher suggested, involved the role of professionals. As he defined them, the professions, rather than being simply a body with specialized skills, became invested with the aura of a religious calling: practitioners not only had to be "duly qualified" but needed a high sense of responsibility for shaping the intellect of the nation, forming its conscience, and regulating "its affection, heart, and action." Professionals had to be "wise and understanding hearts, consecrated to the work," self-denying and disinterested. More than this, professionals had to pursue their task "embracing the experience of the past, and the accumulating knowledge of coming generations." While referring specifically to teachers, the role as Beecher defined it might equally well apply—and would subsequently be applied— to any learned profession in its highest sense. This sense, Beecher implied, required that professionals be trained in institutions that shared those high values.

Transforming Calvinism

Beecher's social activism was more than a pragmatic response to disestablishment. It was anchored in Calvinist doctrines of moral agency as they had evolved since the seventeenth century. Since Calvin's time, theologians—most notably Jonathan Edwards—had struggled to reconcile the possibility of moral agency with the doctrine of original sin. Calvin's formulation of moral agency had been fatalistic: fallen man was incapable of moral action, since everything he did was tainted by his sinful nature. This view may have made sense when Europe still lay under the shadow of feudalism, but was out of step with the spirit of the Enlightenment. Influenced by the ideas of Newton and Locke, New England Calvinists strove to reinterpret mankind's duties and responsibilities in the light of new scientific discoveries about the natural and social worlds.

The problem, as Edwards put it, was to reconcile Calvinistic fatalism and moral passivity with the activist ideas of "human liberty, moral agency, accountableness, praise and blame" that were reshaping politics and markets in the eighteenth century.[37] The core of the problem was the doctrine of imputation, which burdened descendants of Adam and Eve with responsibility for sin which they had no agency in committing. Edwards did not deny original sin, but his reading of Locke enabled him to argue for a distinction between man's "natural ability" to make choices and his "moral inability" to make the right ones—his habitual inclination to sin.

Where the old Calvinists believed that man's sole freedom was the freedom to sin, Edwards argued that man was naturally able to choose not to sin, but morally unable to do so.

Edwards's followers labored to resolve this paradox by pecking away at the doctrine of imputation. While not rejecting imputation, Samuel Hopkins (1721–1803) and Nathaniel Emmons (1745–1840) argued that individuals' sense of guilt stemmed not from Adam's sinful acts, but from their own—thus highlighting free will and personal accountability. Their arguments enabled Dwight to entirely reject imputation and to expand on Edwards's conception of the twofold nature of sin—the individual ability to choose and the habitual tendency in acting to choose evil over good. Dwight refined this distinction by characterizing selfishness—"the preference of ourselves to other, and to all others; to the universe, and to God"—as the "universal sin."[38] The regenerate, in surrendering themselves to God's will, would find their selfishness replaced by "Disinterestedness, Love, God-will, Benevolence."[39] Dwight did not suppose that either regeneration or disinterested and benevolent actions could lead to salvation. But they could help believers obey God's commandments—obedience that God demanded of all, saved and unsaved alike.

Beecher understood the implications of these ideas for the kind of pluralistic and voluntary public arena he was beginning to envision in the wake of disestablishment. To engage the theological issues, he worked closely with his best friend, Nathaniel W. Taylor (1786–1858), pastor of New Haven's First Society and professor of theology at Yale. Having studied theology with Dwight and served as his private secretary, Taylor considered himself the bearer of his theological legacy.[40] As such, he was a particularly appropriate person to assist Beecher in his efforts.

In a letter to Beecher in 1819, Taylor mapped out his theological calling, promising to settle "points which Edwards did not aim to settle, and which will, to some extent, change the current of theological sentiment" in a series of jointly authored essays to be published in the *Christian Spectator*.[41] These points centered around "unsettled, and almost untouched" aspects of moral agency, volition, and free will. If sin consisted of specific intentional acts, Taylor argued, one could not infer "a sinful heart in any moral agent, distinct from his own sinful choices, determinations, or preferences." As he would put it in his 1828 sermon *"Concio ad Clerum,"* "guilt pertains exclusively to the voluntary action."[42] According to his biographer, Taylor "opposed the teaching which was held by most Calvinists, that sin was the necessary means to the greatest good. He sought to substitute for it the supposition that, owing to the nature of moral agency, God could not prevent sin, or at least the present degree of sin, in a moral system. In such an argument lay the germ for a new freedom for the will of man, making him no longer a mere automaton in the hands of God."[43]

Religious historian Sidney Mead has argued that Taylor was able to expand the range of choices men could make by reassessing the authority of scripture.[44] Edwards was able embrace the paradox of man's capacity to choose the good yet his moral inability to do so because scripture revealed this to be the case. Taylor argued that scriptural truth was not self-evident and that revelation had to be "tried at the bar of human reason."[45]

Reconciling Calvinist fatalism, which preached the uselessness of work in the world, with the idea of the individual as an active moral agent, was no easy task. It came perilously close to the heretical notion that salvation could be achieved through good works. Taylor and Beecher avoided this hazard. They never asserted good works were a means to salvation. Rather, like Edwards, they insisted that faith was the precondition for moral agency—the capacity to freely choose to do good (which God demanded, irrespective of his ultimate judgment). They went beyond Edwards in their understanding of the institutional dimensions of moral agency, specifically, the extent to which voluntary associations, religious and secular, could both transform people into moral agents and create the social and political conditions for expanding the possibilities of moral agency.

Beecher and Taylor's theological innovations directed believers' energies into the world—transforming every occupation and activity into a ministry. But what made these innovations especially significant was the extent to which they distinguished sectarian proselytizing from secular reform. Reforming social, political, and economic institutions had profound spiritual implications, both for people of faith acting as reformers and for the people affected by reform, but it was not in itself spiritual activity. Rather, it was an expression of the activists' individual spiritual convictions and a way of creating the conditions under which others could begin to make the choices that could lead them to spiritual regeneration. This clear articulation of the relation between the domain of the spirit (the individual's accountability to God) and the world (the stage upon which men were called to act in obedience to God's commandments) gave this form of Protestantism its distinctly civic character. Believing that participation in voluntary associations created opportunities for individuals to make morally informed choices enabled these civic Protestants to put aside divisive sectarianism without diminishing their evangelical fervor.

These beliefs had powerful organizational implications. Most important, it led these Protestants toward a distinctive articulation of the organizational ties between religious bodies and the charitable and educational enterprises they established. Because their theology had shifted the primary arena of spirituality from the church to the individual, formal interorganizational relationships between religious bodies and secular organizations mattered less than participation by people of faith in their affairs. This enabled them to establish a wide range of charitable institutions which, though not formally tied to religious bodies, were linked to them through the faith of the individuals who participated in them. Because they were nonproselytizing, they were able to form inclusive coalitions around reform, charitable, and education issues with other groups, religious and secular.

"Civic" and Sectarian Religion

As theological conservatives overcame their distrust of voluntary associations in the mid-nineteenth century, the pioneering Congregationalist enterprises found themselves in competition with charities, schools and colleges, hospitals, missionary societies, and other associations sponsored by other Protestant groups. This highlighted the differences between the Congregationalists' civic inclusiveness and the theological conservatives' sectarian exclusiveness. During the Civil War, when the Congregationalists and other theological liberals joined forces to create the United States Sanitary Commission, the nonprofit organization that contracted with the federal government to provide public health and relief services to Union soldiers, theological conservatives formed a rival organization, the United States Christian Commission. The two pursued very different agendas: one strictly secular, professional, and scientific, the other explicitly sectarian, spiritualized, and proselytizing. Proclaiming the virtues of volunteers—the system "adopted eighteen hundred years ago by our Lord"—the Christian Commission denounced the Sanitary Commission for using paid agents, who, it claimed, treated soldiers like machines rather than like men.[46] The Sanitary Commission dismissed its rival's efforts as sentimental and inefficient. Both commissions were infused with religiosity, but each expressed its religiosity in a different way: the Sanitary Commission was a secular entity organized and controlled by religious men to serve a broad public; the Christian Commission was a religious charity organized and controlled by religious leaders to provide services to co-religionists and to attract converts.

The contrast between them became even more evident after the war, when the Freedmen's Bureau, the federal agency entrusted with the task of managing the political and economic habilitation of freed slaves, invited volunteers to assist the government in the task of "reconstructing" the South. Organizations of all sorts—some religious, some secular—responded with enthusiasm, sending thousands of volunteers to teach, to preach, and to restore political and economic institutions.

Early in 1865 two of the major "freedmen's" societies, the New York National Freedmen's Relief Association and the American Union Commission, together with elements from New York's Women's Center Relief Association, a branch of the Sanitary Commission, consolidated themselves as the American Freedmen's and

Union Commission.[47] This brought together the eastern elite liberal Protestant advocates—primarily Unitarian and Congregational—on behalf of former slaves who had closely allied themselves with General Oliver Otis Howard's push for rationalization of the benevolent societies' efforts.

By the spring of 1866 the Freedmen's and Union Commission was pushing to bring other voluntary groups under its umbrella but was meeting with resistance. Despite commission pleas for cooperation and for a Christian but nonsectarian emphasis in education and relief efforts, the conservatives, whose organizations were formally tied to denominations, resisted consolidation. As one Methodist minister put it, "Methodist hands should have handled Methodist funds, and been appropriated to pay Methodist teachers, to found Methodist schools, and carry on a work for which the denomination should have due credit."[48] The "unsectarian" groups not unreasonably feared that the sectarians' efforts endangered the credibility of Reconstruction. The South, they argued, needed common schools, not parochial institutions. After all, as one correspondent in the *American Freedman* pointed out, most Southerners were already practicing Christians.

This struggle between civic and sectarian Protestantism would be played out again in the 1880s and 1890s over the question of religious charities in urban social reform. The conservative sectarians would identify with the rescue mission model, which tied relief to proselytizing and assisted people on the basis of professed need, whereas the civic liberals would shift criteria for service provision from neediness to worthiness—with an emphasis on systematic approaches to eliminating the causes of poverty, based on scientific studies of conditions rather than on sentimental and spiritualized efforts to relieve suffering.

This difference of approach would eventually be institutionalized in the divergence of religious charity from scientific philanthropy—a departure that would have an enormous impact on the development of nonprofit institutions in the twentieth century. The scientific philanthropists, virtually all of them members of theologically liberal denominations, would make ever larger commitments of wealth to foundations, universities, and the other secular institutions that came to define public life. The theological conservatives, until the mobilization of the Christian right in the 1970s, would restrict their public commitments to supporting religious and religiously tied institutions.

Conclusion

The historical record indicates that the proliferation of voluntary associations in nineteenth-century America involved groups whose theological convictions and religious practices led them to see secular civil society as the most promising arena for exercising moral agency. This was the product of a creative adaptation of their theology to the challenges of democracy.

To appreciate the centrality of theology to these groups' response to democracy, it is essential to understand that their defense of religious establishment was not based on a belief that church membership ensured salvation. As Calvinists, they believed that God alone had this power. The best the churches could do was to prepare believers to submit to God's judgment. As Dwight put it, "Man is to plant, and water; and then, and then only, is warranted either to hope, or to pray, that God will give the increase." The role of the church was one of preparation, not of sanctification.

Disestablishment forced Congregationalists to reconsider their strategic options. Going head-to-head with other religious groups in a struggle to win converts could, at best, bring only limited success. In any event, since neither they nor any other sect could claim an exclusive power to dispense salvation, the more productive endeavor—in line with their belief that they were not saving souls, but preparing them for salvation according to God's wisdom—was to embrace those activities consistent with preparation: promoting health, morality, and public order, and imparting the literacy that gave people access to God's word and helped to make them useful and productive citizens. All of these were goals that could serve as bases for alliances with other religious groups. All were consistent with a commitment to democracy. All, absent religious establishment, were ways of making democratic life more virtuous—by transforming citizens into moral agents committed to what Leonard Bacon, a protégé of Beecher and Taylor, called "the business of doing good."

The conception of moral agency, as developed by Taylor and Beecher, was able to bypass the Calvinist paradox that credited humanity with free will but denied its ability to choose to do good. They insisted, as Edwards had, that faith was the precondition for moral choice. Adding their own institutional dimension, Taylor and Beecher suggested that voluntary associations, religious and secular, were settings that enhanced believers' capacity to make moral choices. Within this framework, voluntary associations became not only an instrument for doing good but also a means of teaching people how to do so. As such, secular associational activity became incorporated into the religious life of these believers. Because civic Protestants identified secular associations as primary arenas for the acquisition and exercise of faith, civic engagement became as integral to their religious practice as the physical form and internal arrangements of church buildings, the sermon-centered liturgy, and standing rather than kneeling to pray.

It is easier to understand the extent to which religious belief influenced civic behavior at a time when religion was a central part of public and private life than it is today. Grasping the continuing influence of religion is made harder by the fact that contemporary Americans, even if devoutly religious, are less likely than their forebears to be theologically literate.

Yet certain theological orientations continue to be embedded in religious and civic practices and institutions. More important, as Verba, Schlozman, and Brady suggest, the extent and intensity of lay involvement in congregational worship and governance activities affect not only the extent to which adherents acquire civic and organizational skills but their willingness and capacity to exercise those skills in secular settings.

But neither congregational participation nor civic engagement requires a conscious awareness of the theological rationale that shapes and sanctions them. Values in both religious and secular organizations, once institutionalized, have acquired a taken-for-granted status and are unlikely to be altered unless changing circumstances lead people to question them. When those values are challenged in a religious setting, any issues raised are apt to be resolved on the basis of belief, not expediency, because in faith communities belief is the touchstone of authority.

An appreciation for the formative power of Calvinist doctrines of moral agency is essential to understanding not only the distinctive response of nineteenth-century Congregationalists to the challenge of disestablishment but also the legacy of civic engagement that has persisted into our own time, which is the broad context of each of the following eight case studies. Indeed, the remainder of this book, set in the context of America at the turn of the twenty-first century, demonstrates the continuing need to appreciate the power of theology and practice in understanding the uses of contemporary religious groups and values.

Faith Communities

The four chapters in Part Two present case studies of the public roles and functions of religion in congregations and communities, the root context of faith. The first three chapters examine religious practices and social interactions in particular settings, while the fourth analyzes the social patterns of regular Christian churchgoers.

Mary Jo Bane, in Chapter 2, examines an apparent disconnect between the deep resources for moral and social discourse in Roman Catholicism and the lived reality of social capital in Catholic parishes. Combining her identities as a policy analyst and a faithful Roman Catholic, Bane weaves theology and regression results to probe why it is that Catholics, as a group, are less involved than Protestants in civic activities.

In Chapter 3, Omar McRoberts visits an impoverished corner of the Boston neighborhood of Dorchester and studies the attitudes of a cluster of black and immigrant congregations toward service to the community. His study contradicts comfortable assumptions that African-American churches have such service as a primary mission and can be relied upon to mend the safety net. Significantly, McRoberts portrays the inward-looking nature of several local congregations as a function not only of a lack of capacity but of a theology of "the world" as evil and of an ingrained fear of the violence that is a reality of "the street."

In Chapter 4, Brent Coffin studies the variables that shape moral deliberation in one affluent suburb. He tracks the different ways three historic Protestant congregations negotiate religious differences and conflicting moral orientations to generate "thick" moral deliberation on an important social issue: the inclusion of gays and lesbians. Coffin shows that faith-based moral discourse can be compatible with the democratic values of tolerance and mutual respect.

Nancy Ammerman, in Chapter 5, shows how specific traditions provide their members with stories, activities, and practices that link them to the world in different forms of participation. She also shows the importance of religious beliefs and activities as predictors of civic involvement. Ammerman then uses survey data to evaluate styles of civic engagement within several Christian traditions.

chapter 2

The Catholic Puzzle: Parishes and Civic Life

Mary Jo Bane

SOME CATHOLIC BISHOPS seek to deny communion to Catholic politicians who support abortion rights. Catholic parishes mobilized by the Industrial Area Foundations lobby for affordable housing. Lay Catholics occupy important leadership positions in local and national right-to-life committees. Catholic members of Congress divide, mostly but not entirely by party, in votes on stem cell research, partial birth abortion, and welfare reform. National polls show that neither Catholics' demographic characteristics nor their attitudes on public issues are particularly different from the nation as a whole; and that Catholics are less involved with and give less money to religious and nonprofit groups than members of other religions. As part of their Sunday liturgies, tens of millions of Catholics hear scripture readings and homilies urging them to eschew riches and care for the poor.[1]

As these examples indicate, the Catholic presence in American public life takes varied and often contradictory forms. The contradictions and tensions raise all manner of interesting questions from, for example, political strategists confused about what Catholic voters really respond to, clergy complaining that nobody seems to pay attention to Church teachings, and social justice advocates wanting more involvement by Catholics in social and economic issues. My own membership in the last group was part of my motivation for undertaking this study.

But this chapter primarily reflects a more analytical stance, an attempt to evaluate the Catholic presence in American civic life. As I have looked at the research on the role that congregations and other religious groupings play in shaping public life, and done some investigation of my own, I have identified what I call the Catholic puzzle: a strong set of official teachings on social justice and faithful citizenship alongside Catholic participation in various realms of civic life that is no higher than that of other denominations, and in a number of areas, lower. Exploring this puzzle is a valuable enterprise for those of us who care about the Catholic Church, but also for anyone interested in the interplay of theology, organizational forms, and religious practice.

The Catholic Church and its parishes provide particularly noteworthy examples of this interplay. Catholics are the largest single religious denomination in the United States, with over 60 million Americans, almost a quarter of the population, identifying themselves as Catholic.[2] Data on Catholics are available both from specialized surveys of Catholics and from nationally representative surveys such as the Social Capital Benchmark Survey, which I rely on here and which uses samples of Catholics that are large enough for valid analysis. In addition, because of the universal and hierarchical nature of the Church, it is possible to talk about Catholic teachings, worship, and structure independent of empirically observed attitudes and behaviors, in a way that is less possible in other denominations.

There exist, therefore, a rich set of sources for understanding Catholic tradition and the practice of Catholics as they interact in various settings. These interactions illustrate many of the complexities that Nancy Ammerman illuminates in Chapter 5 about how religious narratives influence identity and how the practice of religion predicts levels of participation in civic life. And as I suggest toward the end of this chapter, rather mundane secular realities concerning, for example, the size and structure of parishes, staffing, and resources influence the behavior of Catholics as well. I seek to understand all this—at least to some extent—in an effort to illuminate both Catholic life and the intersection of religious practice and civic life more generally.

Catholic Teaching on Discipleship and Citizenship

In Catholic theology the Church is a timeless sacrament and a global institution as well as the gathered people of God; it has a life that both encompasses and transcends the empirically observable behavior of Catholic men and women. Although Vatican II emphasized that the Church is not defined solely by its hierarchy or its official teachings, the structure and nature of authority in the Catholic Church make it possible to describe its teachings independent of the expressed beliefs and practices of its component parishes and of individual Catholics.[3] My sources for this interpretation of Catholic teachings are therefore the documents of the hierarchical *magisterium* (the pope and the bishops), including especially the Vatican II documents, but also papal encyclicals, especially John Paul II's *Centesimus Annus,* the Catechism of the Catholic Church, and two pastoral letters produced by the National Conference of Catholic Bishops on peace and on the economy.[4] The official documents are not completely consistent, internally or with one another, so I also rely on the writings of Catholic theologians, including biblical scholars, moral theologians, and ecclesiologists.

The following five propositions are contained in Catholic social teaching, accepted by the broad middle of Church leaders and theologians, and more or less reflect the official positions that the institutional Church formally teaches.

1. Christian life takes place in community, reflecting the social nature of the human person as created by God and modeled after the fellowship of Jesus and the early Church, in both small parish units and the larger Church.

Catholics believe that their relationship with God, who created humans as social beings, takes place in community. God's covenants with Abraham, Moses, and David were covenants with peoples. Christian men and women belong to the community of disciples that Jesus founded and to which he continues to give life. Members of the community of disciples are called to worship and to live in a way that models for the world the values and teachings of Jesus. All are called to contribute, in various ways, to evangelization, proclaiming the good news and inviting others into the community, and to the healing and liberating work of Jesus in the world.

The parish is the primary local community in the Church, the place where disciples come together to live out their faith, and for which all have responsibility. At the same time, each parish is part of a larger community of communities, bound together by faith and the notion of discipleship itself.[5] Church structures and leaders shape, promote, and challenge discipleship, and through worship, reflection, and renewal keep it true to Church faith and responsive to the contemporary world.

2. All believers, clergy and lay, are called to discipleship and to holiness, to participate in the community of disciples that is the Church and to contribute to the mission of the Church.

Traditionally, and reflecting an institutional and hierarchical conception of the Church, a clear distinction was made between what was expected of Catholic clergy and what was expected of the laity. Christian living for the laity meant avoiding sin by obeying the commandments and the teachings of the Church. Perfection and holiness were to be pursued by a decision to leave the secular world and enter the priesthood or consecrated religious life, living by the evangelical counsels of poverty, celibacy, and obedience.

Vatican II asserted in contrast that all the faithful, laity as well as clergy, are called as Christians to a vocation of hearing and accepting Jesus' call to discipleship and of shaping their lives in accordance with that call.[6] This new understanding of Christian life also requires attention to social structures and to social justice, themes that permeate a number of Vatican II documents.[7] Sin is breaking the covenant of love with God and with each other. Sin always results from individual decisions and actions, but these can result in sinful structures—social, political, or economic institutions that oppress, violate human dignity, or inhibit full human development. Individuals are responsible if their own actions or failure to take action contribute to the creation or maintenance of "social sin." Lay Christians especially have a responsibility to work for justice and peace in the world, to sow the seeds of the kingdom of the God.

3. The mission of the Church encompasses salvation and liberation, in this world and the next, evangelism and service, both to fellow Christians and to "all nations."

On first reading, two of the most important Vatican II documents, both of which are elaborated in later writings and embodied in liturgy and practice, appear to take quite different positions on the mission of the Church. The first, *Lumen Gentium* (Dogmatic Constitution on the Church),[8] articulates a predominantly otherworldly and evangelical sense of the Church. The Church was established to bring all people to belief in God and in the saving power of Jesus Christ, and through faith, the sacraments, and holy lives, it was to bring them to eternal union with God. Holiness is primarily an interior state, characterized by prayer and a humble and loving attitude toward the world. This aspect of the mission of the Church dominates the Catechism, which devotes the bulk of its pages to doctrine, the sacraments, prayer, the beatitudes, and the commandments.

The second document, *Gaudium et Spes* (Pastoral Constitution on the Church in the Modern World), is quite different. This document focuses on "the joys and the hopes, the grief and anguish of the people of our times, especially of those who are poor and afflicted."[9] It talks in strong and compelling terms about human dignity and social justice, and about the responsibility of the Church for the liberation of humanity, both from personal sin and from oppressive social and economic conditions that prevent men and women from achieving their full human potential. *Gaudium et Spes* applies biblical and Church teaching to contemporary issues such as the protection of marriage and the family, economic development, political participation, and respect for diverse cultures. These issues are accorded less prominence in the Catechism, but appear even there, and are elaborated in both papal writings and documents from bishops' conferences after Vatican II.

A faithful reading of both contemporary and traditional Church teaching and of the scriptures is that Christian faith is about both this world and the next, both personal holiness and social liberation, a relationship to God both through worship and sacrament and through ministry to the poor and marginalized. The importance of both of these dimensions was emphasized at Vatican II and in subsequent writings of the pope, bishops, theologians, and commentators. This reading was stated eloquently by the 1971 Synod of Bishops in *Justice in the World:* "The Church has received from Christ the mission of preaching the Gospel message, which contains a call to man to turn away from sin to the love of the Father, universal brotherhood, and a consequent demand for justice in the world."[10]

Tensions and differences in emphasis in various writings and in the worship and activities of various parishes are apparent. Nonetheless, the mission of social justice is clearly critical to the Church.

4. In community and in service, the Church has a special place, a "preferential option," for the poor and the vulnerable, as part of a consistent ethic that is pro-life, pro-family, and pro-poor.

Catholic social teachings begin with basic moral principles, derived from scripture and from rational analysis, that provide the foundation for discussions of social justice.[11] The American bishops' letter on the economy formulated the basic principles in the following terms: primacy of the principle of human dignity; necessity to realize human dignity in community; right of participation; obligations to the poor and vulnerable; responsibility of society as a whole to enhance human dignity and protect human rights. The bishops emphasize the special claim that the poor and the vulnerable have on the community as a whole.[12]

The basic principle of human dignity is also foundational to Church teaching about the preciousness of life. The teachings on life, on the family, and on social justice all flow from an integrated analysis of the human person, the person in community, and the person in relationship to God. Church teachings are indeed pro-life, pro-family, and pro-poor.[13]

5. Christians are called to be responsible citizens and to participate in civic and political life to promote justice and protect life. This responsibility applies to individual Christians, to congregations, and to the institutional Church.

Much religious writing and talk about obligations to the poor conclude with recommendations that Christians experience a change of heart, love one another, take personal responsibility, and exercise private charity.[14] The assumption seems to be that if business people, public officials, and private citizens simply thought and behaved generously and lovingly toward each other, and if all exercised their responsibilities to themselves and each other, all would be well and the problems of poverty and injustice would disappear.

Catholic social teaching, in contrast, has both a stronger sense of sin and a more sophisticated understanding of the importance of the state, especially of democratic politics, in dealing with social and economic problems. The American bishops' letter recognizes that private charity alone is not sufficient to counteract the "structures of sin" that lead to poverty and oppression. Governments are necessary inventions to mobilize collective resources and effort for the common good and the good of the less fortunate. Christians carry out their responsibilities to the poor both through individual acts of charity and through exercising responsible citizenship in the service of justice.[15]

More recently, the Catholic bishops have elaborated on these issues in a letter on "Faithful Citizenship,"[16] which they produce every four years, before presidential elections. In their 2003 letter they said: "In the Catholic tradition, responsible citizenship is a virtue; participation in the political process is a moral obligation. All believers are called to faithful citizenship, to become informed, active and responsible participants in the political process."[17] The bishops emphasize the responsibility of Catholics to "measure all candidates, policies, parties and platforms by how they protect of undermine the life, dignity, and rights of the human person, and whether they protect the poor and vulnerable and advance the common good."[18]

Are Catholic teachings unique? The puzzle I am exploring concerns the thinness of Catholic civic life in the light of strong teachings on community and social justice. My framing of the puzzle asserts that Catholics ought to show more civic commitment than members of other religious traditions; this assertion presupposes a lack of equally strong social teachings by those traditions.

There have, of course, been many strong social justice statements by Protestant leaders and, more generally, by influential theologians and pastors from many groups. There is one sense, however, in which Catholic social teachings are unique. Only the Catholic Church has a teaching office, exercised by the bishops to disseminate its official teachings, which is unified and presumed to be binding on the faithful. The existence of the teaching office, as part of the hierarchical structure of the Church, means that Catholics should, in theory, receive consistent messages from their pastors in line with official teachings. No such structures exist in other denominations.

What happens in practice, in the hundreds of thousands of pulpits from which religious leaders preach, is another matter, about which there is little information. As we shall see, there are reasons to believe that the preaching that Catholics hear is less sharp than the strength of the official teachings might lead one to expect. And much evidence exists that the social and political opinions of Catholics are only slightly more pro-poor or pro-government than those of others.[19] Nonetheless, the presence of strong official teachings in a hierarchically structured Church is sufficient to pose a puzzle worth exploring, a puzzle that existed prior to and independently of the clergy abuse scandal that broke in 2002 and its aftermath.

The Civic Life of Catholics

The social teachings of the Catholic Church thus lead one to expect that its parishioners would be widely involved in community service and civic life—more involved, one would think, than members of denominations with less well developed or articulated social teachings.[20]

A number of studies suggest that this is not the case. A study by Independent Sector found relatively low levels of volunteering and financial contributions among Catholic respondents.[21] Christian Smith, in a study focused on evangelicals, reported that Catholics scored lower than either evangelicals or mainline Protestants on four of seven measures of social and political activism.[22] Robert Wuthnow, in a study focused on mainline Protestant church members, found that Catholics scored lower than mainline Protestants on nine measures of civic activities and lower than evangelicals on seven of the nine measures.[23]

Ammerman, in Chapter 5, explores the religious correlates of "doing good" in the community—being involved with neighbors, volunteering for service organizations, and contributing to secular charities. She finds that among the churchgoers she studied, these civic activities are enhanced both by particular religious orientations—that is, what she calls *Golden Rule* and *Activist* orientations rather than an *Evangelical* orientation—and by participation in religious activity and organizations. The patterns are interesting. Evangelical churchgoers tend to be less oriented toward broad social justice issues, but they are also extremely active in congregational life and other religious organizations. This explains, according to Ammerman, a level of civic activity among conservative Protestants that is lower than that among liberal and African-American Protestants, but about equal to Catholics. Catholics, in contrast, are more likely than any group to have an activist orientation toward the world, but much less likely to actually participate in parish and other religious activities; the Catholics Ammerman studied display lower levels of civic activity than those of liberal and African-American Protestants. Ammerman suggests a solution to what I have called the Catholic puzzle by pointing to the low levels of activity in Catholic parishes.

Other findings complement Ammerman's and support her general findings. For example, I looked at data on civic activity from the Social Capital Benchmark Survey, a nationally representative survey of about three thousand adults conducted in the fall of 2000 under the leadership of Robert Putnam of Harvard. The survey asked an extensive series of questions about organizational memberships, community engagement, volunteering, giving, and political activity, aimed at understanding social capital in the broadest sense. As such, it represents the best large-scale source of data on many of the elements of faithful citizenship. It also asked about religious affiliation and religious activity, and included a large enough sample of Catholics to permit comparative analysis.

In this study, religious identity was established by asking respondents their religious and denominational preference. For the purposes of Putnam's analysis, Catholics are all those who identify themselves as Catholic; they are not necessarily churchgoers, as are the respondents in Ammerman's study. The advantage of this study is that its Catholics are a nationally representative group, not limited to the two Albuquerque parishes studied by Ammerman.

I looked at six measures of civic activity, several of which are constructed from a number of variables:

- Volunteering for the needy: a yes answer to a question on whether the respondent had volunteered to help the needy or elderly at any time during the past year.

- Any nonreligious volunteering: a yes answer to questions on volunteering for the needy, for culture/arts, health, neighborhood, youth, school, or civic groups.

- Contributions to nonreligious charities: whether contributions were at least $100 for the year.

- Number of formal group involvements, excluding church and religious groups: constructed from answers to individual questions about different types of groups, such as sports clubs, youth organizations, school organizations, and veterans' groups.

- Electoral politics scale: constructed from questions on voting, being registered to vote, interest in politics and national affairs, political knowledge, and reading a daily newspaper.

- Protest scale: constructed from questions on belonging to any group that took local action for reform, attending a political meeting, rally, demonstration or march, signing a petition, participating in a political group, an ethnic nationality or civil rights organization, or a labor union.

I also looked at one measure that combined religious and civic activity, and four measures of religious participation:

- Giving and volunteering summary index: constructed from questions on the amount of volunteering and on contributions, both religious and nonreligious.

- Whether attended religious services at least weekly.

- Any participation in church activities besides services.
- Whether volunteered for religion.
- Contributions to religion: whether contributions for the year were at least $100.

Results appear in Table 2.1, with means reported by three categories of religious affiliation. Religious affiliation is divided for this analysis into three categories: Catholics; those of other religions, that is, those who identify themselves as Protestants or members of a specific denomination, as "just Christians," or as affiliates of another religion; and those who describe themselves as having no religion. I grouped together all other religions to make the contrast with Catholics clearer, but also because many of the categories, like "just Christian," were difficult to specify more exactly. The table shows sample means, not controlling for demographic or other variables.

The survey findings shown in the table show a consistent pattern. In all cases, Catholics' reported participation is lower than that for those describing themselves as members of other religions, but higher than that for those who reported no religion. Catholics were less likely than other religions to volunteer, to contribute to secular charities, to belong to formal groups, to participate in electoral politics, or to engage in political activism. The differences in civic participation are in some cases not large, but they are consistent. With regard to participation in religious organizations, activities, and giving, the differences are much larger.

I next analyzed the data on informal social interaction, nonreligious volunteering, and contributions to nonreligious charities controlling for age, gender, education, race, income, whether married, and presence of children in a regression equation that also included variables for Catholic and no religious affiliation.[24] With the demographic controls included, the coefficients on Catholic affiliation were statistically nonsignificant, meaning that Catholics differed little from members of other religions. In all cases, those with no religious affiliation were significantly lower than other religions.[25] In

Table 2.1 Civic participation by religious affiliation

	Catholic	Other religion	No religion
Volunteering for the needy	29%	32%	15%
Any nonreligious volunteering	46%	52%	35%
Contributions to nonreligious charities of at least $100	43%	45%	41%
Number of formal nonreligious group involvements	2.83	3.17	2.40
Electoral politics scale	2.77	3.00	2.32
Protest scale	.98	1.05	1.05
Giving/volunteering summary index	4.89	5.56	2.92
Church attendance at least weekly	48%	52%	0%
Any participation in church activities other than services	33%	50%	0%
Volunteered for religion	28%	33%	0%
Contributions to religion of at least $100	56%	67%	15%

Source: Social Capital Benchmark Survey, 2001.

short, the data from the Social Capital Benchmark Survey show that Catholics are not more likely than adherents of other religions to volunteer, to contribute, or to participate in civic or political life.

The Social Capital Benchmark Survey does not allow for construction of the virtue orientation scales that Ammerman used to explore the ways in which religious orientation interacts with civic participation. It does, however, include information on participation in religious activities, which as Table 2.1 confirms, indicates that Catholics are noticeably lower than other groups both in participation in activities other than services and in financial contributions to religion.

Following the logic of Ammerman's analysis, including a religious participation variable in the analyses should show a strong positive relationship for that variable with informal social interaction, nonreligious volunteering, and nonreligious giving. Including a religious participation variable would also be expected to result in a positive sign on the variable that indicates whether a respondent identifies as Catholic. With religious participation controlled for, this "Catholic" variable should be representing to at least some extent the Golden Rule and Activist orientations that Ammerman found to contribute to civic involvement. This is indeed what happens, although only for nonreligious giving does the effect of being Catholic reach statistical significance.

The simple means and regression results presented above are thus consistent with Ammerman's basic story, and suggest that it is applicable to self-identified Catholics nationwide. Broadly speaking, the Catholic story encourages community and civic participation and service to others. But Catholic parishes do not provide the opportunities and settings for practicing these virtues. Catholics, as a result, are no more likely than those of other religions to carry a mission of service and civic involvement into the world.

Catholic Parish Life

Congregations are places where people come together, converse, interact, engage in projects, and form bonds of cooperation and trust—social capital, in short, constituting perhaps half the social capital that exists in the United States today.[26] They are training grounds for civic skills—participating in meetings, writing letters, planning projects, making decisions, giving speeches. And as Sidney Verba and his colleagues have pointed out, congregations are for many people, especially low-income people, minorities, and women, the primary setting in which these skills necessary for civic life are learned and practiced.[27] The extent to which parishes teach skills, build networks, and shape patterns of participation or fail to do so can have a powerful influence on the civic behavior of Catholics.

St. William's. My own parish, St. William's, provides an example of a Catholic parish which, if not strictly representative, is typical of many parishes.[28] St. William's serves a territory of about one square mile in north Dorchester, part of the city of Boston. The neighborhood is an old Irish enclave, heavily Catholic, which is increasingly home to immigrants, especially from Vietnam. It is mostly working and middle class, with some professionals, some subsidized housing for the elderly and families, and some poor, especially among the immigrants. Mass attendance on a typical weekend is about 1,500, spread over one Vietnamese (by far the largest attendance) and four English masses.

The parish budget is about $400,000 per year. Both the percentage of parishioners who contribute and the percentage of income given by those who do contribute are estimated to be quite low.[29] The parish has no endowment, and almost no funds set aside for contingencies; finances are very tight and a continual source of concern. The parish runs a school for about 240 children, financed by tuition, an enormous bingo game, and some tuition scholarship funds from the archdiocese. The staff of the parish includes two priests, one of whom is Vietnamese, a secretary, a part-time business manager, a youth minister, and some additional paid part-time help. Two older priests who are retired from active parish work assist with weekend liturgies. The parish makes extensive use of volunteers to support basic programs and services; over a hundred volunteers serve in one capacity or another.

The parish's mission statement, a product of the parish council, is printed every week in the bulletin:

> Gathered in common praise and worship of God, we the community of St. William's Parish affirm Jesus as the center of our lives and the reason for our being. Thankful for God's goodness, we live as generous stewards of the gifts of time, talent and treasure entrusted to us. We promote unity within our parish and celebrate the richness of our diverse culture. We are and we minister to people of all ages. We are committed to excellence in our school and religious education programs. We work with others to address the concerns of the wider community and the needs of all our brothers and sisters. With God's help we strive to live out these gospel ideas, in this place, in these times.

The pastor places a good deal of emphasis on liturgies and homilies. Homilies generally reflect on the day's scriptural readings and attempt to convey both a sense of God's love and graciousness and some practical lessons for everyday life. For example, the homilies for the first weeks in 2000 reflected on the first few chapters of the Gospel according to Mark or Paul's first letter to the Corinthians. One homily spoke strongly about the need for repentance and conversion, using as examples people who changed their lives by overcoming alcoholism or by devoting more time to their families. Another talked about reducing anxiety and stress through prayer and through experiencing and accepting God's love. A third reflected on Jesus' ministry of healing and our call to be healers in our daily lives. The pastor from 1996 to 2003 delivered occasional homilies on social justice, including quite specific homilies on campaign finance reform and on a ballot initiative to cut taxes, both in the summer and fall of 2000. In the spring of 2002, the pastor preached a number of times on the clergy abuse crisis in the church. A new pastor came to the parish in 2003; he seems not inclined to speak to social or political issues.

Music at the liturgies is quite professional, with a good choir and desultory congregational singing. Liturgies on the major feasts are bilingual in English and Vietnamese, as is a fall multicultural celebration. There are strong religious education programs, in both English and Vietnamese, and a small program for adults who want to become Catholics. The parish sponsors sports teams and hosts AA meetings; it also sponsors a parent-to-parent group. It has a committee for service to the poor, which has attracted a small number of volunteers for service at a homeless shelter. A group of parishioners and the pastor participated in two work retreats in Haiti, which other parishioners support through donations of cash, medical supplies, and school supplies. The parish is a member of the Greater Boston Interfaith Organization, and some parishioners are part of that group's organizing efforts for improved education and affordable housing. During the summer and fall of 2000 the parish made voter registration available in the church. There is a reasonably active parish council and a finance council, in addition to various ad hoc committees to plan, for example, a seventy-fifth reunion for the parish and school, and renovations to the church.

The pastor from 1996 to 2003, who was in his mid-forties (young for a pastor; indeed, young for a priest these days), was quite liberal, both politically and theologically. The parishioners are a mixed lot. The Vietnamese immigrants bring with them a conservative culture and attitude toward church. The English-speaking parishioners are quite diverse, but many combine old-line conservative Democratic party politics with an approach to Catholicism that has its roots in the pre-Vatican II Church. The neighborhood is very active politically, with high voter turnouts and a strong civic association that deals with local issues such as crime, traffic, and the condition of the subway stop. The changing demographics of both neighborhood and parish introduce some interesting class and ethnic diversity that the parish is dealing with; it is clearly a more diverse congregation than it has been in the past. I am an active member of the parish, and thus not an unbiased observer, but it seems to me a warm and lively community, supportive and not particularly demanding, that is also, in many ways, profoundly ordinary.

Patterns of parish activity.[30] As at St. William's, the basic connection that most Catholics have with their parishes is through Sunday worship services. Most parishes celebrate four or five weekend liturgies. In the National Congregations Study, the median parish reported holding eleven worship services over the course of the week, including weekend liturgies, weekday masses, funerals, and weddings.[31] All parishes also celebrate the other sacraments: baptism, confirmation, reconciliation (confession), marriage, and anointing of the sick. These worship services and sacraments absorb a significant amount of the ordained staff's time.[32]

In addition to liturgies, parishes sponsor a myriad of activities, as described for St. William's. The majority of these are directed at the parish membership itself, both to educate members and to build community. Examples are religious education classes for children and adults, study groups, community social events, and the still common bingo games.

The National Pastoral Life Center conducted surveys of parish staffs in 1992 and 1997, gathering for information on parish activities, among other topics.[33] Nearly all those surveyed had religious education activities in both years. In 1997, 84 percent (down from 90 percent in 1992) reported having picnics, potlucks, or social events for the whole parish. Thirty percent had bingo games. (The 1992 survey reported 56 percent with bingo. The change may represent a real decline.)

The National Congregations Study asked a series of questions about congregational activities in its survey of congregational leaders. In addition to the median eleven worship services per week, the median parish reported sponsoring twelve classes and five group and five committee meetings over the course of a month. Respondents were also asked a series of twenty-seven questions about specific nonworship activities. At least a quarter of the Catholic parishes responding to the survey (weighted by size) reported having a "group or meeting or class or event" devoted to: discussing a book other than the Bible (33 percent), discussing parenting issues (68), physical healing (55), cleaning or maintaining the building (66), organizing or encouraging volunteer work (75), learning about their own tradition (73), informing new members (83), prayer (86), putting on a performance of some type (51), attending a performance (40), training religious education teachers (80), learning about other religious traditions (28), twelve-step or self-help groups (46), or discussing congregational finances (58).

The National Congregations Study also asked about social services programs. Mark Chaves and colleagues found that 82 percent of Catholic parishes report participating in some kind of social service, community development, or neighborhood project. These include food programs (59 percent), housing (33), clothing (19), helping the homeless (17), and health care (14).

Politics are also present. Chaves reports that in 45 percent of parishes people were told at worship services about opportunities for political activity and that 26 percent had distributed a voter guide.[34] Some parishes, including my own, are engaged in community organizing activities, often under the auspices of the Industrial Areas Foundation. These community organizing groups, such as Greater Boston Interfaith Organization, Communities Organized for Public Service (better known as COPS) in San Antonio, and South Bronx Churches, are ecumenical, congregation-based organizations, often involving dozens of congregations and tens of thousands of participants. They tend to focus on local issues, and have been quite successful in pressuring local officials, for example, to develop affordable housing or to build water systems.[35] Many observers consider these organizing efforts among the most promising in the country.[36]

Parishes, of course, vary enormously. My own parish of St. William's is moderately active for a parish of its size. Others are both larger and more active. In 1993 a reporter for the Long Island newspaper *Newsday* looked for a lively Long Island parish to serve as the focus of a series. He found St. Brigid's, which he described as "nothing like St. Rigid's" (his fictive name for lifeless and rule-bound parishes).[37] St. Brigid's is a large, diverse parish of about 23,000 Catholics, four priests, and five deacons. The parish, according to Robert Keeler, produces an astounding level of activity—as reflected in a Sunday bulletin that often runs twenty-two pages, compared with four to eight for the average parish. On one typical Monday evening, the peace and justice committee and the program for bringing adults into the Church met; the rock band and the children's choir practiced; boys played basketball; the church itself had an Italian mass and a candlelight rosary; and the Haitian community offered religious education.[38]

But despite the diversity, and despite what looks like a fairly high level of activity in most Catholic parishes, the National Congregations Study shows that when compared with Protestant congregations of similar size, especially evangelical congregations, Catholic parishes are much less active. Catholic parishes, relative to other congregations, are very large and appear to have a great deal going on. To understand patterns of activity more clearly, we need to adjust for size. I looked at all the congregations in the national study that reported having at least 1,000 regular participants: for Catholics, 203 parishes, for evangelical, 72 congregations, and for mainline, 42 congregations. There were only 7 large black Christian congregations in the sample, so I exclude their data as not sufficiently representative. These data were collected on congregations, normally through reports by the pastor or leader of the congregation. Table 2.2 shows some of the more interesting comparisons.

Large Catholic parishes are much larger than even large Protestant congregations. They also have a much larger number of worship services per week, an average of fourteen compared with about three for other denominations. (Parishes have one or two masses on weekdays, and an average of four masses on weekends.) Interestingly, however, they have a much smaller number of participants in more than one worship service than evangelical congregations—70 compared with 300. (Most parishes have a small but regular daily Mass crowd.)

Looking at activities other than worship services, we see that Catholic parishes have a smaller number of classes, choirs, and groups, and a much smaller number of members reported participating in these activities. They also report a much smaller number of people in leadership roles. (The same patterns appeared when I constructed per capita variables on these same dimensions and analyzed the whole sample.) The only category for which Catholic parish participation appears to be higher than for conservative Protestants is for volunteers for social services or community programs, but even here the per capita number is slightly higher for conservative and much higher for mainline Protestants.

Associated with these differences in activity are large differences in resources. The median Catholic large parish (which, remember, is considerably larger than the large Protestant congregations with which I compared it) reports an annual income of $671,000, compared with $1,600,000 for white conservative/evangelical Protestant congregations and $990,000 for large white liberal/mainline Protestant congregations. The median Catholic parish reports eight full-time staff, compared with twenty for conservative/evangelical and nine for liberal/mainline Protestant congregations. Whether lower resources cause the lower levels of activity or vice versa (or neither) is an interesting but unanswerable question.

All this suggests that if congregations are schools for citizenship

Table 2.2 Characteristics of large congregations

	White Catholic	White conservative/ Evangelical Protestant	Liberal/Mainline Protestant
Regular participants	2,500	1,900	1,900
Number of worship services	14	3.5	3
Number of participants in more than one worship service	70	300	25
Number of classes	14	25	23.5
Number of adults participating in classes	30	400	100
Number of choirs	3	6	6
Number of participants in choirs	40	120	125
Number of groups	7	13.5	13.5
Number of participants in groups	130	400	300
Number of persons in leadership roles	100	225	180
Number of volunteers for social services programs	40	32.5	100
Income	$671K	$1,600K	$1,000K
Full-time staff	8	20	9

Source: National Congregations Study, 1999.

through their community life, Catholic parishes are not doing a good job of providing this education. Why not?

Catholic Sacramental Life

It is certainly misleading to think of any church as a social service agency or a community organization. In describing the Church, the important Vatican II document *Lumen Gentium* defines it first as a mystery and as a sacrament—"a sign and instrument of communion with God and of the unity of the entire human race" with the mission of "proclaiming and establishing among all peoples the kingdom of Christ and God." The Catholic Church is a sacramental church, with the Eucharist at its center.

But seeing the sacramental nature of the Church as inconsistent with teaching and practicing community and social justice is a misreading, I believe, of the character of Catholic worship. In both history and contemporary documents, the themes are intertwined. In the Acts of the Apostles, probably written toward the end of the first century, the Christian community on the day of Pentecost, when according to tradition the Holy Spirit came to the community, was described as follows: "They devoted themselves to the apostles' teaching and fellowship, to the breaking of the bread and the prayers . . . All who believed were together and had all things in common; they would sell their possessions and goods and distribute the proceeds to all, as any had need . . . they broke bread . . . with glad and generous hearts, praising God and having the goodwill of all the people" (Acts 2: 42–47).

The first document issued by Vatican II was *The Constitution on the Sacred Liturgy*.[39] While noting that "the sacred liturgy is not the Church's only activity," it goes on to say, "nevertheless, the liturgy is the summit toward which the activity of the Church is directed; it is also the source from which all its power flows." In the liturgy, the redemption and sanctification of men and women are both remembered and accomplished; the community of disciples is assembled and united; and a moral framework for all of life is taught and exemplified.[40]

The first part of every Sunday liturgy in every parish, following opening hymns and brief prayers, centers on three scripture readings, from the Old Testament, the apostolic letters, and the Gospels.[41] The Gospels are read more or less in order over a three-year cycle, thus ensuring that all of Jesus' teachings and actions are presented at some point, including, of course, his acts of charity and his teachings on the poor. A short homily follows the day's assigned scripture readings. These Sunday homilies are the primary occasions for calling to the attention of Catholics what the Church teaches about doctrine, the virtuous life, morality, charity, and politics.[42]

Homilists have a fair amount of discretion over their Sunday preaching. The official guidance on homilies for America's Catholic parishes comes from the National Conference of Catholic Bishops in the document "Fulfilled in Your Hearing."[43] This document suggests that the task of the preacher is to "speak from the scriptures to a gathered congregation in such a way that those assembled will be able to worship God in spirit and truth, and then go forth to love and serve the Lord."[44] This wording deemphasizes doctrinal instruction and moral exhortation as the central purpose of homilies, and stresses the importance of helping the faithful to recognize the presence of God in their lives.

A number of guides, and indeed prepared homilies, are available for those who choose to use them.[45] They tend to focus on the development of character, the importance of faith, and the performance of personal acts of witness and charity.[46] Perhaps the most "activist" advice on homilies, and countless examples of actual homilies, comes from the project of Walter J. Burghardt, S.J., on "Preaching the Just Word," which he describes as "an effort to improve significantly the preaching of justice issues."[47] Burghardt's published homilies, which he offers as examples of ways to achieve this goal, are scriptural, attentive to virtue and character, nonpartisan, and seldom explicitly political. They often include both statistical and anecdotal descriptions of social and economic problems. Burghardt sees the job of the homilist as helping his listeners "hear the cry of the poor" in their heart and respond consistently with the Gospels, which of course contain a good deal of material on compassion and justice for the poor.

The liturgy of the Word closes with the communal recitation of an ancient creed followed by a series of short prayers, usually of the form: "For *x*, we pray to the Lord; Lord, hear our prayer." Prayers typically reflect general concerns for the community (for the poor and the sick), current public concerns (for peace in the Middle East and Northern Ireland; for public officials, that their votes may reflect a respect for life) or parishioners' needs (for Mary Smith as she undergoes chemotherapy).

Most parishes take up a collection between this first part of the liturgy and the second. Sometimes, following the practice of the early Church (and the urgings of at least some contemporary liturgical theologians), the collection is for the poor; usually, however, the collection is for the support of the parish with periodic second collections for various diocesan, papal, or charitable activities.

The second part of every Sunday liturgy is the liturgy of the Eucharist, a ritual meal, in which bread and wine are brought to the table, blessed, transformed, broken, and distributed to the community in celebration of the death and resurrection of Jesus and of his continued life in the Church. The blessed and transformed bread and wine, now, for Catholics, the body and blood of Jesus, are distributed to the congregation, nearly all of whom typically come forward to receive. Receiving communion both symbolizes and makes real the continuing presence of God in the community and in each person's life.

The Eucharistic liturgy is full of the symbols and prayers of community, reflective of the inclusive table fellowship of Jesus. Parishes vary somewhat in their liturgical style for the Eucharist, with some emphasizing more the reenactment by the priest of Jesus' sacrificial death and others emphasizing the shared meal of the community, though both, by virtue of the common rubrics, are intrinsic to the liturgy. Parishes also vary in the extent to which they are and aspire to be inclusive communities. Jesus scandalized his contemporaries by eating and drinking with "tax collectors and sinners," and by inviting all manner of people to share his table, together. Contemporary Catholic parishes, being geographically based, are as homo- or heterogeneous as the geographic areas they serve. In addition, some parishes are less welcoming to various groups because of their styles of liturgy, patterns of dress and behavior, or attitudes toward different lifestyles. Others make serious efforts to be inclusive and to be multicultural, and at least at the Eucharistic table to break down divisions of race, class, age, and lifestyle.

The liturgy is also full of pointers to the moral life. Scripture readings and homilies tend to be quite explicit in their moral teachings. Prayers emphasize peace, unity, love, charity, and gratitude. The liturgy closes with the words, "Go in peace to love and serve the Lord," to which many add, "and one another." Pastors and parishes vary in their emphases on different aspects of the moral life, especially in the extent to which homilies and prayers are focused on issues of social and economic justice, personal rectitude and acts of charity, individual spiritual development, or sexual morality.

By placing worshippers in the presence of God and bringing God fully to life in them, the liturgy can exercise tremendous power in building community and transforming lives to become full of love and service.[48] If liturgy is done well and consistently with Vatican II liturgical thinking, it should embody and enhance the communal and justice-oriented teachings of the Church, rather than compete with them. Even if parishes did nothing else, the character of the liturgy would still lead one to expect to see these themes echoed in the lives of Catholics.

Understanding the Patterns

Catholic engagement in civic life presents a complicated reality, indeed a puzzle. Official Catholic teachings stress involvement especially on behalf of the poor, through both personal charity and public policy, and individuals' responsibility to their communities. The liturgy reinforces these themes. But the practice of Catholic men and women in civic and political life is at best undistinguishable from, and more likely lower than, that of others. The life of Catholic parishes varies considerably, but exhibits levels of organization and activity considerably lower than in other traditions.

How do we understand these patterns? The sacramental character of the Catholic Church does not provide a good explanation. Another hypothesis, suggested by Verba and his colleagues as an explanation for their findings about low levels of civic skills among Catholics, has to do with size. Catholic parishes are much larger on average than Protestant congregations, and assemblies for worship are also much larger, making the development of intimate community more difficult and providing fewer opportunities for individual parishioners to exercise leadership.[49] It appears from the data, however, that large Protestant congregations manage to solve this problem. Certainly some megachurches have developed much more extensive programs and ministries, including myriad small groups in which their members can participate.[50]

An alternative explanation has been proposed by Jerome Baggett, on the basis of observational studies of parishes in the Bay Area and the lens of culture production.[51] Baggett's interviews with active parishioners revealed norms of nonjudgmentalism, doctrinal independence, and avoidance of controversial issues. He argues that

> [parish cultures] produce the inability to connect the religious with the civic . . . By giving pride of place to affective commitment, by normalizing commitments to the parish that are tenuous and segmentary, and by institutionalizing norms whereby parishioners are free (even expected) to disagree with the Church on socio-political issues but not engage with one another on these topics, these parishes inadvertently produce institutional cultures that make it more difficult for members to connect the religious with the political, the private with the public.[52]

This analysis is roughly consistent with Alan Wolfe's description of the personalistic and anti-institutional nature of American religion more generally.[53] But it does not fully explain why Catholics appear to be different from adherents to other religious traditions. I suggest that there are structural and organizational features of the American Catholic Church that largely explain the patterns that we see.[54]

1. *Hierarchical structures.* Notwithstanding the emphasis of Vatican II on the Church as the people of God, the Church's hierarchical structure remains one of its most important features. Bishops of dioceses own parish churches and schools, control the assignment of clergy, and prescribe many aspects of parish life. Laity and parish-based clergy often defer to higher levels in the Church to initiate activities and ministries and are fearful of official sanctions if their initiatives are perceived as inappropriate. This pattern can result in passivity in parishes where clergy and laity let it happen. The hier-

archical structure of the Church can make priests or bishops reluctant to give up the power they perceive as theirs, or to welcome lay initiatives.[55]

2. *Specialization by national and regional structures.* Another feature of Church structure is the existence of national and regional charitable and political action agencies, independent of parishes and under the control of bishops. Catholic Charities is the largest social services network in the country; it is professional and centralized and seems to feel little need for participation in its ministries by parishioners.[56] Both Catholic Charities USA and the National Conference of Catholic Bishops have lobbying offices that operate in Washington and in many state capitals. They too rely on professionals to do the work and bishops to make the decisions, independent of the parishes that one might have expected to be their grass roots.

Traditionally, lay Catholics have been deferential to priests and bishops, and they in turn reinforced attitudes and structures that preserved their power and status. These centralized and differentiated structures have no doubt also increased efficiency and perhaps effectiveness and the quality of services; certainly the professionalization of social services that occurred in the first half of this century corrected many abuses. But this organizational structure has also meant the loss of opportunities for discipleship by Catholics and the loss of much civic energy to the polity.

3. *Human resource constraints.* Another explanation of Catholic inactivity concerns the shortage of human resources in parishes, a shortage that is exacerbated by Church rules and traditional practices. Ordained priests, required by Church law to be male and celibate, are central to Catholic practice. Only ordained priests can preside at the Eucharist, administer most sacraments, and preach at Eucharistic liturgies. Ordained priests must conduct the daily liturgies that are traditional in Catholic practice, and must preside at funeral masses, wedding masses, and most baptisms.

Since the 1960s, the number of priests has declined dramatically and the average age of priests has increased, while the Catholic population has grown. In the 1950s the ratio of priests to lay Catholics was about 1:1000; now it is about 1:2000 and is moving rapidly toward 1:3000. Two-thirds of Catholic parishes have only one priest.[57] Parish priests are increasingly overworked, and find that the sheer demands of masses, weddings, and funerals leave them little time or energy to improve preaching or parish life.[58]

Pastors have traditionally controlled everything done in their parishes, either doing it themselves or minutely directing the activities. Only recently and sporadically have priests begun sharing mission and authority with women religious and other laypeople. Since the Vatican refuses to entertain the possibility (or even the discussion) of a married or female priesthood, this situation is likely to worsen, at least in the medium term.[59] The short-term answer is much more sharing of ministry with the laity, but Church rules (and in some cases individual bishops) forbid some of the practices (like lay preaching or administering parishes) that could be most helpful. And many priests, especially older priests, have little experience with or inclination toward genuinely participatory parish management. Thus staff constraints in many parishes are serious.

4. *Financial constraints.* Many parishes are also constrained by financial resources, since Catholics contribute such a low proportion of their income to their parishes.[60] As noted above, Catholics are more likely than members of other denominations to give nothing or very small amounts of money to their parishes. The National Congregations Study asked congregational leaders to report both their church income and the number of regularly participating adults.[61] Catholic parishes reported income of $426 per adult; white conservative or evangelical congregations reported $1,286; white mainline Protestant congregations, $1,143; and black Christian congregations, $637. Hence parish budgets are also relatively small.[62]

There is in some ways a vicious circle in place, with overworked priests delivering inadequate services which lead to dissatisfaction, lowered attendance and reduced collections, which in turn lead to fewer staff and more overworked priests. In such a situation, energy and capacity are not available for increased parish activity of any kind, including more active engagement with civic life.

5. *Constraints on preaching and proclaiming the message.* Although there are no studies that I know of on the content of either Sunday homilies or parish discussion groups, personal experience and my examination of the materials and guides that are used in parishes suggest a blandness in discussions of social and political issues. This seems to be especially true for social justice issues, in contrast to the issues of abortion and family life. Homily guides especially emphasize personal morality and avoid pointed political or policy commentary.

This focus may reflect an effort by pastors to please their congregations and not drive people, especially potential contributors, away. The Church by its nature is inclusive, and its parishes are structured to be diverse. The Catholic population is increasingly well educated, suburban, and prosperous; its political attitudes and voting behavior reflect its status. Catholics, like others, may come to church primarily to find meaning and reassurance in their lives. Pastors respond to these needs and desires of their congregations.

Another explanation is that sharp preaching that is also appropriate is hard to do. Translation of the scripturally rooted social teachings of the Church into specific policies is, as the American bishops recognized in their letters on peace and the economy, a complicated and tricky business. Good policy depends not just on right principles but also on empirical assessment and prediction; men and women of goodwill can reach different conclusions about policy even when they agree on goals and principles. Preachers or Church leaders cannot assume that they can get specific policy right enough to teach authoritatively. It is also inappropriate in pluralist democracies, and ineffective with educated parishioners.

The obvious and common solution to this problem is to preach only on the generalities of the teaching and avoid application to specific issues. This approach has clear appeal. It recognizes the areas in which the Church has clear moral standing and avoids political controversy. But it poses a different kind of danger. It inevitably leads to homilies that only present teachings' minimum requirements and miss their fullness and their demanding and dynamic character. Such homilies let parishioners off the hook and deprive those members of the congregation who are active in public affairs of the support and guidance of a faith community.

6. *Constraints on dialogue.* Mature and educated Catholics do not want to be told how to vote, how to manage their businesses, or how to structure their lifestyles. But leaving all these decisions purely to individual conscience may mean that parish members will miss the point of the gospel and too easily act solely in their self-interest. The challenge for pastors is how to formulate the important moral questions and reflect on them while recognizing legitimate differences of opinion. Creating a community of moral deliberation is not something pastors have necessarily viewed as part of their office; the current pope and most bishops do not encourage dissent and debate; nor is moral dialogue something pastors by and large know how to do. Both the general culture of the Church and its practices of pastoral training would have to change for serious moral deliberation to go on in parishes.

7. *Challenges to credibility.* Some aspects of recent Catholic history and some structural aspects of the Church make it difficult for pastors to teach credibly on social issues. The hierarchical teaching office lost a good deal of credibility with both lay Catholics and theologians when it reaffirmed traditional teaching on birth control in the face of objections from nearly everyone, including the commission the pope had appointed to study the issue.[63] Lay Catholics do not obey the teachings on birth control, and pastors by and large neither press nor preach about the issue. The consequence here is a loss of credibility and perhaps a loss of willingness to speak and to listen on more serious issues. The 2002 crisis over the sexual abuse of minors by priests appears to be an even deeper crisis, shaking the faith of the laity in the credibility and responsible governance of the hierarchy, but also leading to interesting and potentially important movements for change within the Church.

The Church may also lack credibility in speaking on the fundamental equality of all people, given the hierarchical nature of the Church and especially given the exclusion of women from ordination and from other important offices. Finally, it is more difficult for the Church to speak credibly about deliberation and democratic decision making when many of its own procedures and practices are anything but; the recent scandals and crises that were first exposed in the Archdiocese of Boston and then appeared nationwide are only one dramatic example of this.

Implications

Catholics make up the single largest religious denomination in the United States, with about 60 million members, and are interesting simply for that reason. But as a case study, the Catholic puzzle also highlights how to think about religion in the public square: that religious traditions are not just collections of autonomous individuals whose beliefs and actions can be surveyed and aggregated, but traditions embodied in practice that both shape and are shaped by their members. The Catholic case is particularly compelling in pointing to the importance of official teachings, liturgy, and parish life, and the organizational and cultural constraints that interact with all of them.

This case also has important implications for Catholics. The Church's role is not to do the business of the state, and the Church should not change its ways simply because that would be good for the polity. Instead the Church should be worried because it is not carrying out its mission as effectively as it might. To carry out its mission it needs to understand what Catholics actually do and how their parish life and life in the world interact. It also needs to understand how various organizational and cultural features of Catholic life impede its ability to serve the vulnerable and proclaim God's kingdom.

The year 2002 was not a good time for the Catholic Church, especially in my own archdiocese of Boston. The failures of closed decision making became painfully and tragically apparent in the clergy sexual abuse scandal. The disillusionment of Catholics was apparent in angry sessions in many parishes and in poll results indicating that a plurality of Catholics thought their archbishop should resign, as he eventually did.

But Catholics believe that the Holy Spirit works through history in the people of God as whole, not limiting her inspiration to the pope or even to the clergy, and making use of the whole spectrum of human knowledge and experience. Despite the tensions and what can only be described as serious and in some cases tragic missteps by the contemporary Church, there is considerable evidence that Catholics love their Church, stick with it, and work for change from within. Catholics believe that the Spirit is with the Church until the end of time, nurturing, sanctifying, and filling it with life. Her action in the future can be neither predicted nor underestimated.

chapter 3

H. Richard Niebuhr Meets "The Street"

Omar M. McRoberts

FOUR CORNERS is a poor, predominantly African-American neighborhood in Boston.[1] A part of the larger neighborhood of Dorchester, Four Corners is known for its high rate of violent crime, its poverty, and its economic underdevelopment. In this sense it is not unlike the kinds of neighborhoods that ordinarily appear in studies of urban poverty or of the "urban underclass." What struck me about the neighborhood when I first began visiting in 1995, however, was the sheer number of congregations in it. Although it covers only 0.6 square miles, Four Corners contained at least twenty-nine congregations, nearly all in commercial storefronts. Although many of the clergy I interviewed fantasized about having large, traditional free-standing churches, most were actually satisfied with their little storefront communities and were even suspicious of larger churches, which they felt might lose some of the spiritual authenticity that comes from gathering as "two or three" in Jesus' name. These combined sacred-commercial spaces thus appeared as fixtures in the landscape.

There was also a good deal of cynicism among neighborhood residents about the presence of so many churches. Churches, rather than being taken for granted as something positive or necessary for the practice of community, appeared as something regressive. They were ubiquitous and yet out of place. They broke tacit societal norms about where and how people should worship. They emerged from the depression of the neighborhood and bluntly reminded people of that depression by occupying otherwise vacant commercial spaces. Perhaps even more unforgivably, the congregants of these churches, many of whom commuted from other neighborhoods and even the suburbs, took up precious parking space on Sundays.

The density and diversity of congregations, plus the fact that most of these churches were in vacant storefronts, led me to coin the term "religious district" to describe Four Corners. Of the twenty-nine churches in this district, twenty-four belonged to the Holiness-Pentecostal-Apostolic constellation of churches. Although the neighborhood was predominantly African American, nearly half of the congregations were composed of immigrants from the West Indies, Haiti, and Latin America. Meanwhile community development corporations, community health centers, and other secular entities were nearly absent in Four Corners, although they were spearheading revitalization efforts in nearby locales. A larger ethnographic study of Four Corners in which I was engaged therefore attempted to understand, among other things, how the presence of so many churches might influence community revitalization and other forms of collective action in Four Corners and neighborhoods like it.

While struggling with this matter, I could not help but think of the historian and theologian H. Richard Niebuhr. His 1951 classic *Christ and Culture* offered a powerful typology of Christian moral responses to the "world" of secular culture and institutions. Niebuhr distinguished five basic stances:

- The *Christ against culture* stance tends toward withdrawal from the world and all its sin. Here, the believer avoids participation in any of the lifeways of secular culture. Niebuhr identifies this impulse with the numerous monastic orders and various purist Protestant sects.

- The *Christ of culture* worldview understands the will of God as something continually unfolding in and through worldly institutions and authorities, including the state and market. There is no contradiction, then, between religious conviction and participation in secular culture, as long as participants uphold the highest values of that culture.

- The *Christ above culture* position holds that all good things in civilization are attributable to God, regardless of whether civilized folk admit as much. The church, as the ordained revelator and discerner of all things good, in turn plays the most crucial role in civilization, and must maintain a position of authority over the institutions of secular society.

- *Christ and culture in paradox,* or in tension, presumes the inherent sinfulness of worldly culture, but recognizes that humans must participate in that culture in order for civilization to survive, if not to evolve toward some godlier state. Humans must therefore maintain standards of holiness in personal life, but otherwise submit to the machinations of secular *realpolitik*. On the cosmic scale of justice, good intentions and God-pleasing outcomes will infinitely outweigh devilish means.

- Finally, *Christ the transformer of culture* seeks to reclaim the entirety of secular life through religious conversion.

Critics charge Niebuhr's typology with being rigid or forced, lacking applicability to actual religious practice, and ignoring the complexity of the cultural world itself. Niebuhr himself admitted to the awkwardness and artificiality inherent in any typological venture. His goal, however, was to provide a map of dominant "motifs," in order that the observer of U.S. religious life might more easily locate particular religious worldviews in relation to each other. With this in mind, I wondered what Niebuhr would have thought about Four Corners, and how an encounter between Niebuhr and the urban "street" might complicate his view of the encounter between "Christ" and "culture." Niebuhr himself might expect the lines between types to blur on the ground or might anticipate the emergence of new types. The question of how and why actual religious institutions defy typologizing, nonetheless, provides a heuristic device through which we might perceive more of the subtlety of religious life. Indeed, it is the heuristic nature of typologies that makes them useful despite their built-in naïveté.

A Niebuhrian encounter with Four Corners might also be useful in today's public policy environment, which increasingly asks, "Can churches save the inner city?" and makes it easier for local religious institutions to do so with federal money. The federal funds are provided under the "charitable choice" provision of the 1996 welfare reform law, a provision President George W. Bush has enthusiastically championed. Much of the rhetoric in support of charitable choice and similar measures presents a localistic variant of the "Christ the transformer of culture" worldview. Note, for example, the evangelical undertones in Bush's declaration that real change is about "people reclaiming their communities block by block and heart by heart . . . Government cannot do this work. It can feed the body, but it cannot reach the soul."[2] Notice a similar tone in this passage drawn from *Rallying the Armies of Compassion,* a 2001 White House missive presenting the rationale for Bush's Office of Faith-Based and Community Initiatives: "The American people support a vital role for government, but they also want to see their federal dollars making a real difference in the lives of the disadvantaged. Americans believe our society must find ways to provide healing and renewal. And they believe that government should help the needy achieve independence and personal responsibility, through its programs and those of other community and faith-based groups."

In these statements Bush and his administration are not asking churches to exist in tension with culture, but rather to be social evangelists weaving a sacred safety net for those who are materially, socially, and spiritually at risk. Ultimately the administration's language is organized around the concept of "reform": the rehabilitation of "the needy," addicts, and perhaps criminals into self-sufficient licit ones. The idea is that individual personalities must change, individual psyches must recover, in order to remedy widespread urban ills. It is no wonder that religious institutions have been mentioned as possible and ideal social welfare institutions. Suffering and lack in inner-city contexts are subtly presented as evidence of collective individual moral lifestyles and moral failures; turning away from these lifestyles, and toward "productive" life, is thus a form of conversion.

This language or logic is not new. The language of individual transformation is related to that which emerged during the Moral Reform Movement, a strain of religious and elite philanthropic social thought originating in the middle of the nineteenth century.[3] According to the philosophy of moral reform, the city's moral pandemonium would inevitably entice recently urbanized masses into lives of vice and violence; that is, unless evangelists were prepared to steer individuals into wholesome, pseudo-pastoral lifestyles with Bible tracts and Sunday schools. This philosophy contrasted sharply with that of the contemporaneous Social Gospel Movement, a liberal Protestant effort that sought to reform industry/labor relations and to address the growing gap between rich and poor. Drawing from the Moral Reform Movement, recent social welfare policy is beginning to look directly to churches to reorient, reform, and rehabilitate struggling urbanites.

At any rate, now that policy and politicians are encouraging local religious institutions to live up to an ideal type (instead of using ideal types to understand better what is already happening on the ground), it is crucial that we subject inherited typologies to some empirical messiness. To begin, although most of the churches in Four Corners lack awareness of the neighborhood as such, they are intensely aware of the spaces immediately surrounding them and do not lack convictions about what to do, or not to do, in those spaces. Four Corners churches conceive of the street in three ways: as an evil other to be avoided at all cost, as a recruitment ground to be trod and sacralized, and as a point of contact with persons at risk, who are to be served. In each case, the street is more than just a physical place—it is a symbolic realm embodying religiously assigned meanings.[4] The meanings that church people, especially clergy, assign to the street in turn help them define what it means to be religious in that particular church. By making sense of the immediate urban space, religious people make sense of themselves.

When Niebuhr discussed "culture" he did not have the urban streetscape in mind. His viewpoint was not that of the local church situated among nearly thirty others in an impoverished 0.6-square-mile neighborhood. As such, he could not imagine what day-to-day, or at least Sunday-to-Sunday, religious confrontations with this aspect of "the world" might look like. Ironically, those who envision "Christ transforming culture" as meaning legions of churches delivering publicly funded social services in poor neighborhoods may not be imagining such confrontations accurately either.

Three main insights emerge from Niebuhr's imagined engagement with Four Corners. First, despite the fact that churches are located in a neighborhood known for the vice and violence that occur there, many fall roughly into the "Christ against culture" category. Niebuhr might have expected these churches to locate as far as possible from this neighborhood and its streets. Second, those churches that view the street as a recruitment ground seem to fit into the "Christ transforming culture" mold, but widespread fear of the street complicates this role in ways that Niebuhr could not have predicted. Finally, the church that most closely enacts the local transformative role currently championed in policy circles simultaneously fits a "Christ in paradox with culture" mold when it comes to local and national politics.

Against (Yet Still Amidst) Culture

Thirteen of the Four Corners churches draw a thick line between themselves and the street and avoid all but superfluous contact with the latter. Ministers do not preach on street corners or go door to door seeking recruits. After services, even on the loveliest spring afternoons, congregants move quickly to cars and church vans in an attempt to avoid exposure to danger. The "evil other" perspective, however, is not just about fear of danger. It takes fear a step further, posing the street as the cosmic nemesis of the church.

Sociologist Timothy Nelson captures the church-based "evil other" sentiment in his insightful ethnography of Eastside Chapel, a black church located in a "ghetto" of Charleston, South Carolina:

> Because of its ghetto environment with its many dangers and temptations, services at Eastside Chapel often had the emotionally charged atmosphere of a besieged military outpost struggling to survive behind enemy lines while preventing defection from within the ranks. Indeed, members used this metaphor of the church as an army encamped in hostile territory to characterize their relationship to the world just beyond their doors. Frequent thefts of congregants' cars and the regular disruption of services by crowds of "unruly" men outside the church further entrenched "[t]he image of the congregation as a tiny piece of God's Kingdom, isolated in the midst of hostile territory."[5] (184)

The Reverend Robert Jameson, pastor of the Church of the Holy Ghost and one of three local clergy who actually live in Four Corners, has had similar run-ins with "unruly" people. Jameson religiously keeps his two used station wagons directly in front of his house, "'cause I don't want any dope dealers . . . hanging around in front of my place. They used to hang out right in front of here. Once they were even selling [drugs] right over the cars. If you let them do it, people think you are involved too." Jameson began taking pictures of the dealers. The dealers would scatter each time they noticed his camera trained on them from the second-floor window. Eventually Jameson's next-door neighbor, an elderly woman whom he called "a great ally," began to call the police when the dealers arrived. The dealers gradually stopped selling in front of the building containing his house and his residence and moved their business further down the street.

In Jameson's worldview, people given to the street life and its decadent values are consistently evil, whether encountered in the street or in the church. When discovered in the church, unrepentant street types are to be expelled. Otherwise, they will promote moneymaking and congregational growth over authentic spirituality, thus derailing the church's mission to save souls. Street people may also corrupt church music with street-associated idioms, as when "people [such as the popular gospel artist Kirk Franklin] try to make gospel music sound like hip-hop."[6] Unlike the church, though, the street is a natural place for such people, and the absolute worst place for holy people. In this view, one can resist the street's chaotic power only by staying out of it, calling the police, or taking pictures. One cannot save those given to the street unless they come into the church seeking salvation.

Julien Duny, assistant minister at the Maison d'Esprit, a Haitian church, echoed Jameson's view when asked how he felt about the church's location in a high-crime, depressed area. "This is a rough area," he reflected. "Maybe God sent us to this area. God wants evil people to come to him—he wants them to get his messages. We have to be there to help the drug addicts, the evil people, people who make others' lives miserable, with no family values." The church does not send missionaries into the street to help the "evil people"—they must come into the church. Duny told me that during the church's seven years at the present location, two drug addicts had wandered in during services. He reported that both had been saved, although neither currently belongs to the congregation.

In churches like Maison and the Church of the Holy Ghost, the street is presented as more than a dangerous place. It is a place where people encounter forces that operate directly against the work of salvation and holiness. Thus clergy in both churches have instructed young people to avoid "running around in the street." Such advice is half literal, half figurative. If one literally lingers in the street, one may encounter drug dealers, prostitutes, and other tempters. But the street also symbolizes sin in general; thus one need not literally hang out on the street in order to be guilty of street behavior—recall that Jameson could encounter evil both in the street and in the church. In short, church people may worship near the street by necessity, but they are decidedly not *of* the street, just as holy people are in, but not of, "the world." In these churches, the street is "the world," the antithesis of spirit.

On that note, it is significant that all of the churches holding the "evil other" perspective are made up of West Indian, Haitian, and Latino immigrants and migrants. For these churches, the streets around them represent the worst the urban North has to offer. This understanding of the street is validated when church members or their children become victims of violence. As migrants realize their vulnerability to such brutality, churches become "safe spaces," shielding members spiritually, if not physically, from an environment that appears as evil incarnate.[7]

Not unlike the religious communities observed by sociologist Mary Waters, immigrant churches in Four Corners urge families "to protect their children from the worst aspects of American city life." Waters speculates that ethnic (as opposed to neighborhood-based) churches offer a reprieve from the types of depressed neighborhoods in which many of her West Indian subjects live. Although valid, this overlooks immigrant sites of worship that fail to remove worshippers from poor neighborhood contexts. Some non-neighborhood-based immigrant churches, by virtue of their location in religious districts like Four Corners, are still located in the more depressed parts of cities. Paradoxically, these churches protect members from the street by preaching against its ills, even, as Waters writes, while bringing the faithful into physical proximity with what Duny calls "the drug addicts, the evil people, people who make others' lives miserable, with no family values."[8]

This group of churches fits Niebuhr's "Christ against culture" type more easily than any of the other four types. None of the other types captures the level of distrust, and distaste, these churches have for the immediate urban world. Still, Niebuhr envisioned "Christ against culture" as an inherently retreatist, if not secessionist, religious worldview. Why would churches that set themselves up as being opposed to the street locate on one of the rougher streets in the city? Why not convene in a more stable part of town, or in a quiet suburb? The answer is that it is relatively cheap to rent a commercial storefront in Four Corners, which matters for these small, majority working-class and working-poor congregations. It is a luxury to be able to remove oneself entirely from the world. These churches therefore accept their lot as those who are definitely in, but most certainly not of, the world. Note that they do not subsequently see themselves as being in tension or in paradox with the world by virtue of their location. Instead of compromising with that world, the faithful view the street as a reminder of how bad the world has gotten. As such, their location in Four Corners actually intensifies the need religious people feel to be against the secular world and its culture. A physical presence and nominal participation in the world may be necessary, but the faithful must be at pains to remain wholly (holy) other.

Fearfully Transforming Culture

If the majority of churches construct cognitive barricades between their sacred spaces and the profane space of the street, at least four churches attempt, often in fits and starts, to overcome the street through outdoor preaching and door-to-door proselytization. These churches, aware that the street is "the world" writ in inner-city dialect, feel it is their duty as people in possession of Truth to transform that space by carrying the Good News into it. In this way, people in the street encounter not only evil, but ultimate good. Failure to proselytize in the street may be taken as evidence that one does not really possess the Truth, or that one is selfish about salvation.

David Roozen and colleagues identify a similar "evangelistic" orientation, according to which religious people "believe that God has given them a message that *must* be shared with friends and neighbors, and the message itself—the need to respond to God's saving action in Jesus Christ—is at the center of congregational life."[9] They do not, however, describe this as an orientation toward the environment immediately surrounding churches—that is, as a way of viewing "the street." And since the evangelical churches in their study were not located in depressed areas, the authors did not notice how fear can make evangelical orientations difficult to *act* on. For that matter, neither did Niebuhr. As I will illustrate, religious persons who view the street as a recruiting ground must perpetually face their fear of violence.

Fear of Violence

In two of the churches in Four Corners, clerics told me that they are torn between complete avoidance of the street and full immersion in it. They feel it is their religious duty to treat the street as a recruiting ground. Nevertheless fear of violence prevents these middle-class churches from fully adopting an interactive stance *vis-à-vis* the world immediately beyond church walls.

Christ Church is one of these religious communities. Here the middle-class status of the church plays a major role in its reluctance to do street ministry. A church leader known as Brother Turner and other church members regularly canvass the immediate area to advertise special gospel meetings. They normally cover the main streets near the church, but "we never venture into" a certain area that is considered especially dangerous. Turner has tried, with little success, to get members to expand their mission radius. He explained that members "are all within five minutes' driving [of the church], yet this is a different world than those that members come from." Church members, including Turner, come from relatively stable, middle-class parts of the metropolis. They are not used to walking around in neighborhoods like Four Corners.

Still, people who have the Truth *must* spread the word where they worship, if only to dispel the "falsehood" being spread aggressively by other churches. As Christians, they must do this work even at risk of death. Turner continued: "If [other churches] are already doing something for the community, and they may not have the truth, if we have the Truth, we should be doing it. We shouldn't sit back and say somebody else is doing it, let them do it. No. If we have the truth, we should be doing it. It's our responsibility. And a lot of folks will disagree with that."

OMM: Not everybody in the church agrees with that?
Turner: Aw, no! That's what *I* think. I think we have a great responsibility. Because once you understand what Jesus has given to you and what he wants you to do with it, you have a responsibility to make sure other people know about it.

OMM: What has gotten in the way of this church doing more outreach?

Turner: Probably fear. I think that's the biggest obstacle to overcome, even for me. When I was entertaining coming back up here [to Boston]—I got spoiled by Parkersburg [Virginia]. I lived in an area where I had forgot to lock my door. And I went home and everything was still in my house. I worry a lot about my wife; I don't like city areas. So it's fear, on my part and on a lot of other members' parts. Because you can't turn on the television at night and not hear about somebody getting killed—in this area! There are some *rough people* that walk up and down the street, and there are some people that come in the church building demanding certain things.

OMM: What kinds of things do they want?

Turner: Well you know, "I need some money to get home," and you know, they've been drinking and they want somebody to give them attention. And they figure, "Oh, a church building, they'll give you money." Well when they don't get it, you know, you have to handle it delicately so you don't have a situation. It *scares* people. It's kind of a paradox because when you're a Christian you say, "O.K., as long as I'm living right, I know if somebody takes my life then I already know I'm going to heaven. But it's hard to get that in your mind when you're out there trying to do what you know you need to do. Even though you know it, it's hard to overcome that fear. And I think that's just something that the devil uses to keep us in check.

Note that while the Jehovah's Witnesses believe that one must endure abuse from people in the mission field in order to enter paradise, Turner feels it is necessary to overcome the fear of death, knowing that death in the field ensures one a place in heaven. The street, in this worldview, is thus imbued with the power to make martyrs as well as sinners.

The Missionary Baptist Church is similar to Christ Church in class makeup. Most members are professionals: nurses, lawyers, doctors, educators, and tradespeople. Unlike Christ Church, however, Missionary Baptist lacks leaders like Brother Turner, who insist on a more intensive street presence. Pastor Carl Winspeare, who works in the investment field and commutes to the church from the predominantly black suburb of Brockton, believes Christians are called to take the Gospel into the street. He theorizes that by doing so, Christians can make people in the street feel more comfortable about coming to church. But Winspeare is afraid of the street; he feels unsafe even inside the church when he works there at night.

One dark winter evening I walked to the church to meet Winspeare for an interview, only to find the doors locked. After a few minutes of waiting, an old brown van pulled up beside me. The driver, whom I did not know, asked, "You waiting for somebody?" I told him I was waiting for Winspeare. The man nodded slowly, as if in disbelief, and drove off. I waited for about twenty minutes on the corner, then walked home. Later that night, Winspeare and I spoke on the phone. He had not shown up earlier due to a mix-up over the time and was not inclined to wait. During the course of the conversation, Winspeare observed that young people from the area were not in church. I asked if he had been walking around talking to young people. He replied, chuckling, "Hmm, brother, I don't do too much walking." I told him how earlier that night a man in a van had questioned me, and I had left the church after waiting for some time. "I know you *did*," he replied, "because it's a very—so much goes on in this area. Like when I pulled up there tonight there were two guys standing out across at the other church on the corner. And I was like, O.K., what are they up to, what are they doing, this and that, you know. So I pull up, and they walk off. And I get up and go in the church and I always lock myself inside. And one of the members came, the late pastor's wife came, and she said, 'Why you got this door locked?' And I said, 'I'm being wise as a serpent and humble as a dove.' And wise means to look out for yourself. I would not dare be in that area and just leave the door unlocked. I don't know who's gonna walk up in there."

In this remark, Winspeare refers to a scriptural passage that captures his simultaneous fear of, and evangelical call toward, the street: "Behold, I send you forth as sheep in the midst of wolves: be ye therefore wise as serpents, and harmless as doves" (Matthew 10:16). Winspeare feels "sent forth" by God to this church and its environment. He thinks it is necessary to go into the street with the Word of God: "Some people in the community would never come inside the church . . . Them that are walking, them that are standing on the corner doing their own thing, smoking, drinking, whatever the case may be." Yet he feels he has been set in the midst of wolves. He feels unsafe in his own church. And as of that conversation, he had yet to proselytize in the street.

These churches, all ostensibly identifiable as "Christ transforming culture," actually must work to prevent slipping into a "Christ *against* culture" mode of behavior vis-à-vis the street world. It is not so much that their theology depicts the secular world as an evil other to be avoided at all cost, despite an unavoidable propinquity between church and street. Rather, these churches struggle with the visceral theology of fear, with its hard-wired doctrine of fight or flight. That impulse to avoid pain, suffering, and death is palpable as these would-be "transformers" try to make sense of the call to bring culture to Christ. In Niebuhr's language, the "Christ transforming culture" institutions are "optimistic" that culture can be "redeemed," and that humanity can, and must, return to its original intimacy with God. But most of the transforming institutions in Four Corners are more like reluctant martyrs who struggle to go joyously, Bible in hand, into a world that straightforwardly assaults the mind and body.

In Paradox with Political Culture While Transforming Street Culture

Members of one church, the Azusa Christian Community, co-opt what they feel are aspects *of* the street in order to reach persons at risk of being consumed by violence *in* the street. They take the street neither as an inherently evil space nor as a space good only for recruitment. To the contrary, the street is the place where Jesus tests the faithful's commitment to those poor and vulnerable. Put differently, Azusa draws a perforated line between church and street, across which certain norms and idioms drift both ways. It is still a *line*. Members still feel they have something that street people lack: a proper relationship with God. For this reason, Azusa's work in the street per se does not represent an "in tension" stance. Azusa members seek to transform the street, not become it. But they attempt to engage the street in its own apparent terms, rather than openly proselytize it or avoid it altogether. They ultimately want to offer spiritual salvation to all, but in the meantime attempt, through preemptive and palliative social services, to treat the causes and consequences of youth violence.

The material culture of the Azusa sanctuary signifies its attitude toward the street and indicates the place of the street in the religious identity of the church. No traditional religious symbols or artifacts mark this space as a sanctuary. Instead a visitor is bombarded with images of the Four Corners streetscape. Lining the walls are black-and-white photographs of police officers, speed-blurred ambulances, littered alleyways, and deserted storefronts. Behind the simple wooden lectern hangs a shot of a brick wall upon which "RIP LARRY" has been spray-painted. This sanctuary stands out in a neighborhood where many churches try to keep images and idioms associated with the street out of the church. Through the photographs, not to mention the actual content of sermons and prayers, worship is suffused with an acute awareness of poverty and violence, and of the role of Christians in addressing these problems.

The emphasis on order is evident in the way the building is run. Everyone who enters—me, a semi-retired beat police officer, an architect from London helping church members design a proposed science center, as well as the young men who regularly circulate in the building—is asked to remove his or her hat. Cursing is strictly forbidden. Male staff are required to wear neckties. By creating a highly ordered space, Azusa is able to offer its Ella J. Baker House as a "gang-neutral space" and "safe space" for young people trying to avoid trouble. Throughout any given day, young people walk in off the street to take advantage of Azusa's tutoring and job placement services, or just to hang out.

Some of Azusa's programs directly incorporate secular activities that, in many churches, would be considered decadent. For instance, in the safe space of the Baker house basement, young men hold pseudo boxing tournaments, which frequently serve to settle "beefs" between individuals and members of rival crews without resorting to armed struggle. It is the high level of order in the building that allows Azusa to metabolize "beef" into boxing without worrying about the fight escalating. "Nothing's gonna happen in here," the Reverend Eugene Rivers, the church's well-known pastor, once assured me. "No fights are going to break out in this church." Just that day, a teenager had broken Baker House protocol by taking a couple of bare-fisted swings at his opponent, initiating an actual fight. Staff pulled the two young men apart. I asked him if this was not evidence of something "breaking out." "Here's how the religious piece comes in," he replied. "If this wasn't a church, [the initiator] would have got *mashed*." In previous scuffles outside the church, the young man had "gotten his ass kicked." For transgressing against the safe space, though, he was temporarily banished from Baker House.

While the boxing matches and other Baker House programs deliberately expose young people to the church and church people, and while young "clients" sometimes come to Sunday services, none of these efforts involves direct proselytization. The key here is that the individuals who frequent Baker House have faith in the stability of the order established in that community space. It is not that they have converted to Pentecostalism and joined Azusa, or that they have a generic respect for church buildings. It is a faith in the reality of order in the building, a faith in Rivers and the younger mentors at the House, that propels the young men to socialize peacefully and help maintain order among themselves. Rivers averred, "It's not a leap of faith, but a walk across a bridge built relationally"—that is, Rivers and his workers prove themselves trustworthy through ongoing relationships. Baker House regulars prove themselves trustworthy as well, over time. Furthermore, order is subtly and explicitly enforced, through everything from the hats-off, neckties-on policy to temporary banishments.

Again, this work is inherently transformative. The Azusa/Baker

House work is, in fact, related to the kind of work that George W. Bush and others have in mind when they lift up the local church's role as a source of "salvation" for broken lives in devastated urban neighborhoods (although advocates of Bush's approach might favor direct proselytization more than do Baker House workers). It is Rivers's work outside the neighborhood, however, that breaks the transformative mold and begins to resemble Niebuhr's "Christ and culture in paradox" worldview. Over the years, Rivers has managed to secure public, private nonprofit, and private for-profit funds for Azusa's work, not because he is perpetually preaching the Gospel in high and low places, attempting to convert those from whom he might later request donations, but rather through very effective personal lobbying. Rivers is a shrewd, cynical player who shuns uncritical loyalty to political camps in favor of a strictly utilitarian, pragmatic politics. He hides neither his personal faith nor his belief in the emancipatory, life-transforming power of a strict, evangelical Christianity. Even so, when lobbying those in "the world" for political or monetary support, he invokes more diffuse moral themes to make his point. At times he even takes advantage of the fear people in positions of political and fiscal power may have of places like Four Corners. He might, for example, warn agents of the state that urban chaos, uncontained by neighborhood boundaries, will ensue if they do not support preventative work on the "front lines." In other words, Rivers subverts the visceral theology of fear as it appears in the halls of power and uses it to the advantage of people doing transformative work in Four Corners.

What is interesting about Azusa's split stance toward with "culture" is precisely that it is split, rather than combined or blurred. This local church engages with the world using two distinct strategies, one in service of the other. Both views are held simultaneously without any hint of contradiction. Recall that critics have charged, among other things, that Niebuhr's framework lacks a sophisticated understanding of "culture." Here we find that the "Christ" in Niebuhr's equation is perhaps more complicated than expected as well. Asuza, a particular institutional agent of Niebuhr's Christ, may enjoy a kind of blessed schizophrenia, allowing it to confront an immensely complicated secular world in ways far more strategic than any one worldview, or amalgam of worldviews, would permit.

Conclusion

The foregoing exercise is enlightening for two reasons. First, it identifies three ways that actual churches fail (as Niebuhr himself might have anticipated) to fit neatly into one type or another. Churches that intensely reject aspects of the secular world may nonetheless locate in the midst of places where they feel secular culture has taken its greatest toll. They locate there not in order to transform this "street" world, but because such areas offer the cheapest rents. The "Christ against culture" type is therefore complicated by mundane organizational imperatives, producing a "Christ against, but still in, culture" mode.

Churches that do attempt to transform the street world through evangelization do not fit smugly within the "Christ transforming culture" type either. Instead, a visceral *fear* of the street forces public proselytizers to struggle constantly with themselves, lest they slouch into the more isolationist "Christ against culture" posture. Those who assume that churches evangelizing in the street are especially "at home" in their inner-city contexts, and are therefore primed to deliver social services, should be aware of how much this fear can impede even evangelism. Finally, church people may also appear as "transformers" in local contexts, yet present a "Christ in paradox with culture" persona when operating in citywide or even wider political arenas.

Second, and by extension, this exercise challenges policy formulations that implicitly accept a social services–oriented "Christ transforming culture" type as the empirical norm in poor urban contexts, uncomplicated by the "Christ against culture" and "Christ and culture in paradox" stances. The abundance of churches in poor urban settings does not indicate their openness to hands-on transformation work. Rather, many of these churches may take a radical "in but not of" stance, drawing a thick line between their holy spaces and an irredeemably evil street world, thus making them less likely to institute programs serving nonmembers in the fashion encouraged by policies like those connected with Charitable Choice. Indeed, these religious communities located in the midst of the greatest need may also require, as a matter of spiritual survival, that members avoid contact with people who have not committed their lives to the path of salvation.

Among those churches given to transformative work, many will limit their activities to street prosyletization. A few, like Azusa, may combine local social services with broad-ranging, shrewd, "Christ in paradox" political engagement. On the one hand, they will take the street as a kind of social service area where the faithful are supposed to go to meet the material and social needs of marginalized persons, including ex-offenders. They may even be willing to put aside explicit proselytizing to do so. On the other hand, these churches may frame local social problems in terms of a larger politics of resource distribution and act accordingly by entering the world of political advocacy. Given this, we can expect such churches not only to take advantage of church-friendly social welfare policies in their local contexts but also to critique and manipulate those same policies with considerable gusto in the public square and halls of policy formation.

To be sure, church-based social welfare programs may take advantage of what religious institutions and their leaders do best. Since these programs draw on religious traditions that affirm the values of human life, community, and faith, their efforts may be uniquely equipped (although not necessarily better equipped) to deal with the social and emotional challenges faced by urban poor people. What these findings suggest, however, is that the individualistic, reformer role promoted by recent policy is unlikely to materialize in any pure typological form among inner-city churches. There will be no revival of early-twentieth-century moral reform movements. Rather, transformative roles will be complicated by other roles and stances that are equally, if not more, alluring to religious organizations in neighborhoods like Four Corners. Policymakers would do well to view this complication not as a subversion or evasion of ideal roles, but as an opportunity to refine policy formulations and expectations to account for the actual dynamics, motivations, and realities of inner-city churches.

chapter 4

Moral Deliberation in Congregations

Brent Coffin

CATHOLIC PRIESTS instruct the faithful to lobby against gay marriage; many liberal Protestant groups, citing their theology, urge legislators to endorse it. One religious lobby denounces capital punishment; another says that it fulfills God's plan for justice. What are we to make of these and other discordant voices of religious morality in American public life?

Liberal democracy is widely assumed to be endangered by revitalized public religion. As more faith-based organizations work with government, Americans worry about discrimination and proselytizing. Public leaders refer to their personal piety but avoid discussing specific (and thus potentially divisive) religious beliefs. Policy analysts draw upon philosophical ethics but eschew religious morality. Underlying these patterns is the deep suspicion that religious morality is inherently authoritarian. The presumption is that if one's moral commitments and reasoning are derived from one's religious understanding of the world, one is authorized, perhaps required, to impose moral judgments on others.

If that view is accurate, then religious morality is fundamentally incompatible with the pluralism generated by liberal democracy.[1] Such a situation would require one of two strategies to be pursued. The first confines religious morality to the private sphere—the interiority of individuals, families, and voluntary associations—in order to maintain the civic tolerance and cooperation required of diverse citizens in the public sphere. The second calls upon religious citizens to exercise their faith in the public sphere, even at the risk of engendering non-negotiable conflicts. One domesticates religious conviction for the sake of civic tolerance. The other undermines civic tolerance to allow citizens to pursue their highest allegiances. The problem is that neither of these options bodes well for the future of American society, a liberal democracy in which the vast majority of citizens are, in fact, religious.

I focus here on moral deliberation as opposed to moral discourse. The study of moral discourse analyzes different modes of reasoning that individuals use to persuade one another of what is right, good, or fitting in a given situation. The study of moral deliberation attends to the actual practices of negotiating different interpretations of facts, values, and purposes.[2] To assess whether religious moralities pose a threat to the civic tolerance and mutual respect so crucial to sustaining liberal democracy, I examine practices of moral deliberation as they occur in the context of three Protestant congregations in one town.

I chose my hometown of Lexington, Massachusetts, as the site of this study for reasons of proximity and access to religious leaders. Several forms of data were collected from October 2000 to March 2001. An empirical survey was sent to all twenty-five local congregations; twenty-one responded, providing data on membership, finances, programs, and theological orientation. Fourteen interviews lasting one to two hours were conducted with the senior leaders of faith communities other than the three congregations described here. Twelve informational interviews were conducted with ministers and key participants of the three focal congregations. Participant observation was conducted in worship services, congregational meetings, church forums, and two civic events. Finally, relevant information was collected through church publications, Web sites, town archives, and newspapers.[3]

I began research on moral deliberation with no particular "litmus test" issue in mind, having long been chagrined at researchers and activists who approach religion with pet agendas. Yet one issue quickly stood out: sexuality, particularly the inclusion of gay and lesbian families, was being debated extensively in Lexington congregations, school committee meetings, and public forums. Although the debate was being framed differently in these settings, it could be summarized by one question: Should gay and lesbian individuals and families be included fully in the religious communities and civic life of Lexington?

This focus provided a window into the broader public debate being waged nationwide. Most Americans hold ambivalent moral attitudes with regard to homosexuality. About 70 percent of the population believes sexual relations between members of the same sex are wrong.[4] Middle-class Americans also believe by a factor of more than two to one that schools should teach either positive understanding or genuine respect for the rights of gay and lesbian persons—not condemnation and intolerance.[5] Many citizens thus face the conundrum of how to reconcile disapproval with respect. Theologians and religious scholars have continued to argue over how to interpret the Jewish, Protestant, and Catholic traditions concerning homosexuality, reinforcing moral fissures with deep hermeneutical roots.[6] At the level of church polity, debate over whether to admit gay and lesbian believers to ordained religious offices has strained denominations to the point of schism.[7] Meanwhile, the declining number of priests in the Catholic Church has raised the issue of barring homosexuals from the priesthood and also focused public attention on the substantial number of clergy and seminarians following the model of "don't ask, don't tell." As the debate continues in religious bodies, it has entered a new stage in the polity as courts and legislative bodies contest the equal rights of gay and lesbian couples, civil unions, and the legal, even constitutional, definition of marriage.

The question of who has membership—who constitutes "we"— generates a "thick" form of moral deliberation.[8] How does such deliberation take place in the context of religious congregations? Does religious morality promote moral absolutism that is incompatible with democratic deliberation among citizens?

The deliberations over sexuality in the three congregations I explore involved complex processes of negotiation. Participants negotiated the issues to be framed, the exercise of authority, and their bonds of social cohesion. They also negotiated their religious interpretations of self and other in relation to the sacred, in the end promoting a deep moral pluralism rooted in different traditions. Whether this kind of discourse is compatible with democracy cannot be answered by simply excluding religion from public life. Rather, the civic value of religious morality may depend on whether those who negotiate it in their faith communities are able to transfer those skills to other settings.

Religious Deliberation in Lexington

Lexington is an upper-middle-class community located about ten miles northwest of Boston. It was a farming community until after World War II, when its fields began filling with suburban houses. Population peaked around 1970 at 31,886, and by 2000 had declined slightly to 30,355. Beneath this steady population has been the continuing transformation of Lexington from a working-class community. Today the town attracts affluent families wanting good public schools, manageable commutes, and secure real estate investments. Sixty percent of adult residents hold a bachelor's degree, one-third a graduate or professional degree. During the 1990s Lexington's average annual income rose almost 69 percent from $35,489 to $56,148. Residents also became more ethnically diverse. By 2000, 86 percent of the population was white, 11 percent Asian American, and just 1 percent African American. Among whites, about half claimed English, Irish, Scottish, and German ancestry; the other half included residents of Arab, Portuguese, Russian, Ukrainian, and West Indian origin.[9]

These social and economic changes have been woven on the loom of a New England town culture built, historically and symbolically, around the public square. The Town Green remains the heart of Lexington. This is the site where British infantry encountered local Minutemen at dawn on April 19, 1775. Each year townspeople and visitors gather eight and ten deep around the Town Green to see the reenactment of the fabled "shot heard 'round the world" that ignited the Battle of Lexington and Concord. Claiming this to be a sacred site in the nation's national saga, Lexington's 20/20 Vision Planning Committee states matter-of-factly: "Particular attention is given to preserving the town's strong historical importance as the birthplace of the American Revolution."[10] It is fitting that a thick debate—a debate over who belongs to congregations and to the community in Lexington—should occur in such a setting.

THE RELIGIOUS LANDSCAPE

Lexington has twenty-five houses of worship with a combined membership of 13,220.[11] Among this total congregational membership, Protestants constitute 55 percent, Roman Catholics 23 percent, Jews 18 percent, Greek Orthodox 2 percent, and others 2 percent. Of the Protestant membership, mainline and liberal congregants make up nearly 40 percent; white evangelicals and racial-ethnic minority evangelicals together account for nearly 60 percent.[12] Today the Puritan cradle of liberty looks quite religiously diverse.

Lexington's houses of worship vary in size and resources.[13] At the small end of the spectrum is St. John's Korean United Methodist Church: a congregation with forty members and a meager budget. At the other end is Grace Chapel: a nondenominational megachurch with an annual budget of $3,650,000 and a full-time staff of twenty-five. On a typical week, Grace attracts 2,600 people to its varied worship services, three-quarters of whom come from outside Lexington. Between these two extremes are two clusters, one of large congregations and the other medium-sized. The large congregations include two Catholic parishes, the town's two synagogues, and one of two United Church of Christ congregations. The last are rooted in New England Congregationalism, the civic engagement tradition which Peter Dobkin Hall traced in Chapter 1. In the moderate-sized cluster are ten congregations with memberships of between 200 and 350 and budgets between $150,000 and $800,000. All but one of the town's liberal and mainline Protestant congregations fall into this group.

While they tend to be affluent, Lexington's congregations mirror broader trends. Nationwide, the vast majority of congregations do not see their primary mission as providing faith-based services to the needy. Although they may provide limited services primarily for emergency relief,[14] faith communities "exist primarily as places of worship and fellowship, where building up the spiritual and moral lives of their own members is at the heart of what they do."[15] This is true of Lexington congregations. Across the spectrum, the religious leaders I interviewed agreed on what they saw as their congregations' highest priorities: (1) fostering members' spiritual growth, (2) worship that fosters a close connection to God, (3) passing faith on to children, (4) deepening members' identity as people of faith, and (5) providing a family-like atmosphere for members.[16]

Two other observations reflect wider historical trends. In this comparatively wealthy town, the median congregation enjoys about three times more resources—members, money, facilities, and staff—than the national median congregation.[17] Moreover, residents' high educational and professional levels provide Lexington congregations with social capital and civic skills above the national norm. Yet Lexington's congregations mirror the decline of mainline Protestantism and the growth of evangelical Protestantism. Nationally, two in five Americans today identify themselves as evangelical "born again" Christians.[18] In the heart of Puritan New England, white mainline and evangelical Christians each make up about one-fifth of Lexington's religious membership. However, Lexington's Chinese Bible Church and St. John's Korean United Methodist Church are also evangelical in theological orientation. All combined, evangelicals outnumber their liberal and mainline churchgoing neighbors in Lexington three to two.

Amid such religious diversity, moral debate that is absolutist in nature is unlikely to yield socially constructive results. In the three congregations I studied, leaders and lay members engaged in a complicated process of negotiation that both enabled and constrained moral deliberation. Four overlapping types of negotiation that are needed for moral deliberation in religious congregations within a pluralist society serve as lenses through which to view what unfolded:

- Actors must negotiate their authority.

- Actors must frame the issue of debate.

- Social cohesion and collective boundaries must be negotiated.

- Actors must contest their religious interpretation of self and other in relation to the Sacred.

COMMUNITIES IN TURMOIL

On October 15, 2000, First Parish in Lexington, a Unitarian Universalist church, hosted a communitywide forum, "Respecting Differences: Creating Safer Schools and a More Inclusive Community for Gay and Lesbian People and Their Families."[19] Five months later, on Sunday, March 18, 2001, and partly in response to the October forum, a group called Concerned Women for America of Massachusetts held a counter-event entitled "A Revolutionary Response to Kinsey-Based Sex Education and Culture." These two events frame the following account of moral deliberation over sexuality in one community.

Two of the three Protestant congregation I followed are located on the Lexington Town Green, looking out on the statue of a musket-bearing Minuteman. They are First Parish, the Unitarian Universalist church that held the forum in 2000, and Hancock United Church of Christ, a mainline congregation in the former Congregational tradition. The third, a few miles away, is Trinity Covenant Church, a relatively moderate evangelical congregation.

First Parish Unitarian Universalist Church. The Respecting Differences forum was hosted by First Parish's minister of fifteen years, the Reverend Helen Cohen.[20] Although its building dates to 1847, First Parish was founded in 1691, twenty-two years before the village of Lexington was incorporated under the Crown.

First Parish's large fellowship hall bears the name of Theodore Parker, a nineteenth-century minister who grew up in the congregation. Parker became a leader in the abolition movement and the Unitarian rejection of Puritan orthodoxy in the name of human dignity, freedom, and progress. Parker's heirs are today a congregation of 350 members with an annual budget of $450,000. Their strongly civic orientation is reflected in the balance of religious and civic activities that take place at the church on a given week. Seven or eight are church related; the other ten are nonchurch groups that meet there. Parker's nineteenth-century liberal values are now articulated on a twenty-first century church Web site: "First Parish Church Unitarian Universalist in Lexington is a liberal church that seeks to recognize and support the worth and dignity of every human being, to embrace an evolving faith in harmony with reason, to comfort and encourage people in their times of sorrow and need, and to help its members live out their values in their daily lives."[21] With a religious heritage aligned with secular values of individuality, civil rights, and tolerance, First Parish seemed the logical setting for the Respecting Differences forum. Yet leading up to that event was a story dating back more than fifteen years.

Cohen received her doctorate in medieval literature and taught at Yale before entering the ministry. Four years after arriving at First Parish in 1980, she faced a ministerial dilemma. The church organist asked Cohen to perform a service of union between himself and his partner in the First Parish sanctuary. Cohen wanted to consecrate the gay union but did not feel free to do so without the approval of the parish board. The sanctuary was the sacred space of the entire First Parish community, not the purview of the senior minister. When the board reacted negatively, Cohen performed the ceremony at Emmanuel Church in Boston.

After a renovation project had been completed in 1990, Cohen again raised the issue of gay and lesbian inclusion. This time the parish board agreed to address the matter. Its first step was to conduct a survey of the entire congregation. Eighty-five percent favored gay unions, and just 13 percent opposed them. Despite the overwhelming support, Cohen and the board felt a deep obligation not to exclude those in the minority as the church sought to become more inclusive. They enlisted the help of a conflict resolution specialist and sponsored a series of adult forums to be sure every voice was being heard. A year and a half later, members of the congregation achieved near consensus, agreeing to authorize their minister to conduct civil union ceremonies for gay and lesbian couples. First Parish had taken a step forward. But a decade would pass before the next step was completed.

In 1998 Cohen decided the time was right to urge First Parish to take up the issue of gay and lesbian inclusion a third time, this time deliberating whether to become what the Unitarian Universalist Association calls a "Welcoming Congregation," a congregation that declares its openness and hospitality to gay members.[22] First Parish drew on Unitarian Universalist resources designed to guide this debate. Cohen devoted a number of sermons to the matter. Educational forums kept the issue at the center of the community's attention. Finally, First Parish declared itself a Welcoming Congregation in the spring of 2000, six months before it hosted the Respecting Differences forum for the larger community.

Why did the progressive heirs of Theodore Parker take so long to declare themselves a Welcoming Congregation for people experiencing subtle, and sometimes not so subtle, exclusion? One reason dates back to the political and social polarization experienced over the Vietnam War. The effects of that period were evident three decades later in the relative scarcity of members of a certain age who had left at that time and never returned. Another factor was a marked shift in the broader religious climate.[23] Twenty years ago, Cohen explained, people came seeking an atmosphere of freedom—freedom to explore their own religious ideas and values. But in a contemporary marketplace awash in spiritual consumption, people are now coming to First Parish "to be held in community," to probe for deeper spiritual meaning. As Cohen put it: "I think people are feeling a tremendous lack of depth, of things that make their life make sense and give it meaning, of being in touch with whatever—call it God, or the holy, or the divine, that which makes us feel lifted up and held."

When I asked for specifics, Cohen's face brightened as she described a once-a-month potluck brunch after Sunday worship. It's "a really great time, because everybody is there . . . older people . . . the kids . . . different people." The example sounded prosaic until I recalled the comment of an Episcopal priest serving in another affluent community: "We're starting to tell our members that eating together is a radically counter-cultural act." Cohen continued: "Eating together is a bonding experience. Hospitality. I've found myself using the theme of hospitality in sermons . . . a lot more.

That's part of being held—the sense that this is a place where your needs will be provided for."

The quest for community, she said, has been altering First Parish's core activity, worship: "We have a lot going on in the church around what style of worship we want. We've changed things about the worship services so that they are more communal. For example, people light candles of joy and concern to share their joys and sorrows with the congregation if they wish to . . . Some people still are very uncomfortable with it as being too emotional. We're talking New England, Yankee Protestants out of the Calvinist tradition. Trying to move people into integrating emotion and reason . . . is a challenge. But it's actually been a wonderful addition. I really think the candles have contributed a lot to people's sense of belonging and of knowing each other a little better."

Over the years, worship, community-building, and spiritual nurture at First Parish have increasingly come to depend not on formal membership but on active participation.[24] In this setting individuals actively construct spaces of social interdependence. These spaces, which are shaped by an awareness of a transcendent horizon, provided the context where members deliberated over how to be a community more inclusive of gay and lesbian members. That process encouraged a newly active member, herself a lesbian parent with children in the Lexington Public Schools, to play an active role in the interfaith committee that organized the Respective Differences forum. That public forum, Cohen concluded, was the outcome of a long process of thick deliberation: "The church has definitely stayed away from any kind of leadership on issues since the Vietnam War. It's been really scary. It split the church, as with many churches, I'm sure. So it's been really hard for it to engage in difficult issues. This is the main difficult issue that [the congregation] has engaged in. We've emerged, I think, as more clear about what we can bring to the community than we've been for a long time."

Trinity Covenant Church. The Reverend Chris Haydon, pastor of Trinity Covenant Church, was the only evangelical minister to speak at the Respecting Differences forum. Cohen felt it was crucial that he did so. How could a community forum genuinely discuss homosexuality without hearing the views of evangelical Christians, who make up over a fifth of Lexington's religious membership?

Trinity Covenant Church is located not on the Lexington Green along with First Parish and Hancock Church, but two miles from the center of town. Founded in 1897, the congregation belongs to the Evangelical Covenant Church, with "roots in historical Christianity as it emerged in the Protestant Reformation, in the biblical instruction of the Lutheran State Church of Sweden, and in the great spiritual awakenings of the nineteenth century."[25] The congregation relocated from Cambridge in the early 1960s. Its working-class members purchased farm acreage with "the dream of creating some moderately priced homes and an apartment complex, to build a community in what was all woods."[26] Lexington denied permits to build the moderately priced homes. Finding itself strapped with a building mortgage and declining rolls in 1964, the church sold all but two acres of its land to a developer who agreed to build moderately priced homes. The covenant did not hold, however, and the church is now surrounded by homes selling for well over a million dollars. In light of his congregation's original vision, Haydon notes with irony: "Very few of our younger families come from Lexington now. They can't afford to live here."

Trinity has grown steadily since Haydon arrived ten years ago. At that time there were 60 people in Sunday worship and Sunday school. Currently 200 attend worship on a given Sunday and 100 participate in religious education classes. The congregation's $196,000 budget, less than half of First Parish's, supports a pastor, full-time youth minister, and church secretary. It was being stretched to hire another staff member to pursue the congregation's vision: "To be an open, caring family of faith, celebrating the love of God, reaching our community with the Good News of Jesus Christ, developing active disciples through worship, study, fellowship and service, with special focus on youth and families."[27]

The "special focus on youth and families" is key to understanding Trinity's religious deliberation. Virtually every congregation surveyed in Lexington reported that providing "a family-like atmosphere for members" is "extremely" or "very" important. However, a particular understanding of church-as-family guides Trinity's identity and mission. This is evident in each of the congregation's goals: "to increase the worshipping congregation to 250; involve every member in worship, study, fellowship and service; be an even more loving family; expand Sunday School and Youth programs; increase Trinity Preschool by one third; establish evangelism teams; and create a vital sister-Church relationship with an inner-city ministry to encourage their work and broaden our own vision." Haydon sees his congregation growing to no more than 250 members. "They do not want to be worshipping with people they don't know," said Haydon. "That's very important to people . . . [knowing] that you belong to one family where the majority of people know you by name."

Unlike evangelical megachurches, Trinity belongs to the Evangelical Covenant Church in America, with roots going back to the Swedish Free Church Movement. The denomination, which has about 100,000 members and 625 congregations, summarizes its theological beliefs in five "covenant" affirmations: the centrality of the word of God, the necessity of the new birth, the church as a fellowship of believers, a conscious dependency on the Holy Spirit, and the reality of freedom in Christ.[28]

Haydon personifies the challenge of diversifying an ethnic church while renewing its identity as a "family" rooted in evangelical affirmations. On the one hand, he was educated at Dartmouth, Princeton, and Harvard, attending the denomination's North Park Seminary in Chicago only to fulfill his ordination requirements. An adopted son of the Covenant, Haydon eagerly embraces others who come from outside the traditional Swedish clan. Of those who have joined the church during his pastorate, 90 percent did not grow up in "the Covenant." On the other hand, Haydon remains committed to the traditional identity of his changing congregation: "Church, for me, is family. I learned how to do church because it was family. I wanted to re-create for other people the welcome I got when I was a kid, when we were outsiders."

In Haydon's congregation, church-as-family requires living in a tension generated by two sensibilities: the willingness to embrace others who are different, and the readiness to delineate a clear boundary separating those who do and do not belong to the church family. When the issue of sexuality arose, this tension generated thick religious deliberation in Trinity Church.

In 1999 Haydon extended his usual invitation to visitors to attend the new members' class and become members of the Trinity family. Among the seventeen who attended the class were three couples who introduced themselves as "fiancés." One couple was in their fifties and had four children, two of whom were active in the pastor's youth confirmation class. As was his custom, Haydon met with the couple on two different occasions to become better acquainted and to discuss the two essential affirmations required of all members: acceptance of Jesus Christ as Lord and Savior and a commitment to live under the authority of scripture. He also explained his understanding that a biblical lifestyle required the couple to enter into the covenant of marriage. The couple said that they did not want to become married; they did wish to become members of the church, where their family felt at home. Haydon responded: "That's fine, but I cannot recommend you to do that . . . We love you. We love your kids. But I cannot say that your lifestyle is in accordance with our best understanding of the teaching of scripture." Theologically, the couple was prepared to confess Christ as Lord and Savior, said Haydon, but not to submit to the authority of scripture on the matter of marriage.

"That's when the issue opened up," Haydon recalls. He brought the dilemma to the church council, and a painful debate ensued. How was the Trinity family to embrace a couple and their four children who were already active participants, while holding to the core affirmations that constituted its identity as a church family? In the ensuing months, the church held three forums on sexuality, marriage, and membership. Members aired disagreements on issues that included marriage, membership, and interpretations of the scriptural requirements for a Christian lifestyle. Some stressed the primacy of love and maintaining unity in the church; others stressed the need for a clearer list of guidelines for determining who shall become members. Deliberations continued over an entire year. By the end, one couple had chosen to be married and join the church. A second couple split up; one member left and the other joined the church. The third couple with four children painfully left Trinity to join another congregation.

When the pervasive issue of sexuality emerged, it was defined in a radically different way than at First Parish. At Trinity, the issue was the sanctity of heterosexual marriage, not the inclusion of gay and lesbian families. Still, the deliberative process by which both congregations focused and framed the issue was not dissimilar. Behind Cohen's "welcome to all" at the October forum was an extended process of thick deliberation that resulted in the alteration of members and the church's collective identity as a Welcoming Congregation. So too, behind Haydon's involvement in the October forum was an extended process of thick religious deliberation in the Trinity family. As with First Parish, this process involved much more than a voluntary organization recruiting new members and resources to maintain its programs. It involved contesting and clarifying the core religious affirmations that constitute the identity of the Trinity family, a religious identity very different from that of First Parish.

Hancock United Church of Christ. On the afternoon of October 15, 2000, the Reverend Peter Meek walked from his church across the Town Green to First Parish, where he joined the panel of religious leaders. The son of a minister himself, Meek had been serving for twenty years as the senior minister of Hancock Church. The event he was about to attend focused on a new issue, but the heritage of his congregation went back to the Puritan vision of John Winthrop in 1630: "[W]e shall be as a City upon a Hill; the eyes of all people are upon us."

Of the 1,000 people who belong to Hancock Church, more than 80 percent reside in Lexington. At the center of the congregation's life is its worship, which is distinguished by strong preaching and an extensive music program. Yet the ratio of active worshippers to formal members reflects Hancock's mainline predicament. Ninety percent of Trinity's 212 members attend weekly worship;

almost 50 percent of First Parish's 350 members do so; but just about one-third of Hancock members are in worship on a given Sunday.[29]

With a budget of $750,000, Hancock is served by three full-time ministers who seek to address the diffuse interests and needs of a large congregation. "We are basically a community church," said Meek. "We have everybody in this congregation from Unitarians to evangelicals, with 80 percent of the congregation plunked somewhere in the middle." Along with size and internal diversity, Hancock Church has a Congregational polity that stresses participation, diffusion of authority among committees, and democratic decision making. In such a setting, focusing on a single issue in order to generate formative deliberation is both difficult and threatening. It is difficult because of a diffusion of identities, interests, and authority.[30] It is dangerous because focusing on one public issue, as we saw in First Parish, can generate tensions that prompt some to become more invested and others to leave. When Meek told the October forum that Hancock Church had "made it clear that we welcome all who cross our threshold," he was alluding to a long, stressful process of deliberation.

In 1997 Associate Minister Dan Smith, then a Harvard Divinity School student intern, felt deeply that Hancock Church needed to address the issue of its inclusion of gay and lesbian persons. Smith explained his concern and received support from Meek, Associate Minister Gay Godfrey, and from the moderator of the standing committee to convene an ad hoc discussion group. Smith invited ten members of the congregation to share their views of the church's responsibility to gays and lesbians. One participant commented afterward that it was the most substantive conversation she had experienced in her three years as a member of the church.

Smith's group provided an informal social structure for dialogue. It also began to function as a catalyst, stimulating other members to invest themselves in constructing spaces of social interdependence within formal church structures. That fall the ad hoc group invited members to attend a series of informal conversations. The first conversation allowed several members to share experiences of children and friends who were gay; others to voice their difficulties with the issue; and several to articulate their moral opposition to homosexuality. At a subsequent conversation, the clergy reflected theologically on human sexuality and the church as a community of diverse believers reconciled by God's grace.

By the spring of 1998, the ad hoc group had gained committed members, become formalized as the "Open Hearts, Open Minds Committee," and expanded the arenas in which Hancock members were being challenged to construct bonds of social interdependence by engaging in deliberation. The church's board of deacons and Christian education committee agreed to include the issue in their planning agendas for the coming year. The committee held four educational forums to engage the broader congregation. The fourth event, in May 1998, proved to be particularly significant. "The Human Face of Homosexuality" provided the opportunity for three lesbian members of Hancock Church to discuss their personal difficulties raising children in Lexington and attending Hancock Church. Then two parents, pillars in the congregation and community, shared painful memories of their gay son growing up in this mainline congregation. Hancock members began to see the varied "human faces" of the issue. "General others" were becoming "concrete others."[31] In Meek's words, "It is the self in community. The self in committed community; not accidental community, not the community like a college fraternity of people that you tap somebody and bring him in because he's just like me. It's people who commit themselves to a community that is bound together by a tradition of faith, but necessarily diverse."

Yet these selves and their community were experiencing growing tension—possibly creative, possibly destructive—as the process of negotiating a "tradition of faith" spread throughout a diverse Hancock Church. Tensions rose between those who felt passionately that their prominent congregation needed to take a leadership role in the UCC by becoming an "Open and Affirming" church, publicly welcoming gay, lesbian, bisexual, and transgendered people into the church's full life and ministry.[32] Others believed with equal intensity that such a course of action would polarize the congregation and foreclose the dialogue. In the second camp was Hancock's senior minister. Meek described his position:

> If you bring this to a vote, several things are happening. You are not voting on an idea; you are voting on human beings. And the church has neither the moral right to do that nor is it theologically legitimate to put itself in the position where practicing Christians vote aye or nay on their fellow sisters and brothers in Christ . . . If you bring it to a vote, you have created a *terminus ad quo,* from which people then can go on and say, "I voted against it, so I no longer have to deal with it. I've made my position clear. It's a done thing. Let those folk over here do what they want. I'm going to be over here." We eliminated that.

As in First Parish and Trinity, Hancock Church members were faced with negotiating a difficult tension: how, on the one hand, to contest and clarify the core affirmations that constitute an authentically religious way of living; how, on the other, to sustain and reconstruct bonds of social interdependence needed for a community to debate "who we are" and "how we live"?

Unlike Trinity Church, where Haydon precipitated the debate by exercising his authority, more initiative came from the laity at Hancock Church. Janet Manning and her husband, Bill, the couple with the gay son who had spoken at the "human faces" forum, were soon at the center of Hancock's debate over gay and lesbian inclusion. Their son had painful memories of growing up in Hancock and had left the church entirely. Bill, who had served on the town's Board of Selectmen, was among those who believed strongly that Hancock should play a leading role in the wider United Church of Christ denomination by designating itself to be an Open and Affirming Congregation. Janet was a member of the Open Hearts, Open Minds Committee. When the process seemed at an impasse because Meek opposed the congregation's taking a vote "on who's in and who's out," Janet began working on a religious statement of the church's values. She found no inspiration in hours of scouring archives and denominational materials. It came one Sunday morning in worship. "I went to church and the [choir] did this very moving piece about not being silent . . . It was fabulous!" she recalled. "I was so excited to go home from church, I rewrote that last thing [from the anthem]: 'This calls Hancock members not to be silent in the face of prejudice, and exclusion, but to express our faith.'" Building on her first draft, the Open Hearts, Open Minds Committee went on to draft Hancock's Covenant of Welcome:

> Hancock United Church of Christ of Lexington, Massachusetts welcomes all who seek to know God. We believe that, although we are many members, we are one body in Christ. We have been called as well as challenged by God to respect and reconcile our differences.
>
> We recognize and love each individual as a child of God. We welcome, respect, support and lovingly encourage people of every race, ethnicity, creed, class, gender, sexual orientation, age and physical and mental ability to join us on our journey of faith.
>
> This faith journey indeed calls Hancock members not to be silent in the face of prejudice, injustice, and exclusion, but to express our faith, in word and deed, for justice and inclusiveness for all humanity. As Paul wrote to the Galatians, "In Christ there is no longer Jew nor Greek, slave nor free, male nor female, for all are one . . ."[33]

The covenant was endorsed by the board of deacons in May 1999, the standing committee in June 1999, and then disseminated to all Hancock committees. In spring 2001, each committee submitted a proposal identifying five strategies for acting on the covenant. In March 2001, the Covenant of Welcome was formally dedicated in a special service of worship. In the ensuing months, the standing committee would take up the question of whether Hancock should sponsor a new Boy Scout troop. Deep disagreements would emerge over how best to oppose the national Boy Scout policy banning gay leaders—by refusing to sponsor a new troop or by doing so in open opposition to the policy. In either case the debate could not be avoided.

THE TALE OF TWO FORUMS

How did moral deliberation in these congregations affect civic debate over the inclusion of gay and lesbian families? A direct outcome was the organization of two public forums on homosexuality.

Although I agreed to moderate the Respecting Differences forum in October 2000, I was not a member of the interfaith group that organized it. The forum's stated goal was to make Lexington "a safer community for gay and lesbian families and their children."[34] My apprehension rose that fall afternoon as I approached First Parish. I was greeted by protesters holding signs that read "Do Not Turn Your Back on God" and "What Next: Pedophiles in our Schools?" Inside, the sanctuary was filled with about three hundred people. I sensed I was not alone in my apprehension.

The planning committee had invited Congressman Barney Frank to make a brief appearance before the forum began. The congressman denounced homophobia with his trademark acerbic wit. The audience appeared to be largely supportive. I agreed with the substance of Frank's remarks, but his adversarial, take-no-prisoners rhetoric seemed to mirror the polemics outside. Neither, I thought, would create an atmosphere for citizens to express and hear conflicting views on a controversial issue.

To my relief, the diverse voices of spiritual leaders palpably changed the tone. After the congressman left, nine of the community's religious leaders—a priest, two rabbis, five mainline and liberal Protestant clergy, and one evangelical pastor—each gave his or her religious perspective on the civic issues at stake. An open, respectful exchange developed over the next hour, until a moment of candor stretched the limits of civility to a breaking point. A woman who was an antihomosexual activist rose and said: "To be female or male is normal. To be black or white is normal. To be homosexual is NOT normal!"

"No!" screamed another woman in the back, jumping to her feet. "My son is sitting here beside me. He is gay. I can't bear to hear you tell him he is not normal."

A genuine exchange—searching questions, personal experiences, moral convictions—filled the remaining hour. Before the forum concluded, the mother whose son was gay and who had erupted earlier stood again. "I want to apologize to Doris," she said. "My pain got in the way. I couldn't listen to what you were saying. I did the very thing to you I'm asking you not to do to me."

Doris, the antihomosexual activist, was a member of Concerned Women for America of Massachusetts. She and other Lexington residents affiliated with that group began to plan a follow-up event. It was to be called "Respecting Differences, Part II: A Revolutionary Response to Kinsey-Based Sex Education and Culture." The counter-event occurred five months later. Its title had been changed at the request of the first coalition to avoid confusing the two groups. It featured two speakers, who were the only African Americans in attendance. Each spoke about the loss of Judeo-Christian values, the need for parental control, the epidemic of promiscuity and sexually transmitted diseases, and the conspiratorial behavior of public school officials. In contrast to the October forum, the second event was endorsed by no Lexington congregations, and no local religious leader addressed the gathering in the Knights of Columbus hall.

What made the character of these forums different? While the counter-event bore a resemblance to a rally of the like-minded, the October forum opened a space for civic dialogue. Citizens spoke with one another—sharing experiences, articulating deep convictions, admitting their confusion over a charged public issue. Wide-ranging views were voiced, nearly all with respect. What enabled the October event to do this? Was its civil discourse related to what we have observed in three congregations?

Discussion: Moral Deliberation and Competence

Congregations do not exist only for the purpose of moral deliberation. The framework of this book permits us to focus on this function, but requires we do so in a broader analytical perspective. This suggests two preliminary points. Congregations cannot endure the stress of perpetual debate. At best, they sustain contentious deliberation for an extended period of time; but then, like families, they require resolution and equilibrium. And after returning to equilibrium, congregations will be altered by having engaged in moral deliberation. This function does not operate in isolation: it draws upon and affects other functions—religious identity, social capital, and civic engagement—for better or for worse. Our analytical perspective focuses on these dynamics. Accordingly, this discussion explores moral deliberation as a process of complex interactions.

NEGOTIATING FAITH

The processes we observed in three congregations were generated by the interaction of four types of negotiation. In each setting, participants negotiated authority, the framing of issues, social cohesion and boundaries, and interpretations of the sacred.

Moral authority. The exercise of moral authority is deeply contested in the contemporary environment of cultural pluralism. It therefore would be surprising if we found moral authority to be uncontested in these congregational debates. Our case illustrates just the contrary. Clergy played catalytic roles in launching deliberation by using their authority. That authority, however, was clearly limited. Its full actualization required clergy and lay leaders to participate in extended negotiation.

In each of the three Protestant congregations, clergy influenced moral debate by exercising the authority of their ministerial office and by personally embodying community values.[35] Helen Cohen embodied the Unitarian Universalist value of respecting the dignity of persons—working, for example, to make First Parish a place of hospitality for gay and lesbian families without alienating the small minority of members who were finding it difficult to accept this change. Cohen also used the authority conferred by her ministerial office: she did so by inviting members of First Parish to deliberate over gay and lesbian inclusion. What we might call her *invitational authority* was the catalyst for deliberation in 1984 when she proposed doing a service of blessing; in 1990, when she asked the congregation to authorize blessing gay unions; and again in 1998, when she invited the church to identify itself as a Welcoming Congregation for gay and lesbian residents.

In the case of Hancock, seminarian Dan Smith embodied his community's commitment to greater inclusiveness by articulating his distress that the church was not fully inclusive of gay and lesbian participants. Smith exercised *convening authority* when he gathered an informal group to open up dialogue. In addition, Peter

Meek, who embodied the mainline theological conviction that "we are all in this together," exercised the authority of his office as senior minister by authorizing the process to go forward. He later exercised *constraining authority*, prohibiting the debate from being resolved procedurally by a majority vote. Chris Haydon, who embodied Trinity's evangelical commitments to the authority of scripture and to being a loving family, asserted his ministerial authority by provoking controversy with his decision not to recommend families for membership.

However, the moral authority that these clergy exercised by virtue of their ministerial office and personal embodiment of core values was limited.[36] Cohen wanted to exercise her unique liturgical office by performing a ceremony of blessing in the sanctuary but was denied the board's approval. Smith's convening authority and Meek's authorizing authority required the endorsement of lay committees for the debate to expand throughout the congregation. Haydon's bold pastoral stance, far from resolving matters of marriage and membership, sparked a yearlong debate to ratify his action.

Thus the readiness of ministers to exercise their moral authority was necessary but not sufficient to generate formative debate. Having invited, convened, authorized, and provoked, clergy and lay leaders found that they needed to become participants in a protracted, uncertain process of communal deliberation. This suggests that actualized moral authority, that is, the operational authority to define who we are and how we ought to live, resided primarily in the community, not with individual agents.

Framing issues. This in turn meant that the community's effective exercise of moral authority depended on its capacity to negotiate the framing of an issue for sustained debate. Framing is the symbolic interpretation of a public issue as a salient focus for parties to contest identities, values, interests, and courses of action. Never a purely rational process, it engages the capacity of human beings as valuing agents who interpret their circumstances, identities, and purposes.[37] In a culture where individuals are required to exercise their interpretive capacity in many and diverse institutional settings, it would be surprising to find that the process of framing was not participatory in these congregations. It clearly was. In each setting framing evolved over extended periods of time, and did so in ways that avoided the divisive polarization so often characterizing political debates.[38]

When Cohen first raised the issue in 1984, First Parish was still recovering from the polarization of the Vietnam War era. At that time she framed the issue narrowly in terms of celebrating a single gay union. First Parish continued cultivating an ethos of hospitality where diverse men and women could explore their spiritual identities more deeply. When Cohen invited the congregation to revisit the matter in 1990, members were willing to negotiate a broader framing—the blessing of gay unions as a matter of theological and liturgical policy. When the congregation once again engaged the issue a decade later, it did so in terms of the broadest frame: members debated their collective identity and mission as a Welcoming Congregation. Similarly, the process of framing evolved over extended periods in the other congregations. What began at Hancock as a small group discussion about gays and lesbians was reframed as a dialogue among heterosexual and homosexual members, and further reframed as a deliberation over the congregation's identity and mission. Trinity's evangelical culture did not allow the matter of sexuality to be debated in terms of gay and lesbian inclusion. Yet once again we saw an extended period of negotiation in which issues of sexuality were formulated and reformulated for sustained deliberation. A decision about specific couples became a debate over the sanctity of marriage; that in turn was reframed as an even more fundamental debate over how to resolve the tension of living under the authority of scripture as a loving yet diverse family of faith.

Additionally, all three congregations negotiated the framing of controversial issues in ways that avoided divisive polarization. First Parish went to great lengths to respect the dignity of all participants by allowing their voices to be heard and by patiently working to build consensus. Hancock refused to use procedural democracy; it needed to resolve the controversial issue without members voting "aye or nay on their fellow sisters and brothers in Christ." Trinity members held strong convictions constitutive of their evangelical identity. Yet the church family created opportunities to air diverse interpretations of those convictions when they came into conflict. Thus the moral framing in these congregations was not solely for the purpose of defining the "right position" on controversial issues. As a practice internal to the communities, it required negotiating controversial issues in ways that allowed members to "disagree without dividing."[39]

Social cohesion and boundaries. Congregations have been defined as organizations whose mission is to increase the love of God and love of neighbors.[40] Religious leaders are trained to interpret their religious narratives in ways that give fresh, timely meaning to this mission. Often they are less inclined to address the organizational realities of their congregations as voluntary associations required to compete in the civic marketplace for members, money, and legitimacy. Some scholars argue that this dynamic accounts for the exceptional religious vitality in American civil society; others argue it portends the demise of historically religious ways of life.[41] Our concern here is to note how the theological and sociological character of congregations entails an inescapable tension between religious faithfulness and organizational effectiveness. In terms of moral deliberation, congregations face a conundrum of how to generate voluntary participation in a process that involves the high risks of altering individual and collective identity. This poses a challenging dilemma. A congregation that does not actualize its capacity for formative moral deliberation runs the risk of abandoning its mission to transmit authentic religious values. A congregation that generates serious moral debate risks weakening its competitiveness as members withdraw and invest their resources in less costly associations.

How did our three congregations navigate this dilemma? I have noted a dynamic of authority residing primarily in community and a dynamic of framing issues for extended disagreement without division. Both of these interact with a third dynamic—negotiating social cohesion and community boundaries. Our three congregations point to one of their central features, which may be termed *trans-*

formative participation. Transformative participation is a process of ongoing transactions between "insiders" and "outsiders" enabling and requiring both parties to alter their personal and collective identities. Recognizing the salience of this practice may help to explain the power and limitations of congregations as communities of moral deliberation.

In our three churches, the catalytic events deepening moral deliberation were transactions between particular others separated by cultural boundaries. Cohen found herself responding to a church organist who challenged the norm by seeking the blessing of his partnership. Haydon had to respond to three couples active in the church but not wishing to marry. Members of Hancock Church had to respond to church members and loved ones who were gay and felt marginalized in their congregation and community.

Moreover, these "included" and "excluded" others found themselves having ongoing transactions. At Hancock not merely another "interest group" but the whole congregation became engaged in the debate when the issue took on a sustained "human face." Core members of the church disclosed the painful experiences of their gay children; respected members discussed the shaming experiences their children endured in public schools because they belonged to gay families. Such relational engagement placed the "other" in the midst of "us" and deepened the process of formative deliberation. As former "insiders" and former "outsiders" experienced relational integration, parties were enabled and required to reconsider their sense of self and redraw the boundaries of their community.[42]

The dynamic of transformative participation invites us to recognize the capacity and limitations of these congregations as powerful and constrained. They were able to negotiate new forms of social cohesion and boundaries by providing space for ongoing transactions between persons with deep differences over sexuality. They were not able to provide spaces for ongoing transactions across other societal boundaries. For example, while Lexington debated gay and lesbian inclusion, no public debate was taking place over economic inclusion. We might expect that congregations, seeking to be faithful to their tradition of the biblical prophets and Jesus' denunciation of poverty, would frame the issue of poverty or growing inequality for moral deliberation. Interviews with over twenty religious leaders, however, revealed near unanimous uncertainty over how to frame issues of economic fairness.[43] One minister explained: "We've got one couple that built one of these multimillion-dollar homes. I've got to tell you, I'm not going to be nasty to them. We need to replace our sources of income . . . The town is never going to be the same, once you've built those houses, once you've torn down those houses. We are enormously ambivalent about that issue. We are not good at facing issues and having conflict."

When sustained transactions are possible, congregations may have a unique capacity to deliberate issues "with a human face," thereby generating transformative participation that alters individual and collective identities. But when transactions are episodic and symbolic, it is unlikely that transformative participation will occur.[44] Our three congregations had formative deliberation over sexuality: gays, lesbians, and unmarried couples gave the matter a "human face." Religious values notwithstanding, church members generated little serious discussion over poverty or economic inequality: such faces were seldom seen in Lexington. Contact with the less affluent came only episodically, when congregations sponsored programs like Habitat for Humanity.[45]

The sacred. Finally, I consider how these deliberations involved negotiating the sacred. My purpose here is not to enter into a theological discussion on the nature of the sacred, but to explore further how the processes we observed were formative of identity and agency.

As Nancy Ammerman discusses in Chapter 5, religious narratives do not remain inside congregations, nor do secular narratives stay outside communities of faith. As individuals live and work in multiple contexts, their religious narratives are carried into these public settings. Likewise, individuals bring to their religious practices deeply ingrained notions of themselves—rational utility-maximizers, autonomous agents, embodied members of racial, ethnic, and sexual groups, professionals, and so on.

Those who live in the contemporary world of cultural pluralism are pluralist selves with identities shaped by multiple narratives, conflicting goods, and diverse loyalties. To avoid becoming "dis-entities" lacking moral agency, pluralist selves must reflect upon and clarify their values. They not only have multiple desires and aims; they have the capacity to determine what desires are desirable. These "second-order desires," while evolving and changing, are deeply formative of moral agency: they enable individuals to evaluate their desires and make genuinely meaningful choices between better and worse alternatives.[46] In this discussion, the "sacred" refers to these second-order desires, or horizons of strong evaluation, that allow individuals to experience their moral agency as meaningful, purposeful, and accountable.[47]

In a society ever more characterized by transient and instrumental exchanges, religious communities are among the spaces that retain the narratives and rituals to articulate particular visions of second-order desires.[48] In Helen Cohen's words, "People are feeling a tremendous lack of depth, of things that make their life make sense and give it meaning, of being in touch with whatever—call it God, or the holy, or the divine, that which makes us feel lifted up and held." What is significant is that articulations of the sacred in our three congregations did not provide answers to specific problems. They opened spaces for pluralist selves to contest and revise their second-order desires at multiple levels and with different outcomes.[49]

The story of Hancock demonstrates this process at three levels. It emerged at the interpersonal level when a small group was convened to start a dialogue and members began articulating their interests and values to one another. As tensions grew over how the congregation could disagree without dividing, this process could be seen at the intrapersonal level of a pluralist self. Janet Manning was caught between her desire for Hancock to take a leading denominational role and her loyalty to the senior minister who refused to authorize a potentially divisive vote. To resolve these conflicting desires, Manning struggled to articulate the guiding values or second-order desires of her community. She found no clarity reading theological documents, but one Sunday morning in worship the choir's anthem spoke to her conviction "we cannot remain silent in the face of injustice." Manning's articulation inspired the Open Hearts,

Open Minds Committee to draft the Covenant of Welcome. The process spread at the organizational level as committees discussed ways to enact the covenant. It culminated at the collective level when Hancock members recited the covenant as their corporate articulation of moral responsibility in public worship of the sacred.

Negotiating the sacred in these congregations allowed participants not only to articulate but to enact their second-order desires—"the feeling of 'I can do no other' which accompanies a strong value commitment not as a restriction, but as the highest expression of our free will."[50] Those desires were enacted as individuals made decisions to "buy in" or "opt out" of negotiations at multiple levels. In the case of Trinity, one couple chose to marry and join the church; a second split up, with one individual joining and the other leaving; and the third unmarried couple left for a more congenial congregation in town.

Thus while involving similar forms of negotiation, deliberation in the three congregations generated different identities and moral orientations concerning who constitutes the "we" of faithful congregations, civic communities, and the institution of marriage. After articulating its highest values anew, First Parish was again ready to be an activist congregation, inviting the town of Lexington to be more inclusive of gay and lesbian citizens. Hancock was more actively committed to being a welcoming congregation. Trinity reaffirmed the evangelical conviction that faithful members of the church must live in the covenant of heterosexual marriage. Moral deliberation in different congregations yielded deep religious pluralism.

Does this pluralism fuel culture wars, in this case over the legal and constitutional meaning of marriage? Does it generate intolerance between religious groups who hold different understandings of the sacred? Does it weaken the ability of citizens to debate other pressing public issues?

MORAL COMPETENCE

This case suggests the possibility that the practices of negotiation we have discussed teach skills that enable citizens to engage in moral deliberation in other settings—recognizing deep pluralism, disagreeing without dividing, and articulating common second-order values. The religious leaders of our three congregations demonstrated this moral competence in the October forum. Helen Cohen, Peter Meek, and Chris Haydon each articulated their distinct religious identities and their common commitment to the values of tolerance and mutual respect.

Addressing the crowd in her church's sanctuary, Cohen expressed the congruence between her religious ethic of universal human dignity and this forum: "What I think is good about our gathering in this setting is that it offers us an opportunity to hear the truth, the wisdom, the experiences of other people; to learn, as I have learned . . . through conversations within this church, which has become a welcoming congregation for all people, whatever their sexual orientation."[51]

A similar congruence was evident in Meek's remarks. "[The] matters we are talking about here," he began, "will never be fully agreed upon; not in this town, or in this society, or even in the religious traditions that those of us on the panel represent. But there are some important things we need to consider. First of all . . . that we are townspeople together. As a town, we are in many ways like a family. The thing about a family is that they—we—the folk inside, the folk outside, the folk beyond—are stuck with one another. Our success, our happiness, the brightness of our future depends in no small measure upon how generous and how creative we are at dealing with that." After stressing the commonality of Lexington as a civic "family," Meek made reference to the deliberative process in his congregation: "Hancock Church has made it clear that we welcome all who cross our threshold. Christian faithfulness requires of us that we be a loving and safe place . . . That does not mean that those of us in that big stone building across the Green are so foolish or so proud as to assume that we have all the answers. It means that, as Hancock is our church, and this is our town, and this is God's world, we belong to each other. And nothing is as important as that belonging."[52]

The more difficult challenge was that of Haydon, who was active in community affairs but had serious reservations about the forum. He anticipated that Congressman Frank would create a polarizing atmosphere. Haydon also wondered if "respecting differences" would include respecting religious differences—a not insignificant concern in a town where evangelicals outnumber mainline Protestants. Assured by the planning committee that would be the case, Haydon agreed to participate. He spoke first of his commitment to the civic issue of safety and inclusion:

> As president of the Lexington Clergy Association, I feel it's my responsibility, as it is my desire, to insure that the concerns of all our communities of faith, as much as possible, are represented concerning such controversial and potentially divisive issues. With all caring citizens, I wholeheartedly support your efforts . . . to eradicate harassment and intimidation or abuse of any student in any form. Every person should be treated with dignity and their personal choices and convictions accepted with more than tolerance—with respect for their freedom to live as they choose within the framework of school and community.

He then gave voice to the religious ethics of his evangelical congregation:

> However, there are many in our Lexington community who, by personal conviction and/or religious perspective, have sincere and serious concerns about the morality of homosexuality. Though I am in support of your stated efforts for safety in our schools, I join the concerns of others that the current agenda of teaching tolerance is, and perhaps could be, twofold: the advocacy of homosexuality as a normative lifestyle, in contradiction to the moral and spiritual values that many students, parents and religious and community groups [teach]; and, second, the indication or the accusation that those who disagree with the acceptance and advocacy of homosexuality and its inclusion in the school curriculum are bigoted, ignorant, hateful, or otherwise intolerant. I disagree with Mr. Frank. I do not feel that I am dumb or deceptive.

Lexington had been embroiled in controversy over the removal of the holiday crèche from the Town Green. Haydon had been active in the interfaith coalition that sponsored a Habitat for Humanity project to demonstrate shared religious values. After voicing his religious and civic values, Haydon contrasted two ways religious communities can interact in Lexington: "Diversity often creates strong differences, as we have noted this year in the controversy over the crèche on the Green. With the Lexington Habitat for Humanity project, they are attempting to build a stronger sense of cooperation and understanding in our town. I believe that . . . we share core values of concern for our kids and for our quality of life in Lexington that will enable us to embrace our differences with wisdom and respect."

Most of the critical questions were directed to Haydon. A few members of Trinity Church later expressed disapproval that their pastor had chosen to attend and contribute to the forum. But Hancock associate minister Dan Smith praised his colleague: "I think Chris Haydon did an amazing job of standing his ground. Even though I don't agree with it, . . . I don't know how he could have done that. I was proud of him for . . . being there and for allowing some genuine dialogue finally to happen in this community across those differences."

Smith's religious ethics mandated that Lexington become an inclusive community for gay and lesbian families; Haydon's religious ethics rejected a gay-lesbian lifestyle as unbiblical. Did Haydon do an "amazing job" of supporting civic action for tolerance and inclusion at the expense of his church's religious and moral values? Did his citizenship compromise his discipleship?

I raised this question with Haydon in an interview. "My best friend in life is Jewish," he responded. "We have been brothers for twenty years. If anyone should be in the Kingdom of God, it's him . . . I'd die for him, and him for me." But he does not believe in Christ, I noted. "Only Christ judges," Haydon replied. "It's the God of mercy who judges." He said that faith "frees us to serve for the right reasons rather than because we're earning salvation, like a Jehovah's Witness—to get saved is to save a certain number of people, to bring them into the Kingdom Hall. We serve, hopefully, out of joy and gratitude and to honor God, rather than out of necessity of earning righteousness." For Haydon, discipleship and citizenship were not incompatible. He, like Cohen and Meek, demonstrated a bilingual moral competence that cultivates deep religious pluralism and common democratic values of tolerance and mutual respect.

Bilingual moral competence does not mean that pluralist selves have two coherent moral languages and that competence is a matter of knowing how to translate one into the other. Cultural pluralism requires pluralist selves to be multilingual in many respects. Bilingual moral competence is the practice of negotiating the second-order values that sustain moral agency in the multiple public settings of the governmental, for-profit, and nonprofit sectors.[53]

Bilingual moral competence is important for all citizens, because all pluralist selves must negotiate their second-order desires. Such competence includes skills of sustaining one's internal dialogue of interpretive possibilities; judging when to withhold and when to disclose one's thicker moral identity; discerning how different horizons of strong evaluation may overlap to support common public values and purposes; being responsible not to overload public moral debates with sacred claims; and recognizing how the thick values of others, and of liberal democracy, afford a dialogue essential to clarifying and revising one's own moral claims. Cultivating the skills of bilingual moral competence poses an important challenge for all, religious and secular, who exercise moral agency in an ever more diverse American and global society.

CONCLUSION

What capacity do congregations have to be formative communities of moral deliberation? What we observed in three Protestant congregations were not authoritarian declarations of immutable religious truths justifying moral absolutism. Each illustrated processes in which participants were negotiating authority, framing issues, working on social cohesion and boundaries, and interpreting the sacred in ways that shaped individual and collective identities.

Leaders of these congregations invited, authorized, provoked, and participated in these processes. They also demonstrated bilingual moral competence in their collective action—recognizing religious pluralism, disagreeing without dividing, and articulating democratic values of tolerance and mutual respect. Although we must take seriously the prospect that deep religious pluralism may fuel culture wars and weaken the capacity of citizens to debate public issues, these three churches point to another possibility. Moral deliberation in congregations may be a source of bilingual moral competence; and if so, it may serve to strengthen diverse religious communities and common democratic values.

chapter 5

Religious Narratives in the Public Square

Nancy T. Ammerman

TAKING SERIOUSLY religion's role in public life requires a fundamental reorientation toward what it means to be religious in a public context. It means looking in new places and thinking in new ways about what we see. In the past, the public roles of faith have often been misunderstood because conceptual blinders kept us from noticing that faith was there at all. Within the social sciences and humanities, one of those blinders was "secularization theory," which posited an inexorable link between "modernization" and a decline in religious belief and the marginalization of religious institutions.[1] As life gets more enlightened and specialized, we thought, religious ideas and religious authorities would inevitably lose out to science and expertise. Nineteenth- and early-twentieth-century European writers looked around them, and the conclusions seemed inevitable. American academics in the twentieth century, similarly, looked at what their own experience had taught them and concluded that if religion survived at all, it would be confined to private life and sheltered enclaves.[2] As a result we have often been unable to render adequate analyses of religion's public presence, because we have believed the theories that said it could not be so. Only recently has social theory begun to catch up with the fact of technologically sophisticated, publicly active religious movements of all sorts in territories spanning the globe.[3]

The blinders we have been wearing also mistakenly focused our attention on only a narrow understanding of what public religious action might look like. We have defined religious action solely in terms of what religious organizations do and public action solely in terms of politics or "activism." Only when religious organizations were issuing political pronouncements or marching on picket lines did we think we saw "public religious action." And since so few people seemed to pay attention when big mainstream religious organizations issued pronouncements, the image of a privatized and impotent religious sphere was reinforced.

This distorted picture of public activity depends on another theoretical blinder, namely the assumption that public life is something quite distinct from private life, indeed that each sphere of modern activity has its own distinct norms and authorities.[4] That blinder is further reinforced by the assumption that religion's unique function concerns "ultimate meaning" or "sacred truth." By concentrating on religious ideas (and their presumably untenable sources of authority), other aspects of religious life have been ignored and the presumed conflict between rational science (or politics) and religion has been highlighted.[5] If religions are by definition limited to pronouncements of unchanging sacred truth, they will inevitably be at odds with the everyday give and take of democracy. In this accounting, civil society, with its necessary disagreement and debate, is impossible when religion seeks to enter the public debate.

This picture of religion bequeathed to us by twentieth-century social theorists no longer serves us well. Religion, like other aspects of human social experience, is best understood as much more fluid than the differentiated spheres earlier theorists thought would organize our lives; by locating religion in practices rather than in ideas and authorities, we can gain a new perspective that will allow us to see how religious organizations and their members participate in the civic lives of their communities and how religious narratives are present in public action.

Story, indeed, may be a helpful metaphor for understanding the nature of religious social action. "All of us come to be who we are (however ephemeral, multiple, and changing) by being located or locating ourselves (usually unconsciously) in social narratives," claims Margaret Somers.[6] Narratives guide action in ways quite different from ideological or motivational "causes." They are most often unspoken accounts that take an event and give it meaning by implying what has come before and what is likely to come after, thereby identifying the relevant characters and their relation to each other. Although some narratives may become elaborate and public myths, most guiding narratives are simply unspoken stories about who we are and how people like us typically behave.

The narratives that implicitly guide our action are, of course, multilayered, with characters and plots interwoven across and within situations. One set of layers comes from the simultaneous individual and social dynamics at work in any given situation. There are both autobiographical stories, providing continuity for the plots of each individual life, and public stories, which define the groups they collectively constitute.[7] Those public stories are themselves multiple. Every group, category, institution, and culture has its own "public narratives" into which we fit our actions.[8] As a young mother waits with a dressed-up toddler to see Santa, her actions extend her own story (reliving childhood memories, perhaps), repeat episodes seen as typical of her gender and role as a mother, and are shaped by the larger narrative of American commerce (Christmas sales figures are the next day's breaking news). Each child's Santa picture is unique, but the overlapping stories are shared widely enough to make conversations among the parents in line possible. Whether it is the court system or shopping malls, ethnic group or gender, social institutions and categories provide recognized situational "accounts" one can give of one's behavior, accounts that identify where one belongs, what one is doing, and why.[9]

Narratives are not only multilayered but also transposable from one situation to another.[10] The institutional and cultural complexity of our society makes multiple public narratives available to us, with the categories and schemas of one location available to supplement and sometimes critique the plotlines of another. All situations are characterized by a fluidity of boundaries and the presence of story lines gleaned from the multiple contexts in which participants live. In modern, functionally differentiated societies, religious stories have been assumed to be confined either to a recognized religious institution or to the "private" domain. However, if we recognize the necessary intersectionality of all social action, there is no a priori reason to assume that religious episodes will only happen in religious institutions or in private seclusion. If it is true that all social contexts contain multiple narratives, that schemas from one social arena can be transposed into another, then it must be true that under certain conditions religious narratives may appear in settings outside officially religious bounds.[11]

Two key insights, then, help us to approach the task of understanding religious public action. First, all institutional boundaries —including religious and political ones—are porous. But second, what people carry with them across those boundaries are practices and narratives more than ideas and truths. For most people religion is more about living a life than about establishing a tightly argued philosophical system. Religious maxims about "loving one's neighbor" and religiously ingrained practices of charity, for instance, may open avenues of participation and connection that religious ideas about pure doctrine would keep closed.[12] Religious narratives—about, for instance, "good Samaritans" and pilgrims and (for better or worse) crusaders—are simply present in modern life, across institutional contexts. They are among the many sources on which we draw in identifying with each other, in aligning our mutual action, and in imagining how situations might be different.

There are many places we could look for the interweaving of sacred and secular narratives across public and private life, but the work of mobilizing American communities to help needy people provides an interesting laboratory for exploring whether and how such porous boundaries might be present. Not all voluntary service activity is religious, but much of it may be. Different kinds of religious narratives may become part of the everyday public work of doing good. Various practices and institutional structures shape those narratives, as we shall see. At the heart of the connection between religious narratives and community service stand the activities and relationships nurtured in American congregations.

A Survey of Religious and Community Practices

In 1997 and 1998, 4,012 Sunday morning worshippers in 32 diverse Christian congregations were asked to complete a "survey of religious involvement" as part of a project, funded by the Lilly Endowment, called "Organizing Religious Work."[13] While originally designed to serve other purposes, this brief questionnaire included items on individual religious history, current involvement in church and community activities, ideas about what constitutes a good Christian life, and descriptions of religious identity. In each congregation, the pastor had also been interviewed about the church's characteristics, community connections, and priorities; and researchers had collected written materials, convened focus groups, and observed worship services.

Although this provides us with a rich source of data, it is important to note its limits. These are people who are connected with a particular set of religious institutions, so they represent neither the whole U.S. population nor even all those who have some religious affiliation. These results offer no way to assess how churchgoers are different from nonchurchgoers or how people in other religious traditions might compare with these Christians. Nor do survey responses provide the sort of detailed and nuanced body of data that would adequately sort out the autobiographical and public narratives at work in various kinds of service in the community. We cannot, for instance, trace over time how individuals came to tell a particular religious story about themselves. Nevertheless some of the questions asked of this large and diverse group of church attenders offer a glimpse of how and why some religious participants also become active in serving their communities, and what we know of their congregations can roughly place those individuals within particular religious narratives and traditions.

Included in this sample were a wide range of Protestant groups, from conservative to liberal, plus two large Catholic parishes. Four congregations in the African-American traditions were included, and a few of the other churches were ethnically mixed. Because the distribution of worshippers in this sample was not designed to be strictly representative, their responses have been weighted to approximate the denominational distribution of attenders in the nationally representative National Congregations Study.[14]

The narrative quality of religious identity was approximated—even if only indirectly—by a variety of more practice-oriented questions on our survey. We asked about the kind of life Christians should try to live and what they think a church should emphasize most. By asking about the practices and virtues of everyday life, we can see how these churchgoers understand the interplay between their own actions and those of God. We can approximate the internal narratives that may serve as autobiographical scripts for their action in the world.

In earlier work, I have argued that practices of individual and communal Christian living cluster into identifiable orientations that can be described as "Activist," "Golden Rule," and "Evangelical."[15] These are different, but not mutually exclusive, ways of approaching religious life. Individuals tend to value one set of practices more than the other two—to have a dominant mode—but their response to *each* cluster of items tells us something about how they engage in religious action in the world. All three scripts are available to people within the Christian tradition, and individuals may draw more or less on each of the three.

The Activist orientation is one that says good Christians ought to be "actively seeking social and economic justice." It is also strongly corporate, emphasizing that churches should give high priority to supporting social action groups, encouraging their pastors to speak out on social and political issues, providing space for community groups to meet at the church, and cooperating with outside groups for community betterment.

The Golden Rule orientation is one that says good Christians should practice Christian values in everyday life, take care of those who are sick or needy, and share what they have with those less fortunate. This orientation is toward a more personal kind of caring, saying that churches should promote a strong sense of fellowship for their members, but also provide aid and services to people in need.

The Evangelical orientation is one that says good Christians should try to bring others to faith in Christ, and good churches should have a strong evangelism program and support mission efforts in the nation and the world. In addition, this orientation emphasizes personal piety, saying that good Christians should spend time reading and studying the Bible, as well as in prayer and meditation, while also avoiding worldly vices (something they also want their churches to help them do).[16]

These orientations are not equally present among these American churchgoers, as can be seen in Table 5.1. Although very few of our respondents would completely reject any of the three as valid descriptions of Christian living, some are more likely to be endorsed than others. Only a minority place activism at the center of their understanding of the faith, making it their dominant mode, but strong majorities include Evangelical or Golden Rule orientations (or both) in their expectations about how life should be led. For the most part, in fact, people draw on all three narratives, even if they see one as more important than the others. Their first discourse, for instance, may be to say that faith is about personally caring for others, but they recognize that a more Activist story can legitimately be told or that Evangelical virtues are important, as well. In what follows, we will look for the ways each of these orientations is linked both to the public narratives of congregations and to the actions of the individuals who carry and enact them.

Understanding how churchgoers enact the "public" dimension of their faith is, of course, more than knowing how they think about religion. We also want to know something about what they actually do. Again, surveys can offer only an approximation of the subtle story we might be able to tell if we could watch and listen to ordinary daily routines. Even if reports of behavior are less than precise measures of actual behavior, the reports themselves tell us something about how people narrate their lives. We asked people to report how often they participate in "service organizations in the

Table 5.1 Three orientations toward Christian living among congregational participants (in percent)

	Activist orientation	Golden Rule orientation	Evangelical orientation
Not at all important (average <1.5)	3	<1	1
Somewhat important (average 1.5–2.49)	44	6	16
Very important (average 2.5–3.49)	47	66	58
Essential (average 3.5 or more)	6	28	26
Total	100	100	101
(N of cases)	(3,251)	(3,413)	(3,337)
Percentage for whom this is the dominant mode	9	51	40

Note: Not all columns total 100% due to rounding.

community" and how often they offer informal help to people in need. The first question was intended to identify activity that was not directly sponsored by the church but that did have a formally organized base. The second was intended to capture activities like providing transportation, meals, childcare, respite care, and the like—work that might or might not be officially organized and might or might not be connected to the church.[17] Finally, we asked attenders to tell us how much they gave in 1997 to secular charity.[18]

While nearly 80 percent of churchgoers claim that they provide informal assistance at least occasionally, only 59 percent do so through organized community service organizations, and less than half gave more than $100 to organized charities (see Table 5.2).[19] These are three very different ways of trying to make a difference in the world, so different sorts of individual and public narratives may be associated with each.

AUTOBIOGRAPHICAL NARRATIVES AND COMMUNITY SERVICE
Controlling for key demographic factors—education, income, age, presence of children, and rural versus urban residence—actions in

Table 5.2 Participation in service to the community among congregational participants

	Percentage
Frequency of participation in *Community Service Organizations*	
Never	41
A few times a year	33
Once a month	10
2–3 times a month	9
Weekly or more	7
Frequency of participation in *Informal Assistance* for people in need	
Never	21
A few times a year	42
Once a month	13
2–3 times a month	12
Weekly or more	11
Amount contributed in 1997 to *Secular Charity* causes	
Nothing	15
Less than $100	38
$100–$999	40
$1000 or more	8

Note: Not all columns total 100% due to rounding.

service to the community are indeed related to different ways of accounting for life. The orientation most consistently and strongly tied to all three forms of community service activity is the Activist view. Understanding Christian virtue in terms of seeking social justice, and understanding congregational mission in terms of community cooperation and betterment, are ways of thinking about religious life that are linked to participation in organized service agencies and giving to secular charities, but include informal assistance, as well (partial $r = +.20$, $+.15$, and $+.12$, respectively). People who strongly endorse Activist accounts of Christian living are people who think they should be making a difference in the world and who seem to appreciate the way community organizations make that possible.

There is also a positive link between a Golden Rule orientation and each form of community service activity, but the pattern is slightly different. Participation in service organizations is about equally tied to the Activist and Golden Rule orientations (+.20 for the Activist orientation and +.18 for the Golden Rule orientation). That is, both personal and corporate orientations toward caring for the community result in organized volunteerism. But it is the communal, Golden Rule orientation that is more strongly linked to providing informal care ($r = .33$, compared with a .12 link to the Activist orientation) and less strongly related to monetary charitable contributions ($r = .04$, compared with a .15 link to activism).[20] Whether more or less educated, rural or urban, more or less well off, young or old, parent or not, those most invested in this Golden Rule account of virtuous living are more likely to report regular participation in doing just what that account says they should do—person-to-person caring for others.[21]

The Evangelical orientation presents a much more complicated picture. Like the emphasis on caring for others, an emphasis on evangelism and personal piety seems to be linked to high levels of involvement in informal service ($r = .21$) as well as to marginally higher levels of involvement with service organizations ($r = .06$). However, there is a negative correlation between the Evangelical orientation and secular giving ($r = -.13$), and that signals that something different is going on here. Taking both income and overall generosity into account, the stronger the person's commitment to Evangelical virtues, the less likely he or she is to be a generous giver to non-church-based charity.

To fully understand how service and giving are linked to the Evangelical orientation, it is necessary to bring a new set of considerations into the picture. It is not enough to look only at the sorts of demographic differences represented by education and income and place of residence. For all our respondents, the link between orientation and action is mediated by the ongoing religious and secular relationships and activities of which they are a part. Narratives about good Christian living exist in a particular interactional context, so we need to know how community service activities are situated in relationship to networks of membership and participation in the church and beyond.

From the respondents' answers to our survey questions, we know that they at least occasionally attend worship services, but that they vary greatly in their other connections to their congregation and community. We asked them to tell us how often they participate in church-based Sunday school or religious education, in parish fellowship activities, and in church-based mission groups and service activities, as well as in various other church groups beyond Sunday school. In Tables 5.3, 5.4, and 5.5, "church participation" is a sum of the number and frequency of activities in which they participate (standardized item alpha of .73). In addition, some people participate in one or more nonreligious groups in their communities. The category shown in the tables as "community secular group" is a dichotomous variable that identifies those who participate in at least one non-church-based twelve-step, sports (either youth or adult), or scouting group in the community. Not quite a quarter (24 percent) of our respondents reported this kind of activity.[22] The category "community religious group" is a dichotomous variable that identifies those who participate in at least one Bible study or spiritual growth group that is based outside their own congregation. Fourteen percent of our respondents reported this sort of activity. These three different indicators of participation and relationship will further help to situate the community service activity we have found.

More than any other factor we have yet examined, level of church participation is a key to understanding community service activities. It tells us nothing about the amount of money a person is likely to contribute to secular charities, but it tells us a great deal about whether community service organizations and informal forms of helping are included in a person's pattern of activity.[23] People who make time to go to Sunday school or to show up at church picnics or to participate in a church mission group are also likely to make time to deliver meals to a sick neighbor or volunteer at the *ıble 5.3* Effects on participation in informal assistance

	Unstandardized coefficient	Standard error	Standardized coefficient
ɔnstant)	−1.039	.231	
ɹucation	+.050	.021	+.05*
ɔome	−.024	.015	−.03
ɟe	+.016	.028	+.01
ave children	−.202	.053	−.08***
ıral community	+.054	.095	+.01
ɔpport for Activist virtues	+.004	.010	+.01
ɔpport for Golden Rule virtues	+.145	.014	+.28***
ɔpport for Evangelical virtues	−.026	.008	−.09**
ıurch participation	+.123	.007	+.38***
ɹrticipate in at least one community religious group	+.294	.064	+.09***
ɹrticipate in at least one community secular group	+.133	.054	+.05*
ɑtholic	−.054	.085	−.02
ɓeral Protestant	−.052	.097	−.02
ɔnservative Protestant	−.159	.085	−.06
ɗjusted R^2	.248		

* = sig. <.05.   ** = sig. <.01.   *** = sig. <.001.

town soup kitchen. Being part of various small groups in the community—whether spiritual or secular—has similar, if smaller, effects. People who participate in one thing are more likely to participate in other things as well.

That strong connection between church participation and community service is the key to understanding how the Evangelical orientation is related to public engagement. The people who are most likely to be highly active church participants are those with an Evangelical orientation toward life, and their sheer levels of participation increase the likelihood that both informal assistance and organized community service will result. In other words, there are two countervailing forces at work for evangelical Christians. On the one hand, an Evangelical narrative, with its emphasis on personal piety and otherworldly salvation, does not contain the obvi-

Table 5.4 Effects on participation in community service organizations

	Unstandardized coefficient	Standard error	Standardized coefficient
(constant)	−.717	.227	
Education	+.060	.020	+.06**
Income	−.005	.015	−.01
Age	−.000	.028	−.00
Have children	−.196	.052	−.08***
Rural community	+.273	.093	+.06**
Support for Activist virtues	+.049	.010	+.12***
Support for Golden Rule virtues	+.060	.014	+.12***
Support for Evangelical virtues	−.034	.008	−.12***
Church participation	+.130	.007	+.42***
Participate in at least one community religious group	+.311	.063	+.09***
Participate in at least one community secular group	+.251	.053	+.10***
Catholic	+.118	.084	+.05
Liberal Protestant	+.235	.096	+.07*
Conservative Protestant	−.230	.084	−.09**
Adjusted R^2	.233		

* = sig. <.05.   ** = sig. <.01.   *** = sig. <.001.

ous emphasis on this-worldly community service that an Activist or Golden Rule orientation may contain; and when other demographic factors are taken out of the picture, the orientation itself seems to be a negative force. On the other hand, that same Evangelical narrative strongly encourages active participation in a local congregation, through which wider participation in the community may be both expected and facilitated. Because people committed to an Evangelical orientation are the most active participants in churches, the net result is more informal help and at least marginally more community volunteerism beyond the church itself—in spite of the negative impact the orientation itself might have.[24]

PUBLIC NARRATIVES OF SERVICE

All of this raises another set of questions. We have been examining the various strands that may be present in an individual life narra-

Table 5.5 Effects of orientations on giving to secular charity

	Unstandardized coefficient	Standard error	Standardized coefficient
(constant)	−.070	.212	
Education	+.012	.019	+.01
Income	+.260	.014	+.36***
Age	+.163	.026	+.13***
Have children	−.161	.048	−.07**
Rural community	−.298	.087	−.07**
Support for Activist virtues	+.030	.009	+.08**
Support for Golden Rule virtues	+.039	.013	+.08**
Support for Evangelical virtues	−.051	.008	−.18***
Church participation	+.019	.006	+.06**
Participate in at least one community religious group	+.055	.059	+.02
Participate in at least one community secular group	+.063	.049	+.02
Catholic	−.118	.078	−.05
Liberal Protestant	+.223	.089	+.07*
Conservative Protestant	−.182	.078	−.07*
Adjusted R^2	.254		

* = sig. <.05.   ** =sig. <.01.   *** = sig. <.001.

tive and how those experiences and expectations make their way into church participation and work that is aimed at community betterment. We have seen that various kinds of individual religious orientations lead toward different patterns of engagement. But we have also seen that participation in various secular and religious organizations, especially participation in the congregation's own social and spiritual activities, creates scenarios in which community service is more likely. These effects of participation signal the importance of assessing just what church participation means. What are the congregational cultures and narratives within which individuals are working out their strategies of community action?[25]

Because we know something about the congregations these people attend, we are able to look at the public narratives available to them. What sorts of stories do they hear (and see enacted)? Is civic engagement normal and expected or extraordinary, even discouraged? Our most reliable measure of the internal cultural climate in the congregation proved to be the larger religious tradition of which it is a part. Recent research has shown that denominations may be meaningfully grouped into several broad religious families.[26] All but one of our 32 participating congregations falls into one of four of those religious families.[27] Sixteen are within the conservative Protestant family. This group includes the Lutheran Church Missouri Synod, the Southern Baptists, the Assemblies of God, the Churches of Christ, and others in evangelical and Pentecostal traditions. Nine of our participating congregations are within the liberal Protestant family. These are Episcopal, United Church of Christ, United Methodist,[28] and Evangelical Lutheran Church in America churches. Four churches are National Baptist (3) or African Methodist Episcopal (1) churches and thus in the African-American church tradition. And two are Catholic. Although there are differences between and within the congregations in each of these traditions, the tradition itself brings together a constellation of factors that is recognizable even if no given congregation perfectly reflects them all.

Within the conservative Protestant tradition, for instance, people in the pews are more likely to favor an Evangelical orientation, although a substantial minority emphasizes Golden Rule virtues (see Table 5.6). Sunday morning sermons often include tales of lives that have been redeemed, stories of people brought to eternal salvation by the loving witness of a Christian who really lives her faith. Participants in conservative Protestant churches have ample opportunities to absorb such lessons. The majority of them regularly participate in Sunday school, and nearly half are counted among those who are highly active in church programs of all kinds. More than two-thirds give at least $1,000 per year to the church, but very few give that much to secular charities. Their churches, in turn, provide support for an average of only four community service organizations, considerably fewer than the number supported by churches in other traditions.[29] And only a quarter (23 percent) of the members are personally involved on a regular basis with such service organizations.

In some congregations people were explicit about the tension between meeting people's material needs—especially through a secular and/or government-supported program—and doing the work of telling people about salvation. In other places, spiritual and social needs tended to be blurred together. At a strongly evangelical Reformed Church in America congregation, members were encouraged to be involved with people in the community so they could "minister to their needs with the hopes of bringing them into the fellowship in order to disciple them and disciple them to the point where they then can turn around and go back out into the community and do missions and evangelism and ministry in God's name." Participating in such a conservative Protestant congregation provides rich public narratives about helping others in the community, but almost always intertwined with stories about salvation and discipleship. It is no surprise that, in Chapter 8 below, Amy Reynolds and Christopher Winship found more explicitly religious agendas in the most evangelical agency they studied.

Liberal Protestant congregations, in contrast, are dominated by the Golden Rule orientation, with roughly equal (and small) minorities, respectively, in the Evangelical and Activist camps (see Table 5.6). A person in one of these congregations is surrounded by fewer expectations for active intrachurch participation, with only a third of adults participating regularly in church school, less than a quarter counted as active churchgoers, and just under half who give at least $1,000 per year to the parish. Twenty percent give that much to charity (more than in any other tradition), and 39 percent are active in service organizations. Their churches support a plethora of such service groups—eleven on average—and are more likely than not to offer at least one service program of their own and/or to have a congregational group that focuses on social and political issues.

In many of these congregations, the consistent message is that the church should be involved in serving the community—both individually and collectively. The pastor of one of our United Methodist churches said, "The folks in our church who have gotten ahold of the mission [know] . . . that the church isn't there for maintenance;

Table 5.6 Differences among four religious cultures (in percent)

	Conservative Protestant congregations	Liberal Protestant congregations	African-American Protestant congregations	Catholic parishes
Different dominant orientations				
Evangelical	57	13	46	18
Golden Rule	39	68	45	66
Activist	4	19	9	16
Total	100	100	100	100
(*N* of cases)	(808)	(468)	(214)	(1,219)
Different religious participation				
Attend religious education more than once a month	55	34	54	22
Attend once a month or less	45	66	46	78
Total	100	100	100	100
(*N* of cases)	(949)	(598)	(311)	(1,581)
Overall high participation	46	23	48	11
Low to moderate participation	54	77	52	89
Total	100	100	100	100
(*N* of cases)	(891)	(572)	(275)	(1,486)
Give < $100 per year to the parish	13	15	8	21
Give $100–$999	19	36	22	59
Give $1,000 or more	68	49	70	20
Total	100	100	100	100
(*N* of cases)	(907)	(594)	(296)	(1,708)

Table 5.6 (continued)

	Conservative Protestant congregations	Liberal Protestant congregations	African-American Protestant congregations	Catholic parishes
Give <$100 per year to religious charities beyond the parish	47	68	58	66
Give $100–$999	36	24	32	27
Give $1,000 or more	17	8	10	7
Total	100	100	100	100
(N of cases)	(891)	(579)	(280)	(1,644)
Different rates of community service				
Informal Assistance at least monthly	39	40	58	29
Service Organizations at least monthly	23	39	42	23
Give $1,000 or more to Secular Charity	4	20	13	7
Different congregational opportunities				
Congregation has at least one social service program of its own	5 out of 16	6 out of 9	2 out of 4	2 out of 2
Congregation has at least one activity group focused on social or political issues	5 out of 16	7 out of 9	4 out of 4	1 out of 2
Average number of outside service organizations supported	4	12	6	7

it isn't there to have a building; the building's there for the mission of the church. And the mission of the church . . . *is* the community."

At one of our Episcopal congregations, a lay leader talked about all the ways the parish invests in the community.

> We support several community functions that are not necessarily a part of [the parish]—like Alcoholics Anonymous and so forth . . . For as long as I've been here, we've always tried to support an active food pantry . . . We've always had needy people who were part of the congregation. There was a young woman who was schizophrenic, and she had a child, and she just barely could make it on her own. And this church took her on as a project. We'd go clean her house, and stock her pantry, and take care of the medical needs . . . It was not anything that the vestry voted on; this was the people at work.

In a parish like this one, involvement in both formal and informal community service is a natural part of the stories people see in the lives of their fellow parishioners, in the projects sponsored by the church, and in the messages they hear from the pulpit and in their newsletter.

Participants in the African-American churches also hear stories about community service and changing the world. African-American Christians rank Evangelical and Golden Rule virtues almost equally highly; and Activist virtues are rated higher, on average, than in any of the other religious traditions.[30] About half (57 percent) of the participants in African-American churches strongly endorse the notion that seeking justice is what they and their churches should be doing. At a National Baptist church in Alabama, for instance, a proud legacy of participation in the civil rights movement was present in stories everyone knew, and being a pillar of the black community and a lightning rod for change are still realities in the congregation's life. They have long hosted NAACP and SCLC events and brought controversial speakers to town, making clear that seeking justice is central to Christian living.

But so are the Bible and everyday Christian piety. As the pastor of another National Baptist church said, "I would have a problem if I got up and preached Bible stories each Sunday and never made the gospel relevant to what happens out there." Both the Bible stories *and* everyday relevance are what members of these churches hear. An eternal relationship with Jesus, caring for one's neighbor, and changing the world are equally important "plotlines" in their account of a good Christian life.[31]

In keeping with this combination of virtues, African-American churches are like their white conservative sister churches in church participation—over half the members go to Sunday school regularly; nearly half have high overall participation, and more than two-thirds give generously to the church. But members are like their liberal Protestant neighbors in active participation in community service, and they have even higher levels of informal assistance. Like those liberal churches, African-American ones are especially likely to have service programs and social action groups under the church's aegis.

The religious culture of Catholicism is distinctive in other ways. Our picture of the Catholic tradition comes from just two parishes—one predominantly Hispanic, the other a roughly equal mix of Anglos and Hispanics, both in Albuquerque—but the culture they reveal is not at odds with other studies of Catholic life. Themes of caring and justice were often present in the public rhetoric.[32] One of the priests told our interviewer, "The only way you can show you have love for God is the love you have for your neighbors. To have love for your neighbor means you have to want for your neighbor what you want for yourself. Therefore, if I want a nice, warm bed and a shower, health insurance, whatever, I want the same for my neighbors. So you have to become socially active. You can't just sit and watch these poor people over there who are hungry and homeless."

On the Sunday I visited, his announcements included mention of parishioners who serve breakfast at St. Martin's (a local shelter). This won't end hunger, he said, but it does raise our awareness of the need to change unjust structures. His prayer of intercession that day included petitions for persons suffering with AIDS and those who care for them, as well as for persons suffering abuse and their abusers. Both personal caring and action in pursuit of structural change were a part of the public narrative in this place.

This is also a parish with an active parish council and lots of opportunities for community involvement. Still, overall levels of parish and community participation reported by the parishioners we surveyed were quite low, and those respondents are the ones who are likely the most active in the parish. In spite of Vatican II reforms, as Mary Jo Bane notes in Chapter 2, many parishes remain cultures of minimal participation. Fewer than a quarter of adults in these two churches attend any sort of regular religious education, and only 11 percent are in the high-participation category that characterizes half of conservative Protestants. Only 20 percent give more than $1,000 per year to their parish,[33] and barely a quarter (29 percent) report providing informal assistance to others on a regular basis. Despite an explicit theology that valorizes engagement in the world, individual Catholics are no more likely to participate in outside service organizations than are conservative Protestants.

These differences in church culture do parallel demographic differences. The Catholics in our sample, for instance, were slightly less well educated, more likely to have children, and less financially well-off, on average.

And liberal Protestants, by contrast, are older and better educated, on average. But do the traditions themselves have an impact, beyond demographic differences and beyond the individual differences found within them? These traditions represent different families of religious narratives that can be woven into the lives of individual participants. If action is best understood as a multivalent mix of autobiographical and public narratives, then participation in community service ought to reflect that mix. Action in any given instance will be affected by the range of narratives and strategies available to the participants, narratives created in the network of relationships and activity—sacred and secular—of which they are a part.

INTERSECTING NARRATIVES OF SERVICE

Using multiple regression analysis, we can look simultaneously at several dimensions of difference, assessing how each is related to individual (reported) behavior. Statistics can never substitute for the more nuanced analysis that would be possible with in-depth interviews, detailed time-use studies, or actual observation. But sorting out the patterns in a large number of cases can provide hints about how structures, ideas, patterns of interaction, and traditions are related to the work of doing good in the community.

If we look first at informal assistance, we find that demographics tell us very little. Far more important than where one is in the economic and social structure are the Christian narratives of practice one brings to life. With everything else controlled for, endorsing a Golden Rule vision of Christian virtue remains strongly related to the informal practices of care people actually reported. Once one has adopted this religious narrative as a description of how a good life should be lived, actions in various institutional contexts—sacred and secular, public and private—play out the script. This is true across all the religious traditions. Once we take demographics, orientations, and participation into account, there are no significant differences among the four religious families in how much informal care is being practiced. In the case of informal service in the community, different institutional carriers have their effects indirectly. Only as those institutions encourage particular Christian orientations do we see different patterns of engagement in the community.

For instance, with those institutional carriers taken into account and church participation held constant, people who most strongly endorse an Evangelical account of the Christian life are less likely to spend time helping people in need. This is not a matter of differences in demographics or even of what kind of church they attend. It is, rather, the strength of an individual-level narrative that shows up in choices made about how to use one's time. It is as true for an evangelical in a mainline church as for an evangelical in a conservative one. The conservative church itself has its effect only by disproportionately encouraging this particular view of Christian virtue.

Across all religious traditions, including the conservative one, participants who are most involved in community service organizations and in informal help are also those who are most active in the church itself.[34] While the dominant theology in conservative churches may discourage community participation, that effect is largely canceled by the strong and active congregational culture. Far from taking people *out* of the community, active participation in church fellowship, education, and mission groups makes them more likely to get involved in other works of service, as well. Among all religious groups, the overall level of church participation is the single most important factor in explaining involvement in community service organizations. Interactions within the parish thus seem to lead outward. Sheer involvement with fellow parishioners in the give-and-take of church life seems to provide increased opportunity to invest in the well-being of others, within and beyond the church's membership.[35] Over and above the individual's own religious orientation and his or her structural position in the larger culture, participating in a religious community seems both to encourage and to make possible a variety of forms of civic voluntarism.

In part, the level of voluntarism linked to church participation is surely affected by the degree to which the congregation itself is enmeshed in the service delivery network of its community. We found that virtually all congregations had at least one tie to a local organization to which they gave money, space, and other resources, as well as sending teams of volunteers.[36] These interorganizational connections are part of what links church participation with individual community engagement. As Eckstein has noted, volunteerism in some cases is rooted as much in collective activities and ties as in individual values and resources.[37] A variety of earlier studies, in fact, have noted that volunteerism is indeed facilitated by network ties.[38] One of the best predictors of community involvement is whether or not one has been asked.[39]

In addition to the implied networks present among those who participate most actively in the church itself, we also see this (to a much lesser extent) in the effects of participation in small groups in the community. Those who participate in sports, twelve-step, and scouting groups are slightly more likely to volunteer in service organizations and informal care, as well. Community-based small groups focused on Bible study, spiritual growth, and youth religious activities might seem to be a drain on the time and interest a person could devote to more this-worldly forms of community betterment, but that is not the case. At least part of what such groups offer is mutual support,[40] and indeed, people involved in small groups, across all religious traditions, are more involved in informal caring.

But community small-group participants are more involved in organized volunteering, as well. In fact, the small groups themselves may have a strong service component. In our interviews, we found many congregations sponsoring support groups for people who were themselves in need. These gatherings might be parenting or weight loss groups; groups dealing with divorce recovery, birth defects, or disability; or groups for people who have encountered domestic violence or incest, to name a few of those we found.[41] Small groups can be an effective means for sustaining social and emotional bonds and promoting mutual aid.[42] Church participation, being part of a religiously based support group, and service to others are sometimes indistinguishable parts of a single experience.

Both an impulse toward interpersonal care (the Golden Rule orientation) and an impulse toward seeking justice (the Activist orientation) can find expression in community organizations. Even when those orientations are carried individually, never overtly spoken as religious narratives in public contexts of caring and advocacy, they are nevertheless guiding some churchgoers into community engagement, while other religious narratives (specifically Evangelical ones) are discouraging that engagement. Paul Lichterman has observed that among liberal Protestants, "faith" can motivate civic volunteer action even when that faith is not explicitly articulated in religious rhetoric, stories, or maxims.[43] The connections between religious narratives and public service are both subtle and strong. Beyond the effects of individual orientations, participation in particular religious cultures makes organized community service more likely. The heritage of civic engagement carried by mainline churches provides public narratives of service that are tied to individual action in the world.[44]

Catholic culture, like evangelical culture, is more complex. Once one controls for other factors, participants in Catholic parishes are neither more nor less likely to be engaged in the community. It is not that being Catholic, as such, discourages community service. Rather, being Catholic means being far less involved in parish activities than comparable Protestants; and it is that lack of involvement that makes the difference. The most parish-involved Catholics are as engaged in formal and informal community service as are the most parish-involved Protestants, and the least-involved Protestants are no more engaged than the average Catholic. Catholic parish culture provides ample justification for community involvement, but lacks the mechanisms of deep congregational interaction and extensive participation that channel larger numbers of Protestants into formal and informal networks of service.[45] When Catholics do more than come just for worship, they too are likely to be drawn into a web of expectations and activities that connect them with the community.

Particular religious cultures and orientations are the primary mechanisms by which community service is shaped, but demographic and structural differences are not without effect, as well. Both informal assistance and organized volunteer activity are more common among better-educated people and less common when there are children in the household. Having children in the household reduces all forms of community engagement. The picture from this survey is that raising children creates constraints on the time and money available for serving the community in other ways.[46] Service patterns in rural communities are different, as well. Once other factors are taken into account, rural churchgoers are neither more nor less likely to provide informal assistance to their neighbors. They are less generous with their money, but they are slightly more likely to spend time in working in community service organizations.[47] Even when we control for other ways in which rural and urban people are different (income, education, other forms of participation, and so on), the rural context itself does make a small difference.

Rural and urban differences are just one of the ways in which structural and demographic realities shape patterns of charitable giving, the third form of community engagement we have been examining. While income plays no role in levels of participation in community service, it plays a very large role in giving. What better-off people distinctively do, not surprisingly, is give significantly more money to charitable causes. The single strongest factor in the amount given to secular charity—across all religious traditions—is income level. But over and above questions of capacity, urban people give at slightly higher levels, as do those who are part of older cohorts. Once the presence of children in the household has been controlled for, age has no effect on participation in service activities, but it does have an effect on giving. At every income level and across all religious traditions, older people give more to secular charity.

Not all religious traditions equally encourage this kind of giving, however. People in liberal Protestant churches give more, no matter what their individual resources or orientations. And if a person is committed to a Golden Rule or an Activist account of Christian life, giving is encouraged, as well. Caring for needy people and seeking change in the world are narratives that seem consonant with providing money to the variety of agencies that are trying to make a difference in local communities and beyond.

Being in a church culture that encourages giving can make contributions more likely, but active participation in any congregation contributes at least marginally to increased charitable giving. The effects of participation are much smaller, however, when the matter in question is money. Active attendance at church events is strongly related to performing service, but less strongly tied to providing financial support.

Across all three types of community engagement—formal, informal, and financial—participants are sometimes encouraged toward engagement by individual life scripts formed by being well educated or by living in a small town. Such people are sometimes constrained by their lack of income or the demands of child rearing. But their differing ways of accounting for a good Christian life create narrative expectations, as well. Golden Rule narratives of mutual care evolve especially into informal assistance in the community, but also unfold in organized volunteering and giving. Activist narratives of seeking justice and change evolve into organizational participation and financial support for agencies serving the world. Evangelical narratives of eternal salvation and personal piety are unlikely to include such worldly engagement at all, but mediating and facilitating these individual narratives are the religious cultures of the congregations in which people are involved. Liberal Protestant churches provide a public narrative of engagement that encourages individual action, even when nothing else about a person's life would predict civic service. And conservative Protestant churches do just the opposite. But no matter what the church culture and no matter what the individual's own predispositions, the fundamental caring interaction of church life seems to have a force of its own. Because evangelically oriented people are so involved in their churches, their overall average engagement in the community is much higher than the orientation itself would predict. And we can now see that the mystery of Catholic disengagement from community life is not a matter of ideology or of demographics or even of an inherently insular culture. Rather, it is a matter of minimal parish engagement. As Catholics are drawn more actively into parish participation, they are as likely as other religious people to be drawn into community service as well.

Porous Boundaries: Religion in Everyday Action

Serving the needy, feeding the hungry, building neighborhoods—all are actions that are ambiguous in themselves until they are "emplotted" in a story. Often that story is simply that good people or good citizens contribute to building good communities by volunteering time and money in ways that serve others. But almost as often, "serving the needy" is emplotted in the biblical story from Matthew 25 about how, at the end of time, Jesus will recognize those who are truly his followers by the way they have cared for the sick, the hungry, and those in prison. Churches tell these stories, and people who participate in those churches learn to narrate their own lives in those terms. Having come to valorize biblical and other religious heroes who sacrifice, who welcome strangers, and who "go the second mile," the people who are most deeply involved in Christian congregations tend to carry those stories into their communities. These same people provide informal help, volunteer in service organizations, and give their money.

Sometimes their communities of faith provide them with stories that explicitly elaborate the connections between God's action and worldly service. But religiously formed stories of service are not always so explicit, nor do they stay within the confines of church life. Much of the social service sector in U.S. society has very porous boundaries. The public work of providing food, shelter, counseling, training, even recreation and cultural experiences, allows multiple narratives to exist side by side. Rebecca Anne Allahyari writes that the volunteers she observed were simultaneously striving to do "economic, political, social, cultural, religious, ethnic, racial, [and] gender selving."[48] What she calls "selving" is not unlike the narrative process we have described here. She recognizes that a setting may provide its participants with powerful rhetorics about who they are and what they are doing, but they will always bring in other stories, as well.

Lichterman reminds us that sometimes those other stories are signaled by no more than participants' mutual recognition of each other as people who are "religious."[49] That mutual recognition of a common religious identity signals to the actors involved that they each understand themselves to be part of a drama in which (however far in the background) God is present.[50] They do not need to have any explicit biblical story that directly compels their action, but the sum total of biblical stories has already been woven into an autobiographical narrative. The simple use of words like "stewardship" or "calling" or "least of these" signals to others that these acts of service are part of a religious story.

Religious narratives enter public life often without even being noticed. Religious action exists in everyday public spaces not as an alien imposition but as part of the very nature of what many public participants understand themselves to be doing. They need not impose their definitions as an absolute "truth" on others. Every social situation requires negotiating the multiple autobiographical and public narratives at work in it. Some of the narratives that routinely emplot the service rendered to American communities are stories of religious caring, of pursuing justice, of doing ministry. They are carried both by individuals and by institutions, and—like all other narratives—they are transposed across porous boundaries to make their way into and enrich American public life.

part three

Religion at Large

IN THE NEXT four chapters, the focus shifts to the social dynamics and influence of what can be called religion at large: religion as it operates in church networks of social service, nursing homes, individual service programs, and a nationwide movement.

In Chapter 6, Ronald Thiemann looks at the history of two Lutheran child-serving agencies in Pennsylvania that have recently merged to form a new social service agency. Thiemann documents that external constraints, such as changes in federal funding and a more competitive landscape in the broader industry, precipitated the merger. Yet he argues that the formative function of religion as described in our framework remains strong here: the new agency's mission and practices are nevertheless shaped by the intrinsic commitments of Christianity, as understood through Lutheran theology.

Julie Boatwright Wilson, in Chapter 7, examines nursing homes, also in Pennsylvania, as an example of an industry in which, after years of consolidation and increased federal oversight, for-profit, nonprofit religious, and nonprofit secular institutions hold relatively stable market shares. She looks at the differences among nursing homes in these sectors, seeking to determine if religious affiliation makes a significant difference. Her findings on both differences and similarities in operations and quality of care call for further study using the methodology we have proposed.

In Chapter 8, sociologists Amy Reynolds and Christopher Winship evaluate the "faith factor" in four urban programs directed at teenage girls, one a secular program and the others religious to varying degrees. Their small empirical study focuses on whether and how the presence of religion alters program outcomes. They find that, under certain conditions, religion can be an effective component of social service if it helps clients connect their existing value systems (in this case, religion) with more responsible and socially constructive behavior.

Finally, in Chapter 9 Ziad Munson examines a controversial and emotionally charged political phenomenon, the movement against abortion. He examines the attitudes and beliefs of a large sample of movement participants, about both abortion and democracy. Unexpectedly, participants, despite their strong claims for the absolute truth of their positions, also affirm and remain committed to democratic processes.

chapter 6

Lutheran Social Ministry in Transition: What's Faith Got to Do with It?

Ronald F. Thiemann

POLITICIANS and scholars have given increasing attention to the role of religious organizations in public life since the early 1990s. The notion that faith-based social service providers can offer effective and cost-efficient solutions to America's social ills has gained widespread nonpartisan support. Although federal contracts have long been extended to large denominational social service agencies, initiatives put forth by the administrations of Bill Clinton and George W. Bush have sought to expand governmental support to smaller religious organizations.[1] Despite the vigorous rhetoric in support of faith-based social and human services, little research has been conducted to demonstrate the effectiveness of these organizations.[2] In particular, the conviction that the effectiveness of faith-based organizations must be causally related to the faith elements within them has gone virtually unquestioned. In this historical case study, I find the identity and effectiveness of faith-based organizations to be considerably more complex than the current discussion would indicate. Shifting the focus from the beliefs driving these organizations to the work they do, which is where many faith-based providers would say our attention properly belongs, yields a richer and more varied picture of this sector.

As Nancy Ammerman argues persuasively in Chapter 5, individual religious identities are shaped by complex and competing narratives. Being religious cannot be reduced to any single factor or even to a single stable configuration of influences. What is true for religious individuals is true a fortiori for religious communities. Communities of faith develop out of rich, dense, and constantly changing traditions. Internal disputes within these communities lead to the development and revision of doctrine as well as ritual practice, and the complicated relationships between these communities and their host societies contribute to fundamental changes within each. Most religious traditions have emerged from premodern cultures and have been decisively reshaped by their engagement with democratic societies;[3] and democratic societies have been equally influenced by the religious elements within them.[4] Given the complexity of these relationships, one should hardly be surprised that it is difficult to untangle religious and nonreligious elements, particularly within faith-based organizations that serve diverse populations in democratic societies.

Despite the evident complexity of religious organizations, social scientists continue to search for a means by which the "distinctively religious" dimension of complicated social relationships can be identified and isolated. As Ziad Munson observes in his study of the pro-life movement, the use of religion as a causal force to explain other social facts is widespread in sociology. But a causal use does little to elucidate the intricate relationships between religion and pro-life activism, he argues. "Religion and the pro-life movement, it seems, are not so much discrete, distinct social phenomena in which the former influences the latter, but instead are overlapping social processes that impact each other . . . Events can take on multiple meanings, behaviors can take on multiple voices, and ideas can simultaneously express multiple intentions and beliefs. The issue is not to reduce these manifold meanings to one that is primary or more fundamental, but instead to recognize that the polysemy of action can be a major source of social dynamism."[5]

Even as sophisticated an interpreter of religion as the Quaker scholar Thomas Jeavons can fall victim to the reductionist tendencies of social scientific inquiry. In his important study of Christian service organizations Jeavons argues that "the structure and char-

acter of religious organizations . . . should . . . derive from and reflect commitment to central theological principles." He identifies
two basic elements essential to the success of such institutions: mission and service. "Christian service organizations especially tend to
have a sense of mission that has two distinct but inseparable aspects—both to provide service and to give witness to and try to promote the religious beliefs that inspire that service."[6] Moreover, on
the basis of his study of nine (primarily evangelical) social ministry organizations, Jeavons argues that their effectiveness derives in
large part from the primacy of their commitment to the spiritual dimensions of mission.

> Genuinely Christian service agencies whose work is truly an expres-
> sion of faith will, I believe, attend to the spiritual as well as the corpo-
> ral works of mercy in what they do . . . That means they will under-
> take the work they do because of their religious convictions and in a
> way that creates real relationships among the 'servers and the served.'
> It also means opportunities for witnessing about their faith will arise
> out of the works of service performed, and be welcomed. So . . . the
> possibilities for integrating service and witness, will emerge naturally
> and be realized, and will reinforce the distinctive characteristics of
> these organizations.[7]

Jeavons's qualitative study identifies a number of distinctive characteristics, but they remain vague and ill defined. The "core values
would surely include: faith and trust in God; a commitment to dignity, equality, and justice for all people; a commitment to caring
for and empowering people who cannot (presently) care for themselves; and a belief that some ideal of stewardship should define our
relationship to material goods and the natural world."[8] Other characteristics Jeavons highlights are a sense of work as a calling or vocation from God, a close alignment between individual and organizational goals, and policies that allow the hiring and nurturing of
people who share the Christian agencies' mission. Although these
admirable qualities should undoubtedly characterize religious or
faith-based service organizations, it is not clear that they are the
unique defining characteristics of Christian service. Surely many

non-Christian organizations would exhibit similar qualities, and many service-oriented secular institutions might have functionally similar characteristics at work. Does Jeavons's account consist in anything more than an assertion that all social service organizations should be driven by value-shaped mission statements? The conclusion of Byron Johnson of the University of Pennsylvania—that further evaluative research is "desperately needed"—seems inescapable. Johnson cites a particular need for prospective studies assessing multiple dimensions of religion or of being religiously committed: "It is only this kind of accumulated research that will ultimately help us to sort out these complex relationships."[9]

As will be seen in the following account of one faith-based social service agency, the relations between religious and nonreligious dimensions within such organizations are extremely complex—and the reasons for refusing to distinguish them sharply may be as much theological as sociological or historical. In many Christian traditions good works are understood to be an expression of faith but are in no way limited to the faithful.[10] For a theologian like Martin Luther, good works can be performed equally by Christians and non-Christians alike. Luther's doctrine of justification by faith meant that human salvation was accomplished by the work of Jesus Christ alone. Good works, though they may flow from faith, have nothing to do with matters of salvation—either for the doer or for the recipient of the good works. "A good work is good for the reason that it is useful and benefits and helps the one for whom it is done; why else should it be called good?"[11] Thus the goodness of the work stems from the benefit done for the neighbor, not from the faith of the doer. "If you find a work in you by which you benefit God or His saints or yourself and not your neighbor, know that such a work is not good."[12] For this reason Luther argued vigorously against the use of begging by monastic orders as a means of gaining support. Indeed he suggested that institutions that housed monastic beggars should be turned into shelters for the sick and needy of the community. Any act directed to the neighbor in need is a genuine good work; and good works can be accomplished by Christians, adherents of other religions, and even nonbelievers. The work is good because of the benefit it accomplishes for the one in need, not because of the motivation or the faith of the one who does it. If a good work is accomplished and the need of the neighbor alleviated, one should rejoice, no matter who the actor is or what her motivation might be.

Religious traditions that follow this understanding of ethics will therefore resist any effort to distinguish acts of care and compassion by reference to the faith of the actors. It follows that adherents of these traditions will be troubled by the sociological effort to discover and isolate the unique "religious dimension" of the care offered by faith-based organizations. They will also find Jeavons's emphasis upon the integration of faith and works and of witness and service to be theologically suspect. If service of the neighbor is done in order to provide an opportunity to witness to the gospel, it is, according to these traditions, not only potentially a violation of Christian faith but conceivably a violation of the Constitution as well. According to this tradition the effectiveness of Christian social services or social ministries should be evaluated solely by criteria that seek to measure how well the neighbor in need is being served. And those criteria should apply equally to religious and nonreligious social service agencies.

So in the Lutheran social service ministry whose story follows we should not be surprised to find that the religious and nonreligious elements are deeply intertwined and difficult to disentangle. This observation will lead not to a negative assessment of the place of faith-based organizations within the world of social service but to a restatement of their importance among the diverse agencies serving neighbors in need.[13]

Diakon Lutheran Social Ministries

Like a brick Victorian Palace, the Topton Home sits on a knoll overlooking the small town of Topton, Pennsylvania. This grand setting seems appropriate for a service ministry that is one of the oldest Lutheran agencies in America and now serves as the headquarters for a new united organization known as Diakon Lutheran

Social Ministries. Diakon, which draws its name from the Greek word for service, was created in January 2000 by a merger of Tressler Lutheran Services and Lutheran Services Northeast. Affiliated with Lutheran Services in America, an alliance of 300 Lutheran social service organizations, the ministry employs nearly 4,000 people and provides services to more than 50,000 clients. Services range widely and include adoption, behavioral health programs, services for the elderly, family life services, immigration and refugee work, and retirement communities. Diakon sponsors both residential services and community-based programs. The agency acknowledges that the merger was necessitated by "changes in the health care and social service fields, such as decreasing reimbursements and increasing regulation . . . The partnership enabled Diakon to streamline operations and gain needed cost efficiencies. And to begin significant growth."[14]

Although the merger was occasioned primarily by financial considerations, the new organization has begun a serious and systematic rethinking of its mission and ministry. Concerned that sponsoring synods and congregations felt disconnected from their work, Diakon's leaders have begun to strengthen ties with their supporting local bodies and to reassert the distinctively Christian, even Lutheran, identity of the agency. While earlier mission statements and publicity materials described the institution's work in the secular language of "agency, service, and care," the new materials employ strong theological and religious language. Those under care are characterized as "unique gifts of God . . . beloved creature[s] of God." The work is described as "ministry," and the employees are called "faithful stewards" committed to "the community for which God made us." Identifying itself as "a faith-based institution," Diakon strives "to enhance the physical, social, spiritual, intellectual, and developmental potential of the people we serve and those who serve them."[15]

Diakon's leadership team has begun to articulate the clear ministerial character of their organization, and they employ explicit theological and biblical language to identify their basic mission, values, and ethical principles.

Mission

In response to God's love in Jesus Christ, Diakon Lutheran Social Ministries will demonstrate God's command to love the neighbor through acts of service.

Values

Respect: All people are unique gifts of God to be valued.
Service: All work that affirms God's creation has worth and dignity.
Stewardship: We are responsible to God, the church, and society for the use of all our precious resources.
Quality: Teamwork, continual learning, and innovation enhance the quality of service.

Ethical Principles

Whereas Diakon Lutheran Social Ministries:

• values all people as unique gifts of God, we uphold fair treatment and non-discrimination with regard to people we serve and the persons who serve them.

• affirms the whole person as a beloved creature of God, we strive to enhance the physical, social, spiritual, intellectual, and developmental potential of the people we serve and those who serve them.

• affirms both the integrity of the individual and the importance of the community for which God made us, we encourage and assist those we serve to make decisions about their own futures together with staff, family, clergy, and community representatives (for example, legal, medical, and judicial).

• recognizes our call to be faithful stewards, we make ethical decisions in the dynamic tension created by limited resources and unlimited needs.

• is a member of Lutheran Services in America through affiliation with the Evangelical Lutheran Church in America, we strive to conduct our corporate life consistent with our identity as a faith-based organization.

In addition to the mission statement, values, and ethical principles, the Diakon leadership team has developed a code of conduct and an internal educational and evaluational process to monitor the manner in which the mission statement is enacted in the behavior of the employees and volunteers. A new senior staff position, the corporate compliance officer,[16] has been charged with overseeing the implementation of the mission statement in all aspects of the organization's work. Although this process is still in its infancy, this faith-based organization is determined to root its institutional practices in its theology.

National and regional denominational agencies like Diakon have been subject to heavy criticism, both within and without the churches, in the past decade. Congregations, synods, and bishops have expressed concern that these large national agencies have become overly bureaucratized and disconnected from the primary evangelical mission of the church. The heavy reliance of these agencies upon local, state, and federal grants and contracts has led many to believe that such ministry organizations have divided loyalties, and that responsibilities to government regulations have become more important than accountability to the churches. The Diakon leadership team acknowledges that some of these charges are accurate, and they are working to correct these abuses within their own organization.

At the same time organizations like Diakon are often conspicuous by their absence in the current flurry of activity around partnerships between government and faith-based organizations. Even though the vast majority of faith-based social service care is provided by agencies like Catholic Charities, Lutheran Services in America, and Combined Jewish Philanthropies, these national, quasi-independent ministries have been largely ignored in the political fascination with smaller, more intimate faith-based organizations, such as congregations, store-front ministries, and urban coalitions. Large social ministry organizations, criticized by their own churches for their impersonal structure and devalued in the political realm by today's preference for smaller and more local providers, thus stand at a moment of identity crisis. Nonetheless, they continue to be the most influential and effective faith-based organizations for the actual delivery of human and social services.

Here I describe the complex interaction between religious and nonreligious elements in the birth, growth, and development of one

Lutheran social ministry organization. Examining the confluence of factors shaping the identity of this faith-based institution sheds new light on the reasons why such organizations are important in the overall ecology of nonprofits, and also disputes various misguided ways of answering the question, "What's faith got to do with it?"

American Lutheran Theology and Social Ministry

American Lutherans understand themselves to have a unique role among Christian denominations. Though often categorized among mainline Protestants, Lutherans assert that they are a "confessional movement within the church catholic." As the first of the European movements of reform, Lutherans bear a particular responsibility for the divisions created within Christianity by the Reformation. Although Lutheran theology is similar to that of Reformed Christianity, Lutheran liturgical and worship practices are clearly catholic. In addition, Lutherans have played an especially important role in ecumenical relations, both in the United States and worldwide. For more than thirty years, U.S. Roman Catholics and Lutherans engaged in a series of ecumenical dialogues concerning the doctrinal matters that have traditionally separated their churches, culminating in the historic agreement, recently ratified in 1999 by the Vatican, on the fundamental doctrine of justification. Also within the last decade Lutherans have reached "full communion" agreements with both the Reformed churches and the Episcopal Church in the USA.[17]

Lutheran theology and ethical practice thus have a pragmatic, reforming character. Although it is possible to identify distinctive emphases within Lutheranism, Lutherans tend to be eclectic in their work, borrowing insights from every branch of Christianity. Nevertheless certain historical tendencies can be identified, which include:

1. The fundamental Lutheran theological commitment is to the primacy of God's grace offered freely to a fallen and sinful humanity. That grace cannot be earned by any human effort,

but can only be grasped by an act of faith. Consequently all human beings are equal in the sight of God.

2. Lutheran ethics are governed by the motto "Faith active in love." Since God alone can secure the salvation of human beings, works of love are designed not to seek favor with God but simply to serve the neighbor in need.

3. Lutherans tend to be realists in the ethical sphere. Luther's teaching of the "two kingdoms" suggests that in a fallen world perfect love can never be achieved. Indeed, within the "kingdom of the world" it is unlikely that institutions can be built around an ethic of love. Thus Lutheran ethics are dialectical and pragmatic, moving between the poles of sin and grace, realism and hope.

4. "Vocation" is a distinctly Lutheran concept for describing Christian work in the world. Luther took the notion of *vocatio,* which in medieval Catholicism applied solely to clerical vocations, and applied it to the everyday work of the Christian. All Christians, Luther asserted, should understand themselves to be called by God to serve the neighbor through their work.

Lutheran ethics function more as a set of sensibilities enabling its adherents to live a Christian life in the world than as a set of doctrines or divine commands. Thus many of the "principles" by which Lutheran Christians structure their identities remain "tacit" rather than "focal" in the way they live their lives.[18] In order to live a Christian life, the adherent must "rely upon" these tacit principles, but they are made the focus of explicit attention and analysis only when questioned or challenged. Thus they serve as essential "background beliefs" for behavior and action in the world. In the preliminary interviews with the leadership team of Diakon, the tacit character of Lutheran doctrine and ethics was quite evident.[19] Members of the leadership team had so thoroughly internalized their own Lutheran identity that they needed our critical questions in order to articulate their basic religious beliefs.

Although Lutherans have been present in America since the early seventeenth century, they have struggled to establish a clear denominational identity. Catholic in liturgy, Protestant in theology, and Evangelical in piety, Lutherans seem to elude standard categories of classification. Sidney Ahlstrom, in *A Religious History of the American People*, treats Lutherans in a section entitled "Countervailing Religion," along with Roman Catholics and Jews. Lutherans have engaged in serious internal definitional struggles, seeking, in the words of DeAne Lagerquist, "to construct an identity that is simultaneously genuinely Lutheran and authentically American."[20] The effort to be "genuinely Lutheran" spawned a high confessional theology with serious intellectual commitments. The desire to be "authentically American" produced countervailing forms of evangelical piety with more than a hint of anti-intellectualism. These two characteristics—confessional theology and evangelical practice—have created a tension at the heart of American Lutheranism between the assertion of a distinct Lutheran identity and accommodation to trends within mainline Protestantism. These distinctive sensibilities, and their associated tensions, can be seen in the manner in which Lutherans have established social ministry initiatives throughout their sojourn in America.[21]

The first Lutheran settlers immigrated to the Dutch Reformed colony of New Netherlands in 1625. Their attempts to establish Lutheran worship met with severely repressive measures; their children were even rebaptized by the Reformed majority community. Although the first Lutheran congregation was established in 1649 in the New Netherlands, it was only with the surrender of the Dutch New World colonies to the English in 1664 that Lutherans were allowed to develop their own worship practices.

With the arrival of Henry Melchior Muhlenberg in November 1742, the face of Lutheranism in the colonies began to change dramatically. Muhlenberg was sent to the colonies by leaders of the German Pietist movement centered at the University of Halle. The creation of widespread social ministry organizations is one of the most dramatic contributions of Lutheran Pietism. Though often decried for its anti-intellectualism and sentimentality, German Pietism nonetheless established a tradition of institutional care for the needy.

Working under the motto *Ecclesia Plantanda* (the church must be planted), Muhlenberg oversaw a rapid growth of Lutheranism in the colony of Pennsylvania. By 1748 sufficient congregations had been established to warrant the creation of the first Lutheran synod, the United Congregations. By 1765 there were 15,000 Lutheran parishioners in 133 congregations served by 33 pastors—almost all in Pennsylvania.

Like many religious communities in the postrevolutionary period, Lutherans became active in various charitable and humanitarian activities. They cooperated with other Christians in creating societies dedicated to alleviating the difficult conditions facing European immigrants to the new nation. In accord with the biblical injunctions, orphans and widows were special objects of kindly care. Most congregations took up regular weekly collections for the poor, the orphans, and the widows of the community. The first social service organizations established by Lutherans were orphanages. All these activities were understood as matters of charity rather than justice. Although Lutherans preached against the mistreatment of slaves and even opposed the slave trade itself, many Lutherans in the South sought to justify the owning of slaves. As a Lutheran pastor in Georgia argued, "If you take slaves in faith and with intent of conducting them to Christ, the action will not be sin, but it may prove a benediction."[22]

Lutheran benevolent activity was designed along the model first developed within the Pietist movement in Germany. The early Pietist August Herman Francke understood the mission of the church to involve two related activities: the preaching of the gospel and care for the neighbor in need. Thus he established the first German Lutheran social ministry organizations—a school for the poor (1695) and an orphanage (1698), institutions designed to care for both souls and bodies. In a similar fashion early-nineteenth-century American Lutherans developed "home missions," organizations that combined evangelization and benevolent care. With the westward expansion, Lutheran home missions rapidly grew in size and scope, nowhere with greater enthusiasm and success than in Pennsylvania. The founder of the Pittsburgh Synod, W. A. Passavant, founded a hospital and orphanage in 1849 and developed an order of Protestant deaconesses to staff the institutions. During the same time period the first colleges and seminaries of the church were established in Pennsylvania, as the institutionalization of American Lutheranism began in earnest. But despite the broad sweep of benevolent care sponsored by Lutheran churches, "nowhere then was there careful analysis of the underlying causes of social evils, nor any long-range effort to overcome those causes . . . Passavant made no progress beyond his predecessors in analyzing the causes of social ills. The role of the good Samaritan was the highest expression of practical Christian impulses of that day."[23] Even during the height of the Social Gospel Movement at the end of the nineteenth century, Lutherans remained steadfast in their refusal to engage economic and political issues. "From the pulpits of other denominations came calls for the regeneration of society. But the general position of Lutherans at this time was that the work of the church is to regenerate human souls one by one, and that social reform must begin with individuals, not groups. The program to save men by changing their environment was held to be nothing more than golden-rule ethics which forfeits the spiritual worth of the individual."[24]

The Tressler Home and the Post–Civil War Era

Within this social, political, and religious milieu Diakon's originating partners were born. In January of 1868 the Tressler Orphans Home of the Evangelical Lutheran Church of the United States of America was chartered at Loysville, Pennsylvania. Its purpose was "to provide a home for poor orphan children of the Evangelical Lutheran Church and such other poor children as the Board will find funds to justify; to have their temporal wants supplied; to educate them physically, intellectually, morally, and religiously; and to extend over them a wholesome guardianship."[25] The post–Civil War era witnessed the founding of hundreds of orphanages and other institutions of care within the northern states. The terrible conditions created by the war combined with an emerging ideology of domesticity to provide the essential conditions for the sudden increase in institutional care for orphaned and abandoned children. While during the antebellum period children were often given asylum in poorhouses that included adults, some of whom suffered from mental illnesses, during the postwar period children were regularly separated from the adult population of the poor. Orphanages were established both by the states and by religious organizations, but the majority of dependent children were cared for within faith-based institutions.[26]

The Tressler School provides a particularly interesting case study, because it was formed by a partnership between religious and governmental funding. Although the original impetus for the school's founding came from the churches of Perry County, Pennsylvania,[27] these pragmatic Lutherans soon discovered the availability of public monies. Shortly after the school's founding, an opportunity to obtain state funds arose. Pennsylvania governor Andrew Curtin had created an initiative to provide care for "the children of soldiers fallen while fighting for the preservation of their country." In an address to the Pennsylvania legislature in 1862, Curtin asked that government monies be appropriated for the purpose of supporting religious organizations engaged with the care of orphans: "I commend to the prompt attention of the legislature the subject of the relief of the poor orphans of our soldiers who have given, or shall give, their lives to the country during this crisis. In my opinion, their maintenance and education should be provided for by the state. Failing other natural efforts of ability to provide for them, they should be honorably received and fostered as children of the commonwealth."[28]

The funds were finally appropriated by the state legislature in 1866, and the Tressler Home used the monies from 1868 to 1889.[29] Thus Tressler participated in one of the earliest partnerships between government and a faith-based organization.[30] Records show that during the period 1864–1875, 8,277 children were admitted to forty-five soldiers' orphans schools at a cost to the state of more than $5 million. This joint arrangement stayed in force until 1889, when the state finally assumed sole responsibility for the orphans of soldiers.[31] At that time Tressler dropped the word "soldiers" from its name and once again became the Tressler Orphans Home, supported entirely by church funds. Philip Willard, the first superintendent of the school, retired in the same year.[32]

The 1890s marked an important turning point in the development of Lutheran social ministry in Pennsylvania. The years immediately following Willard's retirement were a time of financial challenge and retrenchment for the Tressler Home. The loss of the soldiers' orphans in 1889 reduced the number of orphans to only 147 in 1896, down from 210 at the end of the previous decades. The year 1896 also saw the founding of a new institution, the Lutherans Orphans' Home, which was granted a charter by the Berks County Court in nearby Topton, Pennsylvania. The Home was to be a haven where "the homeless and the destitute may be clothed and fed, and enjoy the advantages of a Christian training." Under its first two superintendents, the Reverend Uriah Heilman and the Reverend John Raker, the Topton Home reached financial stability quite quickly and established itself as a viable institution.

Tressler and Topton in the Progressive Era

The Progressive Era in American social policy (1890–1917) provided the larger context for the next stage of development of the Tressler and Topton homes.[33] These decades witnessed the rapid growth of Lutheranism in America as successive waves of German and Scandinavian immigrants settled in the United States. In 1870 confirmed Lutherans numbered fewer than 500,000; by 1910 their number had swelled to 2.3 million, making them the fourth-largest denomination in America, surpassed only by Roman Catholics, Methodists, and Baptists.[34] Since German Lutherans were already well established in the United States, most German immigrants migrated to those areas of substantial German population: primarily Pennsylvania, Ohio, and Missouri. Scandinavian immigrants, divided from their German co-religionists by both language and culture, started new church organizations along strict ethnic lines. Nearly three-quarters of all Scandinavian immigrants settled in the agricultural region of the upper Midwest. These developments within Lutheranism, while important for the ultimate destiny of both social ministry organizations, did not have a substantial impact on their missions during this era. More important is the broader atmosphere established by the religious and moral arguments set forth by representatives of Progressive Era reform politics.

Inspired by the "Gospel of Child Saving," progressive political and religious leaders launched a nationwide effort to provide better care for dependent children. In many ways the era is a study in contradictions. A White House conference in 1909 unanimously affirmed three fundamental principles: foster care should always be preferred over institutional confinement; private and public agencies should share responsibility for the care of dependent children, but government should provide the administrative and supervisory authority; and earlier practices that intervened in family life to remove children from parents thought to be "unfit" should be completely eliminated.[35] Despite the apparent consensus that institutional care should be phased out, the decade of the 1890s witnessed an explosion in the creation of childcare institutions. "The 1890s may in fact have been more prolific in this respect than any other decade in American history. At least 247 institutions were incorporated during those ten years."[36] The Topton Home, born in the midst of the tensions and contradictions of the Progressive Era, had a flexible philosophy regarding the balance between institutional care and foster home placement. The Tressler Home, committed to an earlier philosophy of institutionalization, coped less well with the changing ethos of dependent childcare.[37]

The debate over institutions versus foster care was structured by a number of important factors. During the Progressive Era the cult of domesticity took root among the leaders of the child-saving movement. The Home was idealized as a haven within a heartless world; women were assigned the essential role of caregivers and moral guardians; and children were seen to be the epitome of innocence and moral purity. The regimentation of the orphanage and the high ratio of children to adults within it made it appear anomalous against the standard of the idealized family. At the same time the rise of the new profession of social work produced a cadre of professionals committed to addressing the plight of the child within a range of public institutions. Often educated in theological institutions, these leaders sought to work out their religious vocations within the public institutions of early-twentieth-century America and helped to develop the professional and scientific standards of the early social work movement. Few of them sensed the potential tension between their belief in the private realm of domesticity and their use of public institutions, including the force of law, to establish those principles in American life. For the most part they saw no conflict between their personal Protestant faith and their enforcement of a Protestant vision and ethic upon a diverse public.

Although many of the criticisms of childcare institutions were valid and well founded (many of them did engage in excessive regimentation, severe punishment, and deleterious child labor practices), the orphanages were also subject to denunciation for their religious indoctrination. It may seem ironic that religiously motivated social work professionals would criticize the orphanages for being religiously doctrinaire, but the irony soon disperses when one recognizes that by the turn of the century the majority of childcare institutions were Roman Catholic. By 1910, 25 percent of all orphanages were run by Roman Catholics and 45 percent of all dependent children were under the care of Catholic institutions. Thus the fulminations against "religious indoctrination" were often thinly veiled criticisms of the rising influence of Roman Catholicism within American life. Religion in these institutions, one prominent critic claimed, was imparted by "a set form of blessings drawled out or mechanically entuned before each meal, and thanks in the same manner after, with chapel exercises twice a day in which psalms or other portions of the scriptures are repeated until they have worn hard-beaten grooves in the brain without penetrating the understanding, a rising prayer in the morning and a retiring prayer at night, all in concert and aloud."[38] The daily regimen of the orphanages was determined by a philosophy built upon three pillars: discipline, industry, and morality.[39]

One major innovation within orphanages that sought to bridge the gap between the idealization of the family and the necessity of institutionalization was the creation of the "cottage" institution.[40] As advocated by Rudolf R. Reeder, superintendent of the New York Orphan Asylum, the cottage was designed to provide a homelike atmosphere for 15–25 students and appropriate staff. Each cottage was to contain the basic rooms and facilities for self-sufficient living: library, dining room, kitchen and pantry, bedrooms, and bathrooms. The cottage was to be run by a "matron," a woman with a "strong natural love for children." Ideally, the cottages should be located in the country so that children would learn the wonders of nature. In addition, the regimentation of the day was to be varied and children were to be given some say in the governance of the cottage. The cottage movement was so successful that by 1910, 15 percent of all orphanages claimed to be structured on the cottage plan. At the 1909 White House conference, some 220 participants approved a recommendation that encouraged the cottage plan for those children who remained within the confines of an institution. "So far as it may be found necessary temporarily or permanently to care for certain classes of children in institutions, these institutions should be conducted on the cottage plan, in order that routine and impersonal care may not unduly suppress individuality and initiative . . . The institution that comes nearest to the home . . . is the one that is successful."[41]

The new leadership of the Tressler Home resisted the innovations represented by the 1909 White House conference. Strongly committed to the fundamental importance of the orphanage, the board of trustees began to expand the physical plant and embarked upon a vigorous fund-raising campaign. Central to this effort was the creation of two traveling musical organizations: the boys' band and the girls' orchestra. In 1917, Tressler's fiftieth anniversary year, the band traveled 6,000 miles, performed at 150 venues, and returned with $13,000 for the school's treasury.[42] The red-coated band became a prominent symbol of the school and helped to establish a national Lutheran constituency for the Home. Indeed, the board continued to insist that the institution remained "a comfortable, Christian Home for orphans of Lutheran parentage who cannot otherwise be well cared for and only such will be admitted."[43]

By contrast, the Topton Home, from its founding, was committed to the care of "the needy and destitute children of Berks County" as well as the "homeless children of our Synod." Under the leadership of the Reverend Jonas O. Henry (1909–1945), the Home adopted a more varied and flexible form of ministry than its older Pennsylvania sibling had. The original building was expanded and modernized in 1911, and a separate infirmary was added that same year. In 1916 the Home moved toward more aggressive use of foster homes and adoptive services and also added a new Memorial Cottage for Infants. The overall master plan dictated that all future physical expansion should follow the cottage approach now broadly accepted throughout the nation. In 1918 a new schoolhouse was erected. The first Boys' Cottage was built in 1926, followed four years later by a new Girls' Cottage. It is clear from the historical record that the Topton Home structured its ministry in a manner far more in accord with the trends of the day than did the older Tressler Home. As J. Russell Hale points out, it was not until the 1940s that Tressler, under the leadership of Luther D. Grossman, began to adopt the innovations first recommended by the White House conference in 1909.

The Child Welfare System and the Decline of the Orphanages

The 1930s and 1940s, though quite traumatic decades in American history, were relatively tranquil times for the two Pennsylvania orphanages. Both institutions expanded their property and physical plants extensively. Resident populations of both homes remained substantial, but in the late 1930s and the 1940s the number of children began to decline (from 350 at Tressler in 1936 to 183 in 1944).[44] Contributions from synods, churches, and individuals grew rapidly, however, and both homes received a substantial number of sizable bequests. The financial success of these institutions was related to the ongoing concern within Lutheranism for the primacy of the family and for the welfare of those children who did not have the advantages of a family upbringing. Charity appeals were often quite touching, even sentimental, and following the success of the Oscar-winning movie *Boys Town* (1938), nationwide awareness of religiously sponsored orphanages soared—and contributions followed.

In the years following the Second World War, harbingers of change were on the horizon. In the Tressler Home newsletter *Echo* Superintendent Luther D. Grossman sounded a note of concern. "More emphasis," he wrote, "needs to be placed on policies affecting admissions, period of residence, foster home placement, adoptions, where possible, and the rehabilitation of the homes from which the children come."[45] At the same time national criticism of orphans' homes began to increase, as children's advocates pointed out the despicable conditions in some homes and condemned the work requirements that bordered on unjust child labor. Henrietta Lund of the National Lutheran Council was a leading voice in this national movement, and her condemnation of the "*Oliver Twist* homes" received widespread attention.[46] "There are orphanages in this country so badly run that they ought to be abolished," she argued, and Lutheranism was "one of the last institutions of the church to turn away from the old type, regimented orphanage."[47]

In the decades of the 1950s both institutions moved vigorously to professionalize their staffs, drawing on the burgeoning social work movement. Dormitory structures were turned into administrative buildings, and smaller individual cottages were constructed for the children. House parents were introduced into the cottages to provide more homelike care. Hale describes the situation facing both homes. "The nation had emerged from the war with a new prosperity. Social security and other welfare legislation were sustaining many families, birth rates were down for the time being, women were marrying later, social work professionals had largely turned against institutional care of dependent children, and the per capita cost of adequate institutional care had skyrocketed."[48]

In February 1953 the trustees of the Tressler Home, responding to these social changes, officially renamed it the Tressler Lutheran Home for Children. That name change signaled Tressler's shift away from the single focus of an orphanage to its new identity as a social service agency attending to the needs of children whether in or out of institutional care.

The histories that document the development of the two Lutheran homes give little notice to the national debates about the relationship between private, primarily religious, institutions and government subsidies. When the first programs to provide direct aid to mothers and children, so-called outdoor aid, were proposed, most private relief agencies offered strong opposition. Not only might such direct aid threaten the stability of these institutions, but it would also challenge the fundamental rationale of charity around which they had been built. Agency advocates were convinced that private institutions could provide vastly better and more humane care than could governmental agencies, but they also argued against the introduction of political manipulation into the provision of assistance for those in need. Their arguments bear an eerie similarity to the rationale offered by twenty-first-century advocates of faith-based private care. Susan Tiffin summarizes the arguments against mothers' pensions:

> Relief was condemned both for its substandard administration and for its detrimental moral effects on the recipients. Officials were poorly trained and badly paid. Their positions opened the door to chicanery and fraud and were susceptible to political manipulation. The aid dispensed was considered expensive and superfluous. It encouraged a tendency toward permanent dependence in those who received it, sapping their energy and self-respect. The poor came to think of the public coffers as bottomless and their claims to its wealth as their rights. Correspondingly, the obligation of the rich toward the poor was made redundant and the gap between the social classes widened, fostering social instability.[49]

Since the entire system of philanthropic institutions rested primarily upon the rationale of Christian charity and *noblesse oblige*, the defenders of the system seemed unable to marshal arguments concerning social justice that might have provided a single moral context for both private care and public funding.

With the enactment of the Social Security Act in 1935, state and federal funding of families with dependent children became a fact of the American welfare state, and the context within which private or religious philanthropic agencies operated changed fundamentally. In addition, the primary moral argument that the major responsibility for social welfare rested with the private and religious sector began to break down. The vast changes in legislation and regulation during the following decades required private religious agencies to adapt to the changing times. With the passage of the 1967 Amendments to the Social Security Act, the relationship between the federal government and nonprofit social agencies was greatly altered, because the law "specifically encouraged states to enter into purchase-of-service agreement with private agencies."[50] Both Tressler and Topton received these funds and thus moved to a new era of financial dependence not primarily upon their founding church bodies but upon public monies distributed by both state and federal governments.[51]

The far-reaching changes of the 1960s had a dramatic effect on the social, cultural, economic, and political context in which Christian social ministry organizations operated. The period from 1960 through 1990 was, arguably, the most secular time in the nation's history. The shift in American culture toward an understanding of public life as secular and neutral toward religion was marked by a number of important developments. The Supreme Court, drawing on the classic 1947 *Everson* decision written by Justice Hugo Black, enshrined the phrase "the wall of separation between church and state" both in First Amendment jurisprudence and in the consciousness of Americans more generally. In a series of decisions dealing primarily with school prayer, the Supreme Court broadened the scope of its establishment jurisprudence, essentially banning the presence of religious language and symbols in public school classrooms. Although the Court struggled unsuccessfully to create a more general framework for religion clause jurisprudence, the clear direction of its decisions supported those liberal political theorists who argued that in a pluralistic democracy the state must be assiduously secular and neutral.

During the 1960s theories of secularization dominated virtually every academic discipline. These theories asserted that as capitalist economies and democratic politics expanded worldwide, the public role of religion would ultimately vanish, and religion would become a matter of personal or private choice. Given the plurality and diversity of ways of believing and acting in the modern world, the dominance of any single religious view would lead to suppressions of freedom contradictory to the aims of democracy. Further, given the religious diversity within democracy, the absolute claims and counterclaims of each religion would portend a return to the religious strife of the post-Reformation era. Religion in the modern world, so the theories argued, can no longer play a public role, that is, a role that provides common ground and shared principles for belief and action. If religion is to survive, it must do so in the private lives of individual citizens. Religion, like the other commodities in the smorgasbord of democratic capitalism, is something you are free to choose or reject as personal preference dictates. Religion in modernity is, as a reviewer once said in disdain of a book, "the kind of thing you like, if you like that kind of thing."[52]

Roman Catholicism, Protestantism, and Judaism all accommodated themselves to this unprecedented suppression of religion in public life. The great Catholic moral theologian John Courtney Murray provided theological arguments in support of the "separation of church and state," asserting that only such a doctrine could allow Roman Catholicism the internal freedom the Church needed to govern its own institutions.[53] A secular neutral state was a state with clear constitutional prohibitions against interference into the internal life of the church. Mainline Protestants by and large also accepted the culture of secularization, believing that their traditional role among the cultural elites protected them from losing all power and influence in politics. Jews also supported the climate of secularity, believing that a neutral state within a culture dominated by Christianity provided the best protection for the minority rights of the Jewish community. Most evangelical and fundamentalist communities had long accepted the theological version of the church/state separation argument set forward by Roger Williams and Isaac Backus in colonial America. Only a separated church could be a place for the gathered elect, a community pure and unadulterated by the destructive influence of a sinful and decadent world. Although that position would change with dramatic suddenness in the 1980s, in the 1960s the evangelical community—with the exception of African-American evangelicals—accepted the growing orthodoxy of secularity within American society.

Thus when the 1967 amendments to the Social Security Act demanded that religious bodies create separate, secular nonprofit corporations in order to receive federal funding, religious bodies quickly acceded to that demand. Eager to gain access to these new funds—indeed, compelled to do so for their survival—Tressler and Topton embarked upon a process of downplaying their religious identities and commitments, following a pattern adopted by nearly every major religious social service agency in the United States.

At the same time that the public context was being transformed, basic changes internal to American Lutheranism also occurred. The decade of the 1960s saw the beginning of the merger movements within Lutheranism that spelled the end of the ethnic enclaves that had dominated the denomination for more than two centuries. In 1960 the American Lutheran Church (ALC), formed primarily out of smaller midwestern Norwegian and German church bodies, was established. Then in 1962 the Lutheran Church of America (LCA), a merger of four smaller Lutheran bodies, was created, and Lutheranism took its first steps beyond its German-Scandinavian ghetto into mainstream Protestantism. (In 1987, the LCA was one of three Lutheran church bodies that merged to form the Evangelical Lutheran Church in America, or the ELCA.)[54]

Once the LCA was established, its leaders began the difficult but necessary project of consolidating the huge number of redundant services the agencies of the merging churches provided. Tressler, which had established a casework department in 1954, thereby extending its ministry into community services, knew that its Home for Children could not easily survive the changing needs of both church and society. At the request of the LCA, the Tressler board ordered suspension of its institutional program, effective August 31, 1962, thus ending ninety-four years of service to homeless orphans. The Home was sold to the Commonwealth of Pennsylvania for $1,160,000.

The Topton Home did not suffer the same fate as the Tressler Home, in part because its leadership skillfully combined the use of its residential facilities as transition homes for adoptive children with a significant community-related family and children service initiative. In addition, the Topton Home, recognizing the movement away from residential care for children, decided to expand into the area of elder care, and the construction of cottages for the elderly quickly followed. This expansion created the need for further professional staffing, and both institutions also began developing significant volunteer organizations. By the mid-sixties the Topton home, facing the realities entailed in elder care, added a 57-bed infirmary. By 1971 the Henry Infirmary had grown to a 121-bed facility, and the demand for further beds continued to increase. The record budget of that year showed expenses of $1,377,000 with an anticipated deficit of $235,000. The financial crisis that was to precipitate the need for the merger some thirty years later had begun to appear on the balance sheets of these institutions.

During the last three decades of the twentieth century, the Lutheran Church sought to consolidate its social ministry programs in southeast Pennsylvania, Maryland, and Delaware. Though essential for financial viability, this consolidation greatly eroded the specific identities of these smaller institutions and severed their connections to their local constituencies. It is impossible to tell the story of these decades with the kind of intimate personal narrative appropriate to earlier years. Many older social service ministries were eliminated and new, merged organizations were created in their place. What were once small institutions with clear identities and local roots became faceless bureaucratized organizations spread over large geographic regions and supported primarily not by church contributions but by government grants and contracts. The professionalization of these social ministries led to significant gains in the scope and quality of care rendered, but these benefits came at a price: the loss of local, more intimate relations with supporting church constituencies and the blurring of what had been a clear religious identity.

Moving toward Merger: A New Beginning

As the 1990s drew to a close, both Tressler and Topton had expanded their ministries—Tressler, for example, launched efforts to improve and increase the adoption of special needs children—and incorporated smaller agencies into their organizations. But changes in the market and in governmental regulations led to serious internal questions about the continuing viability of both agencies.[55] Thus a process began that would lead to the merger of these two organizations and the creation of Diakon Lutheran Social Ministries.

The formal merger combined Tressler Lutheran Services (the successor organization to the Tressler Home) and Lutheran Services Northeast (the successor organization to the Topton Home). The merged organization encompasses five synods within the middle Atlantic region of the Evangelical Lutheran Church in America (ELCA). Within these synods are 1,079 congregations, 561,454 baptized members, and 1,594 clergy. The population of the region served by Diakon is nearly 12,000,000, almost 16 percent of whom are over the age of sixty-five. Diakon organizes its outreach under two service categories: Congregation, Community and Family Services, or CCFS, and Retirement and Health Care Services, or RHCS. CCFS provides ministry outreach in Children's Services, Behavioral Health Services, Family Life and Congregational Service, and Community Service. RHCS ministry includes Home Care, Preventive Care, Long-Term Residence Care, and Comprehensive Rehabilitation services.

Of the two merging organizations, Lutheran Services Northeast had the strongest relationship to its supporting congregations, synods, pastors, and bishops. The long history of the Topton Home as a local and regional residential center allowed local supporting groups to develop a close identification with the organization's mission. Tressler Lutheran Services, in contrast, possessed a strong regional and even national reputation, but its wide geographic reach made it more distant from its supporters. The merger provided an opportunity to reestablish ties with the agencies' supporting organizations. Both merging organizations had similar financial situations, and their boards were primarily elected through the synods of the ELCA. Lutheran Services Northeast had an operating budget of $70 million and assets of $122 million; TLS showed budget figures of $75 million with $133 million in total assets. Thus the union of the two organizations was a merger of equals, rather than a takeover by one stronger party. Leaders in both organizations recognized that the highly competitive marketplace of the 1990s, created by the entry of large for-profit corporations into the healthcare service arena and by dramatic changes in government and insurance funding, would require significant growth by each.[56] Internal studies conducted as part of independent strategic planning within each organization showed that the needed rapid growth could only come from collaboration or merger. The two Lutheran agencies thus launched a process of unification that they hoped would lead to lower costs, greater financial stability, and expansion of both territory and market share.

The similarity in origins, mission, size, and religious affiliation made the merger an obvious option. Still, the two organizations moved carefully and thoughtfully into this uncharted territory. From August through October 1998, the agencies held preliminary discussions with the assistance of a facilitator provided by Lutheran Services in America, the national service organization to which both agencies belonged. This process involved intensive consultations within the boards, the executive teams, the senior management staff, and the bishops of the supporting ELCA synods. Differences in style and approaches to service delivery were faced and methods were devised to address potential difficulties.[57] The needs of different audiences—staff, bishops, pastors, contracting agencies, donors, clients, and the general public—were analyzed and a coordinated approach to communication developed. The board meetings at which the merger agreements were to be approved were scheduled within two days of one another, and the communication effort was launched following the second board meeting. The outcome of these meetings was the signing of a "letter of intent to merge" that would guide the planning of both organizations in the coming months.

During the next six months—December 1998 to May 1999—the merging agencies engaged in systematic investigation of each organization's legal, financial, and operational situation. Crucial to this process was a serious review of the mission objectives of the merging organization, including the distinctive faith-based elements of that mission. In April 1999, the two boards met together for the first time in a two-day retreat. Although ample time was given to financial, governance, and personnel matters, significant discussion also revolved around the distinctive Lutheran identity of the merging organizations. Meetings began with devotions and prayer, and a subcommittee of the board was charged with developing a new mission statement that emphasized the particular Christian objectives of the new agency. Later that month a special "ecclesiastical due diligence" meeting was held that included the board chairs, senior management personnel, and bishops from the supporting ELCA synods. Special attention was given to the relationship between the new merging agency and congregations of the synod.

The question of the religious identity of the new organization was central in all of the discussions associated with the merger. The initial vision statement, however, stressed primarily the formal relationships between the agency and its sponsoring bodies rather than the theological principles that guided its mission: "Tressler Lutheran Service and Lutheran Services Northeast seek to create a new, efficient social ministry organization that would facilitate partnerships with congregations, Synods, Districts, and other social ministry partners to develop a unified, regional faith-based presence, while maintaining local identity and historical allegiances."[58]

One might have expected the new name, Diakon Lutheran Social Ministries, to be the product of an intensive period of theological reflection on the mission of this faith-based social ministry organization. In fact, the name emerged from a study conducted by a public relations firm, a process that Diakon's own newsletter trumpeted as a triumph of niche marketing: "Because naming the new organization is such a critical task—our new name will need to last for many years, capture the essence of our mission and vision, and eventually, help to establish our image or 'brand'—a Harrisburg public relations firm has been hired to develop the name, positioning statement, and branding."[59]

Still, the conversations the firm held with key figures, including the Reverend Dr. Foster McCurley, Tressler's theologian in residence, stressed the central religious aspects of the agency's mission sufficiently to enable the distinctive new name to emerge. As the organization's new CEO, Daun McKee, wrote in its newsletter, "*Diakon* comes from the Greek term for servant or service. It is a unique and succinct way to describe what we do each day . . . Our goal will be preserving local identities, those with which our residents, clients, and supporters are most comfortable." A crucial part of the merger process was the establishment of a "merger ethics committee" that created the momentum for the development of the values statements, the ethics and personnel policies, and the educational programs that the new organization has now implemented. The committee also provided advice for the board in the transition process, during which some employee positions were eliminated. The committee set guidelines for proper notification for position elimination, appropriate severance packages for employees, and out-placement services for those employees who could not be reassigned within the agency.[60]

On January 1, 2000, the new agency was born. As the inheritor of a long legacy of Lutheran service to the communities of Pennsylvania, this newly merged organization began its work with an acute sense of the perilous context within which it was operating and of the essential role of its own religious heritage and identity. The mission, values, and ethical principles of the agency emphasize the distinctive Christian commitments that undergird the organization's work, and the educational and socialization efforts they have undertaken are designed to introduce their diverse employee base to Christian service in the Lutheran tradition. At the same time the primary work of the agency is to provide the highest quality, most effective service to the neighbor in need. While the leadership understands its own motivation and that of the agency in light of the Christian gospel and the obligation to love the neighbor in need, the actual work done by the agency may look remarkably similar to the work done by other value-oriented service organizations, whether religious or secular.

Conclusion

Current debates concerning the value of faith-based organizations in the area of service provision would be assisted by a more complex understanding of the cultures of these agencies. Studies like the ones gathered together in this volume are efforts to engage in "thick descriptions" of various religious communities and organizations.[61] Some of the chapters focus upon worshipping bodies like congregations or parishes—what is termed "organic religion"—while others draw attention to "intentional religion"—religious organizations engaged in political action or social service.[62] But in every case these studies resist oversimplification or reductive explanations.

Political or social scientific attempts to discover the unique source of the effectiveness of faith-based organizations in their faith commitments run the risk of engaging in bad politics, bad social science, and bad theology. The studies in this volume show that the religious identities of these organizations cannot be reduced to a single factor or configuration of influences. Throughout their histories, the organizations I have studied here have responded to social, cultural, and economic changes in their environments. They have struggled to shape identities that are faithful to their founding religious communities and responsive to the changing conditions in which they have provided care. Sometimes their hold on traditional religious values undermined the effectiveness of their care;[63] at other times, innovative responses to environmental changes enhanced their ability to carry out their faith-based mission. The merger in 2000 was, for example, motivated primarily by considerations of financial viability within a rapidly changing economic and political environment, but it became the occasion for a fundamental reconsideration of the religious rationale of the merging organization as well. The newly revised statement of mission, values, and ethical principles will allow the organization to deliver effective social and human services in a manner compatible with the fundamental religious values of the organization, even if those services do not differ in kind or quality from those offered by the best secular agencies. Service that is integrated with mission will be effective service to the neighbor in need. Such service should be valued by the religious community because it fulfills an obligation of the Christian gospel. Such service should be valued by the civil community because it contributes to the well-being of society in general.

Government funding for such service should be continued and perhaps even expanded, but not because government thereby will encourage some particular religious value or service that secular agencies cannot deliver. Rather, funding should go to support faith-based agencies because they contribute to the variety of high-level social services available to a diverse population. Without the continued flourishing of such agencies, the network of social and human services would be seriously diminished in both quality and quantity. This way of viewing public support for faith-based services thus mitigates the constitutional difficulties associated with governmental funding of religious agencies because these agencies deliver a particular spiritual service or inculcate a particular religious value or lifestyle. This view also suggests the need for a more complex social science approach to the study of faith-based organizations. Good studies of such organizations should not seek to identify the unique causal feature that distinguishes religious from nonreligious groups. Rather, they should seek, as the studies in this volume do, to display the complex cultures of organizations that enlarge the mission of their religious communities by service to neighbors in need and thereby contribute to the well-being of the larger civil community as well.

The history of Diakon Lutheran Social Ministries suggests six conclusions.

First, the founding of Lutheran social ministry organizations in America followed the pattern established by Lutheran Pietists in eighteenth-century Europe. Rationales for social ministry thus had a strong evangelical character and stressed the importance of charity, love for the neighbor, and *noblesse oblige*, often to the detriment of larger considerations of social justice.

Second, Lutheranism in America grew through successive waves of immigration in the eighteenth and nineteenth centuries. Eighteenth-century immigrants settled in the eastern states, particularly Pennsylvania and New York, and rather quickly lost the trappings of their ethnic identities. Nineteenth-century immigrants settled primarily in the upper Midwest and held strongly to their ethnic identities well into the twentieth century. The Topton and Tressler homes reflected the early, eastern, liberal, and mainstream forms of Lutheranism.

Third, although doctrinal debates were central to the formation of Lutheran identity in America, these debates had little impact on the self-understanding of these social ministry organizations. Their founding Pietist heritage remained the strongest religious factor shaping their identities.

Fourth, the two homes developed different strategies for growth during the Progressive Era. The Topton Home, born in this era, developed a more flexible policy regarding foster and community care than did its older sibling, Tressler. Topton thus professionalized its staff and diversified its mission before Tressler did, thereby adapting more easily to the changing political and social environment. In the last decades of the twentieth century, however, Tressler became a national leader through its pioneering efforts in special-need adoptions.

Fifth, the external environment of governmental regulation and of social and cultural secularization played a decisive role in shaping these two organizations during the second half of the twentieth century. While holding to their evangelical and Pietist theology of care, these organizations did not develop a distinctively Christian rationale of social justice to guide their missions. The lack of strong theological reflection on matters of justice within Lutheranism and the anti-intellectual tendencies of the Pietist tradition in general made these organizations more vulnerable to secularization during the postwar era. Increasingly their missions became shaped more by the demands of external public demands than by a clearly stated internal theological rationale.

Sixth, the process that led to the merger of these venerable institutions was sparked by the need to expand within the complex market and regulatory context of the twenty-first century. But the merger process also provided an opportunity for the merging institutions to reexamine and reclaim their particular Christian and Lutheran mission and rationale for service. This reexamination may not lead to any dramatic change in the actual services rendered or in the manner in which services are delivered. But it has already strengthened the ties between the agency and its sponsoring synods, congregations, and bishops, and the organization has clarified the values and ethical principles that guide its work. This renewed integration between mission, guiding principles, and service should serve to strengthen the coherence and effectiveness of Diakon's ministry.

Examining the religious, institutional, and operational evolution of Diakon Lutheran Social Ministries helps to demonstrate that the interests of the religious community and those of the civil community converge when faith-based organizations are understood to provide services that benefit the entire society of which they are a part. The effort, by either politicians or social scientists, to identify the religious factors that contribute uniquely to the effectiveness of these organizations may be counterproductive. Faith-based social service organizations should be neither valorized nor dismissed because they emerge from the religious convictions of their sponsoring communities. Rather they should be recognized as an important part of the national network of social and human service provision that is essential to both sound religion and sound democratic government. They should be welcomed not only as service providers but as partners in the task of setting high and humane standards for all agencies that provide assistance for citizens and neighbors in need.

chapter 7

Long-Term Care: Does Religious Affiliation Matter?

Julie Boatright Wilson

ONE OF THE MOST anguishing decisions anyone will make is choosing to put an aging parent or spouse in a nursing home. That home may be run by federal, state, or county government, by a for-profit corporation, or by a nonprofit one. It may be overtly religious, have historical roots in a religious tradition, or not be religious at all. The existence of this variety attests to the interplay of secular and faith-based providers and institutions that is the subject of this book. It also raises the question, a natural one in a market economy such as America's: which institutional profile is best suited to the task? Many individuals look to religiously affiliated homes in the belief that they provide a higher quality of care and more individual attention. But is this the case?

The last fifteen years have been challenging for all nursing homes in America. Over this time, federal and state governments have increased their oversight of quality of care and intensified their efforts to control costs. The care needs of individuals entering nursing homes have increased as hospitals have reduced in-patient lengths of stay and as alternatives such as assisted-living facilities and homecare services have become increasingly popular among healthier and more independent individuals. Although many nursing homes did not survive these challenges, most met them by transforming their organizational structures or ways of operating.

How have these pressures changed the characteristics of nursing homes and the quality of care they provide? Are there observable differences among nonprofit, for-profit, and government providers? Even more important, are nursing homes affiliated with religious organizations distinctive in any way? To examine these questions, I compare three nursing home sectors in one state, Pennsylvania. Investigated are the organizational structures, staffing patterns, patient characteristics, and quality of care among for-profit, religiously affiliated and secular nonprofit, and government-operated facilities.

Birth of the Three-Sector Nursing Home Market

The outlines of the current long-term care market structure have emerged gradually over the course of the nation's history as public leaders struggled with ways to care for those who could not care for themselves. In the seventeenth century, local governments began paying private homeowners to provide room and board for indigent and incapacitated elderly or disabled individuals without family to care for them. Over time, however, the public and many government officials grew concerned about the cost of such arrangements, alleged profiteering on the part of providers, and perceived undeservedness of some care recipients. In the eighteenth century, local governments began responding to these concerns by opening poorhouses—institutions for the elderly, disabled, and other indigent individuals. Although many officials and civic leaders attempted to completely replace the practice of boarding out in private homes with poorhouses, in most of the country private and public care coexisted.[1] Poorhouses quickly developed a reputation for dreadful conditions, and in the nineteenth century many ethnic and religious groups set up residences to provide long-term care for their own elderly members. These nonprofit homes were initially funded by contributions from the group that founded them.[2]

Until the 1930s almost all long-term care was funded either privately or by local governments. For-profit and not-for-profit providers operated small facilities, with for-profit providers usually offering care in their homes to a few individuals. The New Deal brought federal funds into the mix: recipients of Old Age Assistance payments, for example, could use this money to purchase long-term care. Although this additional money encouraged more providers to offer care, it had little impact on the organizational structure of long-term care facilities or the way care was provided. The dramatic changes emerged after World War II, with the availability of federal funding for capital construction in the 1950s and for subacute medical care in the 1960s. The number of providers increased, and for the first time private corporations entered the market in large numbers, displacing individual proprietors. The availability of Medicare and Medicaid funds as well as early regulations regarding the quality of care encouraged providers in all sectors to upgrade the quality of their facilities and increase the number of individuals served. The availability of funds for capital construction made this possible. The funds were available to both religiously affiliated and secular providers.

Although there is a long history of for-profit, government, and not-for-profit provision of long-term care, the relative share of care provided by each has varied over time.[3] By 1999 for-profit organizations owned almost two in three nursing homes in the United States, while not-for-profit organizations owned slightly fewer than three in ten (see Table 7.1). This distribution varied from state to state, however, depending on state regulations and laws and historical experience. Unfortunately, there are no reliable national data on the share of nursing homes affiliated with religious groups.

Survival of the Three-Sector Market

Some economists argue that we should not be surprised that both nonprofit and for-profit nursing homes coexist, because the long-term care market is an imperfect one.[4] A well-functioning market is defined by readily available information on product quality and price, competition among providers, consumer choice, and mechanisms for keeping providers and customers accountable.[5] When these conditions hold, for-profit firms will provide an efficient dis-

Table 7.1 Distribution of nursing homes across states by sector (in percent)

Sector	Across sector: 1999		
	Average of all states	Minimum share	Maximum share
For-profit	64.8	7.1	81.4
Nonprofit	28.6	12.9	82.8
Government	6.7	0.8	41.7

tribution of products; when they do not hold, other types of firms may enter the market.

In the case of nursing homes, providers cannot compete on the basis of price for most residents because government sets the price. (Although nursing homes are free to charge market rates to privately paying patients, most nursing home care is financed through Medicaid, whose reimbursement rates are set by state governments.) Consumers have limited information on product quality, face restrictions on product availability, and have a limited capacity to pressure providers to change the quality of care. For example, research indicates that most people have little information about the quality of care in nursing homes before moving to one.[6] Even those with information may be unable to use it, because governmental efforts to limit the number of nursing home beds combined with excess demand and providers' needs to keep beds filled in order to maximize revenue limit consumer options at any point in time. This is particularly important in the case of critically ill individuals, who may not be able to wait for a vacancy in a preferred home.[7] Once settled in a home, the emotional and physical costs of moving to another are high, which limits the amount of information that can be gained about alternative settings through moving from home to home. Finally, even the most alert nursing home residents lack the leverage of the typical consumer, because of their likely dependence on Medicare or Medicaid to cover the costs of care. These residents cannot withhold payments or threaten to do so to pressure providers to improve the level of care. And those with the capacity to withhold payments on their behalf may not value certain aspects of care as highly as residents or may have difficulty assessing the quality of care.

Economic theory argues that under these conditions, for-profit providers of nursing home care have an incentive to take advantage of information asymmetries to increase profits by reducing the quality of care. This creates opportunities for providers who value the chance to provide high-quality service or to serve a particularly vulnerable group more than they value personal or corporate gain. Such providers will choose to operate in the nonprofit sector, in part because tax law—nonprofits may not distribute or transfer assets or revenue to their owners—requires that it give preference to service over profits.[8] Research indicates that the public is receptive to this signal. Consumers with resources, an understanding of the characteristics of high-quality care, and information about care options choose the most appropriate setting for themselves or their loved ones, whether it be for-profit, not-for-profit, or government run. Those with few resources and little information prefer not-for-profit nursing homes in the belief that such providers are less likely to exploit information asymmetries to take advantage of vulnerable residents.[9]

Current Nursing Home Residents

Although most care for the elderly and disabled is provided by family or friends, nursing homes typically provide custodial and sub-acute health care to several groups of aged and disabled individuals: those who are mentally alert but unable to care for themselves independently,[10] suffer from serious dementia, are recuperating from an episode of acute care, are terminally ill, or are in permanent vegetative states.[11] In 1999, 5 percent of those over sixty-five and 18 percent of those over eighty-five spent at least part of the year in a nursing home.[12] Though a much smaller share of those under sixty-five spend time in a nursing home in any given year, they made up about 40 percent of the 1.6 million residents cared for in nursing homes in 1997.[13]

Most stays in nursing homes are relatively short, lasting less than one year. But the longer stays of a substantial number of residents raise the average length of stay to approximately 2.7 years.[14] Since the average cost of a year of nursing home care in 2002 was estimated to be approximately $55,000 but could easily exceed $100,000, few who need the care are able to pay its full cost for their entire stay.[15] The excess demand for nursing home care in most states allows providers to exercise their preference for filling beds with privately paying residents who can afford higher rates. Most of these residents eventually "spend down" to poverty and become eligible for Medicaid.[16] In 1997 Medicaid paid half the $30 billion spent for long-term care and Medicare another 12 percent. Although most of the remaining costs were funded privately, Medicaid was the primary payer of the costs of care for two-thirds of nursing home residents.[17]

The Perfect Storm

The decade of the 1990s was a critical period for nursing homes. The increasing acuity of residents, external pressures to increase care quality, staffing shortages and increases in labor costs, and the failure of reimbursements to keep up with costs created an equivalent of the perfect storm.

Since 1990 the severity of nursing home resident illness and the extent of incapacity have increased. Efforts by health care funders to reduce costs by limiting the length of hospital stays combined with other measures undertaken by managed care organizations to reduce inpatient hospital use have resulted in a shift to nursing homes of more seriously ill patients who previously would have been cared for in hospitals. At the same time, states have attempted to reduce their Medicaid expenditures by increasing the use of home care for less seriously ill or incapacitated individuals who previously might have moved to nursing homes. As a result the typical nursing home resident of today is much sicker or more incapacitated than her counterpart a decade ago, and the range of services and the amount and complexity of care that she needs have increased.

At the same time as the acuity of their resident population was increasing, providers came under growing pressure to increase the quality of care they provided. A number of sensational scandals in the 1970s and 1980s motivated Congress to pass the Nursing Home Reform Act (OBRA 87), which required that nursing homes receiving Medicare or Medicaid payments "be held to a new standard of care focusing on the 'highest practicable physical, mental and psycho-social well-being of its residents.' "[18] These regulations, many of which were implemented in 1990, required the development of care plans for each resident, periodic resident assessment, and the assurance of specific services at each facility.[19] The act also required annual inspections to determine compliance with regulations on dimensions of quality of care.[20] Nursing homes found to be out of compliance could be fined or even closed, though few were. It is generally conceded that although the quality of care varies from home to home, implementation of the Nursing Home Reform Act resulted in an improvement in the average quality of nursing home care. It is also conceded that implementation of this act pressured providers to adjust the mix of services offered and change their management practices.[21]

While providers were struggling to meet changing demands for care, state and federal governments were struggling with ways to control the rapidly rising costs of and growing demand for long-term care. Throughout the 1980s and early 1990s, providers were successful in using legal action to gain leverage over state rate-setting commissions to increase payments.[22] States addressed the problem of rapidly rising costs through four basic strategies: shifting costs from Medicaid to private insurance or Medicare,[23] increasing efforts to limit the number of nursing home beds[24] or increasing the use of pre-admission screening[25] so that fewer people could enter the system, increasing the amount of home care provided in order to delay nursing home entry,[26] and restricting reimbursement rates.[27] In addition, by the late 1990s most states had moved from a system of flat-rate payments given retrospectively to one of payments adjusted for the difficulty of patient caseloads, often made prospectively.[28]

Using data from the late 1970s and early 1980s, Burton Weisbrod compared proprietary and nonprofit nursing homes along a number of dimensions: use of sedatives to reduce demands on nursing home staff, staff-to-patient ratios, and consumer satisfaction. He found that nonprofits in general, and religious nonprofits in particular, were significantly more positive on all dimensions.[29] But these studies were conducted prior to the dramatic changes that came later. We know that some nursing homes were unable to withstand these pressures and closed. But many more adjusted to the changing environment and survived. Is there any evidence that providers in different sectors responded differently to these challenges? Or was the intensity of the pressure so great that we no longer observe the differences in for-profit, not-for-profit, and government nursing homes that Weisbrod found? Is there any evidence that religiously affiliated homes are distinctive in organizational structure, characteristics of residents served, or quality of care? If so, is there any indication that in this highly competitive market, religiously affiliated nursing homes have influenced the behavior of other providers?

Would We Expect Nonprofit and For-Profit Homes to Be Different?

The absence of a profit motive would seem to argue to many that there is a difference in the quality or characteristics of care provided in the typical not-for-profit nursing home. As noted earlier, many consumers believe this to be particularly true of religiously affiliated homes. Many economists would disagree with these consumers and argue that without a profit motive, nonprofit owners have less incentive to change management practices over time and, rather than converting would-be profits into higher-quality care, may "waste" them through less efficient management practices.

This argument assumes that providers can charge high enough prices to cover costs and earn a surplus without having to change management practices.[30] But they no longer can, unless they serve only individuals who can pay privately for the full costs of their care, because over the last decade, state and local governments and private insurers have exerted considerable downward pressure on financial reimbursements to nursing homes. This has forced all providers to increase management efficiency in order to survive.[31] If not-for-profit providers could realize more gains through increases in management efficiency than their for-profit counterparts, they likely would feel less pressure to reduce the quality of care they provide. Thus we might expect to observe higher-quality care in efficiently managed not-for-profit than in for-profit homes today.

There are other reasons we might expect not-for-profit nursing homes to provide residents a higher quality of care. First, we assume they chose nonprofit status because they valued the provision of high-quality care or service to a particularly vulnerable and underserved group. Their primary mission is thus likely to be more fully focused on quality of care than that of their for-profit counterparts. Second, the lack of shareholder pressure on management to become more efficient also guarantees them more freedom to experiment with different styles of care provision, because, while they must remain solvent, they are not responsible for making a profit. And it may well be, though we have no evidence one way or the other on this, that their boards encourage such behavior by paying attention to issues of care quality. Finally, tax law exempts nonprofit nursing homes from paying certain taxes, which increases the resources they have to spend on care.

The theoretical assumption that not-for-profit homes provide better care, however, may in the end not be supportable. Although more empirical research is needed on this point, it is equally probable that the intensive downward economic pressures and upward pressures on quality cited earlier have eroded the presumed advantages of not-for-profit homes. Nursing home providers have been pushed by increasing regulatory oversight and public release of inspection results to improve the quality of care provided. Economists argue that increasing regulatory oversight of nursing homes is likely to affect performance in two ways. On the one hand, it raises to an acceptable threshold the quality of care of the poorest performers. But, economists argue, it also discourages the best performers from investing in care of a quality far above the threshold.[32] One might expect for-profit providers, who are responsible to shareholders, among others, to be particularly discouraged from making such investments in care above the minimum. But the financial pressures on all nursing homes have been so intense, it is reasonable to expect not-for-profit providers to behave similarly. We might therefore expect to find few differences between not-for-profit and for-profit nursing homes in terms of the quality of care they provide.

Does Religious Affiliation Matter?

Not-for-profit nursing homes can be divided into two groups: religiously affiliated homes and secular homes. Many of today's religiously affiliated nursing homes were started by individual congregations or denominational organizations. As both congregational and denominational membership ebbed and flowed, the resources available for providing care were not always adequate—yet pressures to keep homes open were intense. Over time, Catholic and Protestant denominational hierarchies assumed increasing responsibility for homes affiliated with their churches, creating agglomerations whose component parts were geographically dispersed, had unique histories and organizational cultures, and had different but nevertheless dedicated constituencies. Church leaders who recognized that individual homes were losing money or were housed in facilities that made the provision of high-quality care difficult faced enormous resistance to closing them. In addition, being accountable to so many constituent congregations meant that many of these homes "wasted" resources in inefficient management. External pressures over the last decade, which forced the poorest performing and least economical homes to close, provided leverage for church leaders to restructure organizational relationships to increase management efficiency. But to what extent were religiously affiliated nursing homes able to retain a distinctive identity in the face of these intense pressures?

Ronald Thiemann, in Chapter 6, provides a detailed description of the responses of Lutheran social service organizations in central Pennsylvania to the challenges of the last decade and a half. Two social service providers undertook a multiyear process of merging smaller networks into one, Diakon Lutheran Social Ministries.[33] Diakon, with its nearly 4,000 employees and 12,000 volunteers, currently provides long-term care, retirement, and other senior services as well as a wide range of child and family services, to more than 50,000 residents of central and eastern Pennsylvania, Maryland, and Delaware. Daun McKee, president of Diakon, argues that undertaking multiple mergers in five years forced the organization's leadership to clarify and articulate its distinctive Lutheran identity and mission to constituent congregations and funders. This was important for two reasons. First, economic survival demanded that Diakon eliminate some services and restructure others. The leadership needed the long-term support of congregations "owning" these unsustainable service ministries to ensure the financial viability of the larger organization. Second, the leadership felt that the gospel mandate to serve the neighbor in need challenged it to focus new initiatives on those individuals and families who were not only most vulnerable but also had the fewest sources of care and support.[34] To do this, the financial, volunteer, and spiritual support of congregations would be essential.

While Diakon Lutheran Social Ministries emerged from the challenges of the 1990s with its mission more clearly articulated and its Lutheran identity embedded more firmly in its management structure and service ministry, not all nursing homes affiliated with religious groups were as successful in confronting the challenges of the last fifteen years. As will be seen below, it may be that evangelical congregations lacking the hierarchical structure so essential to achieve management efficiencies struggled the most to remain solvent and maintain their religious identity.

But does this religious identity matter? In what ways, if any, does the quality of care in religiously affiliated nursing homes differ from that in secular nursing homes, particularly secular homes in the not-for-profit sector? In thinking about this, it is useful to visualize two dimensions of nursing home life: quality of care and quality of life. Quality of care encompasses a number of factors, including regular assessments and timely treatment by physicians and other health professionals, timely attention to physical and emotional needs, opportunities for recreational and social activities, and so on. It is primarily this dimension of care that current nursing home inspections assess.

But interviews with nursing home residents have repeatedly identified a second dimension—quality of life. This encompasses how residents are treated, how much independence they have, and how much freedom they have to choose activities and lifestyles. For example, a series of focus groups with nursing home residents conducted for the National Citizens' Coalition for Nursing Home Reform found that "residents have consistently indicated that help, care and meeting personal needs are important to them, but equally valued are personal characteristics and attitudes. Residents want qualified, skilled and knowledgeable staff who have been well trained in the performance of their nursing home care tasks. They also ask that the staff be kind, polite, respectful and friendly to them. The staff person who is caring and sympathetic, making time to talk with residents, is prized."[35] In addition, numerous studies indicate that nursing home residents seek opportunities to make choices about various aspects of daily life, including which activities to participate in, when and what they will eat, and with whom they will associate.[36] This last concern is particularly important, since residents are likely to find themselves sharing living spaces, meals, and free time with individuals exhibiting a wide range of mental and physical incapacities.

Among not-for-profit providers, religiously affiliated nursing homes, because of their scriptural understanding of what it means to be a whole person, are likely to have a broader conception of quality of life. Staff at Diakon Lutheran Social Ministries reported, for example, that they approach those they serve as "whole human beings, children of God." This means they focus on spiritual well-being as well as on physical, emotional, intellectual, and social well-being. For individuals facing pain and death or watching as their neighbors die, this dimension of care may be particularly important—even if they are not religious or do not share the religious affiliation of the nursing home.[37] To the extent that providers act on this conceptualization of their residents, religiously affiliated not-for-profit homes are likely to provide not only a quality of care but also a quality of life that residents perceive to be of higher value than that of secular homes.

We might expect then, first, that this conceptualization of the whole person is more likely to produce levels of care that distinguish religiously affiliated nursing homes from secular homes. It is also reasonable to expect, second, that such a perspective would extend to explicit concerns about the well-being of employees and volunteers. If management philosophy is based on a belief that service to the neighbor provides opportunities for spiritual growth for providers as well as for those being served, and if management practices, performance evaluations, and other forms of recognition reflect this philosophy, we would expect to find that staff respond by providing higher-quality care. Even if wages are comparable across nursing homes, this attention to the quality of work life is likely to provide more day-to-day satisfaction on the part of staff and decrease the probability of high turnover. Satisfaction is likely to be reinforced if staff choose to work in religiously affiliated homes because of their own religious commitment and faith. This is important, because there is considerable evidence that nursing homes with lower staff turnover provide a higher quality of care.[38]

Third, religiously affiliated homes may provide higher-quality care and focus more attention on the quality of life because they often have access to more resources than their secular counterparts. They have access not only to monetary contributions from congregations and members of the religious group,[39] but also to greater numbers of volunteers to provide services and personal attention to residents. The belief that service to the neighbor in need provides opportunities for spiritual growth is likely to encourage religiously affiliated homes to be more proactive in recruiting, managing, and supporting volunteers. In addition, these homes have the support of pastors and congregations who share this belief and may help with volunteer recruitment and management.

Finally, in addition to providing services that enrich the quality of life of residents, volunteers help to monitor the quality of care and report on inadequacies or problems. Such monitoring may serve to keep religious nursing homes on their toes and guarantee that even the most incapacitated residents are more likely to have an advocate. Research suggests that those nursing home residents who have family members or others to monitor their care receive better care, no matter what sector provides the nursing home care. But when quality is not easily measured and no external source is monitoring the care, providers are more able to take advantage of the situation to reduce the quality of care in order to increase profits.[40] Even if they were tempted to do so, providers of religiously affiliated homes would be less likely to deliberately skimp on quality because they are dependent on congregational and pastoral perceptions of their performance for revenue, and these constituencies are likely to be primarily focused on quality of care.

Thus despite the financial and regulatory pressures under which nursing homes have operated for some time, there are a number of reasons we might expect that not-for-profit nursing homes in general, and religiously affiliated nursing homes in particular, might provide care of a higher quality than that provided by their for-profit counterparts.

A Preliminary Examination of Pennsylvania Nursing Homes

To begin exploring these ideas, we examine data on the 626 Pennsylvania nursing homes certified to accept Medicaid residents in the summer of 2002.[41] Pennsylvania provides somewhat higher Medicaid payments for nursing home care than the typical state and has been more aggressive than other states in addressing the inadequacies of nursing home care.[42] Nevertheless, it is sufficiently similar to the typical state to make it a useful site to explore.

My data come from a number of sources, including the On-line Survey, Certification and Reporting (OSCAR) system of the Department of Health and Human Services, the U.S. Census, the Pennsylvania Department of Public Welfare rate-setting commis-

Table 7.2 Number and size of nursing homes in Pennsylvania by sector

	Number of homes	Percentage of all homes	Average number of beds/home	Percentage of beds
For-profit	311	49.7	123	43.5
Nonprofit	273	43.6	127	39.4
Government	42	6.7	357	17.1

sion, and Web sites of nursing homes. In addition, I and my colleagues conducted personal and phone interviews with nursing home staff and religiously affiliated social service organizations. Most of these in-depth interviews were conducted with the leadership of Diakon Lutheran Social Ministries.

Of the 626 nursing homes in Pennsylvania, half are for-profit homes and another 44 percent are nonprofit (see Table 7.2). Only 7 percent of the nursing homes are operated by the government. But at 357 beds on average, government nursing homes are significantly larger than those in the for-profit or nonprofit sectors. As a result, 17 percent of the state's nursing home beds are in government-owned homes.

When asked by the federal government to categorize themselves by type of organization, nearly four in five for-profit homes report being owned by a multi-unit corporation (See Table 7.3). The remainder report being owned privately or by a partnership. Just under three in four nonprofit homes report being a part of a corporation, with most of the rest identifying themselves as church related.

The option of selecting church-related or corporate status, as required by the federal survey, may have been a reasonable choice for this group of nursing homes a decade ago, but it no longer appears to characterize the structure of nonprofit nursing homes. Our search of Web sites and interviews with nursing home receptionists reveal that nearly half (47 percent) of those who did not self-identify on the survey as church related, nevertheless have a religious affiliation. In all, nearly two-thirds of nonprofit nursing homes (64

Table 7.3 Number and size of Pennsylvania nursing homes by sector and affiliation

	Number of homes	Percentage of all homes	Average number of beds/home	Percentage of all beds
For-profit	311	49.7	123	43.5
Corporation	242	38.7	126	34.6
Individual	8	1.3	100	0.9
Partnership	61	9.7	115	8.0
Nonprofit	273	43.6	127	39.4
Corporation	198	31.6	130	29.3
Church/religious	67	10.7	118	9.0
Other	8	1.3	126	1.1
Government	42	6.7	357	17.1
City	5	0.8	414	2.4
County	36	5.8	349	14.3
State	1	0.2	376	0.4

percent) and one-quarter (24.3 percent) of all nursing homes in Pennsylvania are affiliated with a religious group.[43]

The number of religious groups operating nursing homes is extensive. We identified homes affiliated with Catholics, Jews, and mainline Protestants, including Baptists, Episcopalians, Hungarian Reformed, Lutherans, Methodists, Mennonites, Moravians, Presbyterians, Quakers, Unitarian-Universalists, and the United Church of Christ. In addition, we identified nursing homes affiliated with various conservative evangelical congregations, including the Bible Fellowship Church, Brethren in Christ, Christian and Missionary Alliance, Church of God, Church of the Brethren, Church of the Open Door, Evangelical Congregational Church, United Christian Church, and United Zion Church. For the most part these churches owned a single nursing home, but occasionally more than one. Finally, we identified a number of nursing homes that claimed to be religiously affiliated but which were uncertain of the specific affiliation. In most cases those interviewed responded that they were generally Christian or Judeo-Christian.

As the data in Table 7.4 show, half of these nursing homes are

Table 7.4 Number and size of Pennsylvania nursing homes by religious affiliation and sector

	Number of homes	Percentage of homes	Average number of beds	Percentage beds
Religious Homes	177	28.3	121	24.3
Protestant	105	16.8	117	14.0
Catholic	42	6.7	134	6.4
Jewish	6	1.0	156	1.1
Conserv. Evang.	11	1.8	94	1.2
Uncertain	13	2.1	115	1.7
Secular Homes	449	71.7	148	75.7
For-profit	310	49.5	123	43.4
Nonprofit	97	15.5	138	15.2
Government	42	6.7	357	17.1
Total	626	100.0%	140	100.0%

affiliated with a mainline Protestant denomination and another quarter with the Catholic Church. Religious nursing homes are similar in size to for-profit nursing homes, but significantly smaller than their secular counterparts in the not-for-profit sector.[44] Among religious nursing homes, those affiliated with Protestant denominations are on average smaller than those affiliated with the Catholic Church. The six Jewish homes in our sample are on average larger than either Protestant or Catholic homes.[45]

Of the 177 religious homes in Pennsylvania, only 2 percent are affiliated with a conservative evangelical church. Another 2 percent have an "uncertain" religious identity. These two groups are similar in that they have very few homes and those they do operate are on average smaller than those of other denominations and of secular organizations. Without historical or longitudinal data, we cannot determine whether the number of nursing homes and beds affiliated with evangelical churches in Pennsylvania is declining and, if so, whether this decline is a result of the homes closing or a result of their shedding their religious affiliation in order to survive. Likewise, on the basis of the response to our phone calls, we cannot determine if those nursing homes in our "uncertain" category are in the process of moving away from affiliation with their founding religious group in order to survive or whether their religious affiliation is strong at some level but not consciously articulated with sufficient voice to have permeated to the level of the person answering the phone and providing information about the home to the general public.

In summary, it is clear that religiously affiliated nursing homes provide a substantial share of the care to the elderly and incapacitated of Pennsylvania. A wide range of religious groups are involved in this care, though they are primarily Catholic, Jewish, or mainline Protestant. It is difficult to know why only a small number of nursing homes are affiliated with conservative evangelical groups. It may be that there have never been many nursing homes affiliated with conservative church groups in Pennsylvania or elsewhere. Alternatively, it may be that without the larger organizational infrastructure that Catholic and mainline Protestant homes are able to draw on, evangelical nursing homes were less likely to survive the external pressures experienced since 1990. Since we have data from only one location at one point in time, we cannot answer this question. Longitudinal data from states with a greater number of conservative evangelical nursing homes are needed.

Network Affiliation of Nursing Homes

As regulatory requirements increased and reimbursement rates declined, a common strategy for reducing costs was to take advantage of economies of scale by joining with other nursing homes or social service providers to centralize accounting and billing, human resources, and other administrative functions. Although we do not have data on trends in network affiliation, our data from one point in time show that for-profit nursing homes are nearly twice as likely to report that they are part of multi-nursing home networks or chains as their nonprofit counterparts. Among not-for-profits, secular nursing homes are somewhat more likely than their religious counterparts to report being part of multi-unit corporations. Yet nearly four in ten religiously affiliated nursing homes claim a network affiliation.

	Percentage of homes in a network
For-profit	74.3
Corporate	80.6
Other	52.2
Nonprofit	39.6
Religious	37.5
Secular	43.3

Of the 66 religiously affiliated nursing homes reporting that they are part of a multi-unit corporation, 62 were Catholic, Lutheran, Mennonite, Methodist, Presbyterian, or United Church of Christ. The remaining 4 were affiliated with conservative evangelical churches.

	Percentage of homes in a network
Mainline	40.5
Protestant	46.7
Catholic	31.0
Jewish	0.0
Conservative evangelical	31.0
Uncertain	0.0

We identified at least four patterns of network membership among religiously affiliated nursing homes, all of which we believe were perceived as essential to survival over the last decade: affiliating with other homes in one's religious group, affiliating with a secular network or chain, drifting from religious identification and affiliation, and taking over the management of secular homes and imbuing them with a religious identity.

The first pattern, represented by Diakon Lutheran Social Ministries, involves strengthening and/or expanding formal relationships with nursing homes affiliated with one's religious group. Although external pressures to increase managerial efficiency and effectiveness may have motivated this behavior, these social service organizations took advantage of the situation to more clearly articulate their religious mission and strengthen their relationships with individual congregations and church hierarchies.

A second pattern, exhibited by the conservative evangelical churches in our sample, involves increasing managerial efficiency by affiliating with a for-profit network of nursing homes. Two nursing homes affiliated with the Church of God participate in the Extendicare Network, a for-profit chain of nursing homes. A third nursing home, whose Web site identifies it as affiliated with the Church of the Open Door, is affiliated with ACTS Retirement Communities, another for-profit chain of nursing homes. If nursing homes affiliated with congregations that have few homes and whose parent churches have minimal hierarchical administrative structures are able to survive only by affiliating with networks of nursing homes outside their religious community, will they be able to maintain their religious identity over time? Our data, drawn from a single point in time, suggest that a longitudinal examination of this group of nursing homes would be fruitful for understanding what it takes to maintain a religious identity in today's policy environment.

A possible third pattern, exhibited by four nursing homes with historically religious affiliations, is to drift away from a clearly articulated religious identity to a vague "Christian, but nothing specific." Although it is difficult to say much about these homes from data gathered at a single point in time, it is possible that they are drifting away from a religious identity toward a community identity. Were they once affiliated with individual congregations that have declined in size or no longer exist? Were they once part of larger denominations that either failed to articulate their religious identity or needed to sell their nursing homes in order for their social service system to survive? These are questions worthy of further study.

A possible fourth pattern is to partner with for-profit, government, or other nonprofit providers to jointly manage nursing homes. For example, Diakon Lutheran Social Ministries has partnered with a for-profit nursing home and several religiously affiliated but not Lutheran nursing homes. Pennsylvania has stated its interest in privatizing government-owned nursing homes, and Diakon is discussing similar management arrangements with at least one county. In contrast to the apparent loss of religious identities of some homes who partner with for-profit networks, Diakon clearly articulates its Lutheran identity and mission in these secular partnerships and brings its culture of commitment to quality service to these settings.

While further research may reveal more patterns, these preliminary findings suggest that in Pennsylvania there is no sharp distinction in institutional profile between religious and secular nursing homes. Nor is there a sharp distinction between not-for-profit, for-profit, and government-operated homes; rather, we find a blurring of the line between these groups. Further research, particularly historical or longitudinal research, is needed to understand these organizational relationships and to gain an understanding of what happens to these nursing homes' religious identities over time.[46] Why and how have some facilities lost their religious identities in their efforts to survive financially? Why and how have others strengthened or restored their religious identity in response to the pressures of the last decade?

Examining Quality of Care Measures

On the basis of these findings, we categorized the nursing homes in our sample into five groups: for-profit corporation, for-profit other (individually owned or partnership), nonprofit religious, nonprofit secular, and government.[47] Are there differences in the residents they serve? The resources they have available to them? The quality of their care? The outcomes for residents?

We measured the characteristics of residents in two ways—the average case-mix index (CMI) for each category of nursing home and the average share of residents with specific physical characteristics and health problems as measured in the annual inspection of each home. Using information from providers on the condition of residents with respect to the amount of resources needed for their care and rehabilitation, the state develops an index of case-mix difficulty for each home. In general, the higher the CMI, the more complicated and demanding the care of the typical resident in that home.[48]

The Pennsylvania religiously affiliated not-for-profit nursing homes have a lower CMI than other types of nursing homes, suggesting that they have a less demanding caseload than any other category of nursing home.[49]

	CMI
Nonprofit religious	1.10
Nonprofit secular	1.13
For-profit corporate	1.18
For-profit other	1.21
Government	1.14

There are several reasons this might be the case. On the one hand, the religiously affiliated not-for-profits may provide better care. They may accept residents of similar health and capacity status as other nursing homes but care for them in ways that maintain or improve their condition.[50] There is considerable evidence that the health and independence of residents decline more quickly with poor care and are maintained longer or even improved with high-quality care.[51] If religiously affiliated nursing homes provide higher-quality care than their secular counterparts, their CMI at any point in time would likely be lower than that of nursing homes that provide care of lesser quality.

On the other hand, the lower CMI may reflect the fact that the individuals religiously affiliated nursing homes admit are not as sick or incapacitated as those admitted by other homes. This could be a result of overt discrimination against potentially resource-intensive residents. But it could also be a result of statistical discrimination if these homes draw their residents from a pool of individuals that is on average healthier than that drawn on by their secular counterparts.

We can imagine three reasons why this might be the case. First, if individuals with little knowledge about the quality of care and quality of life in nursing homes prefer not-for-profit nursing homes, particularly religiously affiliated not-for-profit nursing homes, on the grounds of trust, we might expect this group of homes to be the first choice of most potential residents. But our data show that there are fewer religiously affiliated nursing homes and they have fewer unoccupied beds on average than their secular counterparts.

	Nursing home occupancy rates (in percent)
Nonprofit religious	91.9
Nonprofit secular	87.7
For-profit corporate	86.8
For-profit other	87.6
Government	85.3

This means that those wanting to move to a religiously affiliated nonprofit nursing home will have a longer wait for a bed. Those in the most serious condition are likely to be the least able to wait, and therefore the more likely to take the first open bed available—which is likely to be in a for-profit or government home.

Second, it is possible that when beds are available, religiously affiliated nursing homes give preference to members of their religious group over others on their waiting list.[52] If the former group is on average healthier, those entering religiously affiliated nursing homes may be healthier. Third, it is likely that different types of nursing homes may employ different methods of recruiting residents in an effort to keep their beds filled. Whereas religiously affiliated providers may recruit from a broad pool of individuals in various states of health and capacity who are affiliated with a specific religious group, for-profit providers may be more likely to depend on relationships with hospitals, HMOs, or physicians for incoming residents. As a result, secular nursing homes may be drawing prospective residents from a more incapacitated pool of individuals.

These are all questions worthy of further exploration. And it would be particularly useful to compare the process of recruiting residents for religiously affiliated homes in areas where much of the population belongs to that religious group with the process for such homes in areas where few adherents reside.

Our second measure of the characteristics of residents comes from the OSCAR data.[53] At the time of a state's annual inspection, data are gathered on the incidence of various conditions among residents of each home. These include the percentage of residents who are bedfast, need significant help with eating, exhibit behavioral symptoms, or have restricted joint motion. Data are also gathered on the percentage of residents who are both bladder and bowel incontinent. This latter measure is an unclear measure of resident characteristics, since residents may arrive at the nursing home incontinent or may become increasingly incontinent in the nursing home due to poor care. Excessive use of restraints or diapering residents rather than taking the time to help them with toileting on an individual schedule can lead to incontinence. Despite the ambiguity of this measure, we have included it here with our other measures of resident characteristics.

When we examined specific characteristics from the most recent inspection data, we found few observable differences between residents of either religious or secular not-for-profit and corporate for-profit homes in Pennsylvania (see Table 7.5). Religious nonprofits are slightly less likely to have bedfast residents, but are similar on other characteristics. Residents of government-owned and proprietary homes are slightly more likely to be bedfast, very dependent in eating, or exhibiting behavioral symptoms. In the case of government-operated homes, residents are only half as likely to have restricted joint motion. Thus, while religiously affiliated nursing homes may have on average fewer seriously incapacitated residents when measured by the CMI, these data suggest this is not due to a substantial difference in symptoms relative to their counterparts in secular not-for-profit or corporate for-profit homes. It also appears that government-owned and proprietary for-profit homes may admit more residents with serious behavioral and dependency problems.

Table 7.5 Characteristics of nursing home residents by sector and affiliation (in percent)

	Not-for-profit		For-profit		
	Religious	Secular	Corporate	Other	Government
Bedfast	3.8	4.3	5.5	6.8	5.6
Very dependent in eating	19.2	19.9	20.4	23.7	25.1
Exhibits behavioral symptoms	29.8	29.5	29.5	33.6	35.2
Restricted joint motion	22.8	22.6	22.2	22.1	10.2
Bladder and bowel incontinence	69.9	68.0	69.2	71.5	70.8

The Nursing Home Reform Act of 1987 required that nursing homes provide "sufficient nursing staff to attain or maintain the highest practicable . . . well-being of each resident."[54] Federal guidelines require that each nursing home, no matter what its size, provide a minimum of eight consecutive hours of nursing coverage (RN) and twenty-four hours of licensed nurse coverage (LPN/LVN) per day.[55] There is no minimum requirement for certified nurse aides, known as CNAs. CNAs provide 80 to 90 percent of the personal care of residents.[56] Their primary tasks are bathing, dressing, feeding, and toileting residents and helping them move from one place to another.[57] It is generally conceded that adequate staffing is the essential ingredient in quality nursing home care, because it reduces the risk of bedsores or falls and enhances the quality of life through personalized support and more frequent and higher-quality personal interaction. A study by Abt Associates reports that the staffing thresholds "below which facilities were at increased likelihood of being in the worst 10 percent for long-stay quality measures and above which there were no additional improvements in quality" were 0.75 RN, 1.3 licensed staff (RNs or LPNs), and 2.78 CNA hours per resident per day.[58]

Our data show that on average almost none of the categories of nursing homes in Pennsylvania meet all of these standards, though government and nonprofit nursing homes—and religiously affilia-

Table 7.6 Hours of staffing per resident day by staff type

	RN	LPN	CNA	Total
Nonprofit religious	0.73	0.67	2.35	3.75
Nonprofit secular	0.70	0.66	2.32	3.67
For-profit corporate	0.68	0.67	2.02	3.37
For-profit other	0.75	0.67	2.01	3.43
Government	0.59	0.81	2.32	3.72

ted nursing homes in particular—come closer to doing so than their for-profit counterparts (see Table 7.6). Religiously affiliated nursing homes have significantly more CNA hours and total staffing hours per resident day than do for-profit nursing homes and significantly more RN and LPN staffing hours per resident day than do government nursing homes.[59]

In a similar study, Weisbrod found much larger differences between religious nonprofit and proprietary homes than are reported here. Several factors may explain this discrepancy. First, Weisbrod's data are from 1978, before nursing homes came under the fiscal and quality pressures described earlier. Second, he measured labor inputs in terms of full-time employees (FTEs) per 100 beds rather than FTE hours of staffing per resident day. If proprietary homes have lower occupancy rates than religious nonprofit homes, and if staff levels are set by occupancy rather than by total beds, the differences between the sectors would be magnified in Weisbrod's study. Third, he used national data from 1978, at a time when staffing requirements varied from state to state. This study examines only Pennsylvania, which has higher standards than many states; this factor would dampen differences in staffing levels between proprietary and religiously affiliated nonprofit homes. Finally, if he is looking at all nursing homes, his sample likely includes not just independents but homes in hospitals, which are designed to take more acutely ill individuals and thus have higher RN and MD staffing rates.

This difference in staffing is likely to reflect the values of these different types of homes, since the Medicaid reimbursement rate is not significantly greater for religiously affiliated homes than for their secular counterparts in the nonprofit and for-profit sectors.[60]

	Medicaid rate/day
Nonprofit religious	$138.38
Nonprofit secular	$139.29
For-profit corporate	$135.33
For-profit other	$137.66
Government	$149.73

Government nursing homes, however, have a significantly higher state Medicaid reimbursement rate than do other types of nursing homes.

In addition to having more hours of paid nursing staff per resident per day than other types of nursing homes, it is possible that religiously affiliated nursing homes have greater access to volunteers to provide care to residents and support to paid staff. While we do not have information on the average number of volunteer hours provided at each type of nursing home, we know that many nursing homes seek volunteers. Our interviews with individuals at Diakon Lutheran Social Ministries reveal that they reach out widely and systematically, particularly to local congregations, to encourage volunteer participation. They give several rationales for seeking volunteers. First, volunteers can provide care that has a certain intimacy that overworked staff cannot provide. Because of their extensive paperwork demands, nursing staff have very little time to interact in a personal way with nursing home residents. Other staff normally have large numbers of residents to care for. Volunteers can focus on talking with and providing services for residents in ways that increase the quality of their lives.

Second, volunteers can devote more time to the most needy residents than can nursing or CNA staff. Diakon identifies the three plagues of nursing homes as "loneliness, helplessness, and boredom."[61] Although volunteers cannot do the work of the caregiving staff, they can spend time with the most lonely and bored, interacting with them in a personal and sustained way that caregiving staff cannot offer. For residents without family close enough to visit, volunteers may play a particularly important role. Finally, nursing homes can easily become "isolated ghettos where residents only see others like themselves." Volunteers potentially bring the broader community into the nursing home.[62] Interviews at the Jewish Home of Harrisburg reveal a similar strategy of reaching out to congregations, focusing on bar and bat mitzvah students, to create sustained relationships across generational lines.[63]

Religiously affiliated nursing homes thus may have residents whose conditions are similar or demand slightly less care than residents in other types of homes and may at the same time have comparable—and potentially greater—resources, so that we might expect them to provide higher quality care. Admittedly the quality of nursing home care is difficult to measure. We use annual inspection data that identify deficiencies in care and characteristics of residents. Specifically, we examine the average total deficiencies for each type of nursing home and the number of deficiencies in each of eight categories: mistreatment, quality of care, assessment of residents, protection of resident rights, nutrition and dietary adequacy, pharmacy services, nursing home environment, and administration. Finally, we look at three specific indicators of care: share of residents with bedsores, share of residents with unplanned weight loss or gain, and share of residents being restrained.

During their annual inspections, nursing homes are assessed along 165 measures of quality and process of care, and deficiencies are noted. While these data do not provide information on which nursing homes are providing high-quality care, they do indicate which homes are providing poor-quality care. The Pennsylvania nursing homes in our sample, on average, have fewer deficiencies than nursing homes in the country as a whole, averaging 4.45 deficiencies in their most recent inspection.

Religiously affiliated nursing homes, on average, had fewer deficiencies in their last inspection than did other types of nursing homes (see Table 7.7), but only in the case of the two types of for-profit nursing homes were these differences significant.[64] On spe-

Table 7.7 Average number of deficiencies by sector and affiliation

	Quality deficiencies	Total deficiencies
Nonprofit religious	1.41	3.66
Nonprofit sector	1.32	4.06
For-profit corporate	1.76	4.95
For-profit other	1.80	5.38
Government	1.60	4.26

cific dimensions of quality of care, nonprofit nursing homes have significantly fewer deficiencies than for-profit corporate nursing homes on four dimensions—those relating to periodic assessments of resident condition, quality of day-to-day care, care in prescribing and giving medications, and safety of the nursing home for individual residents. There are no differences on the dimensions of resident mistreatment, protection of resident rights, or nutritional and dietary adequacy.

When specific characteristics of residents associated with inadequate care are measured, however, the picture is mixed. Residents of religiously affiliated nursing homes are significantly less likely than their for-profit corporate counterparts to have bedsores but significantly more likely to experience substantial unplanned weight gain or loss (see Table 7.8). Bedsores are a particularly tricky measure. They occur when immobile residents are not turned or moved often enough and, in those situations, result from poor quality of care. But many residents enter nursing homes with bedsores that developed while they were in hospitals. The fact that residents of corporate for-profit nursing homes are slightly more likely to be bedfast than their religious nonprofit counterparts and likely to need significantly more resources to care for them may explain these differences. But it is also true that religiously affiliated nonprofit nursing homes have significantly more staff hours per resident day. Since one cause of bedsores is lack of staff to care for, turn, and move residents, the difference might also be explained by staffing differences.

In the case of unplanned weight change, the pattern runs in

Table 7.8 Specific characteristics of nursing home care by sector and affiliation (in percent)

	Bedsores	Unplanned weight change	Unnecessary restraints
Nonprofit religious	12.0	9.1	5.3
Nonprofit secular	12.4	9.4	7.0
For-profit corporate	12.9	7.6	7.8
For-profit other	14.1	7.6	9.6
Government	10.2	7.0	6.3

the opposite direction. This is difficult to understand. Unplanned weight change is often associated with lack of staff to help incapacitated residents eat. When there is too little time for a slow eater to finish a meal, too few staff to cue and help feed those who can't feed themselves, or unappetizing food, residents are likely to lose weight. Because religiously affiliated nursing homes have less incapacitated residents on average and more staffing hours per resident day, one would have expected this relationship to run in the opposite direction.

Our final quality of care measure is the use of restraints. The federal government and advocates for the elderly have long campaigned to eliminate the use of restraints, such as being tied or strapped to chairs. Lack of freedom of movement over time is correlated with decreases in muscle tone and bone capacity, increasing incontinence, and other negative health effects. But where residents have difficulty moving about on their own or become disoriented, staff are needed to help them move about or watch out for them. Religiously affiliated nursing homes are significantly less likely to use restraints than any other type of nursing home.[65] Certainly the greater physical capacity of their residents and the greater number of staff hours per resident day contribute to their lesser use of restraints. But these differences in restraint use are quite large and are likely to reflect a philosophy of care as well.

These inspection data track the amount of poor-quality care in nursing homes but provide few hints about the overall quality of care or quality of life for nursing home residents in different types of homes. It would be useful to undertake more in-depth investigations, through interviews with residents and their families, pastors, and others who regularly visit individuals in a wide range of nursing home types and through observational studies to assess whether the values and missions of religiously affiliated nursing homes are reflected in higher-quality care.

The final question we raised was whether competition has any impact on nursing home behavior. In particular, in highly competitive markets, are there fewer differences between religiously affiliated and secular homes? Is there any evidence that religiously affiliated nursing homes influence the behavior of their secular counterparts? Health care markets tend to be local, so we used counties as our definition of market. We assess competitiveness using the Hirschman-Herfindahl Index (HHI) with a cutoff of 0.15 to separate more competitive from less competitive markets.[66] By this definition, nearly three-quarters of the nursing homes in our Pennsylvania sample are located in highly competitive markets. Religiously affiliated nursing homes are more likely than their secular not-for-profit and corporate counterparts to be located in competitive markets.

	In competitive markets (in percent)
Total	73.2
Nonprofit religious	76.7
Nonprofit secular	61.9
For-profit corporate	69.3
For-profit other	79.7
Government	73.2

When we compare religiously affiliated nursing homes with their corporate for-profit counterparts in highly competitive markets, we find that the patterns we observed earlier hold. In each type of market, the former have residents with a lower average CMI, have a higher occupancy rate, and provide more total staffing hours per

Table 7.9 Differences between religious and secular nursing homes by market competitiveness

	Competitive			Noncompetitive		
	Religious	Secular	Diff.	Religious	Secular	Diff.
CMI	1.09	1.16	−.07	1.13	1.18	−.06
Occupancy rate	92%	88%	+4%	93%	86%	+7%
Total deficiencies	3.49	4.64	−1.15	4.27	5.06	−.79
Total staff hours per resident day	3.72	3.43	+.29	3.86	3.59	+.27

resident day. In addition, they have fewer deficiencies on average. But are these differences smaller in highly competitive markets? As the data show (see Table 7.9), both religious and secular homes have slightly more resource-demanding residents and appear to respond with slightly more total staff hours per resident per day in less competitive markets. And both types of homes had a greater number of deficiencies in their most recent inspection in noncompetitive markets. Although the magnitudes differ by category, differences between religious and secular homes appear to be slightly greater in competitive than noncompetitive markets on the total deficiency measure. This is surprising, because one would have expected the opposite to be the case.

Conclusion

Using data from the late 1970s and early 1980s, Weisbrod, as we saw earlier, compared proprietary and nonprofit nursing homes along a number of dimensions and found that nonprofits in general, and religious nonprofits in particular, were rated significantly more positively. This chapter considers issues similar to those Weisbrod addressed but asks whether there are still observable differences across institutional forms after more than a decade of direct and indirect governmental pressure to reduce costs, improve quality of care, and admit increasingly sick residents. Using publicly available data from 2002 to examine the state of nursing homes in Pennsylvania, our results are much less conclusive.

First, we find that the distinction between religious and secular nursing homes is not always clear. Although we have data from only one point in time, it appears that there is movement across the secular-religious spectrum, with religiously affiliated homes losing their faith identity and religious organizations taking over the management of previously secular homes and bringing with them their values and religious commitments.

Second, we find that the differences between those nursing homes that claim a religious identity and those that do not are not as stark as we might have suspected. The differences we do find are either slight or suggestive in nature. For example:

- Residents of religiously affiliated homes appear to be slightly less incapacitated and need slightly less resource-intensive care than residents in their secular counterparts. It is not clear why this is the case, but these findings are consistent across a number of measures.

- Despite the slightly better medical condition of their residents, religiously supported facilities have higher staffing levels even though there is little difference between religiously affiliated and secular homes in terms of the rate at which the state reimburses them for the care of Medicaid-eligible patients. We can only speculate about additional resources that might be available to religiously affiliated nursing homes, although we hypothesize that they may be able to raise more revenue than their secular counterparts because of their affiliation with congregations.

- The limited interviews we conducted hint that religiously affiliated nursing homes may be able to attract more volunteers and that these individuals may make a significant difference in the quality of life of residents. This additional depth of resources likely rises from and is reinforced by a deep and regularly articulated commitment on the part of the faithful to serve the neighbor in need.

- Finally, the data hint (albeit not persuasively) that religiously affiliated homes may provide better care than their secular counterparts. But, while religiously affiliated homes have significantly fewer deficiencies in their annual inspections, on other measures they do not appear to perform better.

Although some of the findings are provocative, the lack of clear differences between religiously affiliated homes and others leads to further questions. There are a number of directions future research might take in order to build on this initial examination.

First, this study looks at only one state. Despite federal regulations, Medicaid rates and many nursing home regulations vary across states. Pennsylvania has above-average reimbursement rates and higher quality-of-care standards than the typical state. A similar study in one or more states with less demanding regulations and lower reimbursement rates would likely find greater differences between religious and secular homes on many dimensions of quality of care.

Second, this study attempts to examine the impact of recent policy changes on nursing home behavior but uses data at only one point in time. Although it identifies potential patterns of response, these can be fully explored only through a longitudinal examination. To really understand how for-profit and not-for-profit, religious, and secular nursing homes are responding to fiscal and regulatory challenges, it is essential to examine data on individual nursing homes over time.

Finally, this study used primarily publicly available data aggregated to the level of nursing homes. We could get a more precise picture of the impact of nursing home characteristics and quality of care on resident well-being if we had data on the health status of individual residents *when* they entered a particular home and at various points during their stay as well as more detailed information on resources available.

But even with this additional analysis, I would nevertheless expect that the differences a researcher would find today between religious and secular nursing homes, and even between for-profit and not-for-profit nursing homes, would be less clear cut and dramatic than those found by Weisbrod. One reason for this is that the policy changes discussed earlier have forced all types of nursing homes to change. Indeed, new, high-quality models of care are emerging in for-profit and not-for-profit homes, and in religiously affiliated and secular homes.[67] Second, the distinctions between religious and secular, as well as between for-profit and not-for-profit, are not as clear as we might have imagined. In other words, the phenomenon we are trying to explain is no longer a dichotomous variable but rather a range of newly emerging institutional forms.

This suggests that what we really need are a series of detailed case studies, similar to those by Bane, McRoberts, Coffin, and Reynolds and Winship (Chapters 2, 3, 4, and 8), focusing on nursing home life as experienced by residents and employees as well as on organizational mission and management practices. Important questions to address range from exploring how the home's mission is embodied in its personnel practices to patterns of day-to-day interactions among staff, residents, and management. How the death of a resident is handled and addressed is another important question. Ultimately, any benefits from a more holistic or spiritual approach, if confirmed, should be of interest to all parties in long-term care, whether or not they are religious.

chapter 8

Faith, Practice, and Teens: Evaluating Faith-Based Programs

Amy Reynolds and Christopher Winship

THE ESTABLISHMENT of the White House Office of Faith-Based and Community Initiatives in 2002 and the subsequent increase in government grants to faith-based groups is only the most dramatic of many recent developments that have spurred debate about the role of such programs in addressing intransigent social problems. We know little, however, about the effectiveness of faith-based programs. More significant, we know even less about the different types of faith-based programs, how they are constructed, or the ways in which any religious faith inherent in the programs can affect outcomes. It is not well understood, for example, whether faith-based programs that seek to use religious values and motivations as a building block for personal change (and not all of them do this) succeed in connecting religious belief to more socially desirable behavior and thus achieve a successful outcome.

Other chapters in this book address issues surrounding faith-based programs in the public sphere. One challenge we see is the need to understand the religious identities of these organizations and the individuals they serve as a component of their effectiveness. Thus the main topics guiding our research are what role religion plays in these organizations, and how central it is in their operations.[1] Here we analyze one secular and three Christian faith-based programs developed for inner-city teenagers. Our purpose is to understand how these programs differ in the ways they serve youth, in particular whether the specifically Christian character of the three faith-based programs affects their outcomes.

In the debate over faith-based delivery of social services, it is often simply assumed that faith-based social programs have the potential to change the religious understanding or faith of clients, that this can alter how they view moral choices, personal identities, and life plans, and that this, in turn, can affect behavior. Our research explores whether these assumptions are valid and if so, how. In pursuing this question, we do not disagree with Ronald Thiemann's observation in Chapter 6 that the public value of faith-based services may be seen as existing independent of the providers' faith motivations. Thiemann proposes that all programs, faith-based and secular, should be evaluated according to their ability to serve clients, and he argues that many faith-based providers prefer such a focus for their own theological reasons.

That may be the case from the perspective of religious faith, but from the empirical standpoint of social scientific research, the specific religious character and religious motivations of faith-based programs constitute an important variable. Especially in programs that seek to foster personal change, it is also important to measure whether positive outcomes are achieved by tapping into the religious values and beliefs of clients. In Chapter 5, Nancy Ammerman makes a strong case for the pervasive influence of the religious narratives that people bring with them into the public sphere. We would add that these narratives belong not only to the service providers but to the clients as well.

Our approach requires methods to evaluate providers' delivery of services. The model we employ is represented in Figure 8.1. Here we draw on it to ask whether there are linkages between adolescents' religious understandings and faith commitments, on the one hand, and their moral values, personal identities, and life plans, on the other. The three faith-based programs differ in important respects.

In one, Summer of Hope, religion and faith were a key motivating force, and religion permeated the program's environment in im-

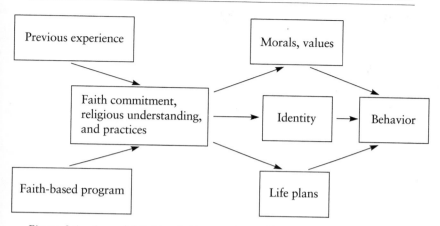

Figure 8.1   A model linking faith, morals, and behavior

portant ways. The program, however, only secondarily focused on changing adolescents' faith commitments, religious understanding, and practices. (The names of all four programs, and of the participants in them, have been changed.)

The goal of the second faith-based program, Discover Yourself, was specifically to help adolescent girls deepen their self-understanding. Among other components of the program were prayer and discussions of personal decisions and life choices.

Connecting Youth, meanwhile, was the most explicitly faith-based program we studied. It might appropriately be called fully faith-infused, in that religion and religious practice fully inform and direct both discussions and program activities. It is also the program that most explicitly is connected to a specific church and the faith practices and commitments of that church.

The fourth program, which serves as the control, was the Boston Project, an entirely secular program administered during both the summer and the academic term by the community service component of a local university. Like the other programs, it serves students from the Dorchester neighborhood of Boston.

On the basis of interviews with program participants as well as participant observation, in three of the four programs we find only weak or moderate connections between individuals' religious understandings and faith commitments and their moral values and life plans. A moderate connection existed in Discover Yourself, where participants were encouraged to link their faith commitment and their behavior. A stronger connection was found in Connecting Youth, by far the most faith oriented of the four programs, where connections were encouraged, religious understanding was emphasized, and religious practices established.

Surprisingly, however, a lack of faith commitment or the need to develop belief was not the primary issue for girls in the four programs. Girls in all four programs report having multidimensional relationships with God. Although their understanding of religious doctrine and teaching was often not extensive, the girls universally believed in God. Most prayed on a daily basis, although few attended church regularly or had evidence of other religious practices. Most girls, however, seemed unable to make a connection between their faith, religious understanding, and practices and their moral values, personal identities, or life plans. These were simply separate, unconnected domains in their life.

Our findings reshape the debate on faith-based programs in contradictory ways. Our analyses suggest, on the one hand, that only the most faith-infused programs are likely to be successful in enhancing the potential of religion to alter individuals' lives. (This supports Ammerman's comment that understanding the role of religion is not just about simply plugging in variables, but about understanding how different aspects of religiosity, or the content of faith, are integrated with certain processes.) On the other hand, our research suggests that such programs need not focus on creating or instilling religious belief. For the girls in this study, a strong degree of faith is already present. Although we recognize that the fully faith-infused program was in large part successful because of the new learning it imparted to the students, the basic beliefs were not contrary to those that girls may have heard before; in addition, the girls were not encouraged to "switch" religions. The issue, then, is helping these girls connect their faith to their moral values and life plans. This finding supports Mary Jo Bane's arguments in Chapter

2 that Catholic institutions must do better at integrating the belief and behavior of Catholics in the public sphere.

Previous Research

A recent review of the efficacy of faith-based programs examines the effect that religion and religious elements have on a number of outcomes.[2] In this report, Byron Johnson and his coauthors at the University of Pennsylvania distinguish the effects of what they term organic religion from the effects of intentional religion, finding that most research has focused on the former. Research on organic religion seeks to determine how people living in religious systems and structures with regular practices are affected by presumably self-chosen religious practices. For example, much of the research on organic religion examines the effects of church attendance on various behaviors. Research on intentional religion has involved evaluating programs that explicitly aim to bring religion and faith into individuals' lives with the intent of changing them, much like the programs we are studying. Johnson's report suggests that organic religion generally has a statistically significant association in the expected directions with criminal behavior, teenage pregnancy, and achievement, while little is known about the possible effects of intentional religion. Within the literature, three research areas are most relevant for youth—teen pregnancy, crime, and drug use.

TEEN PREGNANCY

For teenage girls, early pregnancy and single motherhood are the topics of greatest concern. Youths cite morals and values as important in influencing sexual activity.[3] Ann Meier shows that morals help to explain part of the personal religiosity effect, which is a more effective indicator of behavior than religion alone.[4] She tries to capture the religiosity effect using scales of public and private religion. Public religiosity refers to church attendance and involvement in other group religious activities. Private religiosity refers to belief in God, prayer, and other more interior behavior. When attitudes are controlled for, the significance of private religiosity in decisions about sexual behavior decreases. This suggests that there is a correlation between personal religiosity and variables in attitudes, as we might expect. Participation in religious worship and church programs is also found to influence attitudes.[5] Attitudes alone appear to only weakly affect teens' sexual behavior.

There is little information on the efficacy of different faith programs for teens. Programs that affect the value systems of youth have been found to be more successful than those that do not.[6] Barbara Defoe Whitehead and her colleagues find that faith leaders are able to have an impact on youth sexual behavior through teachings about morality, in activities that provide hope, and in using faith to help youth think about their sexuality.[7]

Recent research has examined the effect of sexual abstinence pledges on youth behavior—a popular program in some religious communities, where they are also known as "sexual purity" pledges.[8] Although the impact of pledges is not uniform, those who pledge earlier in adolescence and who do so within small communities appear to have the highest rates of delayed first intercourse. This effect is found when controlling for religiosity, although youth who pledge often are more religious. For black females in the sample, the effects of pledging appear to be weaker and were less positive.

CRIME

Research finds faith programs do have positive impacts on teens in the areas of crime and violence, although the dynamics of the effect are uncertain. Youth living in neighborhoods of high disorder are the most at risk for criminal behavior. However, recent studies reveal that religious involvement can mediate the effect of the neighborhoods—so much so that religious involvement seems more important than the neighborhood effect.[9] Johnson also finds that religion is most important for teens in at-risk neighborhoods. Many studies that examine the impact of faith on deviant behavior use different measures of religion or faith. Johnson finds through his meta-analysis of different juvenile delinquency studies that the link of religion to less deviant behavior practices increases with more extensive measures of religion.[10] This suggests that religion is a multifaceted variable, and that its different elements need to be measured in order to adequately understand its full effect.

DRUG USE

In a study by Columbia University's National Center on Addiction and Substance Abuse, researchers analyzed the importance of organic religion as a variable in drug use. Researchers found that both church attendance and religious attitudes were significantly associated with various behavior outcomes.[11] Teens who are not involved with drugs (alcohol, marijuana, and cigarettes) are two to three times more likely to say that religion is important in their lives. Teens who think that religion is important are also more likely to involve their parents in their decisions concerning drug behavior. The same evidence exists for religious practice. By a factor of two to three, depending on the drug, teens who attend services were less likely to participate in alcohol, marijuana, and cigarette use. This attendance factor also is connected to peer effects; teens with higher levels of personal and public religiosity are less likely to have friends engaging in drug use.

A 2001 study by Johnson found similar results.[12] Using data from the National Youth Study, he found that religion's restraining effect on drug use increases as youth get older, even when controlling for the effect of social networks, school factors, and neighborhoods. Studies show that religion is related to lower drug use due to a combination of direct and indirect effects. Attitudes about religion are a good predictor of drug use, although attendance may be more important.

Methodology and Program Descriptions

We employ a theory-based evaluation, which involves determining whether evidence can be found for the mechanisms that a theory posits to be important in a program.[13] Specifically, we examine in the context of four programs whether an adolescent girl's faith commitment and religious understanding affect how she thinks about moral issues, personal identity, and/or life plans. We do not assess whether religion affects behavior directly or indirectly, but research reviewed in the last section does support the claim that moral perspective and life plans do affect behavior, even if not perfectly.[14]

On its own, theory-based evaluation takes us only part of the way toward establishing the existence or importance of a particular mechanism, for two reasons. First, without quantitative data, determining the strength of an effect may be difficult. Second, without random assignment to the programs or other methods for controlling for selection into a program, determining whether observed attitudes or behavior are the result of the program or were present prior to the program may be problematic. However, if one can show that a hypothesized mechanism does not appear to be operating, this is potentially strong evidence against the program's efficacy. Likewise, if one can show that a mechanism does appear to be operating, this may be strong evidence of the program's impact.

Our approach is qualitative and ethnographic, based both on interviews and on participant observation. Youth, as well as youth workers, were interviewed from four different programs. The authors were also participant observers in three of the four programs, the exception being Discover Yourself. One of us (Reynolds) was involved in 1999–2002 with interviewing a number of teen girls. These were all youth that were contacted because they were involved with programs in which the researcher had been a participant or because the leaders connected youth with the researcher. Interviews ranged from thirty minutes to an hour. Some were conducted in person, while others were conducted over the telephone, although the length and information did not differ by method. In cases of participant observation, some of the comments come from settings other than interviews. For each program studied, we conducted in-depth interviews with four or five girls. For one of the programs (Summer of Hope), we relied mostly on previous research from interviewed teens. Karyn Lacy was a participant observer in these programs and conducted interviews during our fieldwork, which was done in 2001 and 2002.[15]

BOSTON PROJECT

The Boston Project program consists of a term-time academic program and a full-time summer enrichment program. As noted, it is run out of a local university and is staffed by students. Participants come from local low-income housing areas. In the summer, the program is a type of summer school. The term-time program helps the girls with their schoolwork, and tries to provide them with a mentoring relationship. The program is totally secular. Although the girls are all generally familiar with the Bible, only one participant attended church during the period of our research. They have had opportunities to attend different religious programs, and all seem to have some familiarity with religious practices.

SUMMER OF HOPE

This faith-based program was launched in 1994 by the Ten Point Coalition, a collaboration of black churches in the Boston area, and ran for three summers. An initial goal of the program was to use religion as a mechanism for helping high school students understand their lives. Optional prayer times as well as periodic religious discussions occurred. Youth were often placed at church sites to do work, and the directors were religious leaders. There were also weekly spiritual sessions, though they appear to more typically have involved lectures rather than discussions.

DISCOVER YOURSELF

This faith-based program challenged youth to think about the role of faith in their lives. It involved girls who were at risk for pregnancy, violence, drug use, or court involvement. The program began with prayer. Nevertheless, according to both the director and the girls, it was not a "religious" program. The youth spent time writing and thinking about their lives, reading about the lives of others, having speakers from the community speak/meet with them, and going on trips. The girls typically built strong relationships with the women leaders.

Two groups of teens were studied. One set consisted of girls currently in the program, the other of girls who had completed the program. Generally only a small number of girls were in the program at any one time.

CONNECTING YOUTH

Run through an evangelical nondenominational church in Washington, D.C., this faith-based program has been in existence for fifteen years. We describe the program as it existed at the time when the interviews and fieldwork were carried out. The program focused on many of the same goals as the other programs—community service, breaking of class barriers, and involving faith in personal decisions. The youth were from the area, and fewer than half were involved with the church initially.[16] Of all four programs we studied, Connecting Youth put the most emphasis on faith and prayer. Teaching directly about sexual activity—and even having retreats planned around the theme—set a tone in which many of the youth participated in abstinence pledges. The program is connected with a local academic enrichment center. Although it is similar to the other programs, there are some interesting differences between Connecting Youth and the other three. Most of the youth in Connecting Youth were from low-income black families, but some were from middle-class families; several youth in the program were also white. The mentors, however, much like in the Boston Project, were from middle- and upper-class backgrounds, and only a small fraction of adult workers were not white.

DEMOGRAPHIC AND RELIGIOUS CHARACTERISTICS
OF THE PROGRAMS

The four programs allow us to understand the different contexts in which faith commitment, religious understanding, and religious practices might have an impact on an individual's moral values and life choices. Boston Project, the secular program, allows us to determine whether these connections are naturally present in the absence

Table 8.1 Program descriptions

Program	Data for participants				Data for adult staff			Statistics about program	
	Race	Gender	Grade	Race	Religion	Ongoing	In charge	Size
Boston Project	All black	Mixed, at times separated	6th to 12th	Various races	Not relevant	Yes, summer and term	Local university	50 kids, small groups
Summer of Hope	All black	Mixed	9th to 12th	Mostly black	Clergy among staff	Summer only	Group of black churches	40–70 kids, small groups
Discover Yourself	All black	All girls	8th to 12th	Black	Church members	Yes, several years	AME church	4–8 girls
Connecting Youth	Black and white	Mixed, at times separated	6th to 12th	Mostly white	All attend church	Yes, many years	Evangelical, multi-denominational church	50 kids, small groups

Table 8.2 Program activities

Program	Prayer	Reflection	Bible	Teaching	Service	Community inside	Community outside	Pledges
Boston Project	No	Yes	No	No	No	Some	No	No
Summer of Hope	Some	Yes	No	No	Yes	Little	Little	No
Discover Yourself	Yes	Yes, central	Some	No	No	Some	Little	No
Connecting Youth	Yes, central	Yes	Yes, central	Yes	Some	Yes	Some	Yes

of a faith-based program. Summer of Hope allows us to determine whether these connections are likely to occur in an environment that is supportive of religious belief and practice, but not directly religious. Discover Yourself allows us to see whether these connections exist in a program that specifically encourages participants to think about the relationship between their faith commitments and religious understanding and their moral values and life planning, without any of its own religious pedagogy or practices. Finally, Connecting Youth allows us to test for these connections in an environment where connections are explicitly present in the program, both in discourse and in practice. Tables 8.1 and 8.2 summarize the characteristics of each of the programs.

The Religious Lives of Black Adolescent Girls

BASIC BELIEFS

Regardless of the programs in which they are involved, religion was present in the lives of all of the girls.[17] In many ways, their views of God are more similar than they are different. All of them believe in God, openly profess this faith, and see God acting in their lives. There is little doubt that God exists for these girls, although they do have a lot of questions about God. They overwhelmingly view God as real, present in their lives, and accessible. Research by Robert Coles finds youth understand God in relation to their own needs; girls in our programs identify God as acting in a world of unknowns, equating God with a protector, a provider, and a judge.[18]

The girls in the Boston Project, as well as those in Summer of Hope, insist on the existence of God. Yet after declaring their belief, they would explain some of the questions they had about God. One girl in the Boston Project said she knew that God was there, in part, because "he is looking out for me." Another girl, Mary, captured similar sentiments when she said, "He makes sure I don't get in too much trouble (laugh)." Rashida further commented that "he's a lovable person. He helps us . . . he helps us with everything." Throughout the interviews, God is described as someone who is there for them. One of the staff with Summer of Hope said of the youth, "people need to know there's something larger than themselves . . . our kids know this." Even in complaints that the youth from Summer of Hope often voice about religion, there is a supposition that God is real and there. In addition to believing that God exists, these girls also think that God sees their actions, and that there is a code they should follow. Kamiya talks about how God wants us to do right. Asia brings up the most vivid image of a judge when she describes that God affects her life because of "what I do. He sees what I do. If I do bad things, he knows. Good stuff he knows." Kamiya states that God punishes those who "make trouble."

The girls in Discover Yourself have the same assurance in the existence of God. They are certain of God's existence. "I believe in God 100 percent," asserted Fatima. Chanetta responded to questions about her belief in God by assuring that "God *is* out there." Fatima also commented that "to me there is only one God. To society, there are thirteen different religions that coincide together." God also protects them, although they see themselves as more responsible for their destiny. The idea of God as a judge is more concrete for them. Kaneisha relates a personal story of the time her child almost died. She said, "If it was not for God I would not have been there." Nikia relates that "he works miracles. He does things that a regular human being would not be able to do." She goes on to tell how God wakes her, feeds her, and has even "blessed me with a job." Nikia sees bad situations in her life as deserved, and thinks that God comes at us "as the devil" in those situations. Erica, in a light vein, commented that, because her family does not go to church, "we're all going to Hell." An important difference in the ways that these girls viewed God, as opposed to the other two groups, was that they saw God as a guide. According to Fatima, "I just look at him as my Father. When I go to the crossroads, meet him, he's still here with me only in Spirit."

The girls in Connecting Youth also have a strong belief in God. They have the same assurance of God, and also have questions about who that God is. Unlike the girls in the other programs, however, is the fact that their view of God is tied to a more traditional view of religion. They attest that they want to follow God, and base their belief in God on the Bible. Shaunta, in response to a question about whether she considered herself a Christian, replied, "Yes, I believe in the Word of God." Sarah specifically clarified her belief in God with "I believe in Jesus." While they, like the other programs' participants, may credit God with "waking me up every morning," they discuss more specific ways that God has been active, and view God very personally. Shaunta made her theology personal, stating, "He died on the cross for me. He loves me." Earlier in the interview she also makes the comment that "there is no one above him that I love . . . He's an awesome person. He loves me." Olivia mentions the way that God has been there for her in the toughest moments. Tina first describes God as a friend, then almost as a perfect parent. In talking of God, she says, "He's just like a good being who is perfect and doesn't do any wrong." Sarah said, "I have a relationship with Jesus . . . I think of people—they need Jesus—when I see them doing bad things too."

RELIGIOUS KNOWLEDGE AND UNDERSTANDING

With respect to deeper beliefs, the girls have a hard time understanding or expressing what they believe, and in general have a weak understanding of Christian doctrine. The girls would often respond "I don't know" in the middle of trying to explain some piece of theology, recite commandments, or discuss the Bible. On the whole, the girls seem to want to know more; more than once in the interviews they would ask questions themselves.

Those in the Boston Project asked the most basic questions. Mary, in discussing a miracle of the Virgin Mary, asked how the Virgin Mary was connected to Jesus. Kamiya, presenting the story of Jesus, said, "They [the teen center] showed a commercial of God being killed on the cross. Because he wanted to do good things and they didn't want him to." These girls claim not to think about religious things that often—Shirley, who attends church every week, "doesn't have any views about it [religion]." And Rashida expresses that "umm, I don't know what color he is." These girls have a limited knowledge of the Bible and have mixed feelings about it.

They've been to Bible studies, and seem to think that it is a good thing to study and follow—in theory. When asked to define what was good, Rashida began with "Bible study." Kamiya, in explaining that the Bible did actually have an impact on her life, replied that "it tells you about God and how to respect him and your family. Do what's right for your family and don't be a pain and God will love you for who you are." Shirley, the girl most knowledgeable about the Bible, said, "Some of the stuff in it is true, some I don't understand. I hear about it in church, I read it on my own, but they read it in church." Their religious knowledge comes from random sources—relationships with mothers and grandmothers, the teen center, or their occasional attendance at church. They are open to knowing more, although those who go to church only occasionally discussed wanting to learn more about God.

In some ways the knowledge of those in Summer of Hope seems similar to that of participants in Discover Yourself. Both expect their peers to know about the Bible. One girl who did not know about the Last Supper astonished her peers by asking them what it was. Some of the youth in this program are volunteers at church and know the theology, although they may not believe it all. Lacy, in her assessment of the Summer of Hope, argues that the teens knew the religious teachings quite well but did not understand as easily what they meant and how to apply them to their lives. She indicates that the girls can tell you the stories of Jesus and many would consider themselves Christians who believe in church teachings. Those in Discover Yourself are similar—they describe Jesus as a savior, as Erica says, who "does good and he died for us. Came back." Kaneisha discussed the same savior theology, explaining that "the Lord is going to come back. I believe in that too." They have questions, as some of them relate questions on the difference between different Christian groups.

Teens from both groups are, on the whole, well acquainted with material from the Bible, although there are some in both groups who have little knowledge of it. From Summer of Hope, they made comments such as "if you read the Bible by yourself, you don't need to hear it from someone else," and another argued that "you can read the Bible right." Their base of knowledge is in the church, and this is where most of them have gained the knowledge that they have.

Discover Yourself participants differ in their nontraditional view of God, with a theology furthest away from that of the church. Nikia expresses that she "doesn't have a culture," but instead is all cultures. They asked the most questions. Fatima says: "I wanna go to church and be able to listen and get into God and really have them tell me about God but how can they really tell me. They are just going by what they read. I just don't know what to believe really."

Nikia has turned to investigating the texts of other religions for answers. Several program participants mention the contradictions that exist in the Bible. According to one girl, "the Bible itself has a lot of contradictions in it, if that's what people want to believe . . . but I can't pick out the contradictions exactly. I remember seeing it contradicted itself all over. I don't have a problem with believing it though." At the same time, they still think of religion—even in the more traditional forms—as important. Kaneisha says, "I believe it is the word of God. He put the disciples on the earth to write it. People ask, 'How can you believe it?' All my life, I've been reading it."

Unique to Connecting Youth is a strong tie to beliefs of the church and a more concrete understanding of God, although its participants come from less traditionally religious homes on average. Girls in the program still ask basic questions about theology, but they have a solid understanding of Christianity, probably because of the direct teaching they receive. They give longer, more thorough descriptions of God. Shaunta states, "He died for me and he sent his only son to help me not get punished for the sins I committed." Olivia's understanding of the Bible, the basics of salvation, the reasons she still sins, and why Christians should not have sex is impressive. She explained to the junior high girls, on several retreats, why she has made the decisions she has, and has given mini-sermons at events for the youth. Shaunta discussed the appreciation she has for talking about everyday issues. "One Sunday morning we were talking about hunger. Those are everyday issues. Put it into teaching." Like the other girls, they want to know more, and show this with their continued participation in classes and studies.[19] Their questions are slightly different. One girl, Sarah, commented on God: "He created man and woman, the heavens and the earth. He created Adam and Eve. God is confusing. It's kinda weird, life is weird. He created us and Jesus. He was just here by himself all alone." Tina wrestles with the divine nature of God and states: "I don't know if he would be called a person 'cause he's not really a human being or anything, but more like a being or something."

PRAYER AND RELIGIOUS PRACTICES

The girls in all four programs are similar in that they all believe in their ability to communicate with God through prayer. They pray because they sense that God is there and is answering their prayers —or at the very least, is listening to them. Prayer is not equated with religious activity, but is seen as a normal aspect of life. With the exception of the Boston Project, the girls in all of the programs come from a mixture of religious backgrounds. And again with the exception of Boston Project, all of the programs stress building important relationships with a spiritual mentor.[20]

Most of the girls pray daily. Their prayer lives range from more basic in Boston Project to more involved with Connecting Youth. Rashida, from Boston Project, says she prays regularly, although God "just says hi," talking in a whisper. Shirley prays "just to be able to take care of her son and see another day." Erica, who says she is praying more because of the program, says, "I pray every day before I go to bed . . . I pray for everybody. I pray for myself and my family first and then I pray for other people . . . I pray like to ask God for help, to help me." Nikia prays for "everything good and bad." The girls in Connecting Youth, while they pray more regularly and talk of seeking guidance, offer similar prayers. Tina says:

> I pray at least once a day, sometimes twice a day. I know I always pray over meals, and sometimes I pray at night for the next day or for being able to sleep well. Sometimes I pray for events coming up or if

there is something wrong in my life or someone else's life. Depends on what big event is happening. I pray 'cause praying for them lets God know what I think about and my opinion on it and lets him know what I need help with and that's about it.

Sarah was a little shy in revealing that she prays less than she thinks she should.

The truth—I pray when something bad happens or when I want something. I don't pray like 'hi God.' How often—that's hard. Sometimes I pray in the night or in the morning. When I pray—things about my life . . . Just my family and sometimes the world.

Although most of the girls pray, especially those in Discover Yourself and Connecting Youth, this prayer life is not necessarily equated with a life of religious practices. All of those in the faith-based programs have had exposure to the church, as well as some of those within the Boston Project. Most of those who go to church go because their family does or out of a sense of obligation—this is particularly true for those in the Boston Project and Summer of Hope.[21] Most of those in Discover Yourself rarely go to church. Although they say this, and say they are not religious, those who attend have a sense that this activity is important. Shirley says that she goes because "the rule is that everyone in the house goes to church on Sunday." She also commented, however, that once she was out of the house, she would continue to go occasionally.

A higher degree of involvement in prayer is evident among some of the older girls in Discover Yourself and Connecting Youth. Some of the prayers related to change and transformation came from these girls. Fatima says:

Basically I'm just praying that I am watched over and for him to guide me in the best place, and after death. Just praying for him to be there. Everyone who believes in God turns to him at the best and the worst. Thank him when things are going well, and ask him to be with me when going through hard things.

Olivia provided more specific examples of prayer. Although she too prays for people and situations, she recounts a story about "fasting" by not wearing makeup at school, and how in that time she turned to God through prayer and asked God to help her through that period.

The girls in Summer of Hope and Discover Yourself are the most cynical about organized religion. Those in Summer of Hope talk about the hypocrisy that exists in the church—that they have friends who go who then act differently in school. They also complain about the materialistic attitude that seems pervasive in the churches, and the problem of gossip. Those in Discover Yourself also share this cynicism—but perhaps to a lesser degree. They are not in the churches, because they seem to seek a religious understanding on their own. Farina says, "Home is my church and I pray to my God and for my household." She will go on the "Lord's days" (Christmas and Easter) out of respect. Even those in Connecting Youth spot hypocrisy in their church—Sarah complained that the adult leaders sometimes follow different rules than those that they set for the youth.

The religious involvement of those in Connecting Youth is very different from that of the girls in the other programs. These girls come to church frequently—and for many this might involve taking a bus or walking. Most attend events at church during the week or on weekends, and all of the girls belong to a Bible study. They participate in other events, such as sexual purity pledges, retreats, fasting, and mission projects. They come for a variety of reasons. At one study break, Sarah told her leader, "I'm really missing out on God's word, and on my Bible study friends. So if we can get in contact soon, that would be great." Shauna regularly attends, but does note that if she is coming for an evening meeting at the church, she may attend a different service in the morning.

Those in Connecting Youth believe it is the job of the pastor to make church relevant. Shauna appreciated the teaching on hunger, but dislikes her grandmother's church because there "the preacher doesn't want to make me listen to him." Nikia shares the same appreciation when the minister "speaks in a way that you understand." Girls mention enjoying services when people are into the music, or when "certain people sing and I can just feel the song." Also important is the presence of community. Sarah mentions that "my people" are at the program. And Farina talks of bringing people into the program. Tina talks of how the program "gave me a community." Knowing people at services or activities makes a difference in their attendance. This is especially true for the girls in Connecting Youth—they come most often to activities when they know their friends will be attending.

Moral Values, Personal Identity, and Life Plans

MORAL VALUES

The girls also discussed their sense of right and wrong behavior in our interviews with them. For many of them, good and bad are self-evident. They believe people should be defined in moral terms by their actions rather than by their beliefs. There is variation, however, in how the girls think about their own personal morality.

The girls in the Boston Project had the hardest time defining values, although their ideas are similar to those expressed by girls in Summer of Hope.[22] The girls describe right and wrong primarily in terms of relations with other people or in terms of criminal activity. Getting along with others is an important value. Rawhide gave one of her longer answers to the question of what is bad. "Don't hit, swear, don't hit people, don't fight them. That's all I think." Kamiah, when talking about bad people, says that they don't care about themselves, "parents who give kids up, do drugs, don't care about self, don't have a life." Those in Summer of Hope mention drug use and stealing as bad. They seem to accept the presence of liquor stores as a good thing in their community. One youth in Summer of Hope said that bad people were ones who "needed" to be in church. Youth in Summer of Hope also viewed hypocrisy as a bad thing.

The morality of the girls in both of these programs is only weakly influenced by the teachings and philosophy of the church. Many of them plan to have children without being married. This is especially true for those in the Boston Project. During the interviews, most of the girls said they had boyfriends or admitted they wanted a boyfriend. For all of the girls, going to church seemed to be a "good thing." Those in Summer of Hope accept the teachings of their evangelical churches as mostly valid. Their problem is with people who do not follow church teachings. Interns working in the programs also commented that the youth accept the values of the church and that the youth, in turn, judge them in terms of these values, even if the interns are not personally committed to them.

Interestingly, the Boston Project girls showed the greatest desire to be viewed as doing the right thing. Rawhide, in the middle of an interview, began to yell at a younger brother for cursing because it was not appropriate in the presence of the interviewer. Mary, when having to explain that she was not pursuing college plans at the moment, apologized, since "I know it breaks your heart."

The girls in Discover Yourself, much like those in Summer of Hope and the Boston Project, are partially, but not strongly, influenced by religion in their thinking on morality. Their beliefs are shaped by religion to a greater degree than they are for others. The Bible calls for people to treat others well; Farina said, "It says that everyone should live equally as well as do right by work and to itself and others." She adds that "some of the things I do believe people should follow, like the Ten Commandments." In terms of sexual abstinence, the Discover Yourself participants do claim to want to defer childbearing until later, and most want to be married before having children. However, Mary, one of the older girls, thought it impossible to go a month without a boy. She was skeptical about the program because of its all-girl composition.

Yet the girls in Discover Yourself have developed a thoughtful understanding of their moral choices. Girls often arrive at their values through their own understanding. They believe that Christians are called to high moral standards, even if they do not primarily identify themselves as religious. The program appears to have affected their morality. Nikia believed she received better grades as a result of the program, and said that she got in trouble less for "talking back, being too loud, disrupting the class, not doing work."

Chamita no longer hangs out with the same people who she says were a bad influence, and Farina admits that she had a "filthy mouth" at the beginning of the program, and that she dressed differently and less professionally than she does now. They still struggle, as Kaneohe points out, with doing the things they should; for example, she states, "I need to go to church more. I don't know why I don't."

For girls in Connecting Youth, definitions of right and wrong deal more directly with their personal decisions, and are more closely connected with religious principles. They list the same issues as the girls in the other programs, although they are more likely to mention God as a source of their morality. They see their morality as their own, and their decisions as theirs. The things they believe are wrong are typical: stealing, murder, killing, lying, gossiping. Among good things, they include doing well in school, listening to parents, and helping others.

Specific religion-related morals come up in the area of sexuality. All of the girls made reference to this in discussing bad behavior. Sarah mentions it early on. Olivia has spoken in testimonies before other youth on this issue as well. In terms of proper behavior, Olivia considers dress and even whether or not to be dating boys. Another girl in the program, who was not interviewed, after admitting sexual involvement, decided to change her behavior and meets regularly with a youth worker. Religion for these girls also appears to be about motivation. For some it is a desire to love God—for others, it is because God is a judge and they must do right.

PERSONAL IDENTITY

The girls acknowledge that they are at risk in many ways—many have been referred to as ghetto children. Some even take such names on proudly as their own; others express frustration with such expressions. Most of the girls recognize that these programs exist to prevent them from getting in trouble. The idea that their identity is at risk is quite different for the girls in the church program. They conceive of their identity as more connected with their morality, which is important in understanding their hopes and life plans.

In the Boston Project, one girl had the phrase "Project Born" decorating many of her personal items, taking on the identity of being from the projects. Her and others' circumstances affect not only how they think of themselves, but also how they view their options. Many joined the program because they needed something to do—one girl commented that the best other option was to color at the teen center. Religious identities as such are nonexistent for these girls, and none considers herself religious. Shirley, the only one who attends church, nevertheless claims that she "never thinks about God." The girls in the Summer of Hope program do not identify themselves as religious either. They see their identity as tied with "people who live around here." Some mention the notion and the need for people to come back and give to their communities. Lacy suggests that the teens have a somewhat limited understanding of what it means to be African American, and allow this to place limits on them.[23] Indicative of this attitude was the comment of one student, who explained, "White culture is like, more rich, it has more roots in it."

Girls in the Discover Yourself program do not gravitate toward a typical religious identity. Most of the girls do not define themselves in relation to God and are reluctant to call themselves religious, although quite a few see themselves as spiritual. A few girls do consider themselves Christians. Farina explained that she was religious "100 percent." Erica, who hasn't been to church in years, still responded, "I'm Catholic." These girls think that their individual consciences and sense of morality play a part in shaping who they are. Although they may not see this inner reliance as being connected to spirituality, it seems they do have a religious identity, albeit a nontraditional one.

The girls in Connecting Youth have a religious identity that is based within a community. First, they are in a program that focuses on fostering identity through community. Their relation to God shapes their identity. Shauna has "God's Lil' Child" on her bags and books. Olivia, because of her faith, stopped using makeup during Lent one season to get a better sense of belonging to God. Sarah claims, "I'm a Christian . . . Jesus died for me." She says she "gave my life to Christ" this summer, although she is not sure if she did it previously. Tina relates to the fact that she is a Christian, and explicitly sees herself as religious. At the same time, she claims that her values are her own, shaped by her family and herself, and not dictated by the church. This sentiment—that their values belong to them—was shared by most of the girls.

LIFE PLANS

For many, religion and faith do not appear to significantly affect their thinking about marriage, family, sexuality, and future career plans. Within all of the groups, older girls have more sophisticated visions regarding their futures.

The goals of girls in Boston Project are limited. When Asia described what she would do after graduation, she said, "Go to college. Just to go . . . to learn more and do more." She struggles to have short-term goals—school is going okay "for right now," but she explained that "in the middle of the school year, I might get in trouble." Kamiah commented that she would "go to college and find a job . . . be in a business that makes a lot of money. Need to go to college so you know more when you get the job. Make sure I finish." Shirley, who has begun her first year in college, is also not sure what she will do. Her most specific response is that she wants to "write music. Does matter." Mary, in an early setting, claimed that she was going to Harvard, although weeks later decided that she wanted to be a "construction worker like my grandmother because they make a lot of money."

Most all of the youth mention children as something they want, and most are not worried about having them too soon. Regina wants a nice house, kids, and a nice boyfriend. Another of the girls said that she did not plan on having kids before she graduated, but she didn't know what would happen. Kamiya specifically wants "to not get married, [have] one or two kids . . . nice boyfriend to talk to."

The youth in Summer of Hope think that changed behavior should be part of the life of those who are religious; they discuss actions that the church people do that are not Christian. Yet at the same time, it is difficult for them to see how religion might change their own lives. One girl, in talking about how life choices could be different for younger blacks in their community (concerning food choices), commented, "No. No because it's too late for them. You have to start early teaching them that. The white people start early." Their identity and sense of self appear to be somewhat set, rather than malleable.

The interns in the programs complain about the ways that the youth spend their money, and don't save. One teen exhibited a sense of vision by saving $500 to buy a coat, but even this was a short-term goal. Although one teen captured the broader vision of many by saying that "everyone has dreams about moving out of the projects," the girls seem to have little vision of how to do so. One staff member commented on the attitudes of the youth: "It's an acceptance . . . a lack of faith that anything is going to be changed unless like someone from the outside comes in . . . Just like accepting substandard housing and a lack of education . . . and that's just how it is."

One girl said, "Opportunities . . . come out of nowhere . . . you're going to go for it." Regarding their life plans, it seems that opportunities may come to them, but there is little that they can do to create them.[24]

Within Discover Yourself, there is a direct emphasis on thinking about the future; girls in this program are overall more able to express a vision for their lives. The director of Discover Yourself stressed the following verse as it pertains to the nature of their program: "Where there is no vision, the people perish" (Proverbs 29:18). Although many of the girls share similar goals to girls in the other groups in terms of being wealthy, they have more plans on how to accomplish this. Their short-term sense of vision is also clearer, as in the case of Chanetta, who talks about a desire to be a leader because of the program. Nikia's plans for the future are to be a medical biller, because of the money they make and because "I also like working with computers." She could explain in detail what they do, and also was aware of possible training she might need, and the fact that her goal of a $65,000 yearly income may take five years to reach. She wants to go to college for herself, and to a school to receive training for a medical career. Chanetta spoke of wanting to be an actress, and plans to study drama in college; Fatima wants to open up a hair salon, and is saving wages from her job to be able to go to beauty school. Erica was a little less specific, probably because of her younger age. She does not know what she wants to do, but she does know she wants to decide. "She [her mother] wants me to be a nurse. She doesn't want me to go to school—it doesn't take that long to be a nurse. I don't want to be a nurse."

These girls have other family goals as well. Fatima wants to have children, but as she says, "When I have children, I want to be financially, mentally, and environmentally stable." One of the youth workers mentioned that the girls do not have extremely high standards for the men with whom they are involved. Like the girls in the Boston Project, these girls seem to be hoping for a "nice" partner. But unlike them, they seem to prefer to be married and have children, which they hope happens after high school graduation and moving into employment or careers. Nikia adds the provision that she's "not planning on it [having kids before graduating], but I don't know." Kaneisha, who has a child, has goals for marriage and deferring further children, because "my priority is getting a career, and accomplishing the goals I have for me."

The participants in Connecting Youth have a slightly different idea of their future. Most of them are younger than those in Discover Yourself, but they resemble them in some of their career goals. Olivia was accepted into a number of universities around the country, and is now attending college on a scholarship. Part of her vision for her future involves continuing to invest in the other youth in the program. She frequently comes back to Connecting Youth to assume a counselor role. Other girls in the program, not interviewed, hoped to go to college or to do mission work for a year. Sarah, still in junior high school, selected the school she is attending now because of its entrepreneurial focus. She wants to "own several businesses" after college, and took it for granted that she would go to college. Tina is attending a school with an art focus next year. Shaunta lacks similarly focused goals, though the program has spurred her to aim for better grades, and to improve a report card now laced with F's to one with A's, B's, and C's. The goals of these girls with respect to families are most different from the goals of those of the other groups. As the Connecting Youth girls discuss family, all of them see themselves as having a husband as part of a family, and not as something that may or may not happen. In fact, most were surprised at being asked to describe their future family, since they assumed a husband would be there. The exception is Tina, who is not sure. She wants children, but is also considering the option of adoption. These girls plan to stay sexually abstinent as well. Shaunta talks about not going to parties or having sex outside of marriage, while Olivia and her friends in the program have purchased purity rings.[25] The girls have all signed pledges committing to this chaste lifestyle—not only in not having sex before they are married, but in considering what the pledge means with regard to their dress and behavior. Because of the program, and maybe not their own initiative, they have plans to follow through with some of the plans they have.

Conclusion and Policy Recommendations

Tables 8.3 and 8.4 summarize the teens' religious characteristics and the connections between their faith and religious practice and their lives. From the tables, we see that success in linking religious faith and practice with moral choices and life plans varies with the degree to which a program emphasizes such connections. This pattern belies the view that this connection happens automatically.[26] The Boston Project and Summer of Hope programs make little direct effort to integrate belief and behavior; not surprisingly, their clients often fail to do so. In Discover Yourself, the link is emphasized through discussion, with the result that, to a moderate degree, girls see connections between their religious faith and their lives more generally. Connecting Youth is the most explicit in asking youth to make a connection between religious understanding or practices and their views of themselves, their life plans, and the

Table 8.3 Religious characteristics of teens in programs

Program	Belief in God	Practice of prayer	Religious knowledge	Use of Bible	Church attendance	Church attitudes	Strong relationships
Boston Project	Yes	Yes	No	Rarely	Little/none	Mixed	Weak
Summer of Hope	Yes	Yes	Some	Rarely	Some	Skeptical	Weak
Discover Yourself	Yes	Yes	Some	Little	Little	Good	Good
Connecting Youth	Yes	Yes	Yes	Some	Some/a lot	Very good	Very good

Table 8.4 Faith/practice connections to life

Program	Religious identity	Christian morality	Personal morality	Religious understanding	Sense of vision	Sexual purity
Boston Project	No	Little	Little	None	Little	No
Summer of Hope	No	Some	Some	Some	Little	Little
Discover Yourself	No	Some	A lot	Some	Some	Little
Connecting Youth	Yes	A lot	A lot	A lot	Some	A lot

moral issues they confront, and it is far more successful in getting youth to reexamine their behavior.

These findings suggest the potential influence that the "faith factor" of such programs can have on participants; in order to be effective, however, faith-based providers must actively connect beliefs and behavior. We should not be surprised at this; in her chapter, Bane demonstrates that even the Catholic Church, a setting in which the teaching is clear and members are much more committed, faces a serious challenge in translating social teachings into action.

Our research has a number of implications. First, we found that although religious teaching occurs in some programs (mainly the faith-infused program), this teaching is not in contradiction with previous religious beliefs, and the girls in all our programs are believers. Hence the worry that public money is being used for proselytization may not be a real issue in many circumstances. Rather, the real work of these faith-based programs may lie in determining how best to help individuals make connections between their religious faith and their lives more generally, through means such as teaching, participation in religious practice, or involvement in a community. What our research on these four programs suggests is that only highly religiously infused programs are likely to be successful at making these connections.

Although this research does not speak to the issue of whether public monies should go to faith-infused groups, it does show that the "faith factor" in such programs may be important to their programming and outcomes. The potential importance of this factor does not contradict the idea that faith-based programs should be evaluated in the public sphere on their ability to deliver services, but the research does argue that the religiosity of faith-based programs is essential to their ability to affect life choices and behavior, and may be important for a host of social service providers. This finding is important in discussions about requirements for faith-based programs operating in the public sphere. We must add the caveat that our research dealt with Protestant programs; further studies on other kinds of faith-based organizations in other communities would need to occur to generalize these results.

We make the following policy recommendations.

Increase religious understanding. Although the girls in all programs described themselves as believers, they appeared to have little understanding of their beliefs. They expressed a desire for more opportunities to discuss their faith. Most expressed appreciation of teaching that deals with life issues; it appears that at least some of them responded to such teachings with changed behavior. The Bible also appears to be an underutilized resource. Girls commonly had little understanding of the Bible or how to think about it. Although teaching may be seen as imbuing theological ideas, it was something the girls wanted and would not have been in conflict with their previous religious beliefs.

Support spiritual practice. Most of the girls we studied prayed regularly. Yet for many of the girls, prayer is not something that motivates them, except out of a sense of fear of God. Prayer and worship are spiritual practices that can help individuals connect their religious beliefs with their lives more generally.[27] Lacy suggests that reciting prayers as a group may help the girls see themselves as part of a larger community and help them put concern for others above themselves.[28]

Integrate youth into the church community. Connecting the girls to a church community is not easy. Many who do attend church do not think of it as their community. Although some of the girls are disturbed by faults they perceive within certain churches or traditions, for others the issue may be more one of accessibility. The option to go to church is not easy or readily available; the girls may not feel welcome or connected. Most of the girls report they are willing to be more active in faith programs or enter into religious discussion; all seem to have a high level of respect for clergy. Churches associated with faith-based organizations could do more to be open to youth, letting them know they are welcome. Attendance at church activities like worship, community service programs, and study is often influenced by repeated invitation.

chapter 9

God, Abortion, and Democracy in the Pro-Life Movement

Ziad Munson

"EVERYBODY should be out in front of the [abortion] clinic whether you're Muslim, Christian, or Hebrew, it doesn't matter. You should be out there because it's a human rights issue." Andy, thirty-five, a pro-life activist from Charleston, South Carolina, is arguing that all Americans ought to resist legalized abortion.[1] "Six million Jews died during the Holocaust in Germany," he continues, "but over 100 million children have been murdered by abortion." Andy anchors such ideas in his religious faith. He explains his activism in terms of a personal encounter with Satan, and believes God called him to oppose abortion. This call occurred when "the grieving of the Holy Spirit from the hurt of all the innocent children who have been slaughtered and murdered by abortion came upon me."

Are Andy and others like him a threat to democracy? Certainly his views suggest the dark side of religion's role as a shaper of moral discourse and stimulus to political involvement: the potential for intolerance and exclusion. Yet despite the fervor with which pro-lifers express their views, and the real potential for violence, interviews with pro-life activists also show striking evidence of a simultaneous, perhaps even paradoxical, commitment to democratic principles. The pro-life movement's zealous pursuit of a moral imperative exists in tension with a respect for citizenship.

Andy takes his perceived calling from God seriously; he regularly attends antiabortion protests in different parts of the country, has been arrested several times in front of abortion clinics, was once sued by an abortion provider, and donated money to the families of those imprisoned for antiabortion violence. For Andy, those who are pro-life must answer to a higher law than the statutes protecting abortion rights.

Andy does not represent everyone in the pro-life movement, but his beliefs about abortion—and his faith—reflect common themes in the understandings of many pro-life activists in the United States today. Abortion as the murder of babies, the issue of human rights, analogies to the Holocaust, and the references to God are all common ideas within the movement. Most activists view the issue in starkly black-and-white terms: abortion is the killing of children pure and simple, an act that violates God's law and is always evil.[2] The ideas at stake are thus linked to a moral code that transcends the decisions of the country's legislatures and courts. "It's all because our government is wicked and evil," explains Andy. "They're not following in the footsteps of God as God commanded it." These words reflect a common belief in the pro-life movement that the importance of the abortion issue trumps the decisions made by political and legal institutions.

What makes the case of pro-life activists interesting, however, is that activists express these ideas while simultaneously holding strong commitments to democratic ideals. Intimidation and violence directed against abortion providers are a chilling reminder of the power of popular movements driven by outrage to curb democratically established rights. The view that such violence is justified, however, is surprisingly rare in the pro-life movement given its uncompromising views of the abortion issue. Andy, for example, talks at length about the rights of Americans, rejects the idea that violence—or even civil disobedience—is the proper response to legalized abortion, and believes that education and legislative efforts are the best means the pro-life movement has at its disposal to effect change. "I thank God we have the power to vote," he says. Pro-life activists in fact generally place great value on the very political institutions they vilify and reject for permitting abortion. If activists simply rejected state authority and democratic values as secondary to the evil of abortion, evaluation of the pro-life movement's contribution to the public square would be straightforward. The worldview of pro-life activists, however, is considerably more complicated.

This chapter explores the complex and somewhat counterintuitive absolute beliefs about abortion and equally absolute beliefs about democratic society held by pro-life activists in the United States today. Yet rank-and-file participants in the pro-life movement believe *both* that the moral evil of abortion transcends the democratic process *and* that democratic values must be held inviolate. The inherent contradiction between these two ideas is resolved in several ways within the worldview of activists. First, like Andy, many activists root their beliefs about abortion simultaneously in ideas about God and in principles of the U.S. Constitution and individual rights. The relationship between their religious views and their democratic views is in fact a syncretistic one in which activists embrace a sacralized vision of the American polity. Second, the attitude of activists toward the public square is determined more by their understanding of the most appropriate means to end abortion than by their view of abortion's moral status. In short, beliefs about action differ from moral understandings of the issue itself.

This analysis is based on life-history interview data collected in 1999 and 2000 from eighty-two rank-and-file pro-life activists in four metropolitan areas: Boston, the Twin Cities of Minneapolis and St. Paul, Charleston, and Oklahoma City. These cities were chosen because they vary in their religious composition, degree of pro-life mobilization, and regional location. Interview participants were identified through snowball sampling in each city, with a theoretical sample then selected to maximize variation in age, race, creed, and type of pro-life movement involvement. Interviews typically lasted two to three hours, and all were taped and fully transcribed. Data collection produced over 3,000 pages of transcripts that were then coded and analyzed. More complete information on the study design and data collection is available in Munson (2002). The result is a rich data set that allows us to explore the terrain of beliefs about one of the most contentious social issues in the United States, and to analyze how these beliefs are tied to the political system.

Abortion as an Absolute Evil

"You're killing. You're killing a life. This is life. It doesn't matter whether you get a gun and shoot somebody or do this. They're the same. It's the same thing." Forty-nine-year-old Oklahoma activist Dominique's words reflect the most basic and common understanding of the abortion issue expressed by pro-life activists. The belief that abortion is killing and therefore wrong is central to the movement's moral universe. Mildred, an eighty-year-old in Boston, responded without hesitation when I asked her why she was opposed to abortion. "Well, it's the killing of a life. Life is sacred." An awkward silence followed. This was the end of the story for Mildred; she didn't see any reason to elaborate on such a basic point.

At the core of the pro-life worldview is the belief that the unborn fetus is a person. Abortion is therefore morally wrong because it ends the life of a person. All other beliefs within the movement revolve around this central idea. "Killing an unborn infant is wrong," says sixty-eight-year-old Twin Cities activist John, "killing something is wrong. It's not killing a rabbit or a bird, it's a fellow human being. What do people think it is? A baby is a human being." If the fetus is a person, then others certainly have no right to end its life. Because of this belief, activists are incredulous over arguments about the right to privacy and a woman's right to control her body. If the fetus is as human as a toddler or a child or an adult, then surely its right to life supersedes these secondary rights of others.

This core idea leads activists to reject the notion that there are any circumstances under which abortion is permissible. Although public opinion is divided over where to draw the line between justified and unjustified abortion, the pro-life movement is not. Activists have one ultimate goal: an end to all abortions in the United States. Activists universally agree on this goal, even if their immediate work is focused on stopping only certain cases of abortion. Abor-

tions following rape, incest, and medical/genetic problems with the
fetus are held to be no more justified than abortions in any other
circumstances. Sandra, a thirty-four-year-old in Oklahoma City, reflects this view in her explanation of why even the rape of a ten-
year-old girl cannot justify abortion:

> A good friend of mine's little sister was . . . her mother was ten years
> old. Ten years old! Which is a horrible thing to even think about. A
> ten-year-old child getting pregnant and carrying a baby for nine
> months and laboring to give birth to a child at ten years old. But I
> can't imagine not ever knowing her. And if the woman is raped, and
> then has to go through an abortion also, how is that . . . I think it
> would be very hard to go through a nine-month pregnancy if it was
> rape. But I don't think it's in any way healing to abort it either. Every
> person is their own person in their own right, in their own merit, and
> if a life is conceived it was meant to be conceived, because it has a rea-
> son and a purpose on this Earth.

Sandra's explanation sums up many pro-life understandings of
why abortion must be stopped in all cases: every person is unique,
regardless of the circumstances of his or her conception; abortion
only compounds the pain of a crime like rape; pregnancy is a
unique gift of God, not to be judged as wanted or unwanted.

Abortion in cases of genetic disorders—supported by 78 percent
of the general public—are particularly abhorrent to pro-life activists.[3] They see abortion because of genetic defects as a kind of geno-
cide that weeds out people with undesirable characteristics. "They
were talking about abortion in cases of rape, incest, life of the
mother, psychiatric health of the mother, and defective child. And it
was the defective child one that really upset me the most," explains
Linda, a fifty-five-year-old in the Twin Cities. "That was a eugenics
thing!" Many also worry about a slippery slope in abortion mentality. A gay activist in Boston put it this way: "If they ever isolate a
gene for sexual preference, parents are going to say, 'Well, we live in
Marblehead [an affluent Boston suburb]. And I'm for gay rights,
but I don't want to subject my infant, my child who has this gene
and is going to come out gay, to that. So I'm going to abort to save

him . . . I don't want to bring a gay person in this world because it's going to be hurtful.' So genetics—that's just misguided."

The only crack in this universal consensus comes in cases where the mother's life is in jeopardy. About one-third of the movement say abortion is wrong even in these cases. We can't judge whose life is more important, the mother's or the unborn baby's, and therefore abortion is never justified. Some say that the baby's life is actually more important; the mother has lived her life, but the unborn baby has not yet had that chance. "If you understand that that is another life," says Jeff, a thirty-five-year-old in the Twin Cities, "even at the peril of your own life, you always try to do your absolute best to save that child, to save that other life."[4]

Opponents of abortion thus do not see abortion as a personal choice. Their opposition is an absolute moral commitment, absolute in the sense that it is a moral principle that brooks no exception. Even those active in the political arena, who work to outlaw or regulate abortion in only some cases, see such legislation as an "incremental" milestone toward the final goal of eliminating abortion altogether.[5] The issue is thus not one of extreme versus moderate beliefs about the core piece of the pro-life moral universe. On this issue of the moral status of abortion, the movement stands as one.

A RELIGIOUS EVALUATION OF ABORTION

Many activists, though certainly not all, root these absolute ideas about abortion in their religious beliefs.[6] All but a handful of activists in my sample are weekly churchgoers, and 68 percent participate in religious activities outside of regular worship services.[7] Specific religious traditions are relatively unimportant in activist understandings of the abortion issue. Indeed, even well-educated pro-lifers active in their churches frequently expressed confusion over the theological commitments of their congregations.[8] Activist opposition to abortion is rooted not in particular faith traditions or doctrinal teachings, but instead on the simple, nondenominational principle that God is sovereign over human life.[9] Andy reflects this belief when he notes that all religious people should be trying to stop abortion, whether they are Christian, Muslim, or Jewish.

Christina, a forty-six-year-old in Boston, is representative of what many activists have to say: "It all boils down to the belief that there is a God and he's the author of life, and that for some reason he allowed a life to be created." Because God is responsible for the creation of human life, many activists see it as hubris if not heretical to interfere with God's plans by ending such life through abortion. Ben, a seventy-nine-year-old in Charleston, sees abortion as playing God: "God is the author of life and he has his reasons for things that happen. And we may never know what they are. Even if we don't know, he's a good God, we know that. So we know that he will give you what you need, and this [an unplanned pregnancy] is probably what you need. So we can't play God in that." Human souls are imbued by God at the moment of conception. The abortion issue is thus not one that the politicians or judges are qualified or even authorized to decide. The only acceptable position on abortion, for both individuals and society as a whole, has already been decided by God.

The central tenet of the pro-life understanding of abortion is the belief that the fetus is imbued with personhood and therefore abortion represents the killing of a human being. For many this position is reinforced by a religious understanding of the sanctity of human life based on God's hand in creating life. The result is the idea that there must be an absolute prohibition against abortion and a battle against the system that allows it. "One of the most detestable sins to God is the shedding of innocent blood. And how more innocent is a child, a child inside a mother's womb?"

HITLER AND SLAVERY

On one level, then, many activists suggest that the sanctity of human life—and therefore the immorality of abortion—trumps the value of the government system that permits it. In other words, abortion is such a compelling evil that ending it is more important than support for institutions that have made abortion legal, including state and federal legislatures, the courts, and the electoral system. Activists draw on two analogies in making sense of the moral weight of abortion and its relationship to the political system: the Holocaust in Germany and slavery in the United States. The analogies serve to underscore their belief that the sanctity of human life is a principle that cannot be abandoned even in the face of a political authority that violates it.

Many pro-life activists draw parallels between legalized abortion in the United States and the Jewish Holocaust in Germany. For some, the Holocaust stands as a historical example of the evil to which abortion can lead. "If you read the history of the development of the Holocaust and how it started," explains fifty-eight-year-old Allen in Charleston, "[you will see that] early on, even before Hitler, the German government was doing abortions, they were doing infanticide, and it was getting more and more expansive and permitted. They were already getting into euthanasia before Hitler latched onto the Jews. But that previous business made what he was doing with the Jews even more acceptable . . . to the populace." Allen returns to a concern expressed earlier that abortion is a big step down a slippery slope toward almost unimaginable evil. More common is to actually equate legalized abortion with the Holocaust directly, rather than as merely a step toward a similar kind of tragedy. Typical are the thoughts of Carol, fifty-two, and Nicky, thirty-seven, both activists in Charleston:

Carol: Let's go back to Nazi Germany. And if you think about the horrors that went on there, and how people were shocked when they heard after the war was over what was going on, and why didn't they know when it was going on right under their noses. You have the same situation here. The same parallel going on right here in the United States. You have killing going on every day of the week. So many a day. And everybody is acting like nothing is going on. We're in a free society, but we don't have the freedom to kill. That's not right.

Nicky: And I say to myself, "You're going to decide that someone with an M.D. behind their name should be making ultimate decisions? Who was Hitler's right-hand man? They were very well educated men. And some of them were M.D.s. That does not make them automatically worthy to decide public policy."

The Holocaust serves as a historical point of comparison for activists like Allen, Carol, and Nicky.[10] It defines the moral category in which legalized abortion falls.

The implication of the analogy is that any reasonable person should be compelled to stop abortion, even if this means defying political and judicial authorities. Nicky's previous comments hint at this point; she feels public policy on abortion is morally wrong despite its support by physicians, just as Nazi policies were wrong despite being supported by well-educated men. Others are more direct. Consider the views of Josh, a forty-five-year-old from Oklahoma City: "I look at abortion clinics like I do the gas chambers that the Jews went to. Same type of thing. Except nobody stopped what was happening in Germany, and people are trying to stop it here . . . They go to jail. They may eventually be executed. Hitler was able to [kill], and we say that's a major disaster, but yet here we've murdered millions of our children and nobody wants [to] say, 'Hey, when is the shedding of blood going to stop?' You know? It utterly amazes me." Josh expresses the need felt by many to do something immediately to stop abortion, even if it means going to jail or being executed by the state. Ronald, fifty-four, who lives in Boston, makes the connection to basic democratic principles explicit: "Now certainly any American is going to be very struck by the idea of democracy and what the majority want. But you can't avoid the comparison that all those years when Hitler was doing what he wanted, he had won an election. And after that he had hundreds of thousands of people out there cheering and a negligible opposition and so forth like that. So I don't know if I'm struck by the idea that we just put it to a vote and so forth." Here is a clear expression of the tension between unwavering opposition to abortion and a core feature of the American political system. Ronald suggests that there are certain things that are never permissible, even when those things—the killing of Jews and abortion—are supported by a democratic majority. Abortion must be stopped even if it means certain democratic principles are undermined, because the evil is immediately present and can never be undone. "The only comparison, I think, is the Holocaust of the Jews," Ronald explains. "There are people that are here that are not going to be here. There's not going to be a second choice. It's definitive."

Activists use comparisons with slavery in the United States in the same way. Slavery too is interpreted as a historical example where the evil being done in a democratic system must be stopped even if it requires actions that lie outside the established bounds of the U.S. democratic system. Maria, a forty-nine-year-old in the Twin Cities, explains a common belief among activists:

> How much different is it to say that you have friends who, although they themselves would say they won't have an abortion, they're willing, as a taxpayer, to fund someone else's abortion or drive someone else there who is in need? How is that different than someone who might say, "Well, I probably would never have a slave myself, but I'm going to support someone else, or I'm going to keep laws that keep slaves from escaping, or I'm going to . . ."? How is that different? They're both oppressive of human rights and basic things.

The analogy extends to the historical consequence of continued slavery in the United States: civil war. Frank, fifty-eight, who lives in Boston, puts it this way: "Okay, 'I don't own slaves but I'll defend anybody's right to own slaves,' that's a crock of bullshit. Do you believe in abortion or not? Do you believe in slavery or not? We have the Civil War right there. So it's that simple. It's as simple as that." Frank's perspective highlights not only the direct comparisons made between legalized abortion and legalized slavery, but also the all-or-nothing perspective that activists take toward the abortion issue. Abortion is either right or it is wrong, just like slavery is either right or wrong, just like the Holocaust is either right or wrong. In all these cases, the answer is clear and sufficiently compelling to outweigh even the decisions of courts or the results of referendums and elections that have allowed each of these phenomena to occur.

The sanctity of life is not only a value that can trump the value of democratic institutions in cases like abortion, it is also understood as a value on which democracy itself is predicated. The sanctity of life is seen as logically prior to democratic values—thus abortion represents a threat to the political system. Only by ending abortion, therefore, is the continued health of the American system possible. Fifty-nine-year-old Barbara, an activist in the Twin Cities, puts the argument in its simplest form: "There is nothing more important than life. Everything else—peace and justice and church and everything else—none of it matters if you don't have life first." "If you look at what causes a society to disintegrate, I think the abortion issue is the most serious," echoes Dorothy, sixty-seven, an activist from Twin Cities, "because it's at the core of our person." Without protecting the sanctity of life by ending abortion, this argument goes, the entire society is in jeopardy.

Underlying the beliefs put in these simple terms is a more complex understanding of the foundations of civic life. Not only does abortion take the lives of individual human beings, but it also has the larger social effect of cheapening the value of human life more generally. "I think the broad picture of the abortion issue isn't thought through," explains Joan, sixty-nine, also from Twin Cities. "All aspects of life are being affected in our society by the decline of the respect for life." George, a sixty-eight-year-old in Charleston, expresses a similar view: "Sooner or later a nation that kills its own children legally will end up going down the tube. I think that once abortion became so prevalent and became legal, it so cheapened life in the United States, that I think it mainly—and I'm sounding real philosophical—so cheapened life that it also cheapened morality and everything." The idea that the whole country will "end up going down the tube" if abortion isn't stopped means democratic values, however cherished they might be, are irrelevant when the value of life is degraded. Abortion leads to a changed social mentality that, in turn, hurts everyone.

Activists will occasionally connect this cheapening of human life directly to the political process. More common, however, is to draw connections to rising violence and abuse in society at large. The massacre at Columbine High School was raised by several activists in this context: "I think this [abortion] is really the foundation of it all. I really truly do. I mean *life*, you take life away. I think of what our kids are growing up with, such a disposable society. I think about that tragedy in Colorado. But what are these kids seeing? They're seeing these kids give birth to babies and wrapping them in garbage bags and getting rid of them, and they've grown up with such a terrible culture."

This is the perspective of Susan, a forty-five-year-old Twin Cities activist. The culture in the United States has sunk so low, she says, that even the basic protections of civilization are no longer respected. "Spiritually we're dead," says Andy. "I mean Columbine. Children are shooting children now. Why? Well because of abortion. We're teaching them that they can kill their innocent children. Why can't they kill each other?" For these and other activists, there is little hope for our system as a whole unless abortion can be stopped.

The link between abortion and democracy is made consciously by those who understand abortion as undermining the system by eliminating those who can't speak for themselves—unborn children. Abortion is seen as a direct threat to democratic principles, because it does not treat people equally. "How can you, I mean, how can you *not* want to defend this most vulnerable, most innocent baby?" exclaims Margaret, seventy-three, who lives in Twin Cities. Activists see many of the arguments for legalized abortion as privileging a certain kind of white, middle-class, educated lifestyle. Glen, thirty-three, a Boston resident, sees the liberal emphasis on diversity and inclusiveness to be contradicted by pro-choice views on abortion: "A lot of the pro-abort arguments are very simple. It's, 'Well, these people are going to lead terrible lives. We have to have abortion so these people don't live these terrible lives.' But what are these terrible lives? Somebody who is living a terrible life is living a life of not being out in the suburbs with 2.2 kids and a white picket fence." Glen's comments typify the view that legalized abortion is rooted in social inequality; that those with a louder or more powerful voice can make their lives more convenient, even at the expense of the lives of others. It thereby undermines basic principles of freedom, equality, justice, and diversity.

Abortion also threatens our system in another way: it jeopardizes our country's relationship with God. "I think abortion is a big one for our country," says Evelyn, a fifty-year-old in Charleston. "I think we'll be judged someday for the lives that are lost." Tim, a thirty-eight-year-old in Oklahoma City, goes into much more detail: "I mean he'll forgive us if we ask him. If we turn from our wicked ways he says he'll come in and heal our land. He's a loving God, but he's also a very wrathful, vengeful God, I believe. And just because we live in the New Testament, not the Old, doesn't mean he's changed . . . He is wrathful, he's vengeful, and he doesn't appreciate people killing his creation." Tim argues that abortion is a sin that takes place not only on the individual level but on the societal level as well. By allowing legalized abortion, the country as a whole puts itself at risk. Ultimately it is God who supports a democratic way of life, and abortion mocks God's laws; it is such a flagrant violation of God's will that American society will inevitably suffer punishment unless it changes its ways. It is therefore not enough to simply convert or persuade others of this point of view. Abortion must be universally eliminated on behalf of society and on behalf of God.

Pro-life activists understand the abortion issue in absolute terms. They are absolute not only in terms of permitting no exceptions, but also in terms of not being subject to negotiation or debate. There is no argument or evidence or experience that activists believe will convince them to change their evaluation of the issue. Abortion is evil. It is wrong under all circumstances. Abortion violates God's law, a law that is higher than those made by Congress or the Supreme Court. Like the Holocaust in Germany and slavery in the United States, abortion is such an egregious crime that it necessitates action even in the face of political and legal opposition. In fact, it is abortion itself that is a threat to those institutions and the democratic values that underlie them. Abortion perpetuates an uneven playing field in which the rights of the powerless and voiceless are denied for the convenience of others. It cheapens the value of life generally and the lives of the poor, the elderly, racial minorities, and the handicapped in particular. It also jeopardizes society by inviting God's wrath on a fallen nation. This is a composite summary of the pro-life understanding of abortion as it relates to democratic life. Although no single activist necessarily expresses this moral evaluation in its entirety, it represents the worldview of the movement as a whole.

Democratic Values as Inviolate

There are thus many ways in which activists believe the abortion issue trumps democratic values. The very same activists, however, also express strong beliefs in the rule of law, the principle of nonviolence, and the paramount value of the democratic system as embodied in the U.S. Constitution. There are some notable exceptions, people who support any actions that might stop abortion. Michael, a forty-two-year-old resident of Boston, is a frightening example. Although he doesn't unambiguously endorse killing abortion providers, he is sympathetic to what the killers have done:

> You know, that clinic in Brookline where that guy shot up the place and a couple people got killed?[11] [pause] I don't have any great care for the fact that one way or another a couple people got killed. Okay, it's something that probably shouldn't have happened. But that's as far as I go with that. Those people aren't any great heroes as far as I'm concerned, either the guy who pulled the trigger or the people who got killed. They were all doing something that was wrong as far as I'm concerned. They are not heroes and their families aren't people that I have any great sympathy for, for what happened. Too bad . . . People get killed. It probably shouldn't happen, but the only reason I believe that there shouldn't be any murders of people who are working in those clinics is because it hurts our movement. And that's the only reason I feel, you know, any great regret for people getting killed.

This sentiment stands out in the thousands of pages of interview transcripts because it is so exceptional. Given the absolute beliefs of activists about abortion, one would expect widespread expressions of support for extralegal strategies for ending it. Yet only two of the eighty-two activists interviewed provided any justification for violence against abortion providers.[12] Far more common is the perspective of Doug, thirty-two, who lives in Oklahoma City: "If society says . . . [an abortion provider is] protected, then it doesn't matter if I agree with it or not. I made the choice to live in a country where I support the laws. The law protects him. Whether I agree with them or not, it doesn't mean I can override them."

In fact, activists simultaneously hold the belief that abortion transcends the political process and the belief that democracy is an ultimate value. Concern over democracy is expressed by activists even as they explain how the democratic system has produced and sustained legalized abortion. "I have always had this view, which I still sort of have, that the need for protest underscores some kind of failing of democracy," says Steve, twenty-eight, of Boston. "So I don't see it as particularly productive behavior overall." Steve has a very narrow view of the democratic process; even peaceful protest is largely excluded from the realm of legitimate activity for ending what he calls the killing of innocent human life. Glen, the thirty-three-year-old Boston activist quoted earlier who considers abortion to be "murder," nonetheless is equally clear in how he thinks the movement must approach the issue: "Through politics. Through effective spokesmen and passing legislation and through having debates. Through the debates you can change people's minds, and that leads to more legislation and things like that." Chris, a twenty-nine-year-old in the Twin Cities, agrees: "So I think any way we can fight it, you know, we should do so with the means that we are given as a country. I mean I think we've got a great country . . . You know, this is the country we live in and I'm not going to go out and kill someone. I'm going to try to change the laws of this country." Elsewhere, Chris calls abortion "the greatest sin" and tears fill his eyes when he explains how "so many babies are being killed." These beliefs do not, however, lead him to look for anything but regular, well-institutionalized, legal solutions built on an explicit respect for the democratic process.

Activists thus hold contradictory beliefs with respect to these issues. On the one hand they understand abortion as an absolute evil made possible by a flawed system. On the other hand they place uncompromising value on the system that allows abortion. Two elements of the pro-life worldview make holding these two beliefs together possible. First, although religious beliefs are important in the lives of most activists, much of the moral certainty about abortion comes from ideas about individual rights and the U.S. Constitution. This point is evident in many of the activist quotations already presented. In fact religious beliefs and beliefs about the American political system frequently are elided, and activists understand them to be one in the same value. The activists do not see the issue as an either/or question: either opposition to abortion or support for the system that sustains it. They see God, democracy, constitutional law, and so forth as all elements of the same underlying principle.

Second, there exists a sharp distinction between beliefs about ultimate values—the sanctity of human life, for example—and beliefs about the means by which those values might be achieved, for example, the political process. Hence beliefs about abortion and beliefs about politics are different kinds of beliefs, and they operate independent of one another in the moral understandings of activists. Absolute and uncompromising views on abortion therefore need not dictate an individual's beliefs about how to properly participate in civic and political life. The issue is not only that activists see democratic mechanisms as positive in instrumental terms, as a means to an end. They place independent value in procedural democracy itself.

ABORTION AND INDIVIDUAL RIGHTS

Abortion rights in the United States are based legally on the notion that the right to privacy is guaranteed by the Constitution, and laws prohibiting the procedure violate this right for pregnant women. More generally, legalized abortion is understood as part of a woman's right to control her own body—her right to choose.[13] Those who oppose abortion, however, also understand their views in terms of individual rights. From their perspective, the key issue is the "right to life" of the unborn child. Beliefs about abortion, even when held in absolute terms, are therefore not necessarily in contradiction with basic democratic values, because in many cases they extend from those principles. Recall that Andy's comments introducing this chapter refer to abortion as first and foremost a human rights issue, even as his opposition is also rooted in beliefs about the will of God.

References to individual rights, human rights, or the U.S. Constitution are as frequent as references to God in activist discourse about their beliefs. "You have the Constitution which says *everyone* is created equal, and that includes your religious preferences and everything, unless it is detrimental to society. So if your preference is to go kill people [as in abortion], that's not going to work," explains Lisa, a thirty-four-year-old in the Twin Cities. "The Constitution is what guides me in my belief of things," says Mildred, eighty, of Boston, quoted earlier. Activists feel that the principles of the country have been hijacked in making abortion legal—that the Supreme Court has perverted the meaning of the Constitution and the intent of the founding fathers. Bill, a sixty-eight-year-old in Boston, grew increasingly angry as he told me how he felt when *Roe v. Wade*[14] was handed down in 1973: "If somebody said to me in those days, we're going to have within five years a Supreme Court decision that wipes out the laws against abortion on demand in what would have been forty-six states, right across the board, I would have said you're crazy! That can't be done. Because of the Fifth, Ninth, and Fourteenth Amendments to the Constitution and the English common law that preceded those amendments to the Constitution. That can't happen here! *Well, it did!*" By the end of the story he was yelling at me, enraged at what he saw as perversion of a sacred text, the U.S. Constitution. Activists like these don't understand the issue as abortion versus democratic decision making; they understand abortion as possible only because democratic decision making has been circumvented.

Activists also don't always differentiate between the moral authority of God and the moral authority of the Constitution. Consider the following three statements by activists:

I mean each individual is valuable because God created them. And so that's where our one man-one vote, property rights, that's where this idea of human life comes from. If you don't have human life as sacred, then how can you have property rights and all this other stuff? How do you have any other rights if you don't have a right to life? (Suzanne, fifty, Charleston)

I feel like our country was founded on biblical principles. That's where the Constitution came from. (Paul, thirty-four, Oklahoma City)

This country is built up on a foundation, and the foundation of the country is built up on the word of God. And if the Constitution is coming, built up with the Ten Commandments and what they say, "Thou shalt not kill," they should stop that. They should make it illegal and vote for it and not approach it. (Dominique, forty-eight, Oklahoma City)

Such sentiments are representative of the ways in which activists synthesize understandings of their religious beliefs and beliefs about the American system. In Suzanne's case, the two are so thoroughly combined as to be inseparable; she moves back and forth between talking about God and talking about property rights and other individual rights. For Dominique and Paul, the relationship between the two is extremely close, but reflects a belief that the Constitution is an embodiment of God's law, or at the very least derivative of God's design. Activists as a rule do not seek to supplant democratic institutions with their concern over God (and, by extension, abortion). Instead, they see their work as an effort to restore "Godly" American democratic ideals from others who have twisted and subverted them.

Claire, a fifty-nine-year-old Boston woman who was quoted earlier, puts it this way: "I mean I know what the church's position is. But to me it was much more the right to life. 'Life, liberty, and the pursuit of happiness.' It was, 'how can this happen in a just country?' It was much more, not political, but governmental or whatever, than it was religious." Andy says exactly the same thing: "See abortion is a human issue. Everybody wants to make it a ministry but it's not. It's a human rights issue. You're given the right to life, to the pursuit of happiness and that's taken away from those children." Religion and the U.S. constitutional system in each of these comments are viewed as two sides of the same coin. Just as religious ideas undergird opposition to abortion, so too do they legitimate a certain understanding of the Constitution. These values, then, rather than being a source of contradiction, are instead mutually reinforcing.

CONCERN OVER ENDS AND MEANS

There is a second way in which absolute beliefs about abortion are integrated with equally absolute views of democratic institutions. When activists talk about ultimate values, concern over abortion takes precedence over virtually everything else. In translating such beliefs into implications for action, however, activists invoke democratic principles in determining the most effective and morally appropriate ways to end abortion. Democratic values are inviolate in this discussion. Morally activists value the rule of law and submission to democratic decision making. Practically they may also believe politics in general to be the wrong focus for the movement; they concentrate instead on organizing and persuasion within civil society.

Doug is a thirty-two-year-old activist in Oklahoma City quoted earlier who, like many in the pro-life movement, believes that abortion is wrong under all circumstances, even in cases where a pregnancy threatens the life of the mother. "Is there a time that life is going to be threatened? Yeah, there is. But your life is going to be threatened driving down the road too. You don't get rid of cars . . . It's just a part of life that hardships are going to happen." Doug also has a strong religious basis for his pro-life position. He sees abortion as a violation of God's plan for the world and for individual souls. "The Bible says that God knows us even before we're conceived in the womb. And so that means that before we're even conceived, there's a plan set in motion. And the conception is just a part of that plan, God's plan." Doug translates these comparatively extreme beliefs into a mainstream view of what ought to be done.[15]

Although violence against the unborn is evil to Doug, so too is working outside the law to end that violence: "I mean when we try to set ourselves above the law and be the justice system, it's almost like you, you know, there is a justice system and elected government system in place for a reason. So that we're not all vigilantes running around taking the law into our own hands." Many agree with Doug, seeing a moral requirement to keep efforts to end abortion within the limits prescribed by the law. Ruth, seventy-one, from Twin Cities, is deeply disturbed by all the violence and destruction done in the name of the movement: "Hearing in the newspapers about the burning of the clinics, the destruction, and the killing of abortionists. To have anybody pro-life be connected with that makes you ill . . . You cannot kill and be pro-life. No matter how it's done. And what does it solve? It doesn't solve anything. And the same for burning or destruction of any kind, to me is just abhorrent."

Virtually all activists have a moral commitment to acting on their beliefs in ways circumscribed by their democratic values. They see illegal tactics aimed at stopping abortion as morally tarnishing their cause as "un-Christian" and making them "no better than the abortionists."

Nor is everyone in the movement even comfortable with political solutions. Many reject electoral politics as corrupt or not equipped to deal with an issue as important as abortion. These ideas, however, lead them not to reject the value of the system altogether but rather to turn their attention to strategies focused on public awareness and education. Stan, forty-one, from Oklahoma City, helped establish a pro-life organization focusing on public outreach; it provides pro-life speakers to schools, publishes a pro-life newspaper insert, and operates a pro-life exhibit. He summarizes a common view of politics in the movement: "The [abortion] issue is a lot deeper than politics. Politics is just a result. When you look at a plant, what do you see? We see the flowers and leaves and the branches or whatever. We see the top of it. But really what is underneath is a root. Now if you said, 'I hate roots. Get rid of the roots and just stick that plant back in the ground.' What will happen?

Will it thrive? No, it will die without the root. So the root of the problem is not politics. The root of the problem is the hearts of men."

Thus many activists see the problem of abortion as reaching deeper than politics. They reject politics not because it lacks legitimacy, but because it is ineffective, corrupt, or controlled by enemies of the movement. These activists concentrate on bringing the pro-life message to the general public or convincing individual pregnant women to carry their pregnancies to term. The strategy is thus not to circumvent or overturn the system. These activists seek to influence the system—in which they place great value—by addressing what they see as the underlying reasons abortion has become legalized and so common.

Where Does This Leave Us?

Participants in the American pro-life movement possess an absolute and uncompromising belief that abortion is wrong. It is a moral understanding that is rooted in deeply held religious beliefs. Abortion is wrong for many because it violates God's will, it violates scripture, and it violates the teachings of the Catholic and other churches. Abortion, they believe, is evil. Such beliefs raise legitimate questions about how the abortion issue can be negotiated within a democratic system. The actual divisiveness and occasional violence of the public debate since 1973 only deepens these questions. What role can religious ideas play in the public square? How can commitments that are understood to transcend democratic principles be debated in and incorporated into a democratic process? How do activists integrate their beliefs about abortion and beliefs about legitimate authority and action?

To answer such questions with any finality requires further study. But any discussion of them is flawed if it does not recognize that the beliefs of the pro-life movement are not monolithic. The activists' words help us to see the multiple layers of meaning and moral understanding that those in the movement bring to their activism. To some degree, one must look not only at their discourse but at their actions. Activists do express their views on abortion in black-and-white, all-or-nothing terms. Through comparisons and analogy, they suggest that almost any means would be justified for ending abortion. Given this perspective, then, it is noteworthy that the number of those who advocate stepping outside the boundaries of legitimate civil discourse and action is small. Thus even when we can clearly summarize the range of beliefs held about abortion, the implications for participation in the political system are unclear. A more finely tuned analysis of the overall worldview of activists is needed.

Activists couple a belief in abortion as an issue that trumps the ordinary operation of the system with a belief in the moral sovereignty of democratic principles. Moreover, these two beliefs are held simultaneously, with no apparent sense of tension or contradiction. This is possible for two reasons. First, the moral certainty about activists' abortion beliefs comes in part from their ideas about democratic principles, especially as they are embodied in the U.S. Constitution and in myths about the founding fathers and the creation of the American republic. The authority of God and the authority of the Constitution are frequently elided. Outrage over legalized abortion is thus rooted in an understanding of freedom, individual rights, and justice. Activists' beliefs about abortion can therefore transcend the democratic system without actually challenging it. Second, beliefs about abortion and about democracy shift in their meaning in subtle but important ways as activists move from talking about moral beliefs to talking about the practical implications of those beliefs. Although abortion is attached to the moral category of the sanctity of life in abstract discussions of value, beliefs about democracy and moral action take precedence when activists consider how they should actually address the abortion issue.

Ultimately the evidence suggests that the religious basis of pro-life beliefs is not particularly salient to the way in which activists enact their beliefs. Religious beliefs underlie the ideas activists bring to the public debate and are deployed as strategic resources to win public support, legislative action, and legal decisions. At the same time, these religious beliefs are tied to a range of other ideas about the proper functioning of a democratic system and the values on which the system rests. The pro-life movement's participation in the system thus can only be understood by analyzing its overall worldview. From this perspective the movement appears less as an extreme case—certainly less than Andy's opening remarks would suggest—and more like a common, if complex, example of the way in which ideas, religion, and politics regularly interact in the public square.

Engaging and Evaluating Religion's Public Roles

WE BEGAN this project with the realization that academics have generally tended to ignore or underrate religion as a major strand in the fabric of public life in America. Whatever lies behind this oversight, it has meant that students preparing for roles in the public, private, and nonprofit sectors have devalued a huge segment of American associational life and underestimated the pervasive interplay between religion and democracy. As scholars and as public intellectuals concerned about the quality and vitality of American life, we sought to contribute to an emerging conversation that takes religion seriously in the American context.[1]

Our approach to the social contributions of religion in America is one of constructive engagement. We thus invite those who might otherwise overlook it to recognize faith as it functions in religious organizations, civic life, and political affairs. Our perspective requires not only recognizing, however, but also evaluating those contributions, in terms of both the norms religion sets for behavior and how it actually functions, from the vantages of the polity and of religious and secular organizations. We are required, in short, to both engage and evaluate religious organizations and practice.

The nine case studies we have presented seek to do this within our analytical framework, which, as we saw in the Introduction, proposes six related roles or functions:

- Fostering expression: religion fosters expression of personal beliefs and identity.

- Forming identities: such expression shapes the identities, virtues, and commitments of communities, organizations, and individuals.

- Creating social bonds: religious groups and practices create and sustain social bonds and networks.

- Shaping moral discourse: religious groups and practices shape the character and quality of moral discourse.

- Enabling participation: religious affiliation and practice enable civic engagement and political participation.

- Providing social services: religious groups and organizations serve as providers of social services.

Recognizing Religion

The framework helps us accomplish our two goals of engaging and evaluating. In seeking to engage or recognize religion, a number of our cases have shown that this framework helps to avoid distortions of analysis and misunderstandings of religion created by a focus on one role. The concept of "compassionate conservatism," for example, which is currently in vogue with politicians, focuses attention on supporting "armies of compassion" providing social services to those in need. Yet the congregations analyzed in Chapters 2, 3, and 4 reveal how this singular focus can distort the actual capacities of congregations to perform this function. Bane's study of Catholic parishes, including many located in low-income neighborhoods, shows an absence of institutional resources to create social capital in such communities. McRoberts's examination of minority congregations in a low-income neighborhood challenges the common assumption that such faith communities have a pervasive religious motivation to provide social services for the larger community. Of twenty-nine congregations, only a few offered social services, although the most ambitious of these had received vast attention from public officials and the media. Coffin's account of moral debate in suburban congregations notes that congregational social services are limited and episodic and primarily address emergency needs.

Applying the framework has also shown how a singular focus, in exaggerating one of religion's roles, can ignore or devalue others. Bane invites us not to overlook the fact that Catholic parishes, though lacking social capital, sustain a rich liturgical tradition that shapes Catholic identity; they also disseminate an evolving body of Catholic social teachings that inform public moral discourse. McRoberts invites us to consider how "member-serving organizations" may be mechanisms by which disadvantaged groups provide members spiritual, social, and material resources; they may also, in some instances, serve as "bridging social capital," linking marginal to mainstream members of ethnic-racial congregations. Coffin invites us to recognize that as congregations negotiate thick moral discourse over time, they cultivate the skills of citizenship that allow their members to negotiate deep differences with respect in other settings as well.

Our broad framework for constructive engagement deepens understanding of religious practices by attending to how their multiple roles interact and to how their interaction depends on particular institutional and social contexts. Hall's exploration of eighteenth- and nineteenth-century civic Protestantism demonstrates that religion functioned in multiple and interrelated ways during periods of social change to create innovative institutional mechanisms through which diverse citizens of faith pursued common public interests. Ammerman takes up this insight in her examination in Chapter 5 of contemporary American congregations, showing how patterns of religious rhetoric, norms, and polities continue to foster distinct patterns of civic engagement. Thiemann as a theologian and Wilson as a social scientist, in Chapters 6 and 7, extend this line of inquiry to gain insight into how theological identities are transposed onto competitive organizations providing nursing home care for the elderly in a rapidly changing industry.

This framework of constructive engagement enables us to recognize the multiple roles of religion, as well as the interaction of those roles. The enhancement of one role, for example, may be enabled or constrained by others. Our framework also helps us to see that such patterns vary according to institutional and social context.

Evaluating Religion

We have argued that "taking faith seriously" also requires evaluating religious practices, which means we must challenge assumptions that religion's roles are either uniformly positive or uniformly negative. Rather, researchers and practitioners must evaluate the interactive roles of religion in the contexts of government and of secular and religious organizations.

Religious functions can and must be evaluated both normatively and functionally. Those evaluating religion from the perspective of the polity have the normative obligation to determine that policy neither discriminates against nor grants an advantage to religious organizations in achieving public aims. As stewards of public resources, those in government must also evaluate what kinds of public-religious partnerships are likely to draw on comparative advantages and to minimize liabilities, and how such partnerships are to be held accountable for achieving public outcomes. Those evaluating religion from the standpoint of secular organizations must ask whether the missions of religious organizations are compatible with those of their secular counterparts, and what unique resources religious partners might bring to civic partnerships. When religious and secular organizations pursue partnerships, both need to be held accountable by analyzing their operational contributions, limitations, and outcomes.

Religious groups must evaluate their roles according to standards of faithfulness, whether they are expressing their beliefs, shaping the identity of individuals, forming strong communities, engaging civic and political life, or serving others. But here again, normative commitments cannot exclude some functional analysis of how well these purposes are being carried out; how accentuating one role may limit the effectiveness of others; or how the activities of one religious organization affect, or are affected by, the wider society. Constructive engagement thus not only involves openness with respect to religion and American democracy but necessitates, in effect, a three-way conversation among the polity, secular organizations, and religious organizations in which each must evaluate the functions of religion according to their respective missions and needs.

Our cases suggest several ways this process might work. One is that our framework may help to clarify fundamental differences between these three sectors and thus serve to clarify the importance of maintaining boundaries. Chapter 8, by Reynolds and Winship on teen pregnancy, provides an illustration. If only faith-infused, holistic ministries are effective, then it may be wise, for the sake of both religion and the polity, to reinforce the boundary between faith-motivated agencies that focus on secular outcomes and those ministries of service that necessarily promote their own form of religious practice. At the other extreme, careful evaluation may reveal that what are perceived to be explosive "flash points" between religion and democracy are overstated, as Munson's study of the pro-life movement suggests. Finally, engagement and evaluation may reveal ways in which religious and secular organizations are not categorically different but are mutually informative and reinforcing, though different in important ways. For example, secular nonprofit organizations may gain insight from their religious counterparts on how shared narratives sustain their mission; and religious organizations may learn from secular partners how measuring effectiveness supports their mission. This prospect that religious and secular organizations may fruitfully interact deserves further exploration through constructive engagement.

Hypotheses for Taking Religion Seriously

We offer two hypotheses and a proposal, viewing them as guiding theses to be tested by ourselves and others.

The first hypothesis is that, however difficult it may be to calculate, many of religion's social contributions are functionally good for our democracy. A vibrant and pluralist democracy draws its vitality from a rich civic and associational life. In this country, an enormous portion of the deepest and most enduring forms of associational life continues to be religious. Vital democracy also depends upon values and character embodied in a democratic citizenry shaped by families, neighborhoods, and schools. These in turn are influenced by religious traditions and practices.

Constitutionally guaranteed religious freedom in our liberal democratic polity recognizes and safeguards the sacred obligation felt by many citizens of faith to worship and serve God. All of the traditions represented in this volume celebrate both the right and the mandate of religious citizens to worship. Moreover, the diversity captured in this limited set of cases demonstrates the fact that religious freedom yields a deep and richly pluralistic society where citizens may exercise what they perceive as sacred obligations in particularistic settings and practices. Democratic rights are thus concretized for citizens of faith of all traditions, not only those we studied, through practices of worship and service.

But do religious organizations and religious practices actually function in the ways that are mostly good for the functioning of democracy? If so, do their contributions outweigh the dangers of intolerance, moral absolutism, or exclusionary claims or language that prohibit debate? In general the findings of our nine cases are reassuring. They demonstrate, in a variety of contexts, religion's capacity for positive social contributions to civic and democratic life and, in the examples we studied, do not show signs of serious harm.

For example, Ammerman's survey of Christian churchgoers reveals the degree to which differing ways of accounting for a good Christian life create different expectations about whether and what sorts of contributions to the larger community are valued. Golden Rule narratives of mutual care evolve into informal assistance in the community, but also unfold in volunteering and giving. Activist narratives of seeking justice and change evolve into organizational participation and financial support for agencies serving the world. And evangelical narratives of eternal salvation and personal piety may not include much worldly engagement, but may still provide member-serving edification, bonds, and social support.

The religious cultures of individual denominations and congregations also influence what people do for their communities. Liberal Protestant churches provide a public narrative of engagement that encourages individual action, even when nothing else about a person's life would predict civic service. And conservative Protestant churches offer less support of the kind that promotes social engagement. But no matter what the church culture and no matter what the individual's own predispositions and resources, the interaction of church life seems to have a force of its own. Across all the traditions we examined, those who are most involved in their churches are also most engaged in serving the community. Even when the social capital being generated does not seem to be of the "bridging" variety, it may have bridging effects nonetheless.

Ammerman's findings are supported by several of the case studies: for example, Bane's study of Catholic parishes and Coffin's description of Lexington congregations. The most interesting example of the generally benign interaction of religion and democracy, however, is Munson's study of the pro-life movement in Chapter 9. This case demonstrates that even firmly held, non-negotiable beliefs rooted in inspired truth can be consistent with, and indeed contribute to, the democratic process. Antiabortion activists believe both that legalized abortion is an evil that transcends the democratic process and also that the democratic process is itself a transcendent and inviolable value. Beliefs about God and beliefs about constitutional democracy are in fact closely intertwined in the pro-life movement.

Our case studies support the proposition that religious organizations do indeed contribute to civic life in multifaceted ways; moreover, the tensions they pose in doing so are not particularly worrisome. The findings are also consistent with a developing body of policy thinking that suggests that the wall of separation between church and state is much more porous than many people think. And our findings support a growing willingness on the part of public officials, religious leaders, and civic leaders to explore partnerships for individual welfare and community development on the understanding that even-handed constructive engagement, rather than separation, is the appropriate stance.

A Second Hypothesis

Our second hypothesis is that the instrumental contributions religion makes to our pluralist democracy are anchored in the intrinsic commitments of religious faith. Intrinsic commitments take many forms and are cultivated in many settings. The tradition of constitutional democracy centers on a regard for all members of society as free and equal citizens. So, too, many religious practices involve such intrinsic commitments as trust in and obedience to God, openness to the sacred, and service to the neighbor. Thus we are not merely making the instrumental claim that religion fosters community and good character for the sake of the polity; we propose that many of the same practices that benefit democracy are anchored in faithfulness as practiced in many religious traditions, and not only those examined here.

We worked hard to avoid in our cases and our conversation a stance that regards religion solely in utilitarian terms. We did not ask, at least after a while, what religion could do for democracy or civil society or particular social ills. Instead, we determined to study and present religious practices and religious organizations in their own terms, to examine them in the context of their own missions, and to assess them on the dimension of faithfulness. This stance required us to view the six roles of our framework in a different light. We came to recognize that these roles may be understood as integral dimensions of religious practice. From one perspective, they may be valued and evaluated as an instrumental contribution to civic and political life. From another, they may be valued and evaluated as aspects of faithful religious discipleship. Religious traditions obviously vary enormously, and no general statements can be made about "religion." But we found in our research examples of religious traditions articulating and practicing the virtues of pluralist democracy in the context of their own commitments and missions.

The limited cases in this book fail to reflect the vast diversity of religious communities in which American citizens seek social, moral, and spiritual edification. The cases do inform us, however, that religious communities are not merely the settings for autonomous individuals to engage in self-expression and spiritual improvement. Religious communities are thick cultural spaces of narrative, ritual, and social interaction. They serve not merely to express individuals' values but to form their particular identities, values, and motivations.

In McRoberts's study, we see the churches in a predominantly poor, black neighborhood socialize members to interpret the proximate public areas in a variety of ways. Only one of these interpretations inspires "service" to local populations, and that sole interpretation only awkwardly fits the type envisioned by many advocates of faith-based social welfare. All of these churchly ways of understanding the street, however, are infused with religious meanings that help the faithful make sense of themselves in the context of the devastated environment in which they worship. If policy is to envision the public role of churches mainly in terms of welfare provision, it should not base this vision solely on the generic religious imperative to "do good works." Policy must also consider the lived aspects of church life in poor neighborhoods, especially those facets of faith undermined by religious people's fearful encounters with the street.

Our studies allowed us to explore still other aspects of our framework from the perspectives of religious engagement in society. Hall's historical study in Chapter 1 contrasts sectarian and civic Protestants in eighteenth- and nineteenth-century America. As the quest for salvation took ever more diverse forms, civic Protestants articulated a religious understanding of being called to public service—not to proselytize but to reform social, political, and economic institutions. To do so, men and women needed to found nonsectarian, voluntary associations to work together effectively for common aims. Civic Protestantism thus helped to inspire the architecture of a voluntary sector in which citizens had the choices necessary to exercise their religious calling to public service.

Thiemann's study of Lutheran services provides an important perspective in keeping with Hall's historical analysis. He argues that Lutheran theology, which sees salvation as a free gift from God rather than as a product of human good works, mandates care based solely on need. Its goal is the salvation of neither the neighbor in need nor the person providing the care. Lutherans judge the quality of the services they provide by criteria of effectiveness that do not look particularly different from those used by good secular agencies. This fact is not an accommodation to secular incentives but instead an outgrowth of Lutheran theology.

When viewed from an instrumental stance, a broadened framework for understanding religion allows us to recognize multifaceted roles, their possible contributions, and tension points in the polity. When viewed in terms of intrinsic religious commitments, the framework allows us to recognize how different types of religious practice engage the polity and how different dimensions of religious practice influence one another.

Ammerman's survey suggests that the challenges of transmitting religious narratives of community engagement are different for liberal Protestants than for Catholics, who are in turn different from members of African-American churches or conservative Protestants. As Hall has shown, the culture of liberal Protestantism provides both deeply ingrained narratives of civic engagement and ample congregational connections with the larger community. Most challenging for liberals is their relatively lower level of investment in their own churches and traditions as well as the declining membership of their churches. Ammerman's findings suggest that higher investment in church participation might further enhance and deepen liberal engagement. Bane's study shows how this can occur. Catholics are highly invested in their own religious tradition, and that tradition provides them with a rich store of ideas and narratives of service, but Catholic parishes fail to provide the structures and activities through which social capital can be generated and expended in behalf of the community. As Bane argues, the parishes' challenge is to create active communities where broad-based participation can connect Church teaching with everyday life. Coffin's study demonstrates how such active participation in religious communities can yield beneficial civic by-products.

Conservative Protestants, for much of the twentieth century, created church cultures dominated by narratives of individual salvation and piety, but those very cultures also taught practical virtues of participation and caring. In recent years those virtues have increasingly been put to work in service of the larger community. The intense church participation that conservatives foster is an asset that could also be a liability—if, for example, their care of others was contingent on some degree of religious belief. Their challenge is to find ways to share in caring for the larger community while maintaining their particular religious commitments. In doing that, they might learn from their African-American counterparts. There the emphasis on salvation and piety is equally high, and church participation is a central component in many members' lives, but so is community service and political participation. America's historically black churches are its best examples of religious traditions that combine concern for the well-being of the polity, sacred stories that mobilize this-worldly action, and local congregations that care for, and build up the civic skills of, their members. The continuing influence of these evolving traditions calls us to recognize that religious practices are not a reservoir of resources the polity can leverage to achieve its objectives. Each practice is anchored in intrinsic commitments that inform the ways in which individuals and organizations engage the polity. Members of those traditions claim the independence to do so as partners, resisters, or prophetic critics.

A Proposal

Our proposal emerges from our two hypotheses. Because so much of religion's contributions are good for democracy and because these contributions are anchored in faithful religious practices, we propose that creative initiatives to strengthen the intrinsic religious practices of faith communities will also serve the instrumental aims of helping to strengthen pluralistic civil society and participatory democracy.

With the recent decline in denominational loyalty, many Americans today experience less religious bigotry and intolerance than did their parents and grandparents. This supports our judgment that contemporary American society is not only more religious but also more religiously tolerant than many other societies, as studies have shown.[2] At the same time, the arrival of new immigrant groups, particularly those from Muslim countries, is challenging this tolerance in new ways.

We have also seen a reemergence of public religiosity in America: not solely in the social justice visions of the civil rights era or the emergence of the religious right, but in diverse other expressions of religious identity and values. One possibility is that this trend will contribute to the polarization that characterizes American politics and culture.

We do not believe either that tolerance will neutralize religion or that religion must be walled off from public life. Rather we should recognize and strengthen those forms of religious practice that nurture strong identities and strong commitments to democratic tolerance and mutual respect. In that spirit, we make these recommendations.

To religious leaders and their counterparts in civil society. Our case studies illustrate what appears to us to be missed opportunities in terms of religious organizations' faithfulness to their own traditions. One example comes from Bane's description of Catholic parishes, where the rich Catholic social justice tradition often fails to be translated into effective action in the world. She suggests that this failure may reflect insufficient appreciation of two key components: structures and activities that support associational life, on the one hand, and models within parishes of effective practices of democratic participation, on the other. Bane suggests that more parish participation, volunteering, and service will enrich American civic life, but, more important, that faithfulness to the Catholic tradition requires more attention to these issues. In this context our advice to religious leaders, both within the Catholic tradition and outside it, is to do a better job at your core mission, which incidentally will have benefits for society.

Another example comes from Thiemann's discussion of the response of the Topton and Tressler homes to the financial incentives provided by government as funding expanded for child welfare services. Thiemann suggests that the agencies' eagerness to adapt to secular norms for service delivery led for a time to a diminution of religious motivation and of ties to other religious bodies. This did not necessarily diminish the quality of service to the neighbor in need, which is in fact the Lutheran theological mandate, but it did modify the religious character of the organizations and thus, perhaps, some of the unique qualities of its service. Here the advice is not to compromise the core mission in the service of a public good; doing so helps neither the religious organization nor the public.

A third example comes from the four churches in McRoberts's case that articulate their mission as evangelizing the street but fail to overcome the fear that keeps them from doing so effectively. Here the missed opportunity is that of saving souls, in the language of the church, which might have the incidental benefit for society of beginning a process of transformation from social disruption to good citizenship. From our broader perspective, we observe that some of these churches fail to take advantage of the public and neighborhood resources that might help them deal with their fears and allow them to more effectively pursue their mission. Our advice is to recognize the inherently public context and character of religious practice and the need to develop tools for more effective action within that context.

Our advice to religious leaders, then, is to be true to and good at what you do, recognizing that your ability to do so is shaped by the inherently public character of religious organizations and activities. The theology of most, though not all, of the religious groups described in our cases articulates the notion of God's mission to the world and the brotherhood and sisterhood of all humanity under God. Such ideas have a powerful capacity to build ties between people. And healthy democratic pluralism rests on a civil society in which ties of some kind, even weak ones, stretch across groups. Both religious leaders and their secular counterparts in the nonprofit world therefore need to figure out ways to build these bridges. One can imagine, for example, ties between the churches in McRoberts's study and nonprofit health, social services, and community organizations, to their mutual benefit.

Coffin's study of Lexington raises another set of issues related to religious and secular civil society. Liberal and conservative churches in Lexington were able to structure a civilized dialogue on an important public issue, the inclusion of gays and lesbians in the community. The exploration of serious moral issues is, of course, central to the practice of many religious communities. It is also central to the ideal of deliberative democracy. Yet no religious leaders in this affluent town were able to generate moral deliberation over issues of economic exclusion or inequality, either in their congregation or in the broader community. Many congregations in affluent communities face a challenge that is both religious and civic: how to articulate and act on moral visions of just participation for all citizens of American liberal democracy.

To the polity. One set of implications for the American polity is clear: recognize religious organizations for the unique, diverse institutions that they are, and respect them as such; also understand that they exist to fulfill their own missions, not to serve expectations of the state. Recognize that a flourishing religious life, including worship, fellowship, service, moral dialogue, and sometimes prophetic confrontation, is good for pluralist democracy; and that religious life can flourish when the state is even-handed in its dealings with religious groups.

Our cases also raise more specific issues about public/religious partnerships with regard to service delivery. An important lesson from McRoberts's account is that only one of the twenty-nine churches in Four Corners saw engagement in transformative social service as part of its mission; thus only one would seem to be a plausible partner with government, even if the issue of mixing service with evangelization could be worked out. This case supports the emerging viewpoint that a great mass of small congregations ready to rise to the challenge of charitable choice may in fact not exist—because of inconsistency in mission as much as lack of resources. An equally important lesson comes from the Wilson and Thiemann cases: that the large mainstream religious social service organizations have accommodated very well to government requirements and incentives, perhaps so well that they have lost some of their distinctively religious character. The most important lessons may come from the Reynolds and Winship case. Their examination of programs for teenage girls suggests that faith motivation does not in itself lead to greater effectiveness. The program that seemed to be more effective, however, was fully faith filled, thus raising all the difficult questions about separating religious from secular activity—a fundamental necessity if federal funds are to be made available for the one but not the other. This case suggests that an assumption that religious sponsorship and motivation will result in positive outcomes in areas where secular service programs have traditionally failed is naïve. Thus the construction of such partnerships is likely to be more difficult and controversial than some expect. Constructive engagement between religion and polity will require ongoing engagement and evaluation from multiple perspectives.

Postscript

Looking back over our multiyear discussion, we realized that we have been attempting to practice constructive engagement. In the process, differences among our disciplines and the assumptions rooted in them became clearer. So too has been our need to draw on one another's insights. We have realized, for example, the importance of combining analytical and narrative approaches. We have found it necessary to find better tools to understand complex realities—for example, analyzing how individuals build identity and develop agency across many social settings; or learning how to assess the influence of religious values on complex organizations. Above all, we have realized the importance of grounding serious discussions of religion and polity in empirical studies of lived experience in different locations.

As we noted at the outset, our limited set of cases omits many important forms of religious life; and, with two exceptions, the cases have not placed the interaction of religion and polity in historical perspective. Despite these limitations, we believe our cases and collective discussion warrant the broader argument we have made. American polity, as it has evolved, has never been the construct of a secular society, nor is it being constructed by one today. Beyond the mythic wall of privatization, religious communities continue to pursue their own missions, in most cases respecting the fundamental right of fellow citizens to pursue theirs.

Thus we have proposed an alternative to dogmatic secularism, on the one hand, and what we have called faith-based boosterism, on the other. The alternative we propose invites us to adopt a stance of critical openness toward religion's place in public life, to develop a broader framework for recognizing its multiple roles, and to engage in critical assessment from the standpoints of the polity, secular institutions, and religious communities. Our hope is that constructive engagement will allow us to understand better how religion and liberal democracy continue to construct each other in the American context, and how the American case both informs and is informed by other societies in our global context.

Notes / Bibliography / Contributors / Index

Notes

Introduction

1. The Introduction was written by Mary Jo Bane, Brent Coffin, and Richard Higgins, and draws substantially from a longer working paper by Martha Minow and Mark Moore.
2. See Jose Casanova, *Public Religions in the Modern World* (Chicago, 1994); Nancy Rosenblum, ed., *Obligations of Citizenship and Demands of Faith: Religious Accommodation in Pluralist Democracies* (Princeton, 2000); Christian Smith, ed., *The Secular Revolution: Power, Interests, and Conflict in the Secularization of American Public Life* (Berkeley, 2003). The *American Sociological Review* published a symposium on religion in spring 2003. The *American Journal of Sociology* published about a dozen reviews of books on religion in 2002 and 2003; the *Journal of Politics* also reviewed several books on religion. Economists have also begun studying the effects of religion. The National Bureau for Economic Research recently published working papers on religion and education, religion and economic growth, and religion and economic attitudes.
3. John Rawls, *Political Liberalism* (New York, 1996).
4. David Tracy, *The Analogical Imagination: Christian Theology in the Culture of Pluralism* (New York, 1981), 13.
5. George Gallup Jr. and D. Michael Lindsay, *Surveying the Religious Landscape: Trends in U.S. Belief* (Harrisburg, PA, 1999), 9–11; Robert Putnam, ed., *Democracies in Flux: The Evolution of Social Capital in Contemporary Society* (New York, 2002), 66.

6. Diana Eck, *A New Religious America* (San Francisco, 2001).
7. Martha Minow, *Partners, Not Rivals: Privatization and the Public Good* (Boston, 2002).
8. Zelman v. Simmons-Harris, 536 U.S. 639 (2002). See also Good News Club v. Milford Central School, 533 U.S. 98 (2001); Mitchell v. Helms, 530 U.S. 793 (2000); Agostini v. Felton, 521 U.S. 203 (1997); Rosenberger v. University of Virginia, 515 U.S. 819 (1995); Zobrest v. Catalina Foothills School Dist., 509 U.S. 1 (1993); Witters v. Washington Dept. of Services for the Blind, 474 U.S. 481 (1986).
9. Stephen R. Glassroth v. Roy S. Moore, 335 F.3d 1282, 2003 U.S. App. LEXIS 13412 (2003); Stephen R. Glassroth v. Roy S. Moore, 242 F.Supp. 2d 1067 (M. D. Ala. 2002); John Johnson, "Panel Removes Alabama's 'Ten Commandments Judge,' " *Los Angeles Times* (November 14, 2003).
10. Putnam, *Democracies in Flux,* intro.
11. Michael O. Emerson and Christian Smith, *Divided by Faith: Evangelical Religion and the Problem of Race in America* (New York, 2000); Robert Wuthnow and John H. Evans, eds., *The Quiet Hand of God: Faith-Based Activism and the Public Role of Mainline Protestantism* (Berkeley, 2002).
12. Sidney Verba, Kay Lehman Schlozman, and Henry E. Brady, *Voice and Equality: Civic Voluntarism in American Politics* (Cambridge, MA, 1995).

1. The Rise of the Civic Engagement Tradition

1. W. Lloyd Warner and Paul S. Lunt, *The Social Life of a Modern Community* (New Haven, CT, 1941).
2. E. Digby Baltzell, *Puritan Boston and Quaker Philadelphia: Two Protestant Ethics and the Spirit of Class Authority and Leadership* (New York, 1979).
3. Joseph S. Davis, *Essays on the Earlier History of American Corporations* (Cambridge, MA, 1917).
4. Robert D. Putnam, Robert Leonardi, and Raffaella Y. Nanetti, *Making Democracy Work: Civic Traditions in Modern Italy* (Princeton, NJ, 1993).
5. Robert D. Putnam, *Bowling Alone: The Collapse and Revival of American Community* (New York, 2000), 66.
6. Ibid., 76–78.
7. Thomas H. Jeavons, "Identifying Characteristics of 'Religious' Organizations," in *Sacred Companies: Organizational Aspects of Religion*

and Religious Aspects of Organizations, ed. N. J. Demerath III, Peter Dobkin Hall, Terry Schmitt, and Rhys H. Williams (New York, 1998).

8. Laurence R. Iannacone, "Why Strict Churches Are Strong," in Demerath et al., *Sacred Companies,* 269–291; quotation from 270.

9. Ibid., 277.

10. David Swartz, "Secularization, Religion, and Isomorphism: A Study of Large Nonprofit Hospital Trustees," in Demerath et al., *Sacred Companies,* 330.

11. David C. Hammack and Peter Dobkin Hall, "Panel on Trends in Civic Leadership in Six American Cities" (paper presented at the annual meeting of the Social Science History Association, November 2003).

12. Conrad Edick Wright, *The Transformation of Charity in Postrevolutionary New England* (Boston, 1992).

13. Alexis de Tocqueville, *Democracy in America,* vol. 1, trans. Henry Reeve (New York, 1945), 305–306.

14. Lee Soltow and Edward Stevens, *The Rise of Literacy and the Common School in the United States: A Socioeconomic Analysis to 1870* (Chicago, 1981), 159.

15. Timothy Dwight, *Travels in New England and New York,* 4 vols. (Cambridge, MA, 1969), 4: 410–411.

16. Bruce C. Daniels, *The Connecticut Town: Growth and Development* (Middletown, CT, 1979).

17. Richard Bushman, *From Puritan to Yankee: Character and the Social Order in Connecticut, 1690–1765* (New York, 1967).

18. Gordon S. Wood, *The Creation of the American Republic, 1776–1787* (New York, 1969), 427–429.

19. Rhys Isaac, *The Transformation of Virginia, 1740–1790* (Chapel Hill, NC, 1982).

20. James Madison, "Memorial and Remonstrance against Religious Assessments," in *The American Enlightenment,* ed. Adrienne Koch (New York, 1965), 382–385.

21. Richard J. Purcell, "Connecticut in Transition, 1775–1818," published by the American Historical Association, 1918, 11.

22. Wood, *Creation,* 427–428.

23. M. Louise Greene, *The Development of Religious Liberty in Connecticut* (New Haven, CT, 1905).

24. Zephaniah Swift, *A System of the Laws of the State of Connecticut* (Windham, CT, 1795).

25. Timothy Dwight, "The Triumph of Infidelity" (1788), in *The Connecticut Wits,* ed. Vernon L. Parrington (New York, 1969), 236.

26. Timothy Dwight, "Greenfield Hill" (1794), in *The Connecticut Wits,* ed. Parrington, 272.

27. Charles I. Foster, *An Errand of Mercy: The Evangelical United Front, 1790–1837* (Chapel Hill, NC, 1960); Clifford S. Griffen, *Moral Stewardship in the United States, 1800–1865* (New Brunswick, CT, 1960); and David F. Allmendinger, *Paupers and Scholars: The Transformation of Student Life in Nineteenth-Century New England* (New York, 1972).

28. Dwight, *Travels,* 4: 283. Subsequent quotations from 4: 403, 405, 406; 3: 64–67.

29. Lyman Beecher, *Autobiography,* vol. 1, ed. Barbara M. Cross (Cambridge, MA, 1961), 175–176. Subsequent quotations from 177–184.

30. Tocqueville, *Democracy,* 2: 110.

31. William Ellery Channing, "Associations," *Christian Examiner,* September 1829.

32. Beecher, *Autobiography,* 1: 192. Subsequent quotations from 1: 190–193, 253; 2: 107, 108, 109–110.

33. Allmendinger, *Paupers and Scholars.*

34. Mary P. Ryan, *Cradle of the Middle Class: The Family in Oneida, New York, 1790–1865* (New York, 1982), 105.

35. Dwight, *Travels,* 3: 64.

36. Lyman Beecher, *A Plea for the West* (Cincinnati: Truman and Smith, 1835), 11. Subsequent quotations from 10, 15, 16, 23, 30, 44, 20.

37. Jonathan Edwards, *The Works of Jonathan Edwards,* vol. 1 (Andover, MA, 1842), 482.

38. Dwight, *Travels,* 1: 622.

39. Ibid., 1: 561; 2: 8.

40. John Terrill Wayland, *The Theological Department in Yale College, 1822–1858* (New York, 1987), 82.

41. Taylor to Beecher, January 14, 1819, in Beecher, *Autobiography,* 1: 384.

42. Nathaniel W. Taylor, *Concio ad Clerum: A Sermon Delivered in the Chapel of Yale College, September 10, 1828* (New Haven, CT, 1828), 13.

43. Wayland, *Theological Department,* 326.

44. Sidney Earl Mead, *Nathaniel William Taylor, 1786–1858: A Connecticut Liberal* (1942; repr. Hamden, CT, 1967).

45. Taylor, *Concio ad Clerum,* 151–162.

46. George M. Frederickson, *The Inner Civil War: Northern Intellectuals and the Crisis of the Union* (New York, 1965), 107.

47. "A Bone of Contention," *American Freeman* 1 (December 1866): 130, quoted in Henry Lee Swint, *The Northern Teachers in the South, 1862–1870* (New York, 1967), 13.
48. Quoted in Swint, *Northern Teachers*, 13.

2. The Catholic Puzzle

1. The question of Catholic participation in the public square has been the topic of recent research and deliberation, exemplified by the project on American Catholics in the Public Square sponsored by the Pew Forum. Project activities are described at http://www.catholicsinpublic square.org/. Major papers have been published in Steinfels (2004). The examples come both from that collection and from sources cited later in this chapter.

2. Statistics on the Catholic population and on many aspects of Catholic life have been collected in Froehle and Gautier (2000).

3. For discussions of the nature of the magisterium, see Curran (1999), Gaillardetz (1997), Gula (1989), and especially Sullivan (1983). Even those considered dissenters, like Curran, hold that there exists "an authoritative teaching role for bishops and pope in the Catholic Church that also involves moral matters" (Curran 1999, 200). There is debate over the exercise of the teaching office and over the type of assent that Catholics are required to give to the teachings of the magisterium that are not explicitly defined as infallible, as none of the social teachings are. *Lumen Gentium* says, "In matters of faith and morals, the bishops speak in the name of Christ and the faithful are to accept their teaching and adhere to it with a religious assent of soul" (*Lumen Gentium,* Dogmatic Constitution on the Church, para. 25, translated in Flannery (1996)). After carefully examining the Vatican Council debates that led to this particular formulation, Sullivan interprets it as meaning that the teaching of the ordinary magisterium (that is, those teachings not declared infallible) requires "an honest and sustained effort to overcome any contrary opinion I might have and to achieve a sincere assent of mind to this teaching" (Sullivan 1983, 189).

4. Of these documents, the Vatican II documents would probably be considered to have the greatest authority, and the documents produced by conferences of bishops to have lesser authority. The major documents of the Council and bishops' conferences have been collected in O'Brien and Shannon (1998). Major American documents have been collected by Massaro and Shannon (2002). Recent documents from the Ameri-

can Catholic bishops are available at http://www.usccb.org/. Also important is the Catechism of the Catholic Church (1994).

5. Gula (1989) describes three roles of the Church: as shaper of moral character, through liturgy and symbol; bearer of moral tradition and moral teachings; and as a community of moral deliberation.

6. *Lumen Gentium,* Dogmatic Constitution on the Church, translated in Flannery (1996).

7. *Gaudium et Spes,* Pastoral Constitution on the Church in the Modern World, translated in Flannery (1996).

8. Both of these documents are in Flannery (1996).

9. *Gaudium et Spes,* in Flannery (1996).

10. In O'Brien and Shannon (1998), 294.

11. The social teachings differ in their underlying methodology from the official teachings on sexual ethics and reproduction, which rely heavily on concepts of the "natural." The social teachings do appeal to experience and reason assumed to be common to and accessible to all human beings. Consistent with new directions in Christian ethics, the major statements in the social teachings also rely heavily on scripture, not with the methodology of "proof texting" but in an attempt to elicit the deep underlying principles and images. For discussions of methodology, see Gula (1989); on the uses of scripture as a basis for morality, see, for example, Hays (1996), Spohn (1995), and Spohn (1999). On social justice in the Old Testament, see Lohfink (1987); on social justice in the New Testament, see Donahue (1993).

12. In a 2003 statement, "Faithful Citizenship: A Catholic Call to Political Responsibility" (National Conference of Catholic Bishops 2003), the bishops state the themes of Catholic social teaching: life and the dignity of the human person; call to family, community, and participation; rights and responsibilities; option for the poor and vulnerable; solidarity; caring for God's creation. Documents of the U.S. bishops are online at www.usccb.org.

13. The Reverend Eugene Rivers of Boston's Ten Point Coalition and political scientist John Diuluio introduced me to the formulation "pro-life, pro-family, pro-poor." They see it as powerful language around which Catholics and evangelical Christians might be able to make common cause. It reflects, of course, John Cardinal Bernardin's notion of a "consistent ethic of life." A number of Bernardin's addresses on this topic, plus responses to them, are collected in Fuechtmann (1988).

14. Christian Smith's discussion of evangelical attitudes toward social

change, in Smith (1998), is especially interesting in this regard. See also Wolfe (1998, 2003).

15. National Conference of Catholic Bishops (1986).
16. National Conference of Catholic Bishops (2003).
17. Ibid., 4.
18. Ibid., 3.
19. See, for example, the data on different orientations in Chapter 5, the poll data presented in Froehle and Gautier (2000, 28–35), and the discussion in Manza and Wright (2003) and Leege and Mueller (2004). On the other hand, Tropman (2002) describes and provides some empirical evidence for a distinctly Catholic ethic.
20. Civic and political activity, rather than attitudes or voting behavior, are my focus here. The latter are the subjects of a set of interesting papers in Steinfels (2004).
21. Hodgkinson and Weitzman (1996), app. D, table 1, p. D152.
22. Smith (1998), table 2.7, pp. 41–42.
23. Wuthnow and Evans (2002), table 15.4, p. 390.
24. Nationally, Catholics are slightly better educated and have slightly higher incomes than other groups. Catholics who identified themselves as Hispanics, who are not as well off, made up about 27 percent of the Catholic respondents to the Social Capital Benchmark Survey. Ammerman's respondents (see Chapter 5) were from two Albuquerque parishes, which were disproportionately Latino.
25. The regressions were performed in SPSS. The full results are available from the author.
26. Putnam (2000).
27. Verba, Schlozman, and Brady (1995).
28. St. William's was the parish in my neighborhood, not the university community where I work. The Boston archdiocese closed it along with other parishes in 2004. St. William's was middle- and working-class and not particularly intellectual or progressive. I was a regular Mass attendee, lector, and member of the Parish Pastoral Council and the Committee on Services to the Poor. I was also occasionally a consultant to the pastor on financial and other issues. Thus my observations on this parish are those of a member, not an objective observer.
29. About 150–200 parishioners contribute using envelopes in a given week. If as many people put cash in the collection plate as use envelopes, then about 50 percent of attendees, who are perhaps 50–60 percent of members, contribute. The average contribution of envelope users is about $15 per week and the average household income about

$40,000 (census data suggest that average household income in the tracts making up the parish was about $35,000 in 1990), suggesting that even those who use envelopes are contributing less than 2 percent of income.

30. The history and theology of parishes are clearly explained in Coriden (1997). Parishes are defined geographically, and are thus somewhat different from the voluntary congregations of other traditions.

31. Chaves (1998). It is not clear whether respondents to the NCS would have included funerals and weddings in their count of worship services. They are liturgical celebrations. The average parish probably celebrates one or two a week.

32. In the Boston archdiocese, decisions about staff assignments, parish consolidations, and so on are made largely on the basis of a "sacramental index" which is meant to measure the workload of parishes or, more accurately, the workload of priests. The sacramental index is equal to the number of baptisms plus the number of funerals plus twice the number of marriages. The logic of this measure is not entirely clear.

33. Murnion and DeLambo (1999).

34. Chaves, Giesel, and Tsitsos (2000).

35. The Industrial Areas Foundation (IAF) is notoriously short on written publications. One helpful one is *IAF 50 Years: Organizing for Change,* published by the Industrial Areas Foundation in 1990. An excellent description is Warren (2001).

36. For example, Putnam (2000) and Warren (2001).

37. Keeler (1997), 7.

38. Ibid., 27. Other lively Catholic parishes are described in Wilkes (2001).

39. Vatican II, "The Constitution on the Sacred Liturgy," in Holtzman (1991), 375–376. That this document was issued first could reflect the importance that the Council gave to the Church as sacrament and mystery. It also reflects, however, the pragmatic decision that the Council might actually be able to reach agreement on the liturgy.

40. The newest official instructions for celebrating the liturgy are laid out in the General Instruction of the Roman Missal, pronounced, by most priests, "germ" (United States Conference of Catholic Bishops, 2003). A more theological discussion of the liturgy and the most recent changes in the rites is Baldovin (2003). An excellent discussion of Catholic liturgy as it is practiced and the controversies surrounding it is found in Steinfels (2003), chap. 5.

41. A helpful source on the lectionary is Bonneau (1998). The official description of the lectionary is found in Lectionary for Mass: Introduction (1991).

42. Respondents to the National Congregations Study reported an average homily length of 13.5 minutes. Chaves (1998).

43. National Conference of Catholic Bishops (1991).

44. Ibid., 49.

45. Searching for "homily services" on the Web generates a number of sources. A major one is that of Saint Anthony's Messenger, which offers a subscription to "Homily Helps for Sundays," discussed below. The website of the National Catholic Conference for Total Stewardship offers "homily guides," which include extensive quotes and explanations related to the week's scriptures in the areas of "internal spiritual formation" and "exterior action." An interesting irony is that many of these are written by women, who are not, in the Catholic Church, permitted to deliver homilies. Homily services are apparently used often enough that bishops are concerned about them. National Conference of Catholic Bishops (1991) includes a section on homily services that disparages their use as not being responsive to local congregations. For example, the Jesuit weekly *America* offers reflections on the week's scripture readings which could serve as the basis for homilies. The monthly *Homilitic and Pastoral Review* offers scriptural exegesis and suggestions for homilies from a more traditionally doctrinal point of view. "Homily Helps," published weekly and available by subscription from the St. Anthony Messenger Press, includes exegeses of the three readings, a suggested purpose and summary for a homily, an "attention getting" story, a number of applications to contemporary life, and a suggestion for transition to the Eucharist. Published volumes that cover the whole lectionary are also available.

46. For example, Bergant (2000) suggests as themes for homilies for the fifteenth Sunday in ordinary time, Year C, when the Gospel reading is the parable of the Good Samaritan: openness to the unexpected and love of the law. For the Sunday when the parable of the rich man and Lazarus is read, it suggests the themes of covenant responsibility, judgment, and the pursuit of righteousness.

47. Burghardt (1996).

48. The essays in Hughes and Francis (1991) explore various aspects of this relationship. In her chapter, Hughes points out that liturgical reform and a new emphasis on social justice took different paths after Vatican II and became the concerns of quite different groups of people. The writers in this collection argue that since liturgy and social justice work have the same ultimate goal, they ought to be thought about in a more integrated way.

49. Verba, Schlozman, and Brady (1995) report that religious partici-

pation develops civic and political skills, such as public speaking, planning meetings, and organizing events, for members of all denominations except Catholics. They hypothesize that the large size and hierarchical structure of Catholic parishes might explain this discrepancy.

50. Miller (1997) describes the activities and philosophy of Calvary, Vineyard, and Hope Chapel. Schaller (2000) advises leaders of large evangelical churches on how to structure programs and activities.

51. Baggett (2003).

52. Ibid., 25.

53. Wolfe (2003).

54. Steinfels (2003) provides an excellent discussion of the current state of American Catholicism, with insights on the role of structural features.

55. The crisis in the church that was generated by revelations in the spring of 2002 of clergy sexual abuse and hierarchical cover-ups led to the formation of a number of lay groups, most notably Voice of the Faithful, seeking a voice. In many places, these initiatives were discouraged if not forbidden by the hierarchy.

56. The story of how Catholic Charities centralized and professionalized is well told in Brown and McKeown (1997). An analogous story about Catholic philanthropy is told by Oates (1995).

57. Froehle and Gautier (2000), 59–60.

58. Cozzens (1999) is a poignant and frank review of the problems of the priesthood, by a longtime priest.

59. It is hard to imagine that sheer necessity will not at some point drive the church to at least a married priesthood, though it is hard to predict when that might be.

60. Greeley (1990); Hoge et al. (1996); and Hoge, McNamara, and Zech (1997).

61. Chaves (1998).

62. Catholic giving has been studied, most notably by Greeley (1990) and Zech (1999). Greeley argues that Catholic giving has declined steadily since the 1970s, and attributes the decline to lay anger at the hierarchy and especially at the Church's stand on birth control. Zech and his colleagues dispute this explanation, arguing that low giving is more a function of the ways money is raised and managed in the church: for example, through Sunday envelopes rather than through stewardship campaigns. Both agree that disclosure of financial information and lay participation in church governance increase contributions.

63. Perhaps the most plausible interpretation of the pope's action is that he was convinced either that the church, inspired by the Holy Spirit, could not have been in error on such a serious matter for so long, or that the

consequences of admitting that the teachings could change would be a serious undermining of the authority of pope and church. For a balanced presentation of this issue see Gula (1989); for a much stronger interpretation see Wills (2000).

3. H. Richard Niebuhr Meets "The Street"

1. This chapter draws on data from a larger ethnographic study of religious congregations in Four Corners. See Omar M. McRoberts, *Streets of Glory: Church and Community in a Black Urban Neighborhood* (Chicago: University of Chicago Press, 2003).
2. From news accounts of George W. Bush's speech at the 2000 Republican National Convention accepting the GOP presidential nomination.
3. See Paul Boyer, *Urban Masses and Moral Order in America, 1820–1920* (Cambridge, MA: Harvard University Press, 1978).
4. "The street" as a counterpoint to the "safe space" of the church is explored in Farah Jasmine Griffin, *"Who Set You Flowin'?" The African-American Migration Narrative* (New York: Oxford University Press, 1995).
5. See Timothy Nelson's chapter, "The Church and the Street: Race, Class, and Congregation," in *Contemporary American Religion: An Ethnographic Reader,* ed. Penny Edgell Becker and Nancy L. Eiesland (Walnut Creek, CA: Alta Mira Press, 1997), 184. See also Melvin D. Williams, *Community in a Black Pentecostal Church* (Prospect Heights, IL: Waveland Press, 1974), 158.
6. This corroborates Nelson, "The Church and the Street," who writes that the pastor of Eastside Chapel compared "the violence of the ghetto streets to the 'spiritual violence' of gossip and discord within the church" (176).
7. See Griffin, *"Who Set You Flowin'?"*
8. See Mary Waters, *Black Identities: West Indian Immigrant Dreams and American Realities* (Cambridge, MA: Harvard University Press, 1999), 202–247.
9. See David A. Roozen, William McKinney, and Jackson W. Carroll, *Varieties of Religious Presence* (New York, NY: Pilgrim Press, 1988).

4. Moral Deliberation in Congregations

1. John Rawls, *Political Liberalism* (New York, 1993).
2. Practices of moral deliberation are "not confined to small face-to-face groups; nor do they imply lack of dissent. They include the public

world of democratic politics and call for vigorous discussion and argument. In such a conversation, tradition provides us with the shared experience and ideals that orient us to the present, but not with answers to present problems." Robert N. Bellah, "The Idea of Practices in Habits: A Response," in *Community in America: The Challenge of Habits of the Heart,* ed. Charles H. Reynolds and Ralph V. Norman (Berkeley, 1988).

3. I am grateful to Jenny Foster for competent and energetic research assistance in the project.

4. Alan Wolfe, *One Nation, After All: What Middle-Class Americans Really Think About* (New York, 1998).

5. Ibid., 76.

6. Saul M. Olyan and Martha C. Nussbaum, eds., *Sexual Orientation and Human Rights in American Religious Discourse* (New York, 1998).

7. See Wendy Cadge's chapter, "Vital Conflicts: The Mainline Denominations Debate Homosexuality," in Robert Wuthnow and John H. Evans, eds., *The Quiet Hand of God: Faith Based Activism and the Public Role of Mainline Protestantism* (Berkeley, 2002). See also "Homosexuality and Religion," the Hartford Institute for Religion Research: http://hirr.hartsem.edu/research/research_homosexuality _religion.htm.

8. In the following accounts of deliberation, "the moral world has a lived-in quality, like a home occupied by a single family over many generations, with unplanned additions here and there, and all the available space filled with memory-laden objects and artifacts. The whole thing, taken as a whole, lends itself less to abstract modeling than to thick description." Michael Walzer, *Interpretation and Social Criticism* (Cambridge, MA, 1987).

9. 2000 Census: http://www1miser.umass.ed/datacenter/Census2000/Census2000Datda.html.

10. "Lexington 2020 Vision," Lexington, MA, 2001.

11. In gathering data for this project, I asked about religious membership of congregations in the geographic boundaries of the town, not the religious affiliation of town residents. A significant portion of Lexington residents may not be members of any religious congregation or may attend congregations elsewhere.

12. The percentage of Jews is higher than reported, because the Orthodox Chabad Center did not return a survey. The Bahai community, Christian Science Church, Reorganized Church of Latter Day Saints, and Jehovah's Witnesses also did not return surveys.

13. Membership included those living inside and outside Lexington.

14. Mark Chaves, Helen M. Giesel, and William Tsitsos, "Religious Variations in Public Presence: Evidence from the National Congregations Study," in Wuthnow and Evans, *The Quiet Hand of God.*

15. Nancy Ammerman, "Connecting Mainline Protestant Congregations with Public Life," in *Quietly Influential: The Public Role of Mainline Protestantism,* ed. Robert Wuthnow and John H. Evans (Berkeley, 2002), 131.

16. Coffin, Lexington Congregation Survey, 2001.

17. The median Lexington congregation had 250 members and an annual budget of between $250,000 and $300,000. The national median congregation has 75 people, according to Mark Chaves and William Tsitsos in "Congregations and Social Services: What They Do, How They Do It, and With Whom," a Nonprofit Sector Research Fund Working Paper published by the Aspen Institute, 2001, 15.

18. George Gallup Jr. and D. Michael Lindsay, *Surveying the Religious Landscape: Trends in U.S. Belief* (Harrisburg, PA, 1999), 40. Not all self-identified evangelicals are Protestant: 20 percent of Roman Catholics consider themselves "born-again" or "evangelical Christians." Moreover, these terms mean different things to different people. "Born again" would more likely be heard in the 40,565 congregations in the Southern Baptist Convention and less likely in the 10,396 congregations in the Evangelical Lutheran Church in America. But the Lutheran denomination, not the Baptists, uses "evangelical" to designate its history and theology.

19. The series was sponsored by a coalition of nine community organizations, including four churches, one temple, and the Lexington Public Schools; it was endorsed by State Representative Jay Kaufman, the Board of Selectmen, and the League of Women Voters.

20. I use the actual names of religious leaders and congregations. The names of other individuals have been changed.

21. First Parish, Lexington, MA: http://www.fpc.lexington.ma.us/.

22. For a description of "Welcoming Congregations," see http://www.fpc.lexington.ma.us/Welcoming.htm.

23. Robert Wuthnow, *Loose Connections: Joining Together in America's Fragmented Communities* (Cambridge, MA, 1998).

24. R. Stephen Warner, "Changes in the Civic Role of Religion," in *Diversity and Its Discontents: Cultural Conflict and Common Ground in Contemporary American Society,* ed. Neil Smelser and Jeffrey Alexander (Princeton, NJ, 1999), 229–244.

25. Preamble to the Constitution, Evangelical Covenant Church.
26. Haydon interview.
27. Trinity Church brochures.
28. "Covenant Affirmations" (Chicago, 1996).
29. Weekly attendance at Lexington's evangelical megachurch, Grace Chapel, is 25 percent more than its formal membership of 2,100.
30. Paul DiMaggio, "The Relevance of Organization Theory to the Study of Religion," in *Sacred Companies: Organizational Aspects of Religion and Religious Aspects of Organizations,* ed. N. J. Demerath III, Peter Dobkin Hall, Terry Schmitt, and Rhys Williams (New York, 1998); Robert Wuthnow, *The Restructuring of American Religion* (Princeton, NJ, 1988.)
31. Seyla Benhabib, *Situating the Self* (New York, 1992).
32. According to the state conference of the United Church of Christ, "Open and Affirming churches are congregations . . . which publicly welcome gay, lesbian, bisexual and transgendered people into their full life and ministry." http://www.macucc.org/about_us/ona.htm.
33. Hancock Church Covenant of Welcome Report (March 2001). See http://www.hancockchurch.org/home.html.
34. This public forum took place in what Rawls calls "the background culture . . . where political matters are discussed, and often from within people's comprehensive doctrines." Though not located in formal political or legal contexts, such public spaces allow us to examine whether incompatible, comprehensive doctrines—religious and secular—are reasonable in that they "express political values that others view as free and equal citizens might reasonably be expected reasonably to endorse." Rawls, *Political Liberalism,* 14, 58–61.
35. On ministerial authority, see Daniel Day Williams, *The Minister and the Care of Souls* (New York, 1961), and James M. Gustafson, *The Church as Moral Decision-Maker* (Boston, 1970).
36. Gustafson, *Church as Moral*; Robert Wuthnow, *Producing the Sacred: An Essay on Public Religion* (Chicago, 1994), 59–66.
37. James M. Gustafson, *Ethics from a Theocentric Perspective,* vol. 1, *Theology and Ethics* (Chicago, 1981).
38. The welfare reform debate offers a good example. Steven M. Teles, *Whose Welfare? AFDC and Elite Politics* (Lawrence, KS, 1996).
39. Cadge, in Wuthnow and Evans, *The Quiet Hand of God,* 279.
40. H. Richard Niebuhr, *Christ and Culture* (New York, 1951).
41. For the former, see Rodney Stark and Roger Finke, *Acts of Faith: Explaining the Human Side of Religion* (Berkeley, 2000); for the latter, see

Alan Wolfe, *The Transformation of American Religion: How We Actually Live Our Faith* (New York, 2003).

42. For a penetrating analysis of "discrimination in contract" and "discrimination in contact," see Glenn C. Loury, *The Anatomy of Racial Inequality* (Cambridge, MA, 2002).

43. I explored this possibility through twenty-one interviews with senior religious leaders by asking two open-ended questions: "The gap between rich and poor is widening in our country and internationally. Lexington congregations are located in the wealthier part of the equation. How does your church or synagogue address this? What are the most important resources it has in this regard?"

44. Robert Wuthnow, *Crisis in the Churches: Spiritual Malaise, Fiscal Woe* (New York, 1997); Michael O. Emerson and Christian Smith, *Divided by Faith: Evangelical Religion and the Problem of Race in America* (New York, 2000); Wuthnow, "United States: Bridging the Privileged and the Marginalized?" in *Democracies in Flux,* ed. Robert Putnam (New York, 2002).

45. The Lexington Clergy Association sponsored an interfaith Habitat for Humanity project to build a house in urban Roxbury, MA. For an analysis, see Jerome P. Baggett, *Habitat for Humanity: Building Private Homes, Building Public Religion* (Philadelphia, 2001).

46. In the distinction posed by Harry Frankfurt, a "first-order" desire is a simple wish to do something; a "second-order" desire is a more reflective desire to desire something. Thus a second-order desire can override a first-order impulse. See Frankfurt, "Freedom of the Will and the Concept of a Person," *Journal of Philosophy* 67 (1971): 5–20.

47. This philosophical anthropology draws on Charles Taylor, *Sources of the Self: The Making of Modern Identity* (Cambridge, MA, 1989), and Hans Joas, *The Genesis of Values* (Chicago, 2000).

48. DiMaggio, "Relevance of Organization," and Warner, "Changes."

49. For an insightful analysis of levels of authority in moral discourse, see Charles E. Curran, "Relating Religious-Ethical Inquiry to Economic Policy," in *The Catholic Challenge to the American Economy,* ed. Thomas M. Gannon (New York, 1987).

50. Joas, *Genesis,* 5.

51. Respecting Differences forum transcript, p. 14.

52. Respecting Differences forum. In a culture in which legitimacy and authority are established primarily through the exercise of consent and voluntarism, "family" is a powerful metaphor. It generates interpretive frames that establish the normative dimensions of public discourse.

Affectively, the synecdoche of "family" has deep resonance with the personal history, identity, and aspirations of individual citizens. Normatively, it signifies the possibility of reconciling autonomy and community, identity and belonging, being and doing. Haydon invokes the metaphor to privilege unconditional commitment over autonomy: that of God in Christ and that of converted believers in Christ and to one another; however, autonomy is not obliterated. Meek's rhetoric exemplifies using the metaphor to privilege respect for the autonomy of others; but once again, autonomy does not exclude community: "[all of us] are stuck with one another." In our political and popular cultures, the metaphor of family continues to frame policy debates, with conservatives doing so more effectively than liberals.

53. The distinction of "primary and secondary" moral languages in *Habits of the Heart* posited empirically coherent religious and ethical traditions, a claim that has come under strong criticism (Bellah et al., Berkeley, 1985). In this context, "bilingual moral competence" is a normative proposal that includes a view of moral agency (Amartya Sen, "Well-being, Agency, and Freedom," *Journal of Philosophy* 82 [1985]: 169–221; Taylor, *Sources;* and Joas, *Genesis*); a view of the relation of theology to ethics, the relation of religion to morality, and practices by which people of faith become "bilingual." This discussion has focused on the last aspect. See James M. Gustafson, *Can Ethics Be Christian?* (Chicago, 1975), and Nancy Ammerman, *Congregation and Community* (New Brunswick, NJ, 1997).

5. Religious Narratives in the Public Square

1. Peter L. Berger, *The Sacred Canopy* (Garden City, NY: Anchor Doubleday, 1969); Frank Lechner, "The Case against Secularization: A Rebuttal," *Social Forces* 69, no. 4 (1991); Max Weber, *The Protestant Ethic and the Spirit of Capitalism,* trans. Talcott Parsons (New York: Scribner's, 1958).

2. This link between the social location of the observers and the secularization that was observed is made by R. Stephen Warner, "Work in Progress toward a New Paradigm for the Sociological Study of Religion in the United States," *American Journal of Sociology* 98, no. 5 (1993). The prediction of "privatization" is theorized in Emile Durkheim, "Individualism and the Intellectuals," in *Durkheim on Religion,* ed. W. S. F. Pickering (London: Routledge & Kegan Paul, 1975); Peter L. Berger, "From the Crisis of Religion to the Crisis of Secularity," in *Religion and America,* ed. Mary Douglas and Steven Tipton (Boston:

Beacon, 1982); Phillip E. Hammond, *Religion and Personal Autonomy: The Third Disestablishment in America* (Columbia: University of South Carolina Press, 1992); and Talcott Parsons, "Religion and Modern Industrial Society," in *Religion, Culture, and Society,* ed. Louis Schneider (New York: Wiley, 1964).

3. Berger himself has changed his mind. See his chapter "The Desecularization of the World: A Global Overview," in *The Desecularization of the World: Resurgent Religion and World Politics,* ed. Berger (Grand Rapids, Mich.: Eerdmans, 1999); and Peter L. Berger, *A Far Glory: The Quest for Faith in an Age of Credulity* (New York: Free Press, 1992).

4. An important critique of this assumption is found in Nancy Fraser, "Rethinking the Public Sphere: A Contribution to the Critique of Actually Existing Democracy," *Social Text* 25, no. 26 (1990).

5. Religion that "compromises" on truth is, to this way of thinking, but a pale reflection of its essential self. This equation of "religion" with an institutional logic of "truth" is a mistake made, for instance, by Roger Friedland and Robert R. Alford, "Bringing Society Back In: Symbols, Practices, and Institutional Contradictions," in *The New Institutionalism in Organizational Analysis,* ed. Walter Powell and Paul DiMaggio (Chicago: University of Chicago Press, 1991). It also underlies the theory of religion promulgated by Rodney Stark in *One True God: Historical Consequences of Monotheism* (Princeton, NJ: Princeton University Press, 2001).

6. Margaret R. Somers, "The Narrative Constitution of Identity: A Relational and Network Approach," *Theory and Society* 23 (1994): 606.

7. Somers identifies four relevant narratives: "ontological" (roughly equivalent to what I call autobiographical narratives), "public" (collective and institutional), "conceptual" (the categories used by observers to analyze social action), and "metanarratives" (the overarching schemas that shape how other stories are told).

8. These public narratives reside in what Bourdieu would call "fields," the operative arena that determines which forms of cultural capital and which habitus will come into play. On Bourdieu, see David Swartz, *Culture and Power: The Sociology of Pierre Bourdieu* (Chicago: University of Chicago Press, 1998).

9. C. Wright Mills, "Situated Actions and Vocabularies of Motive," *American Sociological Review* 5 (December 1940); Marvin B. Scott and Stanford Lyman, "Accounts," *American Sociological Review* 33, no. 1 (1968).

10. I borrow the idea of transposability from William H. Sewell Jr., "A

Theory of Structure: Duality, Agency, and Transformation," *American Journal of Sociology* 98 (1992). Martha Minow points to "intersectionality" as a way multiple narratives allow us to connect and communicate across lines of social division. See Minow, *Not Only for Myself* (New York: New Press, 1997).

11. This argument about the formation of narrative religious identities is made in more detail in my chapter "Religious Identities and Religious Institutions," in *Handbook of the Sociology of Religion,* ed. Michele Dillon, 207–224 (Cambridge: Cambridge University Press, 2003).

12. Ammerman, "Golden Rule Christianity: Lived Religion in the American Mainstream," in *Lived Religion in America: Toward a History of Practice,* ed. David Hall (Princeton: Princeton University Press, 1997).

13. A full description of the project may be found at www.hirr.hartsem .edu. The larger project included attention to congregations outside the Christian tradition, but the survey of individuals was conducted only in Christian congregations.

14. Mark Chaves et al., "The National Congregations Study: Background, Methods, and Selected Results," *Journal for the Scientific Study of Religion* 38, no. 4 (1999). Note that *descriptives* have been weighted, but where denominational tradition is a variable being controlled, unweighted responses are used.

15. Ammerman, "Golden Rule Christianity," and Ammerman, "Organized Religion in a Voluntaristic Society," *Sociology of Religion* 58, no. 3 (1997).

16. The standardized item alphas for the three scales are .78, .76, and .84, respectively.

17. Responses ranged from "never" (0) to "weekly or more" (4).

18. Categories ranged from nothing (0) to $5,000 or more (7).

19. The levels of community involvement we report appear to be quite comparable to those reported by a massive new study of American churchgoers. These researchers report 38 percent having donated to secular charities, for instance, while our overall figure is 41 percent. See Evan Silverstein, *Survey Finds High Rate of Turnover in the Pews,* January 17, 2002, available at www.churchbusiness.com and www.wfn.org.

20. A "partial *r*" is a correlation coefficient that has taken multiple variables into account. It varies between zero and one, with positive values indicating variation in the same direction and negative values indicating variation in opposite directions. Larger absolute values indicate stronger relationships, so a value of +.20 is stronger than +.12, and

both indicate that as one variable increases, the other variable also increases.

21. M. A. Musick, J. Wilson, and W. B. Bynum, Jr., "Race and Formal Volunteering: The Differential Effects of Class and Religion," *Social Forces* 78, no. 4 (2000): 1539–71, found that people who think helping others is important in making life worth living were more likely to volunteer. Ours is a more elaborate and religiously based measure, but their findings support the notion that ways of talking about what constitutes a good life are linked to strategies of voluntary action.

22. Although the categories we used parallel those used in Robert Wuthnow's study of small groups, it is not possible to compare the rates of participation he reports with these. He does not systematically separate congregationally based groups from others. In addition, his is a population sample, rather than an attender sample. See Wuthnow, *Sharing the Journey* (New York: Free Press, 1994).

23. If education, income, age, presence of children, and rural residence are controlled for, the correlation between church participation and informal help is +.38 and between church participation and community service organization participation is +.30.

24. Differences between "evangelical" and "mainline" Protestants (using denomination as the measure) are also documented in Robert Wuthnow, "Mobilizing Civic Engagement: The Changing Impact of Religious Involvement," in *Civic Engagement in American Democracy,* ed. Theda Skocpol and Morris P. Fiorina (Washington, DC: Brookings Institution Press, 1999). As Penny Edgell Becker and Pawan H. Dhingra point out, it is important not to assume therefore that evangelicals are not involved in the community; they are just less likely to engage in these particular types of community activity. See Becker and Dhingra, "Religious Involvement and Volunteering: Implications for Civil Society," *Sociology of Religion* 62, no. 3 (2001). Brian McKenzie documents a similar pattern in nonelectoral political participation. Those he calls "fundamentalists" go to church services more frequently, and it is that self-selection effect that accounts for an apparent positive relationship between attendance and political activism. He curiously posits that religious orientation is the actual exogenous variable, but does not test a model so specified. See McKenzie, "Self-Selection, Church Attendance, and Local Civic Participation," *Journal for the Scientific Study of Religion* 40, no. 3 (2001).

25. On the power of congregational cultures to shape individual and corporate action, see Penny Edgell Becker, *Congregations in Conflict: Cul-*

tural Models of Local Religious Life (Cambridge: Cambridge University Press, 1999).

26. Brian Steensland et al., "The Measure of American Religion: Toward Improving the State-of-the-Art," *Social Forces* 79, no. 1 (2000).

27. One Greek Orthodox parish was also part of our study. These respondents are included in overall summaries, but not grouped with any of the four categories used here.

28. The very small United Methodist church in rural Alabama is an exception to this overall pattern. Given its southern evangelical heritage and culture, we have included its eight respondents in the conservative Protestant camp.

29. Susan Eckstein describes the relative isolation of the one evangelical church in the community she studied. Other parishes had deep ties to other community organizations, but this one did not. See Eckstein, "Community as Gift-Giving: Collectivistic Roots of Volunteerism," *American Sociological Review* 66, no. 6 (2001); also Wuthnow, "Mobilizing Civic Engagement."

30. That there are, however, differences *among* black churches can be seen in Jo Anne Schneider, "The Kenosha Social Capital Study: Churches, Nonprofits, and Community" (Indiana, Penn.: Indiana University of Pennsylvania, 2001); and in Richard L. Wood, "Religious Culture and Political Action," *Sociological Theory* 17, no. 3 (1999). Different views of how to respond to injustice are documented in C. Eric Lincoln and Lawrence H. Mamiya, *The Black Church in the African American Experience* (Durham, NC: Duke University Press, 1990).

31. Wood has shown how the culture of a congregation can provide cultural tools that can be mobilized for political action. See also Mary Pattillo-McCoy, "Church Culture as a Strategy of Action in the Black Community," *American Sociological Review* 63 (1998).

32. Catholic life is described by James C. Cavendish, "Church-Based Community Activism: A Comparison of Black and White Catholic Congregations," *Journal for the Scientific Study of Religion* 39, no. 1 (2000); William V. D'Antonio et al., *American Catholics: Gender, Generation, and Commitment* (Walnut Creek, CA: Altamira, 2001); Michele Dillon, *Catholic Identity: Balancing Reason, Faith, and Power* (New York: Cambridge University Press, 1999).

33. The average for Catholic households was reported at $819 in the early 1990s by Dean R. Hoge et al., *Money Matters: Personal Giving in American Churches* (Louisville: Westminster John Knox Press, 1996). This compares with $2,479 for Baptists and $1,635 for Presbyterians.

34. The importance of church attendance for community participation and volunteering is also documented in Wuthnow, "Mobilizing Civic Engagement." His findings show that "regular" attenders differ from infrequent attenders in joining community organizations, volunteering for some types of service activities, and voting. Robin Gill, *Churchgoing and Christian Ethics* (Cambridge: Cambridge University Press, 1999), works from both theories of Christian ethics and British poll data to show how church participation affects morality. See also Becker and Dhingra, "Religious Involvement"; Virginia A. Hodgkinson, Murray S. Weitzman, and Arthur D. Kirsch, "From Commitment to Action: How Religious Involvement Affects Giving and Volunteering," in *Faith and Philanthropy in America: Exploring the Role of Religion in America's Voluntary Sector,* ed. Robert Wuthnow and Virginia Hodgkinson (San Francisco: Jossey-Bass, 1990); Musick, Wilson, and Bynum, Jr., "Race and Formal Volunteering"; Jerry Park and Christian Smith, " 'To Whom Much Has Been Given': Religious Capital and Community Voluntarism among Churchgoing Protestants," *Journal for the Scientific Study of Religion* 39, no. 3 (2000): 272–286, also find that participation in "church activities" (presumably beyond worship) is a strong and consistent predictor of volunteering in nonchurch organizations. Michael Stoll, "Race, Neighborhood Poverty, and Participation in Voluntary Associations," *Sociological Forum* 16, no. 3 (2001), shows that church attendance is a key link in channeling poor blacks into other voluntary organizations. John Wilson and Thomas Janoski, "The Contribution of Religion to Volunteer Work," *Sociology of Religion* 56, no. 2 (1995), present a more complicated picture, arguing that church activism has positive effects on nonchurch volunteering only for liberals and Catholics.

35. This coincides with what we know about how congregations nurture "civic skills." Sidney Verba, Kay Lehman Schlozman, and Henry E. Brady, *Voice and Equality: Civic Voluntarism in American Politics* (Cambridge, MA: Harvard University Press, 1995), 328–330, highlight, for instance, the opportunities for leadership (and therefore enhanced civic skills) experienced by even the least well off churchgoers. They make the point that structures do make a difference, either enabling or constraining action. At the national level, a similar point about structural constraints on voluntary activity is made by Evan Schofer and Marion Fourcade-Gourinchas, "The Structural Contexts of Civic Engagement: Voluntary Association Membership in Comparative Perspective," *American Sociological Review* 66, no. 6 (2001).

Paxton reports that members of religious groups were especially likely to be members of other voluntary organizations, and such "connected" membership is especially beneficial for sustaining democracy. Pamela Paxton, "Social Capital and Democracy: An Interdependent Relationship," *American Sociological Review* 67, no. 2 (2002).

36. See also Mark Chaves, "Congregations' Social Service Activities," Urban Institute, Washington, DC, 1999; Ram A. Cnaan, "Social and Community Involvement," University of Pennsylvania School of Social Work, Program for the Study of Organized Religion and Social Work, 1997; Virginia A. Hodgkinson and Murray S. Weitzman, *From Belief to Commitment: The Community Service Activities and Finances of Religious Congregations in the United States: 1993 Edition* (Washington, DC: Independent Sector, 1993).

37. Eckstein, "Community as Gift-Giving."

38. Becker and Dhingra, "Religious Involvement"; Park and Smith, "To Whom Much Has Been Given."

39. Musick, Wilson, and Bynum, Jr., "Race and Formal Volunteering."

40. Wuthnow, *Sharing the Journey*, 327ff.

41. For a complete report on these connections, see Ammerman, *Doing Good in American Communities: Congregations and Service Organizations Working Together* (Hartford, CT: Hartford Institute for Religion Research, 2001).

42. Wuthnow, *Sharing the Journey*.

43. Paul Lichterman, *Elusive Togetherness: Religion in the Quest for Civic Renewal* (Princeton, NJ: Princeton University Press, 2004).

44. Robert Wuthnow and John H. Evans, eds., *The Quiet Hand of God: Faith-Based Activism and the Public Role of Mainline Protestantism* (Berkeley: University of California Press, 2002). On the societal-level effects of Protestantism, see James E. Curtis, Douglas E. Baer, and Edward G. Grabb, "Nations of Joiners: Explaining Voluntary Association Membership in Democratic Societies," *American Sociological Review* 66, no. 6 (2001).

45. Cavendish, "Church-Based Community Activism," notes that parishes that have lay-led parish councils and local leadership training programs are also more involved in providing service to their communities.

46. This stands in contrast to the argument by Putnam and others that middle-aged parents are especially likely to volunteer. See Robert D. Putnam, *Bowling Alone: The Collapse and Revival of American Community* (New York: Simon & Schuster, 2000). Thomas Rotolo, "A

Time to Join, a Time to Quit: The Influence of Life Cycle Transitions on Voluntary Association Membership," *Social Forces* 78, no. 3 (2000), however, reports that for women, volunteering drops off during the child-rearing years. The need for specificity in predicting parents' volunteering is also seen in Becker and Dhingra, "Religious Involvement."

47. This coincides with Park and Smith's finding in "To Whom Much Has Been Given" that size of county population is negatively related to the community voluntarism of Protestant churchgoers.

48. Rebecca Anne Allahyari, *Visions of Charity: Volunteer Workers and Moral Community* (Berkeley: University of California Press, 2001), 205.

49. Lichterman, *Elusive Togetherness,* chap. 7.

50. This is reminiscent of the strategies of mutual recognition described by Michel Maffesoli, *The Time of Tribes* (Beverly Hills, CA: Sage, 1995).

6. Lutheran Social Ministry in Transition

1. A 2002 study by the Hudson Institute and the Center for Public Justice surveyed "charitable choice" initiatives in fifteen states and found 726 grants totaling more than $123 million. No comprehensive study of contracts with faith-based organizations has been completed. In March 2004, however, the White House Office of Faith-Based and Community Initiatives reported that federal grants to faith-based providers by Health and Human Services and the Housing and Urban Development rose a total of $144 million in fiscal 2002–2003 over the prior year.

2. "While there is a working assumption that faith-based organizations are effective, until very recently there had been little research proving the effectiveness of faith-based programs." Byron R. Johnson, *Objective Hope: Assessing the Effectiveness of Faith-Based Organizations,* Manhattan Institute, 2002, 9.

3. This is as true of evangelical communities as it is of more liberal ones. See Nathan Hatch, *The Democratization of American Christianity* (New Haven: Yale University Press, 1989) and Diana Eck, *A New Religious America* (New York: HarperCollins, 2001).

4. Among the discussions of religion's role in the founding of the American Republic, see Gary Wills, *Explaining America: The Federalist* (New York: Penguin Books, 2001), *Inventing America: Jefferson's Declaration of Independence* (New York: Vintage Books, 1979), and

Under God: Religion and Politics in America (New York: Vintage Books, 1991). I addressed this issue in *Religion in Public Life: A Dilemma for Democracy* (Washington, DC: The Century Fund/Georgetown University Press, 1996).

5. Ziad Munson, "Becoming an Activist: Believers, Sympathizers, and Mobilization in the American Pro-Life Movement" (diss., Harvard University, 2002), 236, 245–246. See also Chapter 9.

6. Thomas H. Jeavons, *When the Bottom Line Is Faithfulness: Management of Christian Service Organizations* (Bloomington and Indianapolis: Indiana University Press, 1994), xvi, 2, 51.

7. Ibid., 51.

8. Ibid., xviii.

9. Johnson, *Objective Hope*, 22.

10. The Catholic tradition of natural law reasoning is perhaps the best-known example of this phenomenon.

11. *D. Martin Luthers Werke: Kritische Gesamtausgabe* (Weimar: H. Boehlau, 1883), 39:5.

12. Ibid., 41:5.

13. The work of Amy Reynolds and Christopher Winship reported in Chapter 8 analyzes the relation between religious faith and associated values, life plans, and behavior. But the authors admit that the evidence is mixed and that further quantitative research will be necessary.

14. Diakon Web site.

15. Ibid.

16. Although the term "compliance officer" may have bureaucratic overtones, the person who holds this job is a graduate of a Lutheran seminary and a university law school. She is keenly aware of the importance of applying the Diakon values and principles in the personnel structure of the organization.

17. The agreement with the Roman Catholic Church: "Joint Declaration on Justification," *Evangelical Lutheran Church in America Documents,* October 31, 1999. The agreement with the Reformed churches: "A Formula of Agreement," *Evangelical Lutheran Church in America Documents,* 1997; with the Episcopal Church: "Called to Common Mission," *Evangelical Lutheran Church in America Documents,* 1999.

18. This distinction is drawn from Michael Polanyi, *Personal Knowledge: Towards a Post-Critical Philosophy* (Chicago: University of Chicago Press, 1958) and *Meaning* (Chicago: University of Chicago Press, 1975). It is also compatible with the notion of "background beliefs" as employed in "holist justification." For the use of holism in the justification of beliefs, see W. V. Quine, *Word and Object* (Cambridge: MIT

Press, 1960), *The Web of Belief* (New York: McGraw-Hill, 1978), and *Ontological Relativity and Other Essays* (New York: Columbia University Press, 1969).

19. The preliminary interviews were conducted with Julie Wilson, director of the Wiener Center for Social Policy at Harvard's Kennedy School of Government and the author of Chapter 7.

20. L. DeAne Lagerquist, *The Lutherans* (Westport, CT: Greenwood Press, 1999), 2.

21. Materials for this historical sketch were drawn from Sidney Ahlstrom, *A Religious History of the American People* (New Haven and London: Yale University Press, 1972); E. Clifford Nelson, *Lutheranism in North America, 1914–1970* (Minneapolis: Augsburg Publishing House, 1972); Abdel Ross Wentz, *A Basic History of Lutheranism in America* (Philadelphia: Fortress Press, 1955); Lagerquist, *The Lutherans*; J. Russell Hale, *Touching Lives through Service: The History of Tressler Lutheran Services* (Mechanicsburg, PA: Tressler Lutheran Services, 1994); Donald A. Miller, *A Gift of Love: The First Hundred Years of the Lutheran Home at Topton* (Topton, PA, 1995).

22. Wentz, *Basic History,* 55. Wentz notes, "it is indicative of the religious genius of the Lutheran church and her essential conservatism that up to this time [1862] she had not allowed the purely economic and moral issue of slavery to split her organization" (141). Ahlstrom argues that the localism of American Lutheranism meant "that extreme views often did not meet at this level." Lutheranism held within it both abolitionist sentiments (especially in the General Synod and the Franckean Synod) and defenses of slavery (especially in the churches of the South). But the overwhelming American Lutheran sentiment was anti-slavery. "The Lutheran Synods organized by new immigrant groups were for the most part in free territory, and they tended to oppose slavery, though they naturally preferred not to commit the church on what they regarded as secular political issues." Ahlstrom, *Religious History,* 667.

23. Wentz, *Basic History,* 321.

24. Ibid. This emphasis was not unique to Lutheran institutions but was the dominant ideology of social assistance in mid-nineteenth-century America. "The new institutions all rested on optimistic assumptions . . . that institutions could improve society through their impact on individual personalities." Michael B. Katz, *In the Shadow of the Poorhouse: A Social History of Welfare in America* (New York: Basic Books, 1996), 11.

25. From founding charter available at the Tressler Home. Although this period is notorious for the forced removal of children from the homes

of their impoverished parents and their placement in orphans' homes, there is no evidence that the Tressler Home ever participated in such efforts, even though the Society for the Prevention of Cruelty to Children (SPCC), one of the prime agents of poor-family breakup, was quite active in nearby Philadelphia. See Katz, *In the Shadow*, 107–113.

26. Census statistics regarding orphans are not well established until the early twentieth century, but it is clear that the second half of the nineteenth century saw an explosion of religious child-care institutions, particularly among Roman Catholics. By the turn of the century more than half of all dependent children were cared for within religious institutions, and a full 90 percent were housed by privately run organizations. "According to the figures for 1910, Catholics ran 24.4 percent of children's institutions, caring for 45 percent of the nation's dependent children; Protestants ran 23.7 percent, caring for 15.1 percent; Jews ran 2.2 percent, caring for 4.5 percent. The remainder was divided among other private organizations (39.7 percent, caring for 24.2 percent) and public institutions (10 percent, caring for 11.3 percent)" (U.S. Bureau of the Census, *Benevolent Institutions 1910*, p. 69). Susan Tiffin, *In Whose Best Interest? Child Welfare Reform in the Progressive Era* (Westport, CT: Greenwood Press, 1982), 84.

27. A classic example of the Lutheran rationale for the care of orphans can be found in the 1866 sermon of the Reverend John George Butler of St. Paul Lutheran Church in Washington, D.C. Butler, who would later become chaplain to both the House of Representatives and the Senate, as well as the president of the Lutheran General Synod, played an important role in the advancement of Lutheran social ministry in the postbellum era. Borrowing liberally from Lincoln's "Second Inaugural Address," Butler wrote, "With malice toward none; with charity for all; with firmness in the right, as God gives us to see the right, let us strive on to finish the work we are in; to bind up the nation's wounds; to care for him who shall have borne the battle and for his widow and his orphan, to do all which may achieve and cherish a just and lasting peace, among ourselves, and with all nations." Quoted in Hale, *Touching Lives*, 18.

28. Hale, *Touching Lives*, 10. The scope of the devastation created by the Civil War is difficult to comprehend, even by modern standards of warfare. The Union side alone suffered 364,511 mortal casualties, a ratio of 18 northerners killed per thousand in the population. These figures compare with 1.31 American per thousand who died in World War I and 3.14 per thousand who fell in World War II. Another

281,881 northern soldiers returned home wounded or with disabilities, accounting for another 14 per thousand of population. Theda Skocpol, *Protecting Soldiers and Mothers: The Political Origins of Social Policy in the United States* (Cambridge: Harvard University Press, 1992), 103–104. Even as late as 1910 Civil War pensioners accounted for nearly 25 percent of the population aged sixty-five and older in the state of Pennsylvania. Ibid., 133.

29. On state-church partnerships in the mid- to late nineteenth century, see Theda Skocpol, "Religion, Civil Society, and Social Provision in the U.S.," and Ronald Thiemann, Samuel Herring, and Betsy Perabo, "Risks and Responsibilities for Faith-Based Organizations," in *Who Will Provide? The Changing Role of Religion in American Social Welfare,* ed. Mary Jo Bane, Brent Coffin, and Ronald Thiemann (Boulder, CO: Westview Press, 2000), 21–72.

30. The Tressler Home's origins show that the provision of direct government funding to religious organizations is not, as its supporters claim, a recent Republican Party initiative. In *Protecting Soldiers and Mothers* Skocpol notes that under a 1862 Federal law, "widows, orphans, and other dependents of those who died for causes traceable to their Union military service also received pensions at the rates their relatives would have gotten for total disabilities" (107). Thus it is conceivable that the Tressler Home received not only direct state funding but also indirect federal funding by means of the orphans' pension payments. This observation is supported by Patrick J. Kelly, *Creating a National Home: Building the Veterans' Welfare State, 1860–1900* (Cambridge, MA: Harvard University Press, 1997). "Dependents of veterans received some, but not all, of the benefits available to ex-soldiers. Upon the death of a veteran, for example, his widow and any orphaned children became eligible for a government pension" (4).

31. "The 1890's mark the start of a new era in the history of social welfare . . . The first major alternative was child-saving. Child-saving not only shifted the focus of social welfare; even more, it rested on a new psychology, a series of major strategic innovations, an enhanced role for government, and a reordered set of relations between families and the state." Katz, *In the Shadow,* 117.

32. The minutes of the Board of Trustees indicate that the "retirement" was not altogether voluntary. "In view of the discordant and demoralized state of affairs at the Home since the opening of the new year . . . largely due to the incapacity of the venerable Superintendent, incident to the growing infirmities of age, it has become the duty of the Board to

consider the question and if possible provide some remedy." J. Russell Hale, *Touching Lives*, comments, "The board resolved to request Philip Willard's immediate resignation, as well as that of his wife, Nettie, then matron of the home" (33).

33. "Between the 1880s and 1916, fascination with the needs of children ignited an explosion of activity that produced juvenile courts, child labor laws, child guidance clinics, babies health contests, free lunch programs, kindergartens, the playground movement, experiments in progressive education, numerous child study groups, a profusion of organizations (such as the Big Brothers and Big Sisters, the Boy Scouts, Girl Scouts, and Lone Scout(s), the formation in 1912 of the United States Children's Bureau, and . . . new institutions and associations concerned with the special needs of dependent children." Leroy Ashby, *Saving the Waifs: Reformers and Dependent Children, 1890–1917* (Philadelphia: Temple University Press, 1984), 4.

34. "No Protestant communion was so thoroughly transformed by the later nineteenth-century immigration as was the Lutheran. Three million immigrants came from the diverse provinces of Germany, perhaps a half of them at least vaguely Lutheran, 1.75 million from Scandinavia, nearly all of them at least nominally Lutheran, and a heavy scattering of others from Finland, Iceland, and various parts of the Austro-Hungarian empire. They settled in every section of the country, in cities and on farms, but, of course, overwhelmingly in the North." Ahlstrom, *Religious History*, 756.

35. Katz, *In the Shadow*, 119.

36. Ashby, *Saving the Waifs*, 13. Ashby argues that the growth of such institutions indicates the "variety and diversity of Protestant voluntary activity" during these years. Ashby's work shows how deeply and pervasively religious motivations and rationales influenced the work of the "child savers" during the Progressive Era. See also Tiffin, *Whose Best*, 55. "Much of this altruism had a religious orientation. As was mentioned earlier, a fair number of welfare reformers entered social work via the ministry. To many others, welfare work was a practical substitute for a life in the church, a way to carry out a sense of mission to society that had been nurtured in their youth."

37. Susan Tiffin argues that the preference for foster-home care "was not logically necessary, nor was it based on any systematic empirical demonstration of the benefits of this type of care for the child's growth and development. The research efforts of these years were superficial and narrow in scope; their conclusions were tenuous" (*Whose Best*, 62).

The political pressure for change was, however, nearly overwhelming, based as it was on the abuses discovered in many orphanages and upon the "cult of domesticity" that dominated late-nineteenth- and early-twentieth-century America.

38. Byron C. Mathews as quoted in Tiffin, *Whose Best,* 75–76. Such criticism could easily be applied to the Tressler and Topton homes as well, and portends the increasing secularization of the social work movement.

39. Tiffin, *Whose Best,* 68–72.

40. Ibid., 79–83.

41. *Proceedings of the (1909) Conference on the Care of Dependent Children,* Washington, D.C., January 25–26 (repr. New York: Arno Press, 1971), 194.

42. Hale, *Touching Lives,* 41.

43. Ibid., 49.

44. This decline lags nearly two decades behind the nationwide movement to move children from orphanages into foster homes. In Massachusetts, for example, between 1876 and 1900 the proportion of dependent children living in state institutions dropped from 51 percent to 15 percent. Katz, *In the Shadow,* 125.

45. Hale, *Touching Lives,* 86.

46. Her article in the nationally distributed Sunday newspaper supplement *This Week* caused a national sensation.

47. Quoted in Hale, *Touching Lives,* 88–89. At this time Lutherans supported 73 orphanages serving 10,000 children. Of the 1,600 orphanages nationwide in 1950, more than half were church related.

48. Hale, *Touching Lives,* 91–92.

49. Tiffin, *Whose Best,* 127.

50. Steven Rathgeb Smith and Michael Lipsky, *Nonprofits for Hire: The Welfare State in the Age of Contracting* (Cambridge, MA: Harvard University Press, 1997), 55. The result of this law was a proliferation of contracts with nonprofit organizations to provide government services. The new approach to delivering government services was financed by a threefold increase in federal social welfare spending from 1965 to 1970 ($812 million to $2.2 billion). Government contracting with nonprofits grew throughout the 1970s, increasing from 25 percent of total public social service expenditures in 1971 to 49 percent in 1978. To take only a single example: between 1962 and 1973 government payments to Jewish agencies grew twentyfold, from $27 million to $561 million. See Katz, *In the Shadow,* 270.

51. Inevitably both homes began to exemplify the more general pattern within nonprofit agencies described by Michael Katz. "Partly as a consequence of decreased contributions, partly as a result of government policy, voluntary agencies have become increasingly dependent on public funds . . . As so much of their income came from government sources, voluntary agencies more frequently became service contractors, rather than innovators and pioneers" (*In the Shadow,* 271–272).

52. See Thiemann, *Religion and Public Life,* 121–173. Theories of secularization are currently undergoing serious critique and reformulation. Among the many volumes written on this topic, see Jose Casanova, *Public Religions in the Modern World* (Chicago: University of Chicago, Press, 1994); Steve Bruce, ed., *Religion and Modernization: Historians and Sociologists Debate the Secularization Thesis* (New York: Oxford University Press, 2001); and Peter Berger et al., eds., *The Desecularization of the World: Resurgent Religion and World Politics* (Grand Rapids, MI: Eerdmans Publishing House, 1999).

53. See Murray's classic work *We Hold These Truths: Catholic Reflections on the American Proposition* (New York: Sheed & Ward, 1988), especially chapter 2, "Civil Unity and Religious Integrity," 45–78.

54. The history of the merger movement within American Lutheranism is complex. It may be said, in summary, that while ethnic and theological divisions within the denomination made merging difficult, Lutherans in America still shared widespread theological and liturgical unity. All the merging organizations acknowledged the authority of the Augsburg Confession (1530) as binding upon their ordained clergy, and many of the groups used a common English hymnal and service book as early as 1890. By 1957 all of the merging church bodies adopted the common *Service Book and Hymnal,* a step that made the eventual merger much simpler and more harmonious.

55. For example, the 1997 Balanced Budget Act, especially the sections involving reimbursements and managed care under Medicare and Medicaid, seriously affected federal grants.

56. "As organizations that provided healthcare services, LSN [Lutheran Services Northeast] and TLS [Tressler Lutheran Services] weathered a storm of industry-related challenges. Managed care, reimbursement, and quality-assurance changes fundamentally altered the way governments and private insurance agencies did business with healthcare providers. They reduced and standardized payments for many services while also reducing the number of clients who are eligible for those services." Fern E. Nerhood, "Two Lutheran Nonprofits Become One:

The Merger of Lutheran Services Northeast and Tressler Lutheran Services," February 25, 2000.

57. For example, the two agencies had different approaches to adoption. Lutheran Services Northeast provided a wide range of adoption services, while Tressler Lutheran Services focused solely on special-need adoptions and thereby became a model for special-need adoptions nationwide.

58. "Merger Vision Statement" for Lutheran Services Northeast and Tressler Lutheran Services, 1999.

59. "Firm Hired to Help Name Newco," *Intersections* Newsletter, June 1999, 3.

60. "While it is often difficult and painful to consider these human issues, it was a great credit to both LSN and TLS that they approached these issues with due consideration of ethics, a desire to be a compassionate employer, and an effort to maintain people's dignity. These issues are especially important since—as faith-based organizations—they had a special commitment to act in a way that affirmed the organization's values and did not damage people's image of the Lutheran church." Nerhood, "Two Become One," 36.

61. See Clifford Geertz, *The Interpretation of Cultures* (New York: Basic Books, 1973), and *Local Knowledge: Further Essays in Interpretive Anthropology* (New York: Basic Books, 1983).

62. These terms are used in Johnson, *Objective Hope,* and discussed by Reynolds and Winship in Chapter 8.

63. The reluctance of the Tressler Home to move beyond the residential orphanage is a case in point.

7. Long-Term Care

1. Michael Katz, *In the Shadow of the Poorhouse* (New York, 1996).

2. Bruce Vladek, *Unloving Care: The Nursing Home Tragedy* (New York, 1980), 35.

3. For a detailed study of the growth of for-profit nursing homes over the last fifty years, see Vladek, *Unloving Care.*

4. I found no references to government providers.

5. Richard A. Hirth, "Consumer Information and Competition between Nonprofit and For-Profit Nursing Homes," *Journal of Health Economics* 18 (1999): 221.

6. William D. Spector et al., "The Impact of Ownership Type on Nursing Home Outcomes," *Health Economics* 7 (1998): 639–653. See also

Mark Schlesinger and Bradford Gray, "Non-Profit Organizations and Health Care: Burgeoning Research, Shifting Expectations and Persisting Puzzles," draft of forthcoming paper; William E. Aaronson, J. S. Zinn, and M. D. Rosko, "Do For-Profit and Not-For-Profit Nursing Homes Behave Differently?" *The Gerontologist* 34, no. 6 (1994): 775–786; Gooloo S. Wunderlich and Peter O. Kohler, eds., *Improving the Quality of Long-Term Care,* Institute of Medicine (Washington, DC, 2001).

7. In addition, many residents depend on hospital staff or families to select a nursing home. The characteristics of care a resident prefers may differ from those preferred by the individual making the decision.

8. For a detailed discussion of the different constraints faced by for-profit and not-for-profit organizations, see Burton Weisbrod, "Institutional Form and Organizational Behavior," in *Private Action and the Public Good,* ed. E. S. Clemens and W. W. Powell (New Haven, 1998), 70. One point he fails to make is that for-profit nursing homes have greater access to capital than do their not-for-profit peers.

9. Spector et al., "Impact of Ownership"; Schlesinger and Gray, "Non-Profit Organizations and Health Care."

10. As used in the industry, "activities of daily living" refer to tasks involved in caring for oneself and usually include bathing, dressing, eating, transferring in and out of a bed or chair, and using the toilet. "Instrumental activities of daily living" refer to slightly more demanding tasks involved in living independently. They usually include shopping, cooking, light housekeeping, money management, taking medications, and communicating with others verbally, in writing, or over the phone.

11. Robert L. Kane, "The Evolution of the American Nursing Home," in *The Future of Long-term Care: Social and Policy Issues,* ed. R. H. Binstock, L. E. Cluff, and O. Von Mering (Baltimore, 1996), 149.

12. AARP, *Beyond 50: A Report to the Nation on Trends in Health Security* (Washington, DC, May 2002), 68. A much smaller share of those under sixty-five needed nursing home care.

13. Wunderlich and Kohler, *Improving the Quality of Long-Term Care,* 42.

14. Mark Merlis, "Financing Long-Term Care in the Twenty-First Century: The Public and Private Roles," Commonwealth Fund, September 1999, 5; and Richard Kaplan, "Financing Long-Term Care in the United States: Who Should Pay for Mom and Dad?" Illinois Public Law and Legal Theory Research Paper Series, Research Paper no. 00-14, December 2001, 68.

15. AARP, *Beyond 50*, 87; Wunderlich and Kohler, *Improving the Quality of Long-Term Care*, 63.

16. Medicare is available for short-term posthospital nursing home stays. Medicaid covers long-term nursing home care. In order to be eligible for Medicaid, residents must meet income requirements. Those not initially eligible for Medicaid may become eligible after "spending down" their income or assets on care.

17. Josh Wiener and David Stevenson, "State Policy on Long-Term Care for the Elderly," *Health Affairs* (May/June 1998): 82.

18. Louis B. Hays, Associate Administrator for Operations, HCFA, in hearing before the Subcommittee on Aging of the Committee on Labor and Human Resources, United States Senate, June 13, 1991.

19. These include "nursing, dietary, physician, rehabilitative, dental and pharmacy services." Wunderlich and Kohler, *Improving the Quality of Long-Term Care*, 143.

20. The 165 inspection items fall into eight groups: mistreatment, quality of care, resident assessment, resident rights, nutrition and dietary, pharmacy service, environmental and administration deficiencies. Inspections are conducted approximately once a year at unannounced times. Although many states had state inspections prior to the implementation of OBRA 87, the new inspection standards exceeded those of many states.

21. Wunderlich and Kohler, *Improving the Quality of Long-Term Care*, 76.

22. Throughout the 1980s states were allowed to develop their own methodology for reimbursing providers, if their rates were reasonable and adequate. Because "reasonable" is an ambiguous term, state reimbursement rates were highly litigated and courts often mandated higher payments. In 1997 Congress repealed the Boren amendment that had included the "reasonable and adequate" requirement in the hope that states would be able to reduce the amount of money paid to nursing homes.

23. States pay approximately 43 percent of the cost of Medicaid but none of the cost of Medicare.

24. Normally states used the Certificate of Need process to limit the construction of new facilities or the expansion of existing ones.

25. Judith Feder, Harriet L. Komisar, and Merlene Niefeld, "Long-Term Care in the United States: An Overview," *Health Affairs* 19, no. 3 (May/June 2000): 40–56.

26. Ibid.

27. Wiener and Stevenson, "State Policy on Long-Term Care," 83. Although nursing homes have considerable leeway in determining what they will charge privately paying individuals for care, the amount of reimbursement for Medicaid and Medicare residents is set by state and federal governments, respectively.

28. Reimbursement rates are based on a hierarchy of medical conditions, level of dependency, and other needs. Pennsylvania uses the Resource Utilization Group III system (RUGS III), which assesses residents on forty-four categories in seven hierarchies: need for rehabilitation, extensive services or special care, clinically complex, impaired cognition, behavioral problems, and physical functions reduced. *The Pennsylvania Association of Non-Profit Homes for the Aging, Long-Term Care 2000: Statistics and Information,* Winter, 2000.

29. For a summary of his findings, see Weisbrod, "Institutional Form and Organizational Behavior," 69–84.

30. For-profits would consider this surplus a profit that could be distributed to shareholders or reinvested in the company. Not-for-profits are legally required to reinvest this surplus.

31. It has also encouraged providers to reach out to private pay patients who can initially pay higher rates until they "spend down" to Medicaid.

32. Peter Blau, *The Child Care Problem: An Economic Analysis* (New York, 2001).

33. See also David A. Miller, *A Gift of Love: The First Hundred Years of the Lutheran Home at Topton, 1896–1996* (Topton, PA, 1995); J. Russell Hale, *Touching Lives through Service: The History of Tressler Lutheran Services* (Mechanicsburg, PA, 1994); Fern E. Nerhood, "Two Lutheran Nonprofits Become One: The Merger of Lutheran Services Northeast and Tressler Lutheran Services," ms., February 25, 2000.

34. J. M. Childs, Jr., *Joined at the Heart: What It Means to Be Lutheran in Social Ministry,* Lutheran Services in America, St. Paul, MN, 2000.

35. National Citizens Coalition for Nursing Home Reform, "A Consumer Perspective on Quality Care: The Resident's Point of View," ms., 1985, II-23.

36. Shu-Chiung Chou, Duncan P. Boldy, and Andy H. Lee, "Measuring Resident Satisfaction in Residential Aged Care," *The Gerontologist* 41, no. 5 (2001): 623–631; Celeste Shawler, Graham D. Rowles, and Dallas M. High, "Analysis of Key Decision-Making Incidents in the Life of a Nursing Home Resident," *The Gerontologist* 41, no. 5 (2001): 612–622; Susan Eaton, "Pennsylvania's Nursing Homes: Pro-

moting Quality Care and Quality Jobs," Keystone Research Center High Road Industry Series, no. 1, April 1997; Timothy Diamond, *Making Gray Gold: Narratives of Nursing Home Care* (Chicago, 1992).

37. Linda Emanuel, "Palliative Care: A Weak Link in the Chain of Civilized Life," in *Aging: Decisions at the End of Life*, ed. David N. Weisstub et al. (Dordrecht, 2001), 31–47.

38. General Accounting Office, "Nursing Home Quality of Care More Related to Staffing than Spending," GAO-02–431R, June 13, 2002; Chou, Boldy, and Lee, "Measuring Resident Satisfaction"; Joan Fitzgerald, "Better-Paid Caregivers, Better Care," *American Prospect* 12, no. 9, May 21, 2001, Web version, 1–6.

39. In contrast to for-profit nursing homes, not-for-profit homes registered as 501(c)(3) organizations can receive tax-exempt donations. For a detailed discussion of this, see Weisbrod, "Institutional Form and Organizational Behavior," 72.

40. Shin-Yi Chou, "Asymmetric Information, Ownership and Quality of Care: An Empirical Analysis of Nursing Homes," *Journal of Health Economics* 21 (2002): 293–311.

41. The data are taken from the On-Line Survey, Certification and Reporting system of the Department of Health and Human Services as of July 2002. In total, 134 nursing homes accepting Medicare patients only or located within a hospital were excluded from this analysis. Nursing homes that do not accept Medicaid or Medicare were not included in the data set, but represent only a small share of all homes.

42. Pennsylvania investigates complaints within two days and is one of only a few states that have taken advantage of federal guidelines allowing states to refer chain-owned homes for sanctions if any home in the chain has an actual-harm deficiency on an inspection. William Scanlon, Senate testimony (USGAO).

43. When data on religious identification were not available or unclear on a nursing home's Web site, we called the home. We chose to interview the receptionist, rationalizing that if the receptionist reported the home was not religiously affiliated or was uncertain whether it was religiously affiliated or not, the home had either no or little public religious identity.

44. Difference of means for Protestant versus Catholic nursing homes: $t = -1.9275$; $p < t = 0.0275$. Difference of means for Protestant versus Jewish nursing homes: $t = -1.5740$; $p < t = 0.0592$.

45. Mainline Protestant versus Catholic: $t = -1.5384$; $p < t = 0.0631$. Mainline Protestant versus Jewish: $t = -1.5740$; $p < t = 0.0592$.
46. Further research is also needed to more accurately identify networks of nursing homes. We believe some providers may be confused about whether they are part of a network. For example, one nursing home in our sample reports being part of a network affiliated with the Evangelical Congregational Church (ECC). The ECC has two nursing homes in Pennsylvania, one of which reports being part of a network and one of which does not.
47. The Diakon partnership with a for-profit home is coded as religious.
48. Pennsylvania's Medicaid CMI is based on the RUGS III system, which classifies residents by medical conditions and dependency; see note 29. For a detailed discussion of the Pennsylvania system, see the Pennsylvania Association of Non-Profit Homes for the Aging, *Long-Term Care 2000*.
49. Nonprofit religious versus Nonprofit secular: $t = -1.7363$; $p < t = 0.0428$. Nonprofit religious versus For-profit corporation: $t = -4.2649$; $p < t = 0.0000$. Nonprofit religious versus For-profit other: $t = -5.3398$; $p < t = 0.000$. Nonprofit religious versus Government: $t = -1.7268$; $p < t = 0.0482$.
50. It would be better to have CMI data for residents at the time they entered the home. Unfortunately, such data are not available and we are limited to examining resident CMI at a point in time.
51. Wunderlich and Kohler, *Improving the Quality of Long-Term Care*; Abt Associates, "Appropriateness of Minimum Nurse Staffing Ratios in Nursing Homes: Overview of the Phase II Report: Background, Study Approach, Findings and Conclusions," December 2001; Eaton, "Pennsylvania's Nursing Homes"; Susan Reinhard and Robyn Stone, "Promoting Quality in Nursing Homes: The Wellspring Model," The Commonwealth Fund, January 2001.
52. This might occur naturally if the nursing home is part of a continuum of care and those in the affiliated assisted living settings are predominantly members of the same religion.
53. The On-Line Survey and Certification Assessment Reporting system (OSCAR) provides information on state inspections of nursing homes. Inspections are conducted by state officials under guidance from the Department of Health and Human Services. Much of the information for each inspection is initially gathered by nursing home personnel and checked by inspectors. The advantages of using OSCAR data are that they provide similar information on each nursing home and this infor-

mation is reasonably detailed. The disadvantage is that the survey is complicated to complete and the data are not audited. However, since nursing homes can contest the findings, there is a general sense that the data do not err on the side of overestimating problems with care quality. For a more detailed discussion of these data, see Wunderlich and Kohler, *Improving the Quality of Long-Term Care.*

54. Abt Associates, "Appropriateness of Minimum Nurse Staffing Ratios."

55. Frederic H. Decker et al., "Staffing of Nursing Services in Nursing Homes: Present Issues and Prospects for the Future," *Seniors Housing and Care Journal* 9, no. 1 (2001): 14.

56. Joan Fitzgerald, "Better-Paid Caregivers, Better Care," *American Prospect* 12, no. 9 (May 21, 2001): 1 (Web edition).

57. Joan Fitzgerald and Virginia Carlson, "Ladders to a Better Life," *American Prospect* 11, no. 15 (June 19–July 3, 2000), 3 (Web edition).

58. Abt Associates, "Appropriateness of Minimum Nurse Staffing Ratios."

59. Religious nonprofits versus For-profit corporations: Total staff, $t = 3.8025, p < t = .0001$; CNAs, $t = 5.7925, p < t = 0.0000$. Versus For-profit proprietorships: Total staff, $t = 3.0853, p < t = 0.0001$; CNAs, $t = 4.6428, p < t = 0.000$. Versus Government: RNs, $t = -49.76428, p < t = 0.000$; LPNs, $t = -2.6501, p < t = 0.0043$.

60. The difference in rates is significant at the .10 level only for for-profit corporations. Religious nonprofit versus For-profit corporation: $t = 1.3813; p > t = 0.0840$.

61. "Meet 'Tippy,' New Resident at Topton," *The Lutheran Home at Topton*, vol. 2, no. 1, Winter 2000, 1.

62. Interview with staff of Diakon Lutheran Social Ministries at the Lutheran Home of Topton, February 2, 2001.

63. Interviews conducted by Susan Eaton.

64. Religious nonprofit versus For-profit corporation: $t = -3.4877; p < t = 0.0003$. Religious nonprofit versus For-profit proprietorship: $t = 3.2485; p < t = 0.0007$.

65. The difference in restraint use between Religious nursing homes and Nonprofit corporations: $t = -3.2128; p < t = 0.0007$. Versus Nonprofit: $t = -3.4743; p < t = 0.0007$. Versus Secular nonprofits: $t = -1.5493; p < t = 0.0612$. Versus Government: $t = -0.6652; p < t = 0.2533$.

66. The Hirschman-Herfindahl Index is the sum of squares of the market shares of the nursing homes, where market shares are measured by

share of beds in the county. The HHI varies from 1 to a limit of zero, which would be perfect competition. We chose 0.15 as the cutoff because this is the level below which any corporate merger is exempt from federal scrutiny.

67. For example, see Reinhard and Stone, "Wellspring Model."

8. Faith, Practice, and Teens

1. This chapter presents our preliminary and partial findings.
2. Byron R. Johnson, *Objective Hope: Assessing the Effectiveness of Faith-Based Organizations,* Manhattan Institute, 2002.
3. "Faithful Nation: What American Adults and Teens Think about Faith, Morals, Religion, and Teen Pregnancy," National Campaign to Prevent Teen Pregnancy, 2001.
4. Ann M. Meier, "Adolescents' Transition to First Intercourse, Religiosity, and Attitudes about First Sex," *Social Forces* 81 (2003): 1031–1052.
5. Karin L. Brewster, "Race Differences in Sexual Activity among Adolescent Women: The Role of Neighborhood Characteristics," *American Sociological Review* 59 (1994): 408–424.
6. Isabel Sawhill, "Policy Brief no. 8: What Can Be Done to Reduce Teen Pregnancy and Out-of-Wedlock Births?" Brookings Institution, 2001.
7. Barbara Defoe Whitehead, Brian Wilcox and Sharon Rostosky, "Keeping the Faith: The Role of Religion and Faith Communities in Preventing Teen Pregnancy," National Campaign to Prevent Teen Pregnancy, 2001.
8. Peter Bearman and Hannah Brückner, "Promising the Future: Virginity Pledges and First Intercourse," *American Journal of Sociology* 106 (2001): 859–912.
9. Byron R. Johnson, "The Role of African-American Churches in Reducing Crime among Black Youth," Manhattan Institute, 1998.
10. Some of the ways personal religiosity is measured include the reported frequency of attendance at services, prayer, Bible study, participation in religious activities, and self-reporting about the importance of religion.
11. "CASA National Survey of Teens, Teachers, and Principals," published by the National Center on Addiction and Substance Abuse, Columbia University, 1998.
12. Byron R. Johnson, "A Better Kind of High: How Religious Commitment Reduces Drug Use among Poor Urban Teens," Manhattan Institute, 2001.

13. E. A. Suchman, *Evaluative Research: Principles and Practice in Public Service and Social Action Programs* (New York, 1967); C. H. Weiss, *Evaluation Research: Models of Assessing Program Effectiveness* (Englewood Cliffs, NJ, 1972); and Andrew Sayer, *Method in Social Science: A Realist Approach* (London: 1992).

14. All the girls in our sample are African American and live in urban cities. They range in age from twelve to twenty, with younger and older girls interviewed in each program. We were not able to control for family characteristics, income levels, and life experiences. See James Nonnemaker, Clean McNeely and Robert W. Blum, "Public and Private Domains of Religiosity and Adolescent Health Risk Behaviors: Evidence from the National Longitudinal Study of Adolescent Health," presented at the ADD Health Users Workshop, 2001. Also see Johnson, *Objective Hope*.

15. Karyn Lacy, "The Influence of Boston Freedom Summer on the Religious Development and Value Systems of Teenagers and Young Adults," Department of Sociology, Harvard University, 1997.

16. Only "Tina" from our sample was originally active in the church, because of her family.

17. Some information was missing for those involved with the Summer of Hope program.

18. Robert Coles, *The Spiritual Life of Children* (Boston, 1990).

19. About half of the girls said that this knowledge does not come from their families, who are minimally involved in faith communities. For the other half, it is reinforced through family religious participation, although none of the girls were active in the church associated with this program.

20. Summer of Hope tries to foster these relationships through college-age mentors, many of whom are not active Christians. For those in Discover Yourself, these relationships are important. The woman minister in charge of the program is personally close to many of the girls, who appear to respect her. She has encouraged some girls to return to school or push on with their goals. In Connecting Youth, the youth all have workers involved in the church. Many have specific mentors. For some, these relationships seem as important as those for the girls in Discover Yourself. The difference between these two programs is that in Connecting Youth, the girls come in contact with many different adult leaders.

21. Some youth in Boston Project cite logistics as their reason for not attending religious activities and services.

22. For girls in Summer of Hope, we had to rely solely on their comments on the church and the program to understand their sense of their morality.
23. Lacy, "Influence of Boston Freedom Summer."
24. We do not know about their views of family and marriage.
25. These rings symbolize a commitment to stay sexually chaste until marriage.
26. Peter L. Berger, *The Sacred Canopy* (Garden City, NY, 1969).
27. Robert Wuthnow, *After Heaven: Spirituality in America since the 1950s* (Berkeley, 1998).
28. Lacy, "Influence of Boston Freedom Summer."

9. God, Abortion, and Democracy in the Pro-Life Movement

1. Andy and all other names of activists in this chapter are pseudonyms.
2. It is worth noting that partisans on both sides of the abortion debate view the issue in dichotomous terms. Pro-choice activists are equally fervent in their belief that abortion is an absolute right of women, above and beyond any other moral or legal concerns.
3. Figure derived from the 2000 General Social Survey, variable ABDEFECT; results from other polls on this issue are similar.
4. This statement was made by a man, but those who do not believe in abortion even in cases where the life of the mother is in jeopardy are equally distributed among men and women; however, married people are more likely to believe this is an acceptable justification than those who are single.
5. Fred, a fifty-six-year-old in Charleston, provides a typical expression of this point of view: "I would love to see them right now, this year, pass a federal law that abortions are illegal with the exception of health of the mother and rape and incest. It would be better than what we have now. I would settle for that compromise at this point. I would like to see it completely done away with, but I don't think that will happen at one stroke of the pen."
6. Rank-and-file activists in the movement are much more likely to express a religious basis for their opposition to abortion than are movement leaders. This may be due, in part, to the slightly higher levels of education among the leadership as compared with regular members. Leaders are more sensitive to public relations issues and choose to express more secular arguments that they believe will better resonate with the general public.

7. Compare this number with 59 percent of the general churchgoing population, according to the 2000 Princeton Survey Research Associates Poll (August 24), question 013.

8. Overall 66 percent of my sample is Catholic and 12 percent Southern Baptist, with the remainder spread across the full spectrum of other mainline and evangelical denominations.

9. Exceptions tend to be Catholics, who express the belief that abortion is wrong because the Catholic Church teaches it is wrong. Even in these cases, however, the religious beliefs of rank-and-file activists tend to be theologically unsophisticated and strongly influenced by the pro-life movement itself.

10. Some activists go further and argue that legalized abortion in the United States is far worse than the Holocaust, simply because of the scale of death.

11. On December 30, 1994, John Salvi killed two women and wounded five others at abortion clinics in Brookline, Massachusetts, a suburb of Boston. Salvi committed suicide in prison in 1996.

12. Subjects were not chosen through a random probability sample, but I made every effort in each location to identify and contact the most "extreme" elements of the pro-life movement. I am confident that sympathy for violence against abortion providers is rare even if my data do not allow me to precisely quantify how rare.

13. See Celeste Condit, *Decoding Abortion Rhetoric: Communicating Social Change* (Urbana: University of Illinois Press, 1990).

14. *Roe v. Wade* and its companion case handed down the same day, *Doe v. Bolton,* together deal with the legal status of abortion. They established the conditions under which states can regulate the procedure.

15. Doug's views are extreme in the sense that they are dramatically different from the views of most Americans on abortion and on religious faith.

Conclusion

1. The Conclusion represents the views of the members of the Taking Faith Seriously seminar and was drafted by Mary Jo Bane, Brent Coffin, and Richard Higgins.

2. Mainstream practice is more tolerant in part because of the recent focus in America on spirituality as opposed to doctrine. Among the books that have documented the cultural effects of the spirituality boom are Wade Clark Roof, *Spiritual Marketplace, Baby Boomers,*

and the Remaking of American Religion (Princeton, NJ: Princeton University Press, 1999), Robert Wuthnow, *After Heaven: Spirituality in America since the 1950s* (Berkeley: University of California Press, 1998), and Alan Wolfe, *One Nation, After All: What Middle-Class Americans Really Think About* (New York: Viking Press, 1998). In *A New Religious America* (San Francisco: HarperCollins, 2001), Diana L. Eck documents the overall growth, despite strains, of religious tolerance and pluralism in America.

Bibliography

Ahlstrom, Sydney E. *A Religious History of the American People.* New Haven, CT: Yale University Press, 1972.

Allahyari, Rebecca Anne. *Visions of Charity: Volunteer Workers and Moral Community.* Berkeley: University of California Press, 2001.

Allmendinger, David F. *Paupers and Scholars: The Transformation of Student Life in Nineteenth-Century New England.* New York: St. Martin's Press, 1972.

Ammerman, Nancy. *Congregation and Community.* New Brunswick, NJ: Rutgers University Press, 1997.

Anderson, Elijah. *Code of the Street.* New York: W. W. Norton, 1990.

——— *Streetwise: Race, Class, and Change in an Urban Community.* Chicago: University of Chicago Press, 1990.

Ashby, Leroy. *Saving the Waifs: Reformers and Dependent Children, 1890–1917.* Philadelphia: Temple University Press, 1984.

Bacon, Leonard. *The Christian Doctrine of Stewardship in Respect to Property.* New Haven, CT: Printed by Nathan Whiting, 1832.

Bacon, Theodore Davenport. *Leonard Bacon: A Statesman in the Church.* New Haven, CT: Yale University Press, 1931.

Baggett, Jerome P. *Habitat for Humanity: Building Private Homes, Building Public Religion.* Philadelphia: Temple University Press, 2001.

Baldovin, John F. *Bread of Life, Cup of Salvation: Understanding the Mass.* Chicago: Sheed and Ward/Rowman and Littlefield, 2003.

Baltzell, E. Digby. *Puritan Boston and Quaker Philadelphia: Two Protestant Ethics and the Spirit of Class Authority and Leadership.* New York: Free Press, 1979.

Becker, Penny Edgell. *Congregations in Conflict: Cultural Models of Local Religious Life.* Cambridge: Cambridge University Press, 1999.

Beecher, Lyman. *Autobiography,* ed. Barbara M. Cross. Cambridge, MA: Harvard University Press, 1961.

———— *Plea for the West.* Cincinnati: Truman and Smith, 1835.

Bellah, Robert N. "The Idea of Practices in Habits: A Response." In *Community in America: The Challenge of Habits of the Heart,* ed. Charles H. Reynolds and Ralph V. Norman. Berkeley: University of California Press, 1988.

Bellah, Robert N., Richard Madsen, William M. Sullivan, Ann Swidler, and Steven Tipton. *Habits of the Heart: Individualism and Commitment in American Life.* Berkeley: University of California Press, 1985.

Benhabib, Seyla. *Situating the Self.* New York: Routledge Press, 1992.

Bergant, Dianne. *Preaching the New Lectionary: Year C.* Collegeville, MN: Liturgical Press, 2000.

Berger, Peter L. "The Desecularization of the World: A Global Overview." In *The Desecularization of the World: Resurgent Religion and World Politics,* ed. Peter L. Berger. Grand Rapids, MI: Eerdmans, 1999.

———— *A Far Glory: The Quest for Faith in an Age of Credulity.* New York: Free Press, 1992.

———— *The Sacred Canopy.* Garden City, NY: Anchor Doubleday, 1969.

Blau, Peter. *The Child Care Problem: An Economic Analysis.* New York: Russell Sage, 2001.

Bonneau, Mormand. *The Sunday Lectionary: Ritual Word, Paschal Shape.* Collegeville, MN: Liturgical Press, 1998.

Brown, Dorothy M., and Elizabeth McKeown. *The Poor Belong to Us: Catholic Charities and American Welfare.* Cambridge, MA: Harvard University Press, 1997.

Burghardt, Walter J. *Preaching the Just Word.* New Haven, CT: Yale University Press, 1996.

Bushman, Richard. *From Puritan to Yankee: Character and the Social Order in Connecticut, 1690–1765.* New York: W. W. Norton, 1967.

Casanova, Jose. *Public Religions in the Modern World.* Chicago: University of Chicago Press, 1994.

Catechism of the Catholic Church. Liguori, MO: Liguori Publications, 1994.

Chaves, Mark. *Congregations in America.* Cambridge, MA: Harvard University Press, 2004.

Coles, Robert. *The Spiritual Life of Children.* Boston: Houghton Mifflin, 1990.

"The Constitution on the Sacred Liturgy," Vatican II, 1963. Translated in *The Liturgy Documents: Volume One*, ed. Elizabeth Hoffman, 375–376. Chicago: Liturgical Training Publications, 1991. See also Rynne (1968).

Cooper, Lee R. "Publish or Perish." In *Religious Movements in Contemporary America*, ed. Irving I. Zaretsky and Mark P. Leone. Princeton, NJ: Princeton University Press, 1974.

Coriden, James A. *The Parish in Catholic Tradition: History, Theology, and Canon Law*. Mahwah, NJ: Paulist Press, 1997.

Curran, Charles E. *The Catholic Moral Tradition Today: A Synthesis*. Washington, DC: Georgetown University Press, 1999.

——— "Relating Religious-Ethical Inquiry to Economic Policy." In *The Catholic Challenge to the American Economy*, ed. Thomas M. Gannon. New York: Macmillan Publishing, 1987.

Daniels, Bruce C. *The Connecticut Town: Growth and Development*. Middletown, CT: Wesleyan University Press, 1979.

D'Antonio, William V., James D. Davidson, Dean R. Hoge, and Katherine Meyer. *American Catholics: Gender, Generation, and Commitment*. Walnut Creek, CA: Altamira, 2001.

Davis, Joseph S. *Essays on the Earlier History of American Corporations*. Cambridge, MA: Harvard University Press, 1917.

Deetz, James. *In Small Things Forgotten: The Archaeology of Early American Life*. New York: Doubleday, 1977.

Demerath, N. J., Peter Dobkin Hall, Rhys H. Williams, and Terry Schmitt, eds. *Sacred Companies: Organizational Aspects of Religion and Religious Aspects of Organizations*. New York: Oxford University Press, 1998.

Diamond, Timothy. *Making Gray Gold: Narratives of Nursing Home Care*. Chicago: University of Chicago Press, 1992.

Dillon, Michele. *Catholic Identity: Balancing Reason, Faith, and Power*. New York: Cambridge University Press, 1999.

Donahue, John R. *What Does the Lord Require? A Bibliographical Essay on the Bible and Social Justice*. St. Louis, MO: Seminar on Jesuit Spirituality, 1993.

Douglas, Mary. *How Institutions Think*. Syracuse, NY: Syracuse University Press, 1986.

Durkheim, Emile. "Individualism and the Intellectuals." In *Durkheim on Religion*, ed. W. S. F Pickering. London: Routledge and Kegan Paul, 1975.

Dwight, Timothy. "Greenfield Hill" and "The Triump of Infidelity." In *The*

Connecticut Wits, ed. Vernon L. Parrington. New York: Thomas Y. Crowell and Company, 1969.

—— *Travels in New England and New York.* 4 vols. Cambridge, MA: Harvard University Press, 1969.

Eck, Diana L. *A New Religious America.* San Francisco: HarperCollins, 2001.

Edwards, Jonathan. *The Works of Jonathan Edwards.* Andover, MA: Allen, Morrill and Wardwell, Printers, 1842.

Emanuel, Linda. "Palliative Care: A Weak Link in the Chain of Civilized Life." In *Aging: Decisions at the End of Life,* ed. David N. Weisstub, pp. 31–47. Dordrecht: Kluwer Academic Publishers, 2001.

Emerson, Michael O., and Christian Smith. *Divided by Faith: Evangelical Religion and the Problem of Race in America.* New York: Oxford University Press, 2000.

Farley, Edward. *Good and Evil: Interpreting a Human Condition.* Minneapolis: Fortress Press, 1990.

Finke, Roger, and Rodney Stark. *The Churching of America, 1776–1990: Winners and Losers in Our Religious Economy.* New Brunswick, NJ: Rutgers University Press, 1992.

Flannery, Austin, ed. *Vatican Council II: The Basic Sixteen Documents: Constitutions, Decrees, Declarations.* Northport, NY: Costello Publishing, 1996.

Forell, George W. *Faith Active in Love: An Investigation of the Principles Underlying Luther's Social Ethics.* New York: American Press, 1954.

Foster, Charles I. *An Errand of Mercy: The Evangelical United Front, 1790–1837.* Chapel Hill: University of North Carolina Press, 1960.

Frederickson, George M. *The Inner Civil War: Northern Intellectuals and the Crisis of the Union.* New York: Harper and Row, 1965.

Friedland, Roger, and Robert R. Alford. "Bringing Society Back In: Symbols, Practices, and Institutional Contradictions." In *The New Institutionalism in Organizational Analysis,* ed. Walter Powell and Paul DiMaggio. Chicago: University of Chicago Press, 1991.

Froehle, Bryan T., and Mary L. Gautier. *Catholicism USA.* Maryknoll, NY: Orbis Books, 2000.

Fuechtmann, Thomas B., ed. *Consistent Ethic of Life.* Kansas City, MO: Sheed and Ward, 1988.

Gaillardetz, Richard R. *Teaching with Authority: A Theology of the Magisterium in the Church.* Collegeville, MN: Liturgical Press, 1997.

Gallup, George Jr., and D. Michael Lindsay. *Surveying the Religious Landscape: Trends in U.S. Belief.* Harrisburg, PA: Morehouse Publishing, 1999.

Gamm, Gerald H. *Urban Exodus: Why the Jews Left Boston and the Catholics Stayed.* Cambridge, MA: Harvard University Press, 1999.

"Gaudium et Spes: Pastoral Constitution on the Church in the Modern World." In *Vatican Council II: The Basic Sixteen Documents,* ed. Austin Flannery. Northport, NY: Costello Publishing, 1995.

Geertz, Clifford. *The Interpretation of Cultures.* New York: Basic Books, 1973.

Gill, Robin. *Churchgoing and Christian Ethics.* New York: Cambridge University Press, 1999.

Greeley, Andrew M. *The Catholic Myth: The Behavior and Beliefs of American Catholics.* New York: Charles Scribner's Sons, 1990.

Greene, M. Louise. *The Development of Religious Liberty in Connecticut.* New Haven, CT: Yale University Press, 1905.

Griffen, Clifford S. *Moral Stewardship in the United States, 1800–1865.* New Brunswick, NJ: Rutgers University Press, 1960.

Griffin, Farah Jasmine. *"Who Set You Flowin'?": The African-American Migration Narrative.* New York: Oxford University Press, 1995.

Gritsch, Eric W. *Fortress Introduction to Lutheranism.* Minneapolis: Fortress Press, 1994.

Gula, Richard M. *Reason Informed by Faith: Foundations of Catholic Morality.* Mahwah, NJ: Paulist Press, 1989.

Gustafson, James M. *Can Ethics Be Christian?* Chicago: University of Chicago Press, 1975.

——— *The Church as Moral Decision-Maker.* Boston: Pilgrim Press, 1970.

——— *Ethics from a Theocentric Perspective.* Vol. 1: *Theology and Ethics.* Chicago: University of Chicago Press, 1981.

——— *Intersections: Science, Theology, and Ethics.* Cleveland: Pilgrim Press, 1996.

Hall, Peter Dobkin. "Historical Perspectives on Religion, Government, and Social Welfare in America." In *Can Charitable Choice Work?: Covering Religion's Impact on Urban Affairs and Social Services,* ed. Andrew Walsh. Pew Program on Religion and the News Media and the Leonard E. Greenberg Center for the Study of Religion in Public Life, 2001.

Hammond, Phillip E. *Religion and Personal Autonomy: The Third Disestablishment in America.* Columbia: University of South Carolina Press, 1992.

Hays, Richard B. *The Moral Vision of the New Testament: A Contemporary Introduction to New Testament Ethics.* San Francisco: Seabury Press, 1996.

Hodgkinson, Virginia A., Murray S. Weitzman, and Arthur D. Kirsch.

"From Commitment to Action: How Religious Involvement Affects Giving and Volunteering." In *Faith and Philanthropy in America: Exploring the Role of Religion in America's Voluntary Sector,* ed. Robert Wuthnow and Virginia A. Hodgkinson. San Francisco: Jossey-Bass, 1990.

Hoffman, Elizabeth, ed. *The Liturgy Documents: Volume One.* Chicago: Liturgical Training Publications, 1991. See also Rynne (1968).

Hoge, Dean R., Patrick McNamara, and Charles Zech. *Plain Talk about Churches and Money.* Washington, DC: Alban Institute, 1997.

Hoge, Dean R., Charles Zech, Patrick McNamara, and Michael Donahue. *Money Matters: Personal Giving in American Churches.* Louisville, KY: Westminster John Knox Press, 1996.

Hopewell, James F. *Congregations: Stories and Structures.* Philadelphia: Fortress Press, 1987.

Hughes, H. Kathleen, and Mark R. Francis, eds. *Living No Longer for Ourselves: Liturgy and Justice in the Nineties.* Collegeville, MN: Liturgical Press, 1991.

Isaac, Rhys. *The Transformation of Virginia, 1740–1790.* Chapel Hill: University of North Carolina Press, 1982.

Jeavons, Thomas H. *When the Bottom Line Is Faithfulness: Management of Christian Service Organizations.* Bloomington: Indiana University Press, 1994.

Joas, Hans. *The Genesis of Values.* Chicago: University of Chicago Press, 2000.

Kane, Robert L. "The Evolution of the American Nursing Home." In *The Future of Long-Term Care: Social and Policy Issues,* ed. Robert H. Binstock, Leighton E. Cluff, and Otto von Mering, 145–168. Baltimore: Johns Hopkins University Press, 1996.

Katz, Michael B. *In the Shadow of the Poorhouse: A Social History of Welfare in America.* New York: Basic Books, 1996.

Keeler, Robert F. *Parish!* New York: Crossroad Publishing Company, 1997.

Kingsley, H. C., Leonard J. Sanford, and Thomas R. Trowbridge, eds. *Leonard Bacon: Pastor of the First Church in New Haven.* New Haven, CT: Tuttle, Morehouse and Taylor Printers, 1882.

Kostarelos, Frances. *Feeling the Spirit: Faith and Hope in an Evangelical Black Storefront Church.* Columbia: University of South Carolina Press, 1995.

Lagerquist, L. DeAne. *The Lutherans.* Westport, CT: Greenwood Press, 1999.

Leege, David C., and Paul D. Mueller. "How Catholic Is the Catholic Vote?" In *American Catholics and Civic Engagement: A Distinctive*

Voice, ed. Margaret O'Brien Steinfels. Lanham, MD: Sheed and Ward/ Rowman and Littlefield, 2004.

Lichterman, Paul. *Elusive Togetherness: Religion in the Quest for Civic Renewal.* Princeton, NJ: Princeton University Press, 2004.

Lincoln, C. Eric, and Lawrence H. Mamiya. *The Black Church in the African American Experience.* Durham, NC: Duke University Press, 1990.

Lohfink, Norbert F., S.J. *Option for the Poor: The Basic Principle of Liberation Theology in the Light of the Bible.* N. Richland Hills, TX: Bibal Press, 1987.

Loury, Glenn C. *The Anatomy of Racial Inequality.* Cambridge, MA: Harvard University Press, 2002.

Lumen Gentium (Dogmatic Constitution on the Church), Vatican II, 1963. Translated in *Vatican Council II: The Basic Sixteen Documents,* ed. Austin Flannery. Northport, NY: Costello Publishing, 1996.

Madison, James. "Memorial and Remonstrance against Religious Assessments." In *The American Enlightenment,* ed. Adrienne Koch, 382–384. New York: George Braziller, 1965.

Madsen, Richard, William M. Sullivan, Ann Swidler, and Steven M. Tipton. *Meaning and Modernity: Religion, Polity and Self.* Berkeley: University of California Press, 2002.

Maffesoli, Michel. *The Time of Tribes.* Beverly Hills, CA: Sage, 1995.

Manza, Jeff, and Nathan Wright. "Religion and Political Behavior." In *The Handbook of the Sociology of Religion,* ed. Michele Dillon, 297–314. New York: Cambridge University Press, 2003.

Marsden, George. *Jonathan Edwards: A Life.* New Haven, CT: Yale University Press, 2003.

Marty, Martin E. *Health and Medicine in the Lutheran Tradition.* New York: Crossroad Publishing Company, 1986.

——— *The One and the Many: America's Struggle for the Common Good.* Cambridge, MA: Harvard University Press, 1997.

Massaro, Thomas J., and Thomas A. Shannon, eds. *American Catholic Social Teaching.* Collegeville, MN: Liturgical Press, 2002.

McRoberts, Omar M. *Streets of Glory: Church and Community in a Black Urban Neighborhood.* Chicago: University of Chicago Press, 2003.

Mead, Sidney Earl. *Nathaniel William Taylor, 1786–1858: A Connecticut Liberal.* Hamden, CT: Archon Books, 1967.

Meiners, Mark R. "The Financing and Organization of Long-Term Care." In *The Future of Long-Term Care: Social and Policy Issues,* ed. Robert H. Binstock, Leighton E. Cluff, and Otto von Mering, 191–214. Baltimore: Johns Hopkins University Press, 1996.

Miller, David A., II. *A Gift of Love: The First Hundred Years of the Lu-*

theran Home at Topton, 1896–1996. Topton, PA: Lutheran Home at Topton, 1995.

Miller, Donald E. *Reinventing American Protestantism: Christianity in the New Millennium.* Berkeley: University of California Press, 1997.

Minow, Martha. "About Women, about Culture: About Them, about Us." In *Engaging Cultural Differences: The Multicultural Challenge in Liberal Democracies,* ed. Richard A. Shweder, Martha Minow, and Hazel Rose Markus, 252–268. New York: Russell Sage Foundation, 2002.

—— *Not Only for Myself.* New York: New Press, 1997.

—— *Partners, Not Rivals: Privatization and the Public Good.* Boston: Beacon Press, 2002.

Munson, Ziad. "Becoming an Activist: Believers, Sympathizers, and Mobilization in the American Pro-Life Movement." Ph.D. dissertation, Harvard University, 2002.

Murray, John Courtney. *We Hold These Truths: Catholic Reflections on the American Proposition.* New York: Sheed and Ward, 1986.

Nelson, Timothy. "The Church and the Street: Race, Class, and Congregation." In *Contemporary American Religion: An Ethnographic Reader,* ed. Penny Edgell Becker and Nancy L. Eiseland. Walnut Creek, CA: Alta Mira Press, 1997.

Niebuhr, H. Richard. *Christ and Culture.* New York: Harper and Row, 1951.

—— *The Purpose of the Church and Its Ministry.* New York: Harper and Row, 1956.

Oates, Mary J. *The Catholic Philanthropic Tradition in America.* Bloomington: Indiana University Press, 1995.

O'Brien, David J., and Thomas A. Shannon, eds. *Catholic Social Thought: The Documentary Heritage.* Maryknoll, NY: Orbis Books, 1998.

Olyan, Saul M., and Martha C. Nussbaum, eds. *Sexual Orientation and Human Rights in American Religious Discourse.* New York: Oxford University Press, 1998.

Orsi, Robert A. *Gods of the City.* Bloomington: Indiana University Press, 1999.

Paris, Arthur E. *Black Pentecostalism.* Amherst: University of Massachusetts Press, 1982.

Park, Jerry Z., and Christian Smith. "To Whom Much Has Been Given: Religious Capital and Community Voluntarism among Churchgoing Protestants." *Journal for the Scientific Study of Religion* 39, no. 3 (2000): 272–286.

Parsons, Talcott. "Religion and Modern Industrial Society." In *Religion, Culture, and Society,* ed. Louis Schneider. New York: Wiley, 1964.

Pattillo-McCoy, Mary. *Black Picket Fences.* Chicago: University of Chicago Press, 1999.

Proceedings of the [1909] *Conference on the Care of Dependent Children.* New York: Arno Press, 1971.

Putnam, Robert D. *Bowling Alone: The Collapse and Revival of American Community.* New York: Simon and Schuster, 2000.

————, ed. *Democracies in Flux: The Evolution of Social Capital in Contemporary Society.* New York: Oxford University Press, 2002.

Putnam, Robert D., Robert Leonardi, and Raffaella Y. Nanetti. *Making Democracy Work: Civic Traditions in Modern Italy.* Princeton, NJ: Princeton University Press, 1993.

Rawls, John. *Political Liberalism.* New York: Columbia University Press, 1996.

Reynolds, Charles H., and Ralph V. Norman, eds. *Community in America: The Challenge of Habits of the Heart.* Berkeley: University of California Press, 1988.

Roozen, David A., William McKinney, and Jackson W. Carroll. *Varieties of Religious Presence.* New York: Pilgrim Press, 1988.

Rosenblum, Nancy L., ed. *Obligations of Citizenship and Demands of Faith: Religious Accommodation in Pluralist Democracies.* Princeton, NJ: Princeton University Press, 2000.

Ryan, Mary P. *Cradle of the Middle Class: The Family in Oneida, New York, 1790–1865.* New York: Cambridge University Press, 1982.

Rynne, Xavier. *Vatican Council II.* Maryknoll, NY: Orbis Books, 1968.

"Sacrosanctum Concilium: The Constitution on the Sacred Liturgy." In *Vatican Council II: The Basic Sixteen Documents,* ed. Austin Flannery, 117–161. Northport, NY: Costello Publishing Company, 1995.

Sayer, Andrew. *Method in Social Science: A Realist Approach.* London: Routledge, 1992.

Schaller, Lyle E. *The Very Large Church: New Rules for Leaders.* Nashville: Abington Press, 2000.

Sinnott, Edmund D. *Meeting House and Church in Early New England: The Puritan Tradition as Reflected in Their Architecture, History, Builders, and Ministers.* New York: Bonanza Books, 1963.

Smelser, Neil J., and Jeffrey C. Alexander, eds. *Diversity and Its Discontents: Cultural Conflict and Common Ground in Contemporary American Society.* Princeton, NJ: Princeton University Press, 1999.

Smith, Christian. *American Evangelicalism: Embattled and Thriving.* Chicago: University of Chicago Press, 1998.

————, ed. *The Secular Revolution: Power, Interests, and Conflicts in the*

Secularization of American Public Life. Berkeley: University of California Press, 2003.

Smith, Steven Rathgeb, and Michael Lipsky. *Nonprofits for Hire: The Welfare State in the Age of Contracting.* Cambridge, MA: Harvard University Press, 1997.

Soltow, Lee, and Edward Stevens. *The Rise of Literacy and the Common School in the United States: A Socioeconomic Analysis to 1870.* Chicago: University of Chicago Press, 1981.

Spohn, William C. *Go and Do Likewise: Jesus and Ethics.* New York: Continuum Publishing, 1999.

——— *What Are They Saying about Scripture and Ethics?* rev. ed. Mahwah, NY: Paulist Press, 1995.

Stark, Rodney. *One True God: Historical Consequences of Monotheism.* Princeton, NJ: Princeton University Press, 2001.

Stark, Rodney, and Roger Finke. *Acts of Faith: Explaining the Human Side of Religion.* Berkeley: University of California Press, 2000.

Steinfels, Margaret O'Brien, ed. *American Catholics and Civic Engagement: A Distinctive Voice.* Lanham, MD: Sheed and Ward/Rowman and Littlefield, 2004.

Steinfels, Peter. *A People Adrift: The Crisis of the Roman Catholic Church in America.* New York: Simon and Schuster, 2003.

Sullivan, Francis A. *Magisterium: The Teaching Authority in the Catholic Church.* Mahwah, NJ: Paulist Press, 1983.

Swartz, David. *Culture and Power: The Sociology of Pierre Bourdieu.* Chicago: University of Chicago Press, 1998.

Swift, Zephaniah. *A System of the Laws of the State of Connecticut.* 2 vols. Windham, CT: Printed by John Byrne, 1795.

Taylor, Charles. *Sources of the Self: The Making of Modern Identity.* Cambridge, MA: Harvard University Press, 1989.

Taylor, Nathaniel W. *Concio ad Clerum: A Sermon Delivered in the Chapel of Yale College, September 10, 1828.* New Haven, CT: Printed by Hezekiah Howe, 1828.

Teles, Steven M. *Whose Welfare? AFDC and Elite Politics.* Lawrence: University of Kansas Press, 1996.

Tiffin, Susan. *In Whose Best Interest? Child Welfare Reform in the Progressive Era.* Westport, CT: Greenwood Publishing Group, 1982.

Tocqueville, Alexis de. *Democracy in America,* trans. Henry Reeve. New York: Alfred A. Knopf, 1945.

Tracy, David. *The Analogical Imagination: Christian Theology in the Culture of Pluralism.* New York: Crossroad Press, 1981.

Tropman, John F. *The Catholic Ethic and the Spirit of Community*. Washington, DC: Georgetown University Press, 2002.

Verba, Sidney, Kay Lehman Schlozman, and Henry E. Brady. *Voice and Equality: Civic Voluntarism in American Politics*. Cambridge, MA: Harvard University Press, 1995.

Vladeck, Bruce C. *Unloving Care: The Nursing Home Tragedy*. New York: Basic Books, 1980.

Walker, Williston. "Leonard Bacon." In *Encyclopedia Britannica*. New York: Encyclopedia Britannica Publishing Company, 1911.

———— *Ten New England Leaders*. New York: Silver, Burdett and Company, 1901.

Walzer, Michael. *Interpretation and Social Criticism*. Cambridge, MA: Harvard University Press, 1987.

———— *Through Thick and Thin: Moral Argument at Home and Abroad*. Notre Dame, IN: University of Notre Dame Press, 1984.

Warner, R. Stephen. "Changes in the Civic Role of Religion." In *Diversity and Its Discontents: Cultural Conflict and Common Ground in Contemporary American Society,* ed. Neil Smelser and Jeffrey Alexander, 229–244. Princeton, NJ: Princeton University Press, 1999.

Warner, W. Lloyd, and Paul S. Lunt. *The Social Life of a Modern Community*. New Haven, CT: Yale University Press, 1941.

Warren, Mark R. *Dry Bones Rattling: Community Building to Revitalize American Democracy*. Princeton, NJ: Princeton University Press, 2001.

Waters, Mary. *Black Identities: West Indian Immigrant Dreams and American Realities*. Cambridge, MA: Harvard University Press, 1999.

Wayland, John Terrill. *The Theological Department in Yale College, 1822–1858*. New York: Garland Publishers, 1987.

Weber, Max. *The Protestant Ethic and the Spirit of Capitalism,* trans. Talcott Parsons. Boston: Scribner, 1958.

Weisbrod, Burton. "Institutional Form and Organizational Behavior." In *Private Action and the Public Good,* ed. Walter Powell and Elisabeth Clemens, 69–84. New Haven, CT: Yale University Press, 1998.

Weiss, C. H. *Evaluation Research: Models of Assessing Program Effectiveness*. Englewood Cliffs, NJ: Prentice Hall, 1972.

Wentz, Abdel Ross. *A Basic History of Lutheranism in America*. Philadelphia: Fortress Press, 1955.

Wilkes, Paul. *Excellent Catholic Parishes*. Mahwah, NJ: Paulist Press, 2001.

Williams, Daniel Day. *The Minister and the Care of Souls*. New York: Harper and Brothers, 1961.

Williams, Melvin D. *Community in a Black Pentecostal Church*. Prospect Heights, IL: Waveland Press, 1974.

Wolfe, Alan. *One Nation, After All: What Middle-Class Americans Really Think About*. New York: Viking Press, 1998.

——— *The Transformation of American Religion: How We Actually Live Our Faith*. New York: Free Press, 2003.

Wood, Gordon S. *The Creation of the American Republic, 1776–1787*. New York: W. W. Norton, 1969.

Wright, Conrad Edick. *The Transformation of Charity in Postrevolutionary New England*. Boston: Northeastern University Press, 1992.

Wuthnow, Robert. *After Heaven: Spirituality in America since the 1950s*. Berkeley: University of California Press, 1998.

——— *Crisis in the Churches: Spiritual Malaise, Fiscal Woe*. New York: Oxford University Press, 1997.

——— *Loose Connections: Joining Together in America's Fragmented Communities*. Cambridge, MA: Harvard University Press, 1998.

——— *Producing the Sacred: An Essay on Public Religion*. Chicago: University of Illinois Press, 1994.

——— *The Restructuring of American Religion*. Princeton, NJ: Princeton University Press, 1988.

——— *Sharing the Journey*. New York: Free Press, 1994.

Wuthnow, Robert, and John H. Evans, eds. *The Quiet Hand of God: Faith-Based Activism and the Public Role of Mainline Protestantism*. Berkeley: University of California Press, 2002.

Zech, Charles. *Why Catholics Don't Give . . . and What Can Be Done about It*. Huntington, IN: Our Sunday Visitor Press, 1999.

Contributors

NANCY T. AMMERMAN is professor of sociology of religion in the Department of Sociology and the School of Theology at Boston University.

MARY JO BANE is Thornton Bradshaw Professor of Public Policy and Management at Harvard University's Kennedy School of Government.

BRENT COFFIN is director of the Program on Religion and Public Life at Harvard University's Hauser Center for Nonprofit Organizations.

PETER DOBKIN HALL is Hauser Lecturer on Nonprofit Organizations, John F. Kennedy School of Government, Harvard University.

RICHARD HIGGINS is a writer, book editor, and former longtime *Boston Globe* reporter.

OMAR M. MCROBERTS is assistant professor of sociology at the University of Chicago.

ZIAD MUNSON is assistant professor of sociology at Lehigh University.

AMY REYNOLDS is a graduate student in the Department of Sociology at Princeton University.

RONALD F. THIEMANN is professor of theology and of religion and society, Harvard University.

JULIE BOATRIGHT WILSON is Harry S. Kahn Senior Lecturer in Social Policy and director of the Kennedy School's Malcolm Wiener Center for Social Policy at Harvard University.

CHRISTOPHER WINSHIP is professor of sociology at Harvard University.

Index